Acclaim for Lisa Hilton's

Athénaïs

The Life of Louis XIV's Mistress,
the Real Queen of France

"A fascinating look at a decadent world. . . . Hilton casts Athénaïs as the heroine of a touching love story — which just happens to have taken place at the center of European civilization."
— Pamela Newton, *Entertainment Weekly*

"*Athénaïs* provides the most revealing view yet of a woman who ruled Versailles with her dazzling wit and magnificent looks. . . . Hilton's intensely personal approach lends a novelistic sweep to Athénaïs's tale, which unfolds, not coincidentally, against the rise of Versailles as a center of European politics and culture." — Megan O'Grady, *Vogue*

"Hilton conjures up the arch, self-satisfied world of Paris salons and the Versailles court with considerable panache."
— *The Times* (London)

"Hilton dishes the dirt on several members of the royal court with a sharp, gossipy tongue. But she also makes a strong case for her claim that Athénaïs left a much more powerful mark on her times than did the actual queen. . . . Hilton describes the parties, plays, paintings, tapestries, and architecture of the mistress's homes with an expertise and enthusiasm that is infectious."
— Kristin Latina, *Providence Journal*

"*Athénaïs* is lively, perhaps reflecting the character of its subject. . . . It conveys the flavor of the age." — *Daily Telegraph*

"Hilton brings new color to the cheeks of Athénaïs . . . the woman who named herself for Athena, captured a king, delivered his children, finessed a queen, and fought with ferocious intelligence and political skill to maintain her precarious position at Versailles. Hilton writes with the confidence of a veteran historian. . . . A compelling portrait of an astounding figure." — *Kirkus Reviews*

"Hilton explains just what was so fascinating about Athénaïs. We learn of her role in transforming Versailles and enhancing its splendor." — *Sunday Times*

"Hilton brilliantly shows the labyrinth of customs, protocol, and emotions of the crowds of people inhabiting the court at Versailles. . . . She writes both with accuracy for details and with great style. This debut is exciting and holds the promise of more wonders to come." — Lynn Eckman, *Roanoke Times*

"Hilton has done her best to give Athénaïs her rightful place in the sun. The result is a romp through the courts of the seventeenth century." — *Daily Express*

"A stunning debut. . . . A well-researched, witty chronicle. . . . The story of Athénaïs reads more like a novel than history, an intrigue-packed journey through the Great Century in France." — Andrea Hoag, *USA Today*

Athénaïs

Athénaïs

The Life of Louis XIV's Mistress,
the Real Queen of France

Lisa Hilton

BACK BAY BOOKS
LITTLE, BROWN AND COMPANY
NEW YORK   BOSTON

Back Bay Books / Little, Brown and Company
Time Warner Book Group
1271 Avenue of the Americas, New York, NY 10020
Visit our Web site at www.twbookmark.com

Published in hardcover in the United States
by Little, Brown and Company, December 2002
First Back Bay paperback edition, July 2004

First published in Great Britain by Little, Brown and Company in 2002

Megan O'Grady's article about *Athénaïs* and Lisa Hilton,
which is reprinted in the reading group guide at the
back of this book, first appeared with the title "The Sun Queen"
in the December 2002 issue of *Vogue.* Copyright © 2002
by Megan O'Grady. Reprinted with permission.

Library of Congress Cataloging-in-Publication Data
Hilton, Lisa.
Athénaïs : the life of Louis XIV's mistress, the real queen of France /
by Lisa Hilton.
p. cm.
Includes bibliographical references and index.
ISBN 0-316-08490-5 (hc) / 0-316-77851-6 (pb)
1. Montespan, Françoise-Athénaïs de Rochechouart de Mortemart,
marquise de, 1641–1707. 2. Louis XIV, King of France, 1638–1715.
3. France — Court and courtiers — Biography. 4. France —
Kings and rulers — Mistresses — Biography. I. Title
DC130.M78 H57 2002
944'.033'092 — dc21

[B]   2002073078

10 9 8 7 6 5 4 3 2 1

Q–FF

Printed in the United States of America

To my father

Not all Medea's herbs, not every
Spell and magical cantrip will suffice
To keep love alive, else Circe had held Ulysses
And Medea her Jason, by their arts alone.

Ovid, Ars Amatoria

Cast of Characters

LOUIS XIV, King of France.

ANNE of AUSTRIA, widow of LOUIS XIII and mother of LOUIS XIV.

MARIE-THERESE, Queen of France, wife of LOUIS XIV.

LOUIS, DAUPHIN of FRANCE, called "Monseigneur," son of LOUIS XIV.

MARIE-ANNE-CHRISTINE-VICTOIRE, DAUPHINE of FRANCE, first wife of the DAUPHIN.

PHILIPPE, DUC D'ORLEANS, called "Monsieur," brother of LOUIS XIV.

HENRIETTE D'ANGLETERRE, DUCHESSE D'ORLEANS, called "Madame," first wife of PHILIPPE D'ORLEANS.

ELISABETH-CHARLOTTE, LA PRINCESSE PALATINE, called "Madame," second wife of PHILIPPE D'ORLEANS.

PHILIPPE, DUC DE CHARTRES, then (1701) DUC D'OR-LEANS, son of PHILIPPE D'ORLEANS and LA PRINCESSE PALATINE.

ANNE-MARIE-LOUISE D'ORLEANS, DUCHESSE DE MONTPENSIER, called "Mademoiselle," cousin to LOUIS XIV.

LOUISE DE LA VALLIERE, DUCHESSE DE VAUJOURS, mistress to LOUIS XIV.

ATHENAIS DE ROCHECHOUART DE MORTEMART, MARQUISE DE MONTESPAN, mistress to LOUIS XIV.

LOUIS-HENRI DE PARDAILLON DE GONDRIN, MARQUIS DE MONTESPAN, husband of ATHENAIS.

LOUIS-ANTOINE, DUC D'ANTIN, son of ATHENAIS and MONTESPAN.

LOUIS-AUGUSTE DE BOURBON, DUC DU MAINE, son of ATHENAIS and LOUIS XIV.

LOUIS-ALEXANDRE DE BOURBON, COMTE DE TOU-LOUSE, son of ATHENAIS and LOUIS XIV.

LOUISE-FRANÇOISE DE BOURBON, called Mlle. de Nantes, daughter of ATHENAIS and LOUIS XIV. Married LOUIS, DUC DE BOURBON-CONDE, afterwards known as MME. LA DUCHESSE.

FRANÇOISE-MARIE DE BOURBON, called Mlle. de Blois, daughter of ATHENAIS and LOUIS XIV. Married PHILIPPE, DUC DE CHARTRES, afterwards known as DUCHESSE DE CHARTRES, then (1701) DUCHESSE D'ORLEANS.

FRANÇOISE SCARRON, afterwards MARQUISE DE MAIN-TENON, governess to ATHENAIS's children.

GABRIELLE DE ROCHECHOUART DE MORTEMART, MARQUISE DE THIANGES, sister of ATHENAIS.

LOUIS-VICTOR, DUC DE VIVONNE, brother of ATHENAIS.

COLBERT, minister to LOUIS XIV.

LOUVOIS, minister to LOUIS XIV.

LAUZUN, aspiring husband to MADEMOISELLE.

LA REYNIE, chief of police in Paris.

LA VOISIN, fortune-teller in Paris.

Athénaïs

Prologue

Early in the twentieth century, an antiques dealer living near Nantes heard of two old maids, impeccably aristocratic, but embarrassingly impoverished, who might welcome the opportunity to make a profit on a few old trinkets. Elderly ladies traditionally being obtuse about the value of their possessions, the dealer thought it would be easy to part them from a few good pieces for far less than they were worth. So he was surprised when the women, having overcome their mortification at the idea of entering into any kind of trade, proved astute, if not positively indignant bargainers. No, Monsieur could not possibly believe they would relinquish their precious Louis XIV commode, their rare pewter, their pictures, for such a paltry sum! Really, a most indelicate suggestion. Irritated at having wasted his time, the dealer scrabbled about in a drawer for something smaller he could persuade them to part with, and closed his fingers around a tiny portrait. "Ah," said the ladies, "the Shame of the Family."

This intriguing person proved to be a seventeenth-century lady in the dazzling court dress of Louis XIV's Versailles. Excited, the dealer offered the ladies a much larger sum of money than any he had mentioned so far. What could be the harm in making a little profit from an unknown woman who clearly had some terrible scandal attached to her? Why else would "the Shame of the Family" have remained anonymous for generations, if it were not that even her name were too disgraceful to pronounce? The owners had no idea as to her identity; since their own nineteenth-century childhoods, their ancestress had been known by no other name. The Shame of the Family? It must have been a scandal of distinction all the same, thought the dealer, for its cause to be so exquisitely immortalized. What was the secret of the miniature beauty, that these two respectable country ladies had never been told who she was? The dealer made his bargain, and perhaps the ladies were glad to be rid of a skeleton from the family closet.

The Marquise de Montespan had many names in her life. Athénaïs first, the goddess's name she chose for herself. Circe, after the deadly mythological enchantress who ensnared Ulysses; Alcine, after the ravishing magician in Ariosto. Quanto, meaning "How much?," or "the Torrent" were the famous letter-writer Mme. de Sévigné's code names for her. Her children called her Belle Madame, her admirers La Grande Sultane or La Maîtresse Regnante. Her lover's soldiers called her the King's whore; the poets "Rare Masterpiece of the Gods." Her descendants wrapped much of Europe in a skein of her lineage, but it is not certain as to how her picture found its way through the complicated legacy of her bloodline to lie hidden in a drawer for 200 years as "the Shame of the Family." It is not surprising that the denizens of the straitlaced nineteenth century named her thus, as Athénaïs's disgrace made her the most notorious and celebrated woman of her age. Perhaps the name she liked best was the Real Queen of France.

Chapter One

"Great and glorious events which dazzle the
beholder are represented by politicians as
the outcome of grand designs, whereas they are
usually the products of temperaments
and passions."

Versailles today is rather a sad place. The titanic mass of the château is obscured by the crowds of buses which spew fumes and tourists on to the Cour Royale. The famous gardens retain their magnificent views, but without the attentions of their thousand gardeners they can seem as soulless as a scrubby, shrubby municipal park. Inside, the long coil of visitors shuffles over cheap, squeaky parquet, through huge doorways whose marble mantels have been replaced by painted wood. The crush, the crowd and the heat of the massed bodies in the vast rooms are perhaps all that remain true to the life of the house.

On the evening of 14 May 1664, the first of all the huge gatherings Versailles was to witness assembled for Les Plaisirs de l'Ile Enchantée. That night, Louise de La Vallière was the most envied woman in Europe. For four months, a small army of artisans had labored in the park of the simple hunting lodge that was to become the great palace of Versailles to create "the Pleasures of the Enchanted Isle" — seven days of ballets, banquets and balls which astonished the world with their magnificence. Six hundred gorgeously dressed courtiers crowded together in the cool, early-summer evening to watch the finale of the fête, and the scents of ambergris, rosewater and jasmine melded with the acrid fumes of gunpowder as fireworks swooped great arabesques of intertwining "Ls" across the sky for Louise and her lover, King Louis XIV of France. Aged twenty, this blond-haired, blue-eyed country girl was the beloved mistress of Louis the God-Given, the most powerful monarch in the world.

Louis opened the fête with a procession on the theme of the Italian poet Ariosto's "Orlando Furioso," riding a bejeweled charger and carrying a silver and diamond sword. Louise was lucky in that her lover, as is not commonly the way with kings, was genuinely good-looking, "the most handsome and well-built man in his kingdom."[1] True, at only five feet four, he had not attained quite the regal stature of his cousin Charles of England, but he had inherited the same exotic dark eyes and thick coffee-colored hair — which he wore long and curling before the periwig unfortunately came into fashion — from their Italian grandmother, Marie de' Medici, and he had a good physique and well-shaped legs, a prerequisite for handsomeness before the mercies of the trouser. The great Bernini was to make a bust of Louis that has been called the finest work of portraiture of the century, his eloquent marble capturing the sensuous modeling of the young man's face, simultaneously imperious and slightly louche. Louis appears in his true character, a passionate, proud man, and though his was a dignified beauty, it seems easy, looking at the bust, to imagine him laughing.

And the Queen? Louis, so famously courteous to women that he even touched his hat to the chambermaids, would not have dreamed of openly dedicating his gala to his mistress. The enchanted isle was officially for the pleasure of his mother, Anne of Austria, whose Spanish niece, Marie-Thérèse, was his wife and Queen of four years. Poor Marie-Thérèse. Her most interesting feature is that she was painted by Velázquez. On the diplomatic mission to Spain that preceded the royal marriage, the Maréchal de Gramont commented tactfully on the Infanta Maria Theresa's looks by likening her to Anne, but the spiteful eyes of the courtiers observed that Louis turned visibly pale when he saw his bride for the first time. The Hapsburg genes were exhausted by consanguinity, and Marie-Thérèse was so short as to resemble one of her beloved dwarfs (thoughtfully, Louis included a few in the *tableaux vivants*). She had a lumpy, limping figure and short, stubby legs, black teeth and bulbous eyes, hardly compensated for by her flaxen hair and fine, fair skin. A childish, stupid woman, she would never learn French properly, and was bewildered by the sophisticated banter of the courtiers, which her husband increasingly appreciated. The playwright Molière had produced his risqué anticlerical comedy *Tartuffe* for the fête, and if the pious Queen was not scandalized, like her mother-in-law, it's because she could not understand the jokes.

Was Louise delighted with the enchantments her lover had procured for her? The orchestra played new compositions by Lully, great basins of fruit and ices were served by waiters dressed as fairy gardeners while the Four Seasons and the Signs of the Zodiac danced a ballet. Nymphs and sea monsters and whales emerged from the lake to recite poems; lions, tigers and elephants were led among the delicate pavilions, draped in rippling colored silks, which had been erected amid the trees. Louise loved the King for himself. She was shy, perhaps even ashamed. Or perhaps she realized that it was France Louis aimed to seduce with plays and masquerades and fireworks, since he was a king who would govern through pleasure, whose tyrannies were calculated as elegantly as the measures of a dance.

It is high time that history was hard on Louise de La Vallière. Of all the Bourbon mistresses (and if the kings of France had shown the same taste in wives as they did in mistresses, the country might well be a different place today), posterity has granted virtue only to Louise, the Sun King's first love. Her reign as *maîtresse en titre* coincided with the blossoming of the Great Century, which developed that spectacular combination of genius in the arts which was to make France, and things French, the arbiter of taste in Europe for centuries to come. Louise's "innocence" and "simplicity" have proved an irresistibly sentimental metaphor for that renaissance, in contrast with the dismal conclusion of Louis's reign. In fact, some contemporaries considered her a sorry creature, as this unkind poem demonstrates:

> *Soyez boiteuse, ayez quinze ans*
> *Pas de gorge, fort peu de sens*
> *Des parents, Dieu le sait. Faits en fille neuve*
> *Dans l'antichambre vos enfants*
> *Et sur ma foi, vous aurez le premier d'amants*
> *Et La Vallière en est la preuve.*[2]

This skillful riddle is attributed to one of Louise's fellow ladies-in-waiting, a beautiful, spirited girl named Athénaïs de Montespan. Louise had been Louis's mistress since 1661, the year the young king had come into his own. He had inherited the throne of France aged four, and had suffered a confusing, peripatetic childhood during the series of civil wars known as the Fronde. This conflict, which continued sporadically from 1648 to 1652, set the crown powers against both Parlement and the great nobles of France, notably the Prince de Condé and the Prince de Conti, distant relations of Louis through his grandfather, Henri IV. Although his widowed mother, Anne of Austria, aided by her minister, Cardinal Mazarin, had eventually restored security to the crown, Louis was determined that his kingdom should never again be threatened. When his beloved mentor Mazarin died in March 1661, Louis summoned his councillors and told them he intended to act as his own prime minister. No treaty could be signed, no money spent, no mission dispatched without his personal approval. In this way, as part of the strategy later consolidated by his organization of the court at Versailles, Louis hoped to keep the potentially rebellious aristocracy under control.

France, with a population of 18 million, was the largest nation in Europe, and Paris the continent's greatest city. Released from the influence of the wise but penny-pinching cardinal, Louis was free to address the enormous problems facing the country. The state was practically bankrupt, the army in confusion, agriculture destroyed by years of war. The future looked uncertain, but Louis was passionately determined that France should fulfill her potential as a powerful nation. Despite a cloudy horizon, France was at the dawn of a new age.

And France was Louis, as in Shakespeare's plays, in which France can mean either king or country, or both. This symbiotic relationship was reinforced in the coronation ceremony, in which the Bishop of Soissons placed a consecrated diamond ring on the third finger of Louis's left hand, marrying him to the nation (given the state of the royal finances, Anne had to loan one of her own rings for the occasion). To understand the man, then, is to understand his role.

To be a king of France meant more than exercising a power bestowed by birth, it meant enacting a system of beliefs which governed the monarch's entire understanding of the world. To be royal, much more so than nowadays, was to be divided by a vast psychological chasm from ordinary people. When the courtiers teased the newly arrived Marie-Thérèse about her earlier suitors, she replied sincerely, "There was no king in Spain but the King my father." It was inconceivable to her that she could even look at a man who was not one of God's anointed. This is the primary, crucial aspect of Louis's understanding of his kingship: that it was ordained by God. He was the divine representative on earth. In the words of one of his subjects, "Sire, the place where Your Majesty is seated represents for us the throne of the living God."[3] It was largely agreed (though the limits of monarchical power were certainly disputed — witness seventeenth-century England) that the only stay on the king's divine right was adherence to Christian principle. Accordingly, Louis was also the spiritual governor of his people, and in France, unlike other Catholic countries, the power of the Pope was effectively subordinate to Louis's own, since as king he could vet any papal edict before it was ratified by the Parlement. In short, the king was answerable only to God.

Since the French kings claimed their descent from the Roman emperors, Louis was also considered a demigod by many of his people, a belief which supported the idea that he embodied France. The country, still a collection of provinces with indeterminate borders, had not yet fully emerged as a geographical unit, and Louis's incessant warring on these borders was motivated partly by the need to establish precise national territories.

So the king was not as other men, and this difference was based on something more profound than wealth or political power. Louis well understood how to emphasize his "kingliness" by cultivating an awe-inspiring persona. Petitioners were advised to try to catch a glimpse of the King before approaching him, lest his appearance should strike them dumb, and at his magnificent public exhibitions he would adopt the role of Apollo or Jupiter, the classical gods whose imagery was still a part of the vocabulary of the educated of the time. Versailles itself is as much a testament to Louis's power as a cathedral, a feat of architecture which appears to have been created by a superhuman ego. A French peasant from the medieval squalor of the countryside might easily have believed that this was where God held court. It is characteristic of Catholic culture at the time that faith, in gods or kings, should manifest itself externally, in baroque display, and Louis manipulated this so successfully that the monarchy was not laicized until the mid eighteenth century.

In the early part of his reign, the contrast between Louis the man and Louis the King was distinct. Although graceful, athletic and good-mannered, he was a diffident, if not rather shy young man, uneasy in the company of women, awkward at social chitchat. He was self-conscious about the shortcomings of an education which had been interrupted by the wars of the Fronde, and later tried to compensate by giving his son, the Dauphin, a rigorous classical schooling, although thanks to the assiduous thrashings of his tutors, the poor young man ended up far more foolish than his father. Louis was passionately fond of music, and danced beautifully in the court ballets. He adored hunting, riding out nearly every day when he was not on campaign until the end of his life. But he was shy of intellectuals and had little confidence in his own attractiveness. It was his second mistress who taught him to feel as a king.

In public, at least, Louis was determined to show that he had the resolution to carry out his policy of autocratic government and to keep the aristocracy firmly in their place. He enacted this resolve symbolically in the Carrousel du Louvre, three days of equestrian sports performed in the gardens between the Tuileries palace and the Louvre in 1662. Over 600 riders took part, divided into five companies, and Louis, demonstrating the talent for spectacle which was to become the signature of his reign, headed the first company himself, dressed as a Roman emperor in a gold and diamond tunic with a plumed silver helmet. Louis's brother, the Duc d'Orléans, led the second, the "Persians," in satin and white plumes; a former Frondeur, the Prince de Condé, the "Turks," in silver, blue and black; his son the "Indians," in yellow, and the Duc de Guise, wearing a green velvet suit, blazed the trail of the "American Savages," riding a horse draped in tigerskin. In a strategy he was to perfect at the divertissements of Versailles, Louis dazzled the audience with a dragon, pages dressed as monkeys, satyrs on unicorns and with his motto, *Ut vidi vici* ("I saw, I conquered"). As he was to do throughout his life, he manipulated the vanity of the aristocracy to create a self-regulating order of subjection. Symbolically, the Carrousel enacted the submission of the arrogant feudal privilege which was the source of the Fronde to a new monarchical power that would reside exclusively in the person of the king. It was also, of course, a chance to display himself to advantage to his subjects, and no one in Paris stayed at home. The ladies of the royal household watched from a stand, the colors of the five companies pinned to their fluttering dresses. Would the King notice a shy smile behind a fan, a flirtatiously lowered gaze?

For the present, it was Louise de La Vallière who had the King's attention. In the summer of 1661, the court was at Fontainebleau, the exquisitely decorated palace where François I had launched the renaissance of French art. Amid the elegant Mannerist eroticism of Fiorentino and Primatice, the young court gleefully swept away the cobwebs of the troubled past. The former Queen Regent, Louis's severe, dominant mother, found herself increasingly marginalized, while the dour pieties of dull, dumpy Marie-Thérèse were confined to her circle of Spanish attendants. The King's set was made up of bright young things: the Duc d'Orléans, Louis's attractive, effeminate younger brother (known as Monsieur) and his glamorous wife, Henriette d'Angleterre, the sister of Charles II (known as Madame); the King's cousin by his wicked uncle, Gaston, the Duchesse de Montpensier (Mademoiselle); the Comte de Guiche, who was in love with Madame, and the Marquis de Vivonne, the brother of the unkind poetess Athénaïs de Montespan. None of them was older than twenty-five; Madame, the youngest, was seventeen. Her ladies-in-waiting, known as the "flower garden," were the most beautiful and well-born girls in France, all of them vying to catch the King's eye. Oblivious of political realities, this *jeunesse dorée* abandoned themselves to balls, concerts, moonlight promenades — and to love.

"Behold the reign of love,"[4] wrote the Parisian intellectual Madeleine de Scudéry. Love was everywhere, in the ballets, *La Puissance d'Amour, Le Triomphe d'Amour, L'Amour Malade,* and in the operas and poetry written for the court. The cult of love was conflated with the cult of the monarch, and since there was no more delicate way of flattering the King than by celebrating his prowess as a lover, gallantry, flirtation and intrigue ruled the day. In July, Louis took the role of Spring in the ballet *Seasons,* symbolizing in his person the emergence of new life. Now that the King had revoked Mazarin's law against the use of lace, fashion delighted in gaudy excess, and the courtiers draped themselves gorgeously with gold ornaments, lace collars and shimmering pastel ribbons known, of course, as *galants.* Molière, who had already scandalized the old guard with *Les Précieuses Ridicules,* a send-up of the rarefied manners of Parisian society, gave a new play, *L'Ecole des Maris.* Marie-Thérèse watched the performance in her old-fashioned Spanish farthingale, but she was not amused. Louis had married her dutifully, as an appropriate state alliance, but he needed another queen for his court of love.

"There can be no court without love as there can be no opera without love," proclaimed the gossip newspaper the *Mercure Galant,* so no one considered this odd. Traditionally, French kings had had two wives, one for reasons of state, for duty and procreation; the other for pleasure. Charles VII (1403–61) had inaugurated the "position' of titular mistress with the elevation of his lover, Agnès Sorel, and it was to some extent honorable, after the fashion of a biblical concubine. "Many ladies," wrote Primi Visconti, an Italian adventurer whose memoirs recount his life at court, "have told me it is no offense either to husband, father or God to succeed in being loved by one's prince." In fact, Their Most Christian Majesties were frequently polygamous. Although the position of official mistress was not a formal post, *maîtresse declarée* was a title recognized within and without the King's circle, designating the royal favorite. While some queens, such as Catherine de' Medici and Marie-Antoinette, used their beauty, intelligence or the monarch's youth to their advantage, this was not the case with Marie-Thérèse. Despite her dowry, her dynastic alliances and her dutiful pregnancies, Marie-Thérèse was never to have more influence over Louis than a woman who could offer only her chemise.

Moreover, adultery was a way of life at court, and as the writer Diderot was to remark in the next century, the French have always been terribly good at it.[5] In aristocratic circles, love in marriage was merely a polite formality that glossed over what was essentially a business arrangement, and so, as the playwright Racine observed, it was only possible to believe oneself unfaithful if one believed oneself to be loved. Loving one's husband was in fact considered positively déclassée. One priest, Abbé Coyer, reprimanded one of his penitents who confessed to lusting after her husband with the words: "It is only six months since the sacrament joined you, and you still love your husband. I dare say your dressmaker has the same weakness for her own, but you, Madame, are a marquise."[6] Another writer, La Bruyère, later remarked that it was as easy to identify the women of Louis's court by the names of their lovers as those of their husbands. It could only be a matter of time before Louis followed the example of his famously philandering grandfather, Henri IV, and plucked a pretty flower from Madame's garden to reign as his mistress.

Since she had neither beauty nor wit, Marie-Thérèse had no wiles to keep her husband faithful. The Queen's upbringing had been shamefully inadequate for her future role. For a century and a half,

Spain had been the most important power in Europe, dominating the continent with the support of the plunder of her enormous colonies in the Americas. France was bordered on almost all sides (except for about 300 miles of Switzerland, Savoy and Piedmont) by the Hapsburg empire, and as a result there was near-permanent conflict. Anne of Austria had been married to Louis XIII in an unsuccessful attempt to cement an alliance, and it was her beloved project that Louis should marry a Spanish princess as a means of reducing the threat. After lengthy negotiations with Mazarin, Philip IV of Spain permitted a diplomatic mission by the Maréchal de Gramont, who would woo the Infanta Maria Theresa on Louis's behalf.

Behind their impregnable façade of etiquette, the Spanish had a racy reputation. The laxity of Madrileño morals and the number of prostitutes in the city were a European scandal. Gramont reported drily that the Spanish abstained only from sins which did not give pleasure. Perhaps for this reason, and as a result of the Muslim influence of their former Moorish rulers, the Spanish were highly protective of upper-class women, who lived almost entirely in their homes, venturing out only to go to church. Marie-Thérèse's father, Philip IV, was particularly puritanical, and court etiquette was crushingly formal. Gramont gleefully imagined the courtiers leaping up from funereal feasts and galloping madly off to the bagnio. When the formal marriage proposal was made, in the massive, gloomy throne room of the Alhambra, the contrast between the sober Spaniards, who were forbidden to wear bright colors, and the beribboned, peacocking Frenchmen was comically extreme.

Gramont's description of the performance of a play illustrates the atmosphere in which the future Queen of France was raised:

The King, the Queen and the Infanta entered following a lady who carried a torch. The King raised his hat to all the ladies and then sat down against a screen . . . During the whole comedy, saving a word he addressed to the Queen, he did not move his head, nor his feet, nor his hands, only turning his eyes sometimes from one side to another and having no one near him except for a dwarf. At the exit of the actors, all the ladies rose, and left in single file from each side, joining up in the middle like nuns . . . when they have said their office; they joined hands and made their curtseys, which took several minutes, and one after the other they left, the King remaining uncovered the whole time. At the end, he rose and bowed to the Queen, the Queen bowed to the Infanta . . . the ladies left.[7]

Even a comedy was received like a Mass. What must Marie-Thérèse have thought of the cheerful, anarchic crush of great court gatherings in France? She met Gramont's pretty speeches on Louis's behalf with stiff remarks about the welfare of her aunt Anne, but when Gramont expressed surprise at her taciturnity, he learned that she had spoken more words to him than to any man, excepting her father and confessor, in her entire life.

On arriving in France, the young Queen confessed sweetly that she had fallen in love with her cousin through looking at his portraits, particularly one in which he wore a plumed hat. She called him "my cousin with the blue feather." She was crazy about Louis, and pathetically grateful for any show of kindness. Her placid nature and beautiful manners made her worthy of respect, if not love, and Louis always treated her with consideration and scrupulous courtesy, showing an enlightened affection when he held her hand throughout the delivery of their first child. He came to her bed every night, and performed his conjugal duties regularly, after which the Queen had a special Mass said, coyly delighted to show off the King's love. It was said that the Queen's "hot" Spanish blood made her not averse to her conjugal obligations, and she loved to be teased about them, giggling and rubbing her fat little hands with excitement. It is doubtful, though, that she was a happy woman. Still, she lived quietly with her few Spanish ladies, her devotions and her imported dwarfs. She was an acceptable consort and royal mother, but she was never really the Queen of France.

All the court, then, was desperate to know who would become the King's favorite. Louis already had some experience of affairs of the heart. He had been relieved of his virginity by one of his mother's maids, Mme. de Beauvais, "an old Circe," as the diarist Saint-Simon calls her, who initiated him into the gallant science in a matter-of-fact way as the sixteen-year-old King returned from the bath. She was over forty, and apparently had only one eye, but Louis was gentlemanly towards her, giving her a pension and a house in the fashionable Marais district of Paris, from whose balcony his first crush, Marie Mancini, watched his wedding procession in the company of a certain Mme. Scarron. Marie was Louis's first real love, and losing her gave him his first taste of the conflict between sentimental inclination and royal duty. She was one of three nieces of Cardinal Mazarin, and Louis was deeply attached to this witty, bookish girl before his marriage (though he had a rather less platonic relationship with her sister, Olympe, who became Comtesse de Soissons after their affair was over), and even proposed to marry her, at which idea even the ambitious Cardinal was appalled. Mazarin wrote to Louis: "God has established kings . . . to watch over the welfare, repose and security of their subjects, and not to sacrifice them to their private passions."[8]

Louis sulked and pouted and wrote reams of letters, but he did his duty and renounced Marie, who wept and plotted and wore black. When they finally parted she clung to him dramatically in the courtyard of the Louvre, murmuring, "You love me, you are King, you weep, and I must go." Marie would certainly have made a more exciting wife than Marie-Thérèse: she was persuaded into marrying an Italian prince, from whom she escaped, disguised as a man, to sail to France, avoiding capture by Turkish pirates on the way. She attempted to reach Fontainebleau, but since the King was away on a campaign, the Queen had her detained in the Abbaye de Lys, after which she was encouraged to return to Italy. It was not until 1684 that she was permitted to return to the French court, and by then Louis had forgotten her. Nevertheless, it is the Mancini sisters who are to be credited with really introducing Louis to the pleasures of love, and Olympe de Soissons spent the rest of her life at court scheming to win him back.

Twelve months after his marriage, Louis began to turn his attentions to Madame, his brother's wife. Henriette was attractive rather than beautiful, but her charm and vivaciousness made her the center of attention during the season at Fontainebleau in 1661. She understandably preferred Louis's attentions to the indifference of her flamboyantly homosexual husband, who was far more interested in the Chevalier de Lorraine than in his wife. Monsieur, however, had a less tolerant attitude to his spouse's infidelity than to his own, and complained to his mother and Marie-Thérèse, who, unfortunately for her, had a very jealous temperament. Ironically then, it was Anne of Austria who directed her son's attentions towards Louise de La Vallière.

Anxious to avoid a scandal, she nominated three potential substitutes — Mlle. de Pons, Mlle. de Chimerault and Mlle. de La Vallière — and arranged that they be seated near the King at entertainments to distract his attention from Madame.

Louis and Henriette thought the best way of hiding their mutual affection was to pretend to go along with this scheme, so Louis acted as though he was in love with Mlle. de La Vallière. Unlike the Mancini sisters, and Henriette, Louise was timid and earnest, and Louis believed she loved him for himself. Anne's ruse worked too well, and soon, in the heady atmosphere of Fontainebleau, where the ballroom was decorated with the triumphant crescent moons of an earlier royal mistress, Diane de Poitiers, they became lovers. Louise apparently made the most of the drama of her defloration, begging the King to have pity on her, and bewailing the loss of her virginity aloud. However, the Comte de Saint-Aignan, who had lent his apartment for the seduction, claimed more briskly that the resistance was short and the victory prompt. Either way, the Comte soon found himself governor of Touraine in return for his discreet assistance. This complicated intrigue, and Henriette's anger, is described in Alexandre Dumas's novel *Louise de La Vallière*.

The affair has been idyllically described as a "pastoral," and we might imagine Louise, like a later foolish girl, tripping about on Louis's arm as a burlesque milkmaid. Since she had very little to offer in the way of intellect, it was lucky that her rather insipid, limping beauty was matched by her excellence at country pursuits, of which the King was very fond. Like Louis, who famously brought down thirty-two pheasants with thirty-four shots at the age of seventy-six, Louise was a crack shot, and enjoyed vigorous horse riding. Certainly, the King was infatuated, and it was with Louise that he conceived the only enduring passion of his life, his love for Versailles. As a means of escaping the reproachful glares of his female relations, he organized small parties in the park of his father's old hunting lodge, at the time a collection of just twenty rooms and a dormitory. As it was his greatest love, so it was the least explicable: there was no view, no water, no town; the air was poor, the old house was an inconvenience. But Louis seemed to know that he could make this nondescript spot the center of all that was glorious in French culture, and spent much of his life doing so. He once said: "Versailles, c'est moi." It was his true soul mate.

Louise bore Louis four children, of whom two, Marie-Anne, who was given the title of the first Mlle. de Blois (1666–1739) and Louis, Comte de Vermandois (1667–1683) survived beyond infancy. She was really only a moonlight mistress, a woman for secret assignations and borrowed beds, and she was unable to sustain her role when Louis made their relationship official after his mother's death. In the winter of 1662 she fled to the convent at Chaillot, determined to become a nun, but Louis played the romantic hero with relish, galloping after her to fetch her back.

The fête of 1664 was the inauguration of Louis's project for Versailles, the announcement of his ambition to the world. It was also the public recognition of Louise de La Vallière as *maîtresse en titre,* established, and, for the moment, secure. Yet amid the labyrinth of intrigues, cabals and alliances that made up Louis's court were other ambitions, other dreams, reverberating through the pulse of conversation like the beating of a lady's fan. Athénaïs de Montespan, so contemptuous of her old companion Louise, had ambitions of her own. The novelist Mme. de Lafayette wrote of the court that "If you judge by appearances in this place you will often be deceived, because what appears to be the case hardly ever is."[9] What, in Athénaïs's eyes, did the fireworks illuminate? Perhaps she saw the future.

Chapter Two

"A bourgeois air sometimes wears off in the
army, but never at court."

Athénaïs de Montespan could afford to be sniffy about Louise
de La Vallière's unremarkable connections. Her own family, the
Rochechouart de Mortemarts, were distinguished by two qualities,
their breeding and their charm. Theirs was one of the oldest and
grandest families in France, and they had lived on their estate at Lussac,
in the Poitou region, since the eighth century. The Mortemarts, of
whom a Seigneur is recorded in 1094, were united with the Rochechouarts of Lussac in 1205, when Aiméry, the seventh Vicomte de
Rochechouart, married Alix de Mortemart. The family motto, *Ante
mare ondae* ("Before the sea, the waves"), is a testament to the antiq-
uity of the line. Athénaïs's elder sister, Gabrielle, who married the
Marquis de Thianges, epitomized the family conviction that to be a
Rochechouart was to be superhuman. She considered herself a masterpiece of nature, not only for her external beauty, but for the superior "essence" of which she was composed. She used to tease the
King about the inferior lineage of the Bourbons, who had compromised their quarterings by marrying "trade" in the two Medici
queens, and she only grudgingly admitted the ancient ducal house of
La Rochefoucauld to be equal to the dignity of the Rochechouarts.
Louis was delighted at her impudence, since, like all her family, she
was extremely witty.

Gabrielle's pride appears both petty and absurd in a democratic
age, but the internal logic of aristocratic breeding must have influ-

enced Athénaïs's personal psychology, as well as the circumstances of her life. From the sixteenth century to the French Revolution, there existed a powerful hostility on the part of the nobility to social change as manifested in the "gate-crashing" of aristocratic privilege by politically powerful or wealthy families. François I sowed the seeds of this discontent by creating a *noblesse de robe,* "nobility of the robe," who owed their titles to political or financial service to the crown, as distinct from the *noblesse d'épée,* or "nobility of the sword," the ancient families whose prestige was based upon military power. The nobility of the sword were outraged that anyone should attain aristocratic status by money or hard work — neither of which was considered to be the concern of a gentleman. Relationships between these two types of aristocrat were immensely complex and subtle, but the main principle of the "natural" social hierarchy, in which Louis XIV emphatically believed, was blood. Rank, effectively, was destiny, and a confidence in her own breeding distinguishes Athénaïs de Montespan from the two other chief mistresses of the King, Louise de La Vallière and the Marquise de Maintenon. Indeed, part of her attraction may have been that she considered herself very nearly his equal. Certainly she was the only person in the whole of France who ever dared to scold him.

The connections between the Rochechouarts and the royal family had always been strong. Athénaïs's father, Gabriel de Rochechouart, Duc de Mortemart, Prince de Tonnay-Charente, Marquis de Lussac and Vivonne, was brought up with Louis XIII and held a number of distinguished posts: first gentleman of the chamber, knight of the St. Esprit, governor and lieutenant-general of Metz, Toul and Verdun. He was elevated to his dukedom and peerage in 1650 during the minority of Louis XIV. The Duc de Mortemart was a handsome, sensual man who combined intelligence and cultivation with a taste for luxurious living. He loved hunting and eating as well as music, books and making love. Such vigorous passion for life was in contrast to the more delicate personality of his wife, Diane de Grandseigne, who was descended from the Marsillac family. Diane served as lady-in-waiting to Anne of Austria, and was as pious and virtuous as her mistress, although less dull. She was a celebrated conversationalist and a talented musician who spent much of her time working for charity. From her mother, Athénaïs absorbed the devout Catholic faith which remained with her throughout her life, those "seeds of religion which were never eradicated,"[1] and probably her extraordinary blond hair. The Duc bequeathed her his appetites and a curvaceous, sexy mouth. The characters of her parents were mixed in her temperament as in her face, and the conflict between her father's passions and her mother's piety was to shape her life.

Although the Duc and Duchesse de Mortemart were not a happy couple, they managed to have five children: Gabrielle (born 1634), the superbly snobbish Marquise de Thianges; Louis-Victor (born 1636), the Marquis de Vivonne; Françoise, the future Athénaïs (born at Lussac in 1640), and Marie-Madeleine (born 1645). The life of the fifth child, Marie-Christine, is almost unrecorded: having adopted an early vocation at the convent of Chaillot, she led a sequestered life of fasting and prayer. Clever and good-looking, the other four children shared with their father a famous characteristic of the family known as the "*esprit Mortemart.*" Voltaire wrote of them: "These five persons enchanted everyone by their conversation, an inimitable turn of phrase, a mixture of jokes, pretended innocence and art."[2] The Duc de Saint-Simon, whose memoirs chronicle the reign of Louis XIV, loathed Athénaïs de Montespan, but even he had to admit that her conversation was "the gift of saying things both amusing and singular, always original, and which no one expected, not even she herself as she said them."

As her husband returned from an evening of romancing the maids of his country estate, the Duchesse reproached him, "Do you spend your life with devils?"

"I know that my devils are better-tempered than your good angels," said the Duc, smiling.[3] The Mortemarts were certainly funny; their charm lay in their way of speaking, described by Visconti as their great gift. They adapted their high, cultivated voices at one moment to perfect academic French, the next to the argot of the streets. Their conversation was always daring, always surprising; it privileged amusing untruths over dreary veracity. They delivered the most cutting cruelties in a tone of dreamy naïveté, and though they spared no one, their malice was so delicious that everyone adored it. They invented a private language for their jokes — "*Bourgignon,*" for example, was a terrible insult, stemming from Mme. de Thianges's loathing of her husband's drab country estates in Burgundy. Saint-Simon recalled that well into the following century, Athénaïs's accent, and her particular turn of phrase, could be heard in the voices of her daughters and the daughters of the women who had served her, an ephemeral legacy that whispered in the corridors of Versailles long after her death.

It is sad that conversation is such a transitory gift, for it is impossible to gain a full sense of the captivating Mortemarts from their letters. Athénaïs preferred talking to writing, as is apparent from her eloquent but rather unoriginal correspondence with the Bishop of Soissons in the 1680s, which display a sense of constraint in their unconvincing attempts to support the Bishop's proposal that letters were superior to conversation. Words, Athénaïs wrote, are blown away by the wind, vanishing too quickly into the air, but she took a delight in their insubstantiality which can be appreciated only from contemporary descriptions of her conversation. "You know," Louis once remarked to the Princesse Palatine, "I like clever, amusing people." The Mortemarts, in their way, were artists, and the King admired them.[4]

All that remains of the massive medieval castle of Lussac, where Athénaïs spent her childhood, are the towers of a drawbridge, and very little is known about her early life in the Poitou countryside. The Duc and Duchesse were away for much of the year pursuing their court commitments, and Athénaïs was cared for, as was usual at the time, by nurses and servants. Sometimes the child would accompany her parents to the Louvre, where she would stay in the Grand Logis with her nurse Auzanneau, nicknamed Nono. It is quite possible that during these visits she might have seen the little boy who became king in 1643.

Louis XIV had been initiated into his royal status practically from birth. He performed his first official function at the age of sixteen months, in 1640, when he took a napkin from the maître d'hôtel and handed it to his father, the King. In 1643, now King himself, he was shown to his people in a coach and six, gazing curiously from a pile of cushions at the streets crowded with his cheering subjects. The Venetian ambassador painted a picture of him a few years later:

> His Majesty Louis XIV has a lively and attractive nature which gives promise of virtue. His body is strong, his eyes bright and rather severe, but this severity is full of charm. He seldom laughs, even at play. He insists on being obeyed and respected by his brother . . . aged three. In short, if he lives and receives a good education, he gives promise of being a great king.[5]

It is unlikely that Athénaïs and Louis played together, since the little King preferred his toy soldiers and miniature guns to the hoops and dolls provided for little girls. Already, perhaps, the young Athénaïs was drawn to the excitements of the court, since despite the beauty of her childhood home, she never until the end of her life expressed a great liking for the country.

Aged about twelve, Françoise followed her elder sister Gabrielle to the convent of Ste. Marie des Saintes, founded in 1047, where in the fifteenth century two successive Mortemart ancestors had been bishops. The convent was one of a few great foundations that educated the daughters of the aristocracy at considerable expense. It was an interesting time to go to school, as the education of women, a source of controversy since medieval times, was then being reexamined from both religious and philosophical perspectives.

After the crisis of the Protestant Reformation, the Catholic Church instigated a drive to inculcate good religious practice in children, with a particular emphasis on girls, who would, it was hoped, grow up into influential Catholic mothers. Simultaneously, the radical idea that women's brains might be as intellectually capable as men's was being debated in the Parisian salons, championed by writers like Mlle. de Scudéry and the famous correspondent Mme. de Sévigné. Something of a quiet revolution in female education was taking place in seventeenth-century France, and despite Molière's satires on "learned" women, the movement gained real ground towards the end of the century with the publication of De l'Egalité des Sexes (1673), in which De la Barre proposed that "if women studied in universities . . . they could take degrees and aspire to the titles of Doctor and Master in Theology, Medicine . . . and Law," and Fénélon's De l'Education des Filles (1687), which inspired the curriculum for the girls' school founded by Mme. de Maintenon at St. Cyr. "Nothing is more bizarre," wrote Mlle. de Scudéry, "than the educational system for females. They are taught nothing to fortify their virtue or occupy their mind."[6] Very gradually, it was being recognized that keeping girls in almost total ignorance was foolish, if not dangerous.

However, it appears that neither Athénaïs de Rochechouart's environment nor, for all her cleverness, her temperament, were conducive to making an educational pioneer of her, although her younger sister Marie-Madeleine was to become one of the most truly learned women of the age. Seventeenth-century convents were not the sinister, corrupt prisons depicted in later (Protestant) gothic fiction, and many girls passed through them with no intention of entering the novitiate. Forced vocations were common enough, often as a means of disposing of an excess of marriageable daughters in order to concentrate family funds for dowries, but not all pupils were subjected to religious oppression. Piety was omnipresent though: by far the most important element in the curriculum was religious instruction. "No matter what school a girl went to, there was little danger she would emerge a scholar."[7] Aside from religious studies, Françoise would have learned sewing, reading, arithmetic and writing (the latter none too successfully, since her spelling was flamboyant, even by the standards of the day). For those who could afford it, these lessons were supplemented by private tuition in dancing, history, geography and music. Secular literature was regarded with suspicion, but the arts were valued as a means for a girl to show herself to advantage in the marriage market of the salons. Students may have acted in suitable plays, a good preparation for the court ballets and masques in which they would be expected to participate, and they learned to play and to sing to the harpsichord. Athénaïs was a wonderful dancer, and loved performing at court entertainments. She must have enjoyed reading, particularly history, drama and poetry, as in later life she showed exceptional taste in her encouragement and patronage of some of France's greatest writers. She was adept at writing poetry herself, the playful, witty and sometimes cruel verses which were exchanged at court, and she went on to compose verses for her correspondents.

Domestic economy was also an important skill for girls expecting to manage large households, so an understanding of business letters and basic accounting was taught. Needlework was a wholesome occupation for hands which otherwise might lie dangerously idle. It is hard to imagine that Athénaïs de Montespan spent much time on so tranquil a pursuit, but she appreciated fine embroidery and became a connoisseur of tapestries. Later, she made a contribution of beautiful gold and blue bed curtains for the Grand Dauphin's suite at Versailles, which was so well decorated that it became a popular tourist attraction. She certainly learned to cook, as Mme. de Sévigné records that in 1676, Athénaïs paid a visit to the convent at Chaillot, where she perked up the nuns, including one Sister Louise de la Miséricorde,

with a game of lotto. When supper was served she found the nuns'
provisions rather meager, so she sent out for cream, butter and spices
and cooked a delicious sauce with her own beautiful white hands.[8]
This unconventional enthusiasm for cookery came in handy during
Athénaïs's relationship with the King, who had a gargantuan appetite,
and disliked seeing women refuse food. The consequences for her figure were less convenient, and Athénaïs battled with her weight for
most of her life. A tendency to stoutness ran in the family, and the
Mortemarts' cousin the Duc d'Aumont was notoriously the fattest
man at court. Athénaïs's brother Vivonne was especially large. In a discussion about the value of reading, he once remarked to the King
that books had the same effect on the mind as partridges had on his
cheeks. On another occasion, the King reprimanded his friend, "You
are growing visibly fatter, you don't take enough exercise," to which
Vivonne replied, "What slander! Not a day goes by that I do not walk
around my cousin D'Aumont at least four times."

The most important part of Athénaïs's education began when she
made her social debut, aged twenty, in 1660, under the name Mlle. de
Tonnay-Charente, one of the family titles. Thanks to her mother's
influence with Anne of Austria, on being presented at court she was
given the post of maid of honor to the new Queen, Marie-Thérèse.
One of her first appearances was in Bensérade's ballet *Hercule Amoureux,*
in which she danced alongside the young King, who played the roles of
Mars, the god of war, and the Sun. The most beautiful young woman
of her day, she caused an immediate sensation.

There is some dispute as to her exact physical appearance. Athénaïs
is most often described as a blond, though some commentators,
interestingly the most hostile, claim that her hair was naturally dark,
presumably for the satisfaction of suggesting that she dyed it. She was
of medium height, with bright blue eyes, a straight nose and firm
chin, and at this stage had a perfect figure by the standards of the time,
with slender wrists, waist and neck to set off a full, creamy bosom, an
advantage when wearing the low-cut, tight-bodiced dresses that were
fashionable early in Louis's reign. Her teeth, extremely unusually,
were white and even — "in short, a perfect face," wrote Visconti.
Whatever the true color of her hair, it was thick and luxuriant, and
she invented a becoming new style by wearing it pulled back off the
crown and cascading in delicate ringlets around the face. The Queen

also adopted this hairstyle, which became known as the *hurluberlu,* though she sulkily claimed that she was not doing so to copy Athénaïs, but only because the King liked it.

Mme. de Sévigné describes Athénaïs later, at Versailles:

> Seriously, her beauty is amazing, and her figure is not half as heavy as it was, while her complexion, eyes, lips, have lost none of their beauty. She was dressed from head to foot in *point de France,* her hair done in a thousand curls. From each temple they hung down low over her cheeks . . . in a word, a triumphant beauty to make all the ambassadors admire.[9]

Even the Princesse Palatine, the fat second wife of Monsieur, who hated Athénaïs with all the fury inspired in an ugly woman by a beautiful one, had to acknowledge her "superb *éclat,*" her beautiful fair hair, fine, shapely arms and hands, and her pretty mouth with its charming smile.[10]

What Athénaïs had in abundance was sex appeal, which is apparent in one of the few portraits of her that seem to capture her personality. Reclining on a divan in her château at Clagny, Athénaïs reveals herself as a voluptuous, gorgeous toy who seems to exist for delight. The cupids above her draw back the curtains as on a stage, emphasizing the comparison of their mistress with Venus in her role of erotic display. She is in knowing, negligent *déshabillé,* tantalizingly exposing one strawberry nipple, her slippers kicked away with a courtesan's carelessness from her soft, plump feet; arranged with her splendid palace stretching behind her, demonstrating her wealth and influence, to be approved, admired, desired, envied. Her gaze is expectantly directed to the right foreground, as though awaiting — who? This picture has more in common with Boucher's enchanting erotic paintings of Louis XV's teenage lover Louise O'Murphy than with representations of other *maîtresses en titre* such as Mme. de Pompadour, who seem anxious to regulate their ambiguous social position by representing themselves amid cultural or religious paraphernalia. Athénaïs is unashamed, celebratory, luxuriating in this display of a purely sexual power. It was not until the end of her career that she had herself painted as a repentant Magdalene.

Every scribbler at court vied to produce elegant verses in praise of this stunning beauty. After seeing her at Mass with the King at St. Germain L'Auxerrois, a courtier named Loret called her

> This charming miracle
> This divine paradise of the eyes
> This rare masterpiece of the gods.[11]

He continued in similar vein for another twenty-eight verses of hyperbolic praise. More striking even than her looks was the famous *"esprit Mortemart."* At all court entertainments — dancing as a beribboned shepherdess with Monsieur in the ballet, promenading by torchlight in the Tuileries gardens — Athénaïs's wit flashed out, sharp and sparkling, commanding attention, demanding homage. "Though she might pass for the finest woman in the world, there was yet something more agreeable in her Wit than in her Countenance," one writer later asserted.[12] And in the eighteenth century, Saint-Simon recalled:

> She was always the best of company, with graces which palliated her proud and haughty manner and which were indeed suited to it. It was impossible to have more wit, more refinement, greater felicity of expression, eloquence, natural propriety, which gave her, as it were, an individual style of talk, but delicious, and which, by force of habit, was so infectious that her nieces and the persons who were constantly about her . . . all caught the style, which is so recognizable today among the few survivors.

Athénaïs was ravishing, and yet her modesty and virtue were equally remarkable in this flamboyant, licentious world. Everyone agreed that young Mlle. de Tonnay-Charente was as prudent as she was charming.

Esprit is difficult to translate concisely. It can mean mind, wit, intellect, spirit, but also something which is essentially a combination of all these, the whole talent and energy with which one approaches the world. In France at the time, *esprit* was an "acknowledged power with which all the other powers reckoned,"[13] something of substance that was a valuable social tool. Athénaïs honed her *esprit* at the home of the Maréchal d'Albret in the Rue des Francs Bourgeois in the Marais district of Paris. It was here that Françoise de Rochechouart abandoned her baptismal name and became Athénaïs, a name she picked for herself and which suited her much better. Given her later career, the name of the Greek goddess of virginity was an amusing choice, but perhaps even at this stage a very knowing one. Athena the defiant virgin would accept no mortal suitor. She is associated with wisdom and victory, and with the Muses; she is the protectress of ancient Athens and therefore of civilization. In her helmet and dragonskin tunic, Athena carries on her shield Perseus's gift of the Gorgon's head, the Medusa whose glance turns men to stone. In so naming herself, Athénaïs was conjuring a powerfully symbolic image ideally suited to the classical playfulness of the Parisian salons. It was a name that emphasized her uniqueness, a name to give her courage, and to invite challenge.

The salons, or *ruelles* as they were then known, after the bed alcove in which the hostess traditionally received her guests, were an important intellectual counterculture to the intrigues of the court. In the more relaxed atmosphere of the earlier years of Louis XIV's reign, before the rigid requirements of attendance at Versailles meant social and political death for anyone who received the dreaded royal "I do not know him," it was possible for a socially ambitious person to move in circles beyond the court. The most famous salon hostess was the fragile, cultivated Mme. de Rambouillet. It is clear from Athénaïs's own scanty instruction that enormous effort and initiative were required for a woman to obtain more than a rudimentary education, and Mme. de Rambouillet was inspiring. She was trilingual, well read in literature and theology and interested in painting and architecture — she had designed her own house on Rue St. Thomas du Louvre. Disgusted successively by the coarseness of Henri IV's court and the dullness of Louis XIII's, Mme. de Rambouillet retreated to her own salon at the Hôtel de Rambouillet, where she assembled a circle of like-minded men and women.

The feminine dominance of the salon was its defining characteristic. Here, as nowhere else, women could exercise power by deploying *esprit*. De Rambouillet and her imitators effectively established miniature courts where women, traditionally the arbiters of manners and taste — "Everything that depends on taste is their province," praised Malesherbes — directed high-flown conversation. Accomplished, worldly women were a necessary counterpoint to the boorish, limited arenas of politics and the army, which were of course dominated by men. Even among the upper classes, male behavior was often shockingly uncivilized. In an etiquette manual of 1671, Antoine de Courtins found it necessary to advise aspiring courtiers not only against belching, farting, spitting and scratching, but against exposure of the penis in company. As an adolescent, Louis XIV himself was not above tipping his mother's ladies out of their armchairs for amusement. The salon hostesses aimed to purify language and behavior through the elaborate courtesies they demanded from their male guests, who were cast in the roles of courtly lovers and required to "woo" the leader of the salon with their conversation. Such women soon became known as *précieuses* for the refined ideals of their manners and speech. Some were genuine intellectuals, seriously concerned with ideas, but the term *femme savante* is more indicative of a gracious, socially accomplished woman than a thoroughly educated philosopher. Other salons were monuments to superficial fashion and pretentiousness, where silly society women flattered themselves by playing at knowledge. As a result, the label *précieuse,* originally complimentary, soon took on a derogatory aspect, suggesting an affected hypersensitivity, which Molière was quick to satirize in *Les Précieuses Ridicules.*

Nevertheless, many salons had serious aims, and Athénaïs gained a good deal of her polish and sophistication at the Hôtel d'Albret. Here conversation was taken as seriously as any other art form, and following Pascal's dictum that "*le moi est haïssable*" — it is hateful to speak of oneself — subjects were, in theory, elevated above gossip or personal anecdotes to a more philosophical level, though religion and politics, then as now, were avoided as signs of bad taste. A popular game was the creation of *maximes,* pithy generalizations about human behavior "in a form combining the maximum of clarity and truth with the minimum of words arranged in the most striking and memorable order." The most famous collection of such sayings is that of the Duc de la Rochefoucauld, who produced them during a six-year attendance at the salon of Mme. de Sablé, Mme. de Rambouillet's successor as the leading *précieuse.* Despite Molière's mockery, the influence of the salons on French literature, language and thought in the seventeenth century was immense, and exceptional in that this influence was largely stimulated by women. The salons, it is suggested, transformed the flowery, overelaborate French language of the sixteenth century into what

Leonard Tancock has called "the clearest and most elegant medium for conveying abstract thought known to the modern world."[14]

In attempting to rid their language of any traces of barrack-room coarseness, Mme. de Rambouillet, Mme. de Sablé and their followers bestowed upon it a unique precision and grace. In her thoughtful essay on Mme. de Sablé, George Eliot remarked:

In France alone woman has had a vital influence on the development of literature; in France alone has the mind of woman passed like an electric current through the language, making crisp and definite what is elsewhere heavy and blurred; in France alone, if the writings of women were swept away, a serious gap would be made in the national history.[15]

Much salon discourse centered on complex analyses of love, influenced by (admittedly much simplified) Neoplatonic thought. Love was categorized in minute qualitative gradations, most notably by Mlle. de Scudéry in her interminable symbolic novel *Le Grand Cyrus*. Here, the highest form of love is expressed in a platonic mingling of sympathetic souls (but then, Mlle. de Scudéry was so extremely plain that perhaps this was the best she could hope for). "Love riddles" were a popular stimulus to discussion. For example: "Does the pleasure caused by the presence of the one we love exceed the pain caused by the marks of their indifference?" Or: "Is it more pleasurable to love someone whose heart is occupied than someone whose heart is indifferent?"

La Rochefoucauld's *Maximes* contain numerous thoughts on love, and Athénaïs would certainly have heard witticisms such as "Love lends its name to countless dealings which are attributed to it, but of which it knows no more than the Doge knows what goes on in Venice," quoted to her at the Hôtel d'Albret. In the salons, her natural talent for conversation gained an assurance and a breadth of reference which made up for any deficiencies in her convent education, while her beauty enabled her to take her learning back to court without being considered an earnest old bluestocking like Mlle. de Scudéry. The suppleness of *précieuse* conversation was a form of performance, a means of renegotiating accepted ideas, and one in which women, so unequal everywhere else, could enjoy a discursive equality with men.

All her life, Athénaïs was able to use this talent for repositioning to suit her desires; her gift for speech, as much as her beauty, was her first exercise of power.

Some of the conversational games were more adventurous, involving kissing or the explanation of bedroom dilemmas. A popular pastime was "Jeu de Roman," in which one member of the group began a story continued by the others. Athénaïs must have excelled at this. Written portraits, or "characters," were exchanged among the guests, who would try to guess who was represented therein. They were often arch, if not downright insulting, as was the Cardinal de Retz's observation of La Rochefoucauld: "He has always been chronically irresolute, but I do not even know the cause of that, for in his case it cannot have come from a vivid imagination, since his is anything but lively."[16]

In speaking and writing about love in this fashion, the *précieuses* suggested that women could take an active role in affairs of the heart. The poetry of the sixteenth and seventeenth centuries has been described by Jean-Paul Desaive as "a narcissistic one-man show in which women served as a pretext, but not as a genuine presence."[17] That is, all the Helens and Cynthias of classicized love poetry were reduced to a generic type of the ideal beloved, which had nothing to do with how real women felt or spoke or acted. Of course, the educated, leisured world of the salons was open to only a privileged minority, but their role was important in establishing that women were reasoning, feeling creatures in their own right rather than the passive subjects of male literary fantasy.

It was unsurprising, therefore, that the salon debates often centered on the artificial constraints of marriage. While the Scudéry school advocated the suppression of all physical feeling in order to attain the "pure" love that was the standard of thorough sophistication, a liberal attitude to sex was a further demonstration that one was polished and civilized. The view of marriage as a social tool was widely understood and accepted, but the women of the salons questioned the double standard which permitted men to look elsewhere for sexual gratification. That marriage was usually a choice made for rather than by women was perceived as normal, but a degree of rebellion was posited, not only against women's chastity, but against the "tyranny" of maternity. The social necessity of marriage was rarely questioned seriously, but alternative models for love were suggested; effectively, in Carolyn Lougée's words, "What was advocated here in terms of liberty, nobility and the quest for the perfect friendship was nothing other than the institutionalization of adultery."[18] In the seventeenth century, nothing could be further from the idea of love than that of marriage: Bussy-Rabutin summed this up when he wrote that "the gods of hymen have long been incompatible with the gods of love." And so the lighthearted cleverness of the salon discussions attempted to resolve what seemed an insoluble conflict between virtuous conduct and the inclinations of the heart. To adhere to the mores of one's society, to retain one's moral integrity, and yet to love within a system that made choice almost impossible was the conundrum.

Yet despite such apparent high-mindedness, the *précieuses* did not take themselves too seriously. Mme. de Sévigné, who knew Mme. de Sablé and attended the salon of the novelist Mme. de Lafayette, took great delight in ridiculing her son's amorous misadventures in her letters.

The young wonder [Marie de Champmesle, a famous actress], has not broken off so far, but I think she will. This is why: yesterday my son came from the other end of Paris to tell me about the mishap that had befallen him. He had found a favorable opportunity, and yet, dare I say it? *His little gee-gee stopped short at Lérida.* It was an extraordinary thing; the damsel had never found herself at such an entertainment in all her life. The discomfited knight beat a retreat, thinking he was bewitched. And what will strike you as comic was that he was dying to tell me about this fiasco. We laughed a lot, and I told him I was very glad he had been punished in the part where he had sinned.[19]

That a son could have a good laugh about his impotence with his mother, and for her to relate the news with glee to his sister, provides a balance to the rarefied ideals of the Scudéry school of love, and both attitudes coexisted in the salon jokes. Louis admired wit of the Sévigné style, but was bored by the verbal meanderings of those who attempted to imitate Mlle. de Scudéry. Athénaïs would always be aware of Louis's dislike of *précieuse* pretension, and Primi Visconti observed that if anyone spoke to the King in an elaborately affected manner, he and Athénaïs would mock them together sotto voce.

Mme. de Maintenon, the secret wife of Louis XIV's declining years, took seriously the implications of such an interest in love and sex. When, much later, she came to establish her famous school for aristocratic girls at St. Cyr, she strongly rejected the association of nobility with sophisticated idleness. Old hypocrite that she was, she warned her pupils against the dangers of witty conversation and "expressed most vehemently . . . the antithesis between domesticity and *bel esprit*."[20] The liberated conversation of the salons suggested that traditional marriage and participation in civilized society were mutually exclusive. A refusal to accept the hypocrisies inherent in society marriage, La Maintenon feared, was inimical to Christian virtue.

Athénaïs had already experienced the application of such lax attitudes towards marital fidelity. In 1653, the Duc de Mortemart, already well past fifty, had fallen in love with Marie Boyer, the wife of Jean Tambonneau, head of the Parisian chamber of commerce. He lived with her quite openly for the next twenty years, and the workings of their scandalous ménage at Pré-aux-Clercs must have had a profound effect on the young Athénaïs. Marie was over thirty when Gabriel became her lover, positively ancient by the standards of the time, and despite her elegant dress sense she had certainly passed the bloom of her first good looks, disguising faint traces of smallpox with a good deal of rouge and powder. The aging lovers attracted some sly comic attention.

> *Mortemart le faune*
> *Aime la Tambonneau*
> *Elle est un peu jaune*
> *Mais il n'est pas trop beau.*[21]

Despite her humble social origins (a "nothing," sneered the snobbish Saint-Simon), Marie, too, held a successful salon, where she received "the flower of the court and the town."[22] Witty and dashing, Marie gambled furiously, and pursued amorous intrigue with equal fervor. People joked that her skirts were so light that they blew up at the slightest wind. Tambonneau was fully conscious that he was a cuckold, but he turned his horns of shame into cornucopia by recognizing the advantages of his wife's loose living. Such an adjustment was often the policy of husbands cheated by the King himself. When Louis later cast his eye on the beautiful Princesse de Soubise, her husband prudently made himself scarce for the duration of their fling, and acquired a huge fortune and one of the most beautiful houses in Paris as a reward for his discretion.

Athénaïs must have felt the affront to her mother's dignity keenly. Diane was perhaps less disgusted by her husband's infidelity — after all, adultery was a way of life for aristocratic men — than by his irritating constancy to Marie. Humiliated, she would decamp to Poitou for much of the year. In 1663, she obtained a "separation of bed and board" from her husband, which was an acceptable form of estrangement in a practically divorce-free society, a gesture which shows a good deal of courage and independence. It is extremely unlikely that a young girl would have visited her father's mistress, but Athénaïs must nevertheless have been influenced by Marie's social success. To a sheltered convent pupil, Diane's difficulties might have been the first indication of the fragility of aristocratic marriage, in which love and fidelity were confined to polite appearances. Yet Marie demonstrated that it was possible for a woman to flourish beyond the pale of adultery, provided that her charm and ambition secured her a powerful protector. An inconvenient husband could always be bought off.

Many commentators have observed a certain ruthless cynicism in Athénaïs's character as an adult, a trait which may have originated in the betrayal of her mother. One history places these words in her mouth: "I know well that honor is nothing but a chimera, a pretty fantasy that was invented to hold persons of our sex to their duty."[23] The sophisticated cynicism of the salons can certainly be divined in such an opinion, but the contrast between her father's worldliness and her mother's disappointed fidelity was to be one of the main sources of conflict in Athénaïs's life. She was strongly drawn to the piety and gentleness of her long-suffering mother, torn between the desire to live virtuously and her ambition to exploit the hypocrisies of her society as analyzed by the salons.

One woman who had the courage to practice what the *précieuses* preached was Ninon de Lenclos, Paris's greatest courtesan. Like Marie Boyer, she had been able to attain a position in society despite her disregard for its conventions, and she had also shared Marie's lover, the Duc de Mortemart, who had interceded for her in a legal action in 1651. Along with her paying customers, Ninon selected her own lovers, whom she divided into three categories, "favorites," "caprices" and "martyrs." She was a skillful businesswoman, but her lifestyle was one of restrained good taste rather than the dissipated luxuriousness associated with successful prostitutes. Ninon demonstrated that women's condition could be changed, that marriage could be refused, that love and freedom did not have to remain the prerogative of the male. She played a part in the sophisticated verbal and written culture which grew up around the question of love; Molière sent *Tartuffe* for her approval, and her opinions were influential to writers such as Mere and Saint-Evremond, whose essays discussed the *précieuse* project. In her will, she had the perspicacity to leave 1,000 francs to the twelve-year-old son of her lawyer, who struck her as an intelligent child. His name was Voltaire.

Ninon's *esprit* was famous. The King would inquire after her latest bon mot, and she attracted ministers, society women and the future Regent of France, Philippe d'Orléans, to her salon. Even Mme. de Sévigné admired her, despite the fact that Ninon successively took as lovers the husband, son and grandson of the patient Marquise. Ninon was also known for having "more spirit than heart"; she loved discerningly and never allowed her passions to get the better of her sense. It is delightful to imagine a meeting between Ninon and Athénaïs, the two great sex symbols of the seventeenth century, but even if they did not meet, Athénaïs would have known of the elder woman's brilliant career, and, as in the case of Marie Boyer, observed that *esprit* and skill could bring tremendous success to a woman bold enough to deploy them in love.

Ninon was acquainted with Mme. de Maintenon, whom she pronounced a charming conversationalist, but too clumsy for love. "Mme. de Maintenon," Ninon suggested slyly, "was virtuous by weakness of spirit. I tried to cure her, but she was too afraid of God."[24] It was at the Hôtel d'Albret that Athénaïs first met the young widow of the satirical poet Paul Scarron. In those days, Françoise Scarron was not nearly so pious nor so haughty as the Marquise de Maintenon was to become. The two young women shared a delight in society and polished conversation, and the impoverished young widow was grateful to have so glamorous a friend as Athénaïs. Together, they were the stars of the Maréchal d'Albret's soirées, and here began a friendship that became a conspiracy which led to the most extraordinary marriage in seventeenth-century France. Perhaps they also exchanged confidences on the vagaries of love, since for Athénaïs, marriage was already a reality.

Chapter Three

"Good marriages do exist,
but not delectable ones."

From her convent education to her first entrance into society, Athénaïs, like every aristocratic French girl of the seventeenth century, would have been aware that marriage was the primary goal of her existence. A good match could enhance the prestige of her family, bringing wealth and court appointments, so if Athénaïs sighed over the romantic extravagances of *précieuse* novels, or gossiped with Mme. de Thianges over her partners at court balls, she would never have doubted that her own marriage would be a business contract, arranged for her family's benefit before her own preference.

Romantic love, as conceived of in the twentieth century, had little or no place in courtship, which mainly entailed complex business negotiations between the couple's families over the girl's dowry and the settlements the groom would bestow on his wife. French law laid particular emphasis on parental control of marriages. The Church had ruled at the Council of Trent in the sixteenth century that while it disapproved of marriages contracted without parental consent, they were still valid under ecclesiastical law, but in France, the Ordonnance of Blois subsequently repudiated canonical authority by claiming that such unions were invalid under civil law, privileging obedience to parents over obedience to the Church. This ruling was particularly concerned with protecting the status quo within the aristocracy: since women were important dynastic tools, their disposal in marriage crucially influenced the familial groupings of political power. So as the daughter of a duc, from a family closely linked with the court, Athénaïs might have expected from an early age that her marriage would be arranged with a view to enhancing the Rochechouart prestige.

Desirable unions could be solemnized when their principals reached twelve, the age of consent, in order to cement aristocratic alliances. The size of a girl's dowry — that is, the money settled on her by her family — and the nobility of her birth were the key factors determining matrimonial success. As the *noblesse de robe* and the *noblesse d'épée* became more and more integrated, it was common for these attributes to be "traded," with one partner, usually the man, providing a prestigiously blue bloodline and the other the hard cash. This way, the nouveau riche could boost their aristocratic alliances while impoverished old families received a vital injection of income. The amalgamation of the two classes also made the marriage market more competitive, as the old aristocracy now had to contend with the fortunes of the *noblesse de robe* and the increasingly wealthy bourgeoisie, and as a result bigger and bigger dowries were required for girls from old families if they wished to marry within their class. An impoverished young duke was likely to prefer a wealthy heiress, even if her family had only recently abandoned trade, to an equally impoverished duke's daughter whose quarterings were comparable with his own. A family of marriageable daughters could therefore present a ruinous expense (hence the practice common in large families of sending some more or less willing daughters to a convent, as was the case with Athénaïs's sisters Marie-Christine and Marie-Madeleine). A great marriage could demand up to one third of the family's entire assets.

In Athénaïs's case, the family ambitions were compromised by the gloomy condition of her father's finances. Although the Duc de Mortemart was rich, his extravagances had depleted his resources, and the marriage of Athénaïs's elder sister, the Marquise de Thianges, had stretched them further. By the time Athénaïs had spent two seasons in Paris, her family had settled on a candidate who found her dowry of 150,000 livres (of which one fifth was provided by her mother's independent funds) quite acceptable. Louis-Alexandre de Trémoille, Marquis de Noirmoutiers was well born, solvent and decent-looking. Mme. de Lafayette claims that Athénaïs was attracted to Noirmoutiers and pleased with the match. Given that she was already about twenty-two, quite an advanced age for such a beautiful girl to be single at a time when most women of her class married in their late teens, we might speculate that the famous Mortemart spirit had encouraged her to hold out for a man who appealed to both her pride and her affections. Unfortunately, the second scandal to affect her life was about to intervene.

On the evening of 20 January 1663, a group of young men was leaving the Tuileries palace after a ball given by Monsieur, when a quarrel broke out between the Prince de Chalais and the Marquis de la Frette which quickly developed into a scuffle. Noirmoutiers, Chalais's brother-in-law, stepped in with two friends and blows were exchanged. The result was a challenge, to be satisfied at dawn the next day at Pré-aux-Clercs (not a lucky spot for the Mortemart women). Eight young men turned out in the icy morning: Chalais, seconded by Noirmoutiers, the Marquis de Flamarens and the Marquis d'Antin, and their opponents La Frette, his brother D'Amilly, the Vicomte d'Argenlieu and the Chevalier de Saint-Aignan. Perhaps, to heads still fuzzy with wine, the encounter seemed a romantic game, a chance to act out the ancient code of chivalry that the aristocracy still held dear, but there was nothing glamorous about the consequences. Henri de Pardaillan, Marquis d'Antin, was killed on the spot by D'Aignan, and his three companions were left seriously injured on the freezing ground. When the affair became known, the survivors' prospects looked bleak. The King was furious that his edict against the ruinous practice of dueling had been flouted, and he encouraged Parlement to hand down to the survivors the most severe sentence available: execution. Fortunately, the men were able to flee the country before they were arrested. Noirmoutiers was exiled to Portugal, where he was killed five years later fighting against the Spanish.

Athénaïs had lost her fiancé, but in the process she gained a husband. When the brother of the dead Marquis, Louis-Henri de Pardaillan de Gondrin, Marquis de Montespan, paid her a visit of consolation, their shared sorrow at the catastrophic duel forged an instant bond between them. It soon became clear that, although he might more prudently have married a wealthier woman, the dark young man from Gascony was captivated by Athénaïs. Bussy-Rabutin noted that the talk in Paris was that the Marquis de Montespan preferred her name and her beauty to "a quantity of others who could have much better accommodated his affairs."

Montespan may have been genuinely in love, but he had little to offer beyond passion. His name was an advantage, since the Pardaillans de Gondrin were an impeccably ancient family. The Montespans, to whom they had allied themselves through marriage in the sixteenth century, were related to the kings of Navarre and also claimed links with the royal house of Spain. Montespan's father, Hector-Roger Pardaillan de Gondrin, was a distinguished and influential councillor of state. However, his uncle, the Archbishop of Sens, was a prominent member of the Jansenist sect, a religious group that was in low favor at court. Jansenism (named after its founder, Cornelius Jansen, Bishop of Ypres) had been established in the early seventeenth century as a response to the Jesuit teaching that eternal salvation could be earned through actions on earth. The extent of the influence of human agency on salvation or damnation was essential to all Catholic teaching, but the Jansenists took a more pessimistic view than the Jesuits, arguing that since man was fundamentally corrupt, salvation was practically predetermined, and only a rigorous expulsion of all "human" aspects of man's nature might lead the faithful to heaven. As the Jansenists heartily disapproved of Louis, his religious policies and his lifestyle, particularly his womanizing and his love of the theater, they were personae non gratae at court. This situation altered somewhat in the later part of Louis's reign, as the sect grew in popularity, numbering the writers Pascal and Racine among its members, and indeed eventually prompting the spiritual conversion of the King himself, but in the 1660s, Montespan's family connection precluded any possibility of a court post. He was therefore without influence or position in the world where Athénaïs's family had always been prominent — obviously a grave disadvantage to the marriage.

Whatever the state of the Duc de Mortemart's finances, he could have aimed for a much better future for his beautiful daughter. A Montespan was a poor match for a Mortemart. So why was the marriage allowed to go ahead? Was Athénaïs really in love with Montespan? Both had passionate natures, so maybe the drama and sorrow of the duel caused them to experience emotional excitement as love. Perhaps the Duc de Mortemart wished to marry off his daughter quickly to avoid speculation about the now disreputable Noirmoutiers? Perhaps the family were glad of any replacement, given Athénaïs's age? Or perhaps she herself realized that, as she was relatively poor, a great marriage was becoming increasingly unlikely and that, as a married woman, she would at least have the freedom to turn her social success to advantage.

Was it possible that the marriage was hastened because Athénaïs was already pregnant by Montespan? Their first child was born nine months after the wedding. However, since the contract had been signed in January, it seems unlikely first that even if she had been carrying a baby, Athénaïs could have been aware of it so soon, and secondly that the pregnancy should so conveniently run over term. Since Athénaïs later proved to be highly fertile, it is more likely that her child was conceived on her honeymoon. The modesty remarked upon by all who knew her in her early seasons at court was unlikely to have been compromised, given that Athénaïs knew her virginity was essential currency in the marriage market. She had been tainted already by the Noirmoutiers affair, and must have been anxious to avoid further scandalous rumors, particularly since without, as yet, a powerful male protector, she needed to focus her social ambition on her popularity within the Queen's circle. Beauty can be as tyrannical to those who possess it as it is to those who lack it, and a beautiful woman must often make light of her attractions, attempting to impress by her conduct so as not to be exposed to the envy of her uglier sisters. If Athénaïs's modesty was, as was subsequently suggested, a calculated ploy, it would have been aimed at the cultivation of an unthreatening reputation, and to undo this with a shotgun wedding would have been to undermine that very calculation.

Whatever the respective motivations of their families, the marriage contract between Louis-Henri de Pardaillan de Gondrin and Athénaïs de Rochechouart de Mortemart was signed on 28 January 1663, only a week after Noirmoutiers was exiled. It is extraordinary that such a decision could have been taken in seven days. Among the noble signatures on the contract, those of royalty are noticeable by their absence. No couple of the Montespans' status could be married without the King's consent, and it would have been usual to have at least one royal validation. Yet apparently, none of the royal family, not even Diane's great friend Anne of Austria, could be prevailed upon to sign their names next to that of Montespan's heretical uncle.

Despite the haste of the marriage, some settlements were arranged. Only 60,000 livres of Athénaïs's dowry was paid outright, and not to Montespan but to his parents, who were to give the couple an annual allowance of 5 percent on the capital. The rest of the dowry was to be inherited on the deaths of the Duc and Duchesse de Mortemart: in the meantime, they, too, would pay the Montespans an allowance, raised from the rents on their Brittany estate. Such strict limitations are indicative not only of the Mortemarts' lack of ready cash, but perhaps also of a certain wariness of their son-in-law's reputation for gambling and extravagance. Was the Duc attempting to assuage his conscience about such an ill-considered marriage, and to protect his daughter, by reining in the spending habits of her husband? With a more generous contribution from the Gondrin side of the family, the couple would have an income of 22,500 livres a year, a respectable sum. Its equivalent today would be about $120,000 to $130,000 — wealthy by most people's standards, but nowhere near millionaire status. It would have been impossible, for example, for the Montespans to afford the fifty-three domestic servants considered necessary for an aristocratic couple in *La Maison Reglée,* a conduct manual published in 1692.

However, they did manage a smart wedding. The marriage was celebrated at the imposing church of St. Sulpice in Paris on 6 February 1663. Five days later, the Gondrins gave a reception at the Hôtel d'Antin, and Athénaïs was established in the world as the Marquise de Montespan.

The Montespans took lodgings in the Rue Taranne, on the left bank of the Seine in the St. Germain des Prés district. Although their home was quite modest, the quarter was beginning to supersede the Marais as the most fashionable aristocratic area. Athénaïs continued her court attendance, appearing on 22 February as a shepherdess in a new ballet across the river at the Louvre, along with Louise de La Vallière. Because of his disgraced uncle, it was difficult for her husband to appear with her, and it must have been clear to Athénaïs that the obligation to advance the family cause in royal circles fell on her shoulders. Conventionally, the role of court wives was to promote good relations that could lead to appointments for their husbands and marriage alliances for their children. Athénaïs, unlike other brides, was unable to do this in partnership with her husband, so effectively she had to embark on her career alone.

Unfortunately, it soon became apparent that marriage had not tempered Montespan's appetite for spending, and the newlyweds were in a constant state of financial embarrassment thanks to his carelessness. From the beginning, he involved his wife in his debts. He borrowed 24,000 livres from his mother against Athénaïs's dowry, and another 18,000 on the rents of the duchy of Bellegarde, part of his family's estates, in both their names. The merchants of Paris provided further fuel for his extravagance. He ran up debts of 1,500 livres with one Rémy Marion, 1,800 with Jean Opéron, a carriage-maker, 900 with a master wheelwright named Jean Hebert. Later, on the night before she was due to dance in the ballet *The Birth of Venus*, Athénaïs was forced to take her husband to see two lawyers, Rollet and Parque, to try to prevent him from being arrested for debt. This time he owed 2,170 livres to two merchants, but they were persuaded by 1,000 livres to drop the action. Again and again, Athénaïs was dragged into his sordid machinations to raise money and humiliated into begging for clemency from their creditors. At one point, Montespan even pawned his wife's pearl earrings to a merchant in the Place Maubert.

Montespan had his own ambitions and, seeing that there was little hope of a future at court, he convinced himself that he could make his fortune in the army. Although France was at peace, a political quarrel presented a juicy opportunity for him to realize his aim. By a treaty of the previous year, Charles IV, the Duke of Lorraine, had agreed to cede the town of Marsal to the French King. Cunningly, he then reneged on this promise on the grounds that the treaty had been ratified only by his nephew. Louis, eager to flex his military muscles, declared that he would lead an expeditionary force to convince the Duke to honor his word, and Montespan eagerly volunteered his sword.

War was an expensive business. A gentleman was expected to finance his own retinue of men, arms and horses and to cover his traveling expenses. And Montespan relished the chance to show off his patriotism with the most magnificent entourage he could muster. In August 1663, he borrowed another 500 livres, and then obliged Athénaïs to accompany him to a moneylender in the Rue des Anglais, where he obtained 7,750 livres, on condition that the money was used to finance his military efforts. He took 2,000 livres in advance on his allowance from the Duc de Mortemart, and 500 livres from his brother-in-law Vivonne. Clearly, his wife's father and brother were ignorant of the debts Montespan had already contracted, since both he and Athénaïs were under twenty-five, the legal age for borrowing. Montespan had unscrupulously persuaded three Parisian merchants to underwrite his loans in secret. Although Montespan pompously swore that he needed the money to do his duty to the King, in fact, the war was merely a convenient pretext for raising money to meet his astronomical gaming debts. The expedition departed in great state on 25 August, but by the time it reached Metz the Duke of Lorraine had been persuaded to honor his promise, disappointingly without a single shot being fired. Montespan returned in September in debt to the tune of 13,000 livres, and having failed to do anything to improve his standing with the King.[1]

If Athénaïs was angered by this expensive damp squib, she may not have had leisure to do much about it, for by November she was preparing the apartment in the Rue Taranne as a lying-in chamber in readiness for the birth of her first child. In the rarefied world of the *précieuses* at the Hôtel d'Albret, childbirth was a conversational hypothesis, a symbol of nature's tyranny over love. But no amount of intellectualizing could prepare Athénaïs for the terrifying ordeal to come.

What kind of experience could Athénaïs expect as the birth approached? For a start, certainly a grubby one as bathing, thought to dangerously relax the womb, was discouraged during pregnancy. Regardless of the historical commonplaces which abound about the dangers of childbirth in early modern Europe, we should not overlook what an emotionally and physically daunting prospect it presented on an individual level. *"Femme grosse a un pied dans la fosse,"* ran a French proverb — a pregnant woman has one foot in the grave. Death — of child, mother or both — was a horrifying reality. In sixteenth- and seventeenth-century France, forty women in every thousand died in childbirth. Mortality was particularly high among the upper classes, where the practice of wet-nursing led to a larger number of pregnancies. Some aristocratic women were alarmingly prolific. Two of Athénaïs's contemporaries, the Duchesses de Brion and Noailles, had more than twenty children apiece, and one frighteningly fertile mother, the Presidente de Marbeuf, gave birth thirty-one times. So Athénaïs would undoubtedly have known of women who had not survived childbirth. The fear of giving birth to an abnormal child, interpreted as a punishment for the sins of the parents, was also powerful. Any complication during the birth could mean hours of potentially fatal agony, as seventeenth-century obstetrics could offer no aid in the event of a breech birth or a strangulating umbilical cord. It was not uncommon for a child to be dismembered in the birth canal in order to save the mother. The introduction of forceps — the earliest model was little more than a holy-water pistol, designed to baptize a dying child — often damaged the baby. Caesarean sections were occasionally performed on a mother who was already dead, although if a surgeon deemed it likely that the mother would die anyway, the operation could be performed, with the father's permission, without anesthetic on a conscious woman.

Usually, female friends or relatives came to assist at a mother's lying-in. No one thought it worth recording the details of Athénaïs's first delivery, but perhaps Diane came from the Parisian convent where she was lodging, or Mme. de Thianges from the Louvre. It is likely that Athénaïs would have had a midwife; as, interestingly, she was due to give birth at the same time as Louise de La Vallière, the King's mistress, it is possible that she followed the new trend set by Louis and engaged a male midwife. Whoever was present, if the child's presentation was not normal — that is, head first — there was little that could be competently done. Closeted in an overheated, airless bedroom, fires blazing, the only painkiller Athénaïs could hope for was religion. It was the only recourse. During the birth of Louis XIV, a relay of bishops had prayed around the clock for his mother, Anne. Catholic women often had a Marian girdle placed on their agonized bodies. The mother's friends might support her by reciting the special prayers to the Virgin recommended by the Church: "Obtain for me by Your Grace . . . the favor to let me suffer with patience the pain that overwhelms me and let me be delivered from this ill. Have compassion on me, I cannot endure without your help."

Athénaïs, like most women, may have been especially terrified by her first confinement. In the event, she proved herself splendidly healthy, accomplishing nine live births in total. Her first child, Marie-Christine, was baptized on 17 November at St. Sulpice, where Athénaïs had recited her marriage vows nine months before. Athénaïs was strong enough to return to her society duties almost immediately, a strength which would prove vital in the future. At court, Louise de La Vallière was enduring the same dreadful experience, compounded in her case by the necessity for secrecy. As Louise went into labor, Madame passed through her chamber on the way to Mass, and Louise had to pretend that her groans were caused by colic. As soon as Madame was gone, Louise told her doctor (the rather unfortunately named Monsieur Boucher): "Hurry up! I want to be delivered before she comes back!" The baby was smuggled away before she even had time to hold it in her arms, and she had to be up and in full court dress for an evening party. "Do you feel unwell, Mademoiselle?" inquired the Queen spitefully, noting Louise's pale face. Louise muttered that the strongly scented tuberoses in the room were making her feel sick.

Louis was always anxious that his illegitimate children thrived, at least by the standards of the time. Five of his six legitimate children by Marie-Thérèse died young. He was particularly distressed by the death of "La Petite Madame," his third daughter, Marie-Thérèse, who had managed to live a promising five years. Louis's doctor told him that his children were weak because he wasted his virility on other women, giving to the Queen only "the dregs of the glass," but it is more likely that generations of inbreeding were at the root of the problem. Later, Louis was to interpret the deaths of his legitimate children as a punishment from God for his incessant philandering.

If Athénaïs was to achieve her ambition of advancing at court, she had, like Louise, to be present immediately, since the ladies-in-waiting to Queen Marie-Thérèse were about to be appointed. Athénaïs's job as maid-of-honor had been automatically forfeited on her marriage, and she needed a new court employment. The ladies-in-waiting — two princesses, two duchesses and two marquises or comtesses — were at the center of court life, provided with lodgings and a salary, and forming a constant entourage for the Queen. All the women at the court schemed and intrigued for a position in this circle. By February the field had narrowed to eight, a shortlist that included Athénaïs.

Thanks to the intervention of Monsieur, who was a close friend of her sister Mme. de Thianges, Athénaïs achieved one of the coveted posts, and her days were now completely consumed by court entertainments. That season, she appeared as a charming sea nymph in the Carnival ballet *Amours Déguisés,* though thanks to the improvidence of Montespan, she was reduced to borrowing money for her costume. That summer, she was at Versailles for the famous Plaisirs de l'Ile Enchantée.

Athénaïs had now shared her court life with Louise de La Vallière for four years. Together they had waited on Madame Henriette, dressed for balls and ballets, gossiped as they fastened up their hair and arranged their dresses, rushed to the next party, the next carriage ride, the latest play. But that night, as Versailles sparkled with fireworks for the first time, they were no longer equals, giggling together over the latest scandals. Louise was the star illuminated in the fireworks' quivering light, and Athénaïs a nobody in the crowd. Dull, worthy Louise de La Vallière, Athénaïs thought, was no more qualified than the dumpy little Spanish Queen to dispense the scintillating grace such an event required. Nothing could have done more to emphasize Athénaïs's disillusionment with her husband of just over a year than the contrast between her own position, jostled and inconspicuous, and the elevation of her old companion. That witless wallflower was the King's cherished darling, while she, a Rochechouart de Mortemart, no less, had to put up with a spendthrift provincial. Surely she deserved better. The King, after all, was timid, and she superlatively confident, brilliant, beautiful. Adept and graceful in public, to flatter his pride; seductive in private, to provoke his desire. Athénaïs knew the rules, and it was now, perhaps, that she confessed her ambition to herself. Use all the weapons of coquetry, then, but remain prudent, feign friendship towards her you mean to betray, secure the support of the King's friends. *Et sur ma foi vous aurez le premier d'amants.*[2] Wait.

Chapter Four

"Where love is, no disguise can hide it for long;
where it is not, none can simulate it."

On a hot summer night in Flanders, the Duchesse de Vaujours was weeping again, for shame or for chagrin, who could tell? There had been a time when her tears had been precious to the King, but he was no longer present to witness them. Louise had done very well. She could sit on a stool before the King, on a chair before a grandchild of France, and before a prince of the blood she might recline, if she so desired, on no less than a sofa. In times to come, people would dedicate their lives to the attainment of such privileges, yet Louise seemed to care very little for them. The Queen, meanwhile, lay wide awake, scorch-eyed in the heavy darkness. She was curious as to what kept her husband away so late.

In the two years since the Plaisirs de l'Ile Enchantée, Athénaïs had grown increasingly dissatisfied with her marriage. Still in search of military glory, Montespan had departed for Algiers in the summer of 1664 on an expedition to claim the port of Djidjelli from the Ottoman Empire. Again he used this as an excuse for borrowing, yet another 56,000 livres against Athénaïs's still unpaid and exhausted dowry. Initially, the fleet, commanded by Athénaïs's brother Vivonne, was successful, and the town was taken after heavy fighting. Soon, however, the French found themselves besieged by the furious Muslims and the commanders quarreled among themselves, to the disgust of many gentleman soldiers, including Montespan, who departed fortuitously with their lives before the French suffered a sorry defeat and were forced to evacuate by sea. Once again, Montespan returned ignominiously, loaded with debt rather than honors. Athénaïs was angry, humiliated and anxious. It seemed clearer than ever that the Montespans' hopes of success and security were dependent upon her efforts at court, for which she needed the money Montespan was scattering casually over the gaming tables of Paris. Despite the salary she earned, the maintenance of her position required substantial expenditure, a fact which her boastful, hot-headed husband refused to take seriously. A second child, a son, was born on 5 September 1664, another source of anxiety for his mother. The baby, Louis-Antoine, Marquis d'Antin, would have no inheritance if his father's extravagances continued. More immediately, a larger household was required for the expanded family. Montespan, it seemed, was condemning them all to embarrassing mediocrity, and Athénaïs's Mortemart blood revolted.

Given the circumstances, it would have been understandable if Athénaïs had consoled herself with an affair — she certainly had plenty of admirers — but she continued to live a life of remarkable virtue at such a licentious court. Her decision to do so perhaps marks the beginning of her deliberate strategy to ensnare the King. Louis might tumble into bed with a woman whose reputation was less than spotless, as he did from time to time with Athénaïs's sister, the Marquise de Thianges, but he would never make such a woman a serious mistress. It was at about this time that Athénaïs began to hope that this was what she would become. Just like Mme. de Thianges, Athénaïs was rather *folle,* crazy, in her belief that her good looks and nobility made her superior to other women, and Mme. de Caylus's criticism of her elder sister — "she believed that her beauty and the perfection of her temperament arose from the difference which birth had made between her and the world in general" — would serve equally well as a description of Athénaïs. Modest she might appear, but as Athénaïs realized that her husband risked making her a proxy nonentity, her vanity, her sense of what was due to a Mortemart, began to fuel her every ambition. The King's love might appease her wounded pride, and assuage her most commanding passion. "She does what she can," remarked Louis of the beautiful Marquise around this time, "but I don't want her." Perhaps he protested too much, for during 1666 it became apparent that Louis wanted Athénaïs very badly, with a desire that even a King might fear.

It was a momentous year for Louis. In January, his beloved mother, Anne of Austria, succumbed to breast cancer. Anne had been a formidable influence in her son's life. While retaining the intense piety of her Madrid upbringing, she had proved herself both a patriotic Frenchwoman and an adept politician, saving the kingdom for her son during the wars of the Fronde. Louis's birth had been the great joy of Anne's life after twenty-three childless, hollow years with her indifferent husband. To Anne and to the nation, he had deserved his name of Dieu Donné, God-given: he was the answer to France's anxious prayers for a Dauphin to secure the succession. The relationship between Louis and his mother was close, and they had an affectionate, natural manner with one another. Until Louis was nine years old, Anne heard his lessons, played with him and spanked him when he misbehaved. During the civil wars, she smuggled her children out of the Louvre in the night, wisely recognizing that the possession of the King's person held the key to power, and their uncomfortable peregrinations, sometimes without the most basic necessities, forged a bond between mother and son that endured for the rest of her life.

It was a horrible death. The doctors gouged holes in Anne's cancerous breasts and inserted little pieces of meat into them to "nourish" the disease and prevent it from devouring her body. But there was little they could do to save her. Louis watched over her deathbed, until, as she faded, he collapsed and had to be carried from the room. She was buried in the third-order habit of a nun, and her heart was placed in the church she had built to celebrate her son's birth at Val de Grâce. Louis was deeply affected by his loss, but it was in a sense a liberation, as her increasing disapproval of the pleasures of his court had cast a pall over his enjoyment of them. Nevertheless he was devoted to her memory, and always held her up as his ideal of a queen.

The following month, Athénaïs, too, lost her mother. Diane made a good Catholic death in Poitiers, far from her neglectful husband and his mistress. Athénaïs, too, may have experienced a feeling of sad release, for Diane's religion, and her close friendship with Anne of Austria, may have acted as a check on her daughter's ambitions. More than ever now, Athénaïs was alone in the world, with no one to rely on but herself.

Freed from his mother's restraining influence, Louis was able to make his affair with Louise de La Vallière fully public. Much to the fury of the long-duped Queen, Louise appeared officially at his side at Mass as soon as Anne's body had been removed from the church. Unfortunately for Louise, the mystery that had added a piquancy to their relations was no longer necessary, and beneath the merciless gaze of the court she wilted like a nocturnal flower. As Louis's confidence developed, he took more pleasure in the extravagant witticisms of court conversation, and Louise's deficiencies as *maîtresse en titre* became more marked. She was embarrassed by the obligation to parade what she saw as her shame in public. Pregnant for the third time, she began to lose her timorous good looks, and she felt herself a poor match for the voracious beauties who surrounded her lover. Desperate for a means of retaining his attention, she turned to her old companion Athénaïs de Montespan.

There is very little excuse for the duplicity with which Athénaïs cultivated the favorite's friendship in order to get closer to the King. She willfully deceived Louise with assurances of affection; perhaps she listened with attentive sympathy as the simple girl poured out anxious confidences. Athénaïs was as ruthless as a general, and to her the conquest of Louise was no more than a necessary skirmish en route to her main encounter. There is no greater indication of Louise's foolishness than her choice of such a friend to amuse the King. "Her conversation is so attractive," recorded Mademoiselle. "La Vallière had little. If she had been more prudent, she would have looked for a woman in whom the beauty and charms of her person did not correspond to her wit."[1] The Marquis de la Fare confirmed that Athénaïs did all she could to please the King, an easy task, in the presence of Louise, for a woman with wit.[2] Unlike her naïve undeclared rival, Athénaïs was prepared to fight her campaign *"avec bec et ongles."*[3] Yet she played subtly. With consummate diplomatic skill, she had also won the good graces of the Queen, impressing her with hilarious anecdotes of how she virtuously rejected her numerous suitors. One courtier, the Comte de Lauzun, had had the impudence to suggest meaningfully that Athénaïs had not been "unkind" to him, and although Athénaïs turned the insult into a joke to amuse the Queen, she never entirely forgave Lauzun. Clearly, it would have been impolitic at this stage to annoy the King by succumbing to a lesser lover, and besides, Athénaïs's vanity would have jibbed at the prospect of any man but Louis. She used her flirtations to pique his interest with precision. At the Hôtel d'Albret, Athénaïs had learned that *esprit* was the perfect aphrodisiac, and she knew, as Louise did not, that to make a man sigh with desire rather than boredom it was necessary to stimulate his uncertainty, alternating hope with severity, to confuse in order to beguile, to grant hope only in retreat, to create delight in despair.

It was helpful that Louise was unpopular. Athénaïs was not the only courtier who felt that the official mistress made a poor showing. In spite of her innocent reputation, she had in fact aroused resentment by being responsible for more *placets,* petitions to the King, than any of Louis's subsequent mistresses. Nor, despite her piety, was she altogether averse to the wages of sin. She obtained the Abbey of Chelles for her sister, married her brother to a rich heiress and her daughter to a prince of the blood, and acquired for herself the small but sumptuous Palais de Brion near the Tuileries gardens as well as the title and estates of Duchesse de Vaujours. When Louise complained of a lack of friendly support in maintaining her position, the Maréchal de Gramont responded: "She should have taken care to make others rejoice with her, whilst she herself had cause to rejoice, if when she had cause to mourn, she desired that others should do likewise." Be nice, in other words, to the people you meet on your way up . . .

This unpopularity gave Louise greater cause to turn with relief to the support of Athénaïs. She invited her friend to little supper parties at the Palais Brion, where Louis was entertained by Athénaïs's cultivated conversation. She was delighted with the success of this strategy, for the King seemed to enjoy visiting her more than ever. In October, Louise gave birth to Marie-Anne de Bourbon, styled Mlle. de Blois, some consolation for the early deaths of her previous two children. But any contentment she felt was short-lived. By November, the court gossips had recognized the real focus of the King's interest at the Palais Brion. "We are saying at the court," wrote the Duc d'Enghien, "that he sighs a little after Mme. de Montespan, and, to tell the truth, she well deserves it, because one could not have more spirit nor more beauty than she has, but I, however, have remarked nothing going on there." Louis's interest was apparent to Athénaïs, but she had the sense to keep him waiting. So what were her plans at this interesting stage?

It seems that when Athénaïs became aware of her power over the King, she feared his love as much as she desired it. Some commentators have attempted rather implausibly to cast her as a reluctant victim of the King's passion, while others are determined to see her as a ruthless strategist with a clear mission to seduce him. Montespan's role is thus equally ambiguous. Was her husband's absence a convenience, allowing Athénaïs to pursue her schemes unimpeded, or was it his neglect that left her unprotected and vulnerable? Neither view is incompatible with the other. Though her pride and ambition may have pulled her towards Louis, her religion and sense of social position may have drawn her away. At the end of 1666 she was certainly vacillating between her duty to her husband and her desire for the King. She famously remarked, "Heaven defend me from becoming the King's mistress, but were such a misfortune to befall me, I should certainly not have the audacity to appear before the Queen!," an observation which, despite its obvious hypocrisy, may yet contain a germ of truth. It is true, as Saint-Simon recounts, that she pleaded with her husband to take her to his country estate at Guyenne as she was afraid of the consequences of the King's interest. Montespan, with characteristic indifference to his wife's feelings, did not find the journey convenient, and she remained at court.

If Athénaïs was secretly plotting to attract the King, why would she sabotage her plan just as it was coming to fruition? Perhaps she had a psychological need to believe that her hand had been forced, that her husband's carelessness justified her actions. For all her celebrated boldness and defiance, Athénaïs remained a religious woman. She always adhered, for example, to the fast days of the Church, a particular sacrifice given her greediness, and when the Duchesse d'Uzès once expressed surprise at her strictness, she responded angrily, "What, Madame? Because I commit one sin am I to commit all others?" If Athénaïs could believe that she had honestly attempted to escape disgrace, she could assuage her very real guilt at the prospect of adultery, and appease her conscience without conflict. Mme. de Caylus comments: "Far from being born debauched, the character of Mme. de Montespan was naturally distanced from gallantry, and drawn towards virtue." All the same, the scandalous poet Aretino had suggested that the only roles available to women were wife, nun or whore, and Athénaïs may have concurred with him in finding the last option the most agreeable. She wanted to believe that the King had a genuine passion for her, that she could conquer his love by her spirit, not merely through her machinations. Like Louise, she held the view that true love was the only excuse for sin, but as she was more sensible, when she had made her choice she damned herself with gusto.

If the King were truly in love, what then? Kings are not in the habit of waiting on their desires; as Mme. de Sévigné's cousin Bussy-Rabutin remarked, a King in love does not sigh for long. Some years earlier, Louis had taken a passing fancy to one of the Queen's maids-of-honor, a hussy named Mlle. de la Mothe-Houdancourt, who, despite already having several lovers, put up an enticing show of resistance. The superintendent of the maids, one Mme. de Navailles, had gone so far as to block up the doors and windows of their dormitory to repulse Louis and a party of gallants who were attempting a slithering assault over the roofs of the palace of St. Germain. The reluctant maid had opportunity to preserve her spurious virtue in a convent, while Mme. de Navailles was rewarded with a long and brutal disgrace in exile in the country. Whatever charming manners concealed the King's intentions, he demanded instant submission from women. Unlike his great-grandson Louis XV, he never went so far as to force himself on anyone, but then, he never had to. Monsieur's second wife sniffed that not even the kitchenmaids were safe from his lust. If Athénaïs had really caught Louis's attention, she could not risk backing down. So she hesitated, aware that restraint increased her value, but also of the irrevocable consequences of her decision.

In May 1667, a choice was made for her. Louis began to clear the way for a new favorite. Politically, he was facing the first test of his independent rule with the outbreak of the Devolution war, and before he departed for the front in Flanders, he tidied up his personal affairs. In the Queen's dowry settlement, negotiated by Mazarin before his death, Marie-Thérèse had ceded her right of inheritance to the Spanish territories in the Netherlands in return for the payment of half a million ecus, a sum which, on the death of her father Philip IV in 1665, remained unpaid — just as the canny Mazarin had predicted it would. This gave Louis an opportunity to increase his territories by invading the Spanish holdings in Flanders on the pretext of claiming compensation for Marie-Thérèse's dowry.

Louis had inherited a strong army, but the complications of the Fronde had damaged its discipline and organization. The regiments were under the personal control of their officers, who made a profit on the expenses paid to them, and there were many abuses, from inadequate feeding and clothing of the men to the system of *passé-vivants,* whereby expenses were paid for a full company when about 40 percent of the troops consisted of imaginary soldiers invented for the financial enrichment of the officer. From 1661, Louis and his war minister, Louvois, took the army in hand and tried to combat such feudal abuses, introducing reforms such as paying the soldiers every ten days. Within six years, Louis had 50,000 well-trained men under the generalship of the Maréchal de Turenne. It was the finest army in Europe, and Louis, like a young man with a fast horse, was dying to test its mettle. On 8 May 1667, he sent to the Spanish government a "Treaty on the rights of the Most Christian Queen on diverse states of the monarchy of Spain." It was an incitement to an international conflict masquerading as the most reasonably bourgeois civil right: a husband claiming on behalf of his wife the portion of her paternal heritage to which she, and therefore he, was entitled.

What Marie-Thérèse thought about her husband making war in her own name against her own country was never considered. Louis, meanwhile, was thrilled at the prospect of a real conflict to assert his authority as a king. One of the officers, the Comte de Coligny, sent a dashing description of the campaign to Bussy-Rabutin in the country: "Everything that you have seen of the magnificence of Solomon and the grandeur of the King of Persia is nothing compared with the pomp which accompanies the King on his journey. All that one sees passing in the streets are plumes, golden costumes, chariots, mules magnificently harnessed, warhorses. All the courtiers, the officers and the volunteers have left with sumptuous equipages, one counts thirty thousand horses solely for them."

Louise, described by Mme. de Sévigné as "that little violet which hid itself under the grass and was ashamed of being mistress," was no consort for such a flamboyant warrior, but the King compensated her by making her a duchess and legitimizing her little girl. On 13 May 1667, he issued letters patent on behalf of "our dear and well-beloved and very loyal Louise de La Vallière," giving her the duchy of Vaujours, which would pass to her children after her, and acknowledging his daughter Marie-Anne with "all honors." Louise, who was pregnant yet again with the future Comte de Vermandois, remarked sadly and accurately that it was like a present given to a dismissed servant. Earlier that month, the gossips had observed, Louis had taken Athénaïs for a carriage ride à deux.

The court left St. Germain on 16 May, and on the 24th Louis departed Fontainebleau to join his armies. Marie-Thérèse, who was, as usual, behindhand with the news of Louise's elevation, took the opportunity to exercise some regal spite and maliciously suggested that the Duchesse de Vaujours should depart to inspect her new country estate. Louise left sadly in her duchess's coach, hung, according to strict etiquette, with scarlet fabric (only princesses of the blood might nail it into place), quietly determined to stay in communication with the King. She waited anxiously at Versailles for news of the campaign.

On 25 May, Louis inspected his troops, then took the road towards the enemy, including Athénaïs among the ladies in his carriage. Louis always insisted on traveling with women. He thought a journey with a man too likely to end in an embarrassing petition. Such an invitation, despite its prestige, was rather a mixed blessing, since Louis, who was an impatient traveler, refused to allow the ladies pause for sleep or even to relieve themselves. To aggravate the latter problem, they were also expected to share with gusto his enormous meals. Making amusing conversation for twelve or fourteen hours in a jolting, freezing coach whose glasses were always open — the King loathed stuffiness — with a bloated stomach and a screaming bladder, was a miserable privilege. On one occasion, the Duchesse de Chevreuse traveled with Louis all the way from Versailles to Fontainebleau in the most urgent need. She was so afraid of displeasing the King that she bore it for six hours, almost fainting with discomfort. When at last they arrived, she dashed to the chapel, unable to restrain herself any longer, and relieved herself in a holy vessel while the Duc de Beauvilliers stood guard.

Louis always admired Athénaïs's capacity for endurance in such situations. She was too wise ever to complain, and even when she was pregnant she would follow him on campaign, tolerating the lurching carriages and haphazard accommodation. It was lucky that her health was so strong, as Louis's contempt for physical weakness allowed no exceptions. Years later, he ordered his granddaughter, the Duchesse de Berry, to travel with the court to Fontainebleau when she was three months' pregnant, despite her doctors' advice that the trip would be a risk to the child. His one concession to the Duchesse's condition was that she was permitted to travel by barge, which offered a smoother ride than the coach. But her boat collided with a bridge, and her party narrowly avoided drowning. Unsurprisingly, she miscarried. Louis's view of the matter was summed up in a letter from his sister-in-law, Monsieur's second wife, who wrote that of course the Duchesse's accident was unfortunate, but not upsetting. "After all, she is all right . . . and the child was only a girl."[4]

In 1673, when Athénaïs was expecting her daughter Mlle. de Nantes, the journey to the front took the royal party through the Vosges mountains, on winding, precipitous roads surrounded, as Mademoiselle recalled, by trees "of a green so black and so melancholy that they were fearful." They traveled through seven towns in eight days on routes packed with terrified refugees. On another occasion, Louis's entourage was forced to spend the night in a cottage that was little more than a barn. The Queen took the only bed, and the ladies had straw pallets on the floor. Marie-Thérèse was concerned about the promiscuity of such an arrangement, but Louis remarked dryly that if she left the bed curtains open, no one could get into mischief while she observed them all.

In 1667, Louis's troops, under the command of Turenne, had begun their campaign on the disputed Flanders borders. Their victories were as impressive as their lacy and befeathered outfits. The Spanish quickly surrendered Armentières and Charleroi, and two more towns fell after a few days' fighting. Before attacking Tournai and Douai, the King ordered a pause for the Queen to join him, ostensibly to allow time for the repair of the fortifications at Charleroi. A rendezvous was arranged at Avesnes on the Netherlands border, and the Queen, whom Athénaïs had rejoined at Compiègne, departed on the morning of 7 June. Meanwhile, Louise, still languishing at Versailles, having heard of the King's victories, rashly decided to go and congratulate him in person. In the one defiant and predictably ill-judged action of her life, she set off for Flanders. Her carriage arrived at La Fère, where the Queen's party was resting for the night, on the evening of the 7th. Marie-Thérèse wept with rage and humiliation, and all her ladies, including Athénaïs, professed their shock and disgust at such scandalous impertinence. The Queen had poor Louise locked out of the church where they all heard Mass, and when they broke the next stage of their journey, she gave orders that no refreshments be served to the Duchesse de Vaujours. Luckily, the servants were much more afraid of the King than of the Queen, and Louise was given her lunch in secret. Doggedly, she pursued her goal.

The next day, as the Queen's carriage approached Avesnes, the King and his troops were sighted over a hill. Marie-Thérèse decided to go directly to meet him. Suddenly, a coach broke from the train and dashed over the fields, careering over the hillside at full speed as Louise hysterically urged on her coachmen in her mad rush to meet the King. Desperate for the chance to explain herself, she arrived five minutes before her mistress, disheveled, panting and tearful. It was a grave miscalculation. Louis was outraged by such an affront to the etiquette owed to his wife. He greeted Louise with suppressed fury, merely remarking "What, Madame? Before the Queen?" Louise, in disgrace, was permitted to attend Mass and dine at the royal table, but the King's icy politeness made it clear that these attentions were paid to her rank as Duchess and not to her role as his favorite.

Athénaïs de Montespan was lodged in the household of her friend Julie de Montausier, the elderly daughter of the famous salon hostess Mme. de Rambouillet. It was almost certainly here, at Avesnes, that she finally became the King's lover. One version of the story is that the King, disguised in the livery of one of M. de Montausier's servants, surprised Athénaïs at her bath. Did she know at once who the intruder was, detecting something less than servile in the sooty eyes beneath the slouched cap? Louis was so transfixed by her that he stood dumb and unable to move, gazing upon her until Athénaïs laughed at him and dropped her towel.

One of Mme. de Montausier's rooms was close to the apartment of the King, and after a while, sharp eyes observed that a guard who had been placed at the door was removed downstairs. The Marquise de Montespan rather neglected her duties to the Queen, while the King spent much time in his private rooms. Athénaïs's roommate Mme. d'Heudicourt took to leaving her discreetly alone so that Louis could visit her in disguise. Some days later, the old and the new mistresses attended confession together. It would be interesting to know whose was the more unquiet conscience.

At this time, Louis commenced the series of military successes that for ten years rendered him indisputably the most powerful monarch in Europe. If the Flanders campaign of 1667 marks the real beginning of the Great Century, then it corresponds precisely with the beginnings of the King's greatest love affair. Disguises, midnight assignations, the trumpets sounding the King's victories, love and glory allied — all the accoutrements of a romantic novel surrounded the young man triumphant in his first conquests. Like all lovers, Athénaïs and Louis must have lain at dawn in one another's arms believing the world made new for them. In their case, it was true.

The campaign continued splendidly. Louis's new passion made him more daring than ever, and his troops were inspired. The King personally led the attack on Tournai, advancing in the first line, unflinching even when his page was shot down next to him. The town capitulated quickly, and the army progressed to Douai, where Louis aroused delighted admiration in the soldiers as he led the charge on a white horse, an ostentatious white plume in his hat, fearlessly dodging bullets to be first on to the ramparts. He was not always so reckless as in the enthusiasm of the war of Devolution. In 1676, with the Spanish as the enemy once again, he took the advice of Louvois and remained behind the lines at the Battle of Bouchain. Louvois was afraid that if the King were killed, the country would be left in chaos. But Louis was genuinely a brave and committed soldier, and he was very hurt when he heard that the troops were muttering that his grandfather Henri IV had shown no such caution. Since the battle resulted in a resounding victory for the French, Louis blamed Louvois for making him appear a coward, a grudge that still rankled more than twenty years later.

Four days sufficed for Douai, then Louis rushed to Compiègne to join Athénaïs. Puzzled by the alteration in the King's nocturnal habits, the Queen inquired at dinner what was keeping him from her bed until four o'clock in the morning. Louis replied that he was occupied with his dispatches, turning to his cousin Mademoiselle to hide his smile. She wisely kept her eyes on her plate. It must have been thrilling to conduct a new love affair right under the nose not only of the Queen, but of the *maîtresse en titre* as well. To keep Athénaïs with him, Louis dragged off the long-suffering Marie-Thérèse in the stifling summer heat to inspect the towns conquered in her name. In the King's carriage, Louis and Athénaïs played jokes on Mademoiselle, pretending they had crashed every time she nodded off. When Athénaïs rode with the Queen, Louis could be heard singing as he trotted next to the open window of the carriage. While Marie-Thérèse went off to grumble at God in her newly acquired churches and convents, Athénaïs complained of "faintness," and kept to her rooms during the long, hot afternoons.

Louis's libido was famed for being as tremendous as his appetite, and, indeed, he made love the way that he ate, with a capacity that would have finished most men. Rather conveniently, he considered it a mark of gallantry to "honor" any woman who professed herself in love with him. His innumerable casual liasions were, however, simply the fulfillment of a momentary impulse, an appeasement of the flesh, forgotten as quickly as he was satisfied. In the case of his apparently bulimic appetite for food, it was discovered after his death that his intestines were twice as long as those of a normal man, but his prodigious hunger for sex was not reflected by any special physical attributes, as one of his casual flings, the Princesse de Monaco, reported. None of his women was able to please him as greatly, or for so long, as Athénaïs de Montespan. Despite the rumors that the Queen was less than averse to her marital duties, she was frankly far too unattractive for sex with her to be anything more than an obligation for the King. Louis needed to make love to Athénaïs at least three times a day, and he was sometimes so impatient that he began to undress her even before her ladies had retired from the room, but Athénaïs never showed that she was embarrassed by such ardor, if indeed she was, and matched his enthusiasm with her own. Louis was finally realizing the dreams of military glory which had haunted him since, as a frightened child, he had been hurried away from the battlegrounds of the Fronde, and in a sense the war of Devolution marked his coming of age as a monarch as much as his assumption of personal power in 1660. Perhaps it is no coincidence that the courtiers remarked on a new assurance when he returned to Versailles, a new confidence in his manhood as much as in his monarchy.

After continuing his rush of conquests at Lille and Deinze, Louis ordered the court back to Paris for the winter, to St. Germain and then Versailles. The King quickly saw that he could protect Athénaïs, whose position as a married woman was highly compromising to him, by encouraging his wife to continue in her jealousy of Louise. The more observant courtiers, however, had already seen that La Vallière had been eclipsed by Montespan. During the two-week siege at Lille, when the King bivouacked with his cavalry, including the Marquis de La Vallière, the men joked that in lieu of the sister, the King spent his nights with the brother. But "In truth," wrote the Marquis de Saint-Maurice, "this passion is only imaginary, as everyone believes he has no thoughts other than for La Montespan."[5] One evening after supper in Arras, the Queen announced that she had received an anonymous letter which explained Mme. de Montespan's relationship with the King, and Mme. de Montausier's complicity in it. Athénaïs pretended to be furious, and the Duchesse de Montausier joined her in protesting her innocence. The Queen said that she was nobody's fool, that she would not be tricked into hating two such loyal ladies. She was so delighted in her delusion that the King had dropped La Vallière that she refused to believe the accusations and, luckily for the lovers, looked no further than the end of her lumpy Hapsburg nose.

If success on the battlefield made a king of Louis, it was Athénaïs who made a man of him. Courtiers who had not followed the campaign observed on the King's return that his demeanor, especially towards women, had undergone a radical change. No longer diffident and rather awkward, Louis had added polish and dignity to his fine manners. He became easy and graceful in company, he "began and carried on the conversation like another man."[6] People were more catty about the change in Athénaïs. No longer a fresh and virtuous young bride, she now appeared capricious, coquettish, imperious and difficult to please. This observation may have had more to do with the changed perspective of the observers rather than a real alteration in her personality, as it is hard to believe that her previous commendable behavior was entirely a manipulative affectation. People condemned her because she was not ashamed, just as they had condemned Louise because she was. If her delight in her lover and her magnificent ambitions were now obvious, they were certainly matched by Louis's own. Their new relationship inaugurated the most dazzling and successful years of his kingship, the years which, even the harshest of French historians concede, deserve to be known as the "Age Montespan."

A critic of the Marquise has written that Louis could never have truly loved her since their relationship was governed entirely by desire. Even on such a biased reckoning, if this were the case, Athénaïs must have been a superlative lover for Louis to have adored her as long and as thoroughly as he did. Certainly they both had strongly sensual natures, enjoying gamey, spicy foods, perfumes (jasmine was a mutual favorite), and the caress of delicate fabrics. Athénaïs has also been criticized for replacing the King's tenderness with libertinism: "Her tears moved him, not because she was pained, but because he found her beautiful in tears."[7] It is true that, unlike Louise, Athénaïs did go so far as to study the King's pleasure in every aspect of his life, including his bed. She knew that mere acquiescence, even from a beautiful woman, will not enrapture a man for long, and she sought to please and excite the King to such an extent that his doctors grew concerned about his nocturnal exertions. She took the time to learn her lover's body, to discover what excited him and how he would react. The hagiographers of Louise de La Vallière suggest that Athénaïs was not "truly" sensual because passion did not make her miserable, as love is great only if it is tragic. Athénaïs refused to suffer. She reveled in her sexual power, and for Louis the pleasure of making love to a thoroughly enthusiastic woman after the guilty tears, the persuasions, the repetitive "surrenders" of the clinging Louise must have been intoxicating. It is interesting to observe that Athénaïs is largely responsible for the racy reputation of the "French favorite," so much so that these ladies' "memoirs" are often a byword for pornography. Certainly many of the apocryphal accounts of Mme. de Montespan's life are thinly disguised erotica.

As autumn descended damply on the court, Louise gave birth to her fourth child, her son the Comte de Vermandois. Did Athénaïs pity her vanquished rival as she danced with the King, knowing that the screams of Louise's labor were being stifled by the music of the ball? As was customary, the child was immediately smuggled away, and that same evening, Louis took his *medianoche* — his late supper — in the new mother's room, where she received him in full dress, etiquette demanding that she appear not the least indisposed. The physical agony of a tightly laced, heavy court dress must have been extreme. Athénaïs knew that no less would be expected of her if she were to have a child by the King, and she learned her lesson well. During seven pregnancies by Louis, she never once complained to him of illness or fatigue, knowing that he disliked to be reminded of the consequences of his pleasures. For the present, her own appetite for pleasure was indefatigable, and the King obliged her, with balls at Versailles and the Tuileries, ballets and parties at Monsieur's Palais Royal, plays, racing, masquerades. The court was "a society by nature already selfish, frivolous, infinitely uncharitable, where the fight for favors, that is for life, takes a savage tone."[8] Athénaïs was brave enough and wild enough, she believed, to take on the court and win. That winter she shone so brightly that the court, more or less grudgingly, admitted that she deserved the title by which she was later to be known, "the real Queen of France." However, her conquest was not yet complete. Was she simply an amusement for the King during the favorite's pregnancy, her attractions enhanced by the adrenaline of the military campaign? Although her husband was still mercifully in the dark, her position was precarious. She had won the King's love, but could she keep it?

She was given an elegantly symbolic proof of her success in the Grand Divertissement the King gave at Versailles in July 1668. This time, the official reason was the peace treaty signed on 2 May at Aix-la-Chapelle, which brought the first war in Flanders to a successful conclusion. Yet it was clear that this fête took its tone from the new mistress it aimed to please. The change in Louis's character was reflected in his choice of theme for his party. Its title, "Les Fêtes de l'Amour et de Bacchus," celebrated earthy, rather than ethereal pleasures. The imaginary delights of an enchanted isle give way to sensual gratification. Louis took a good deal of personal trouble over the preparations. He filled the gardens of his father's old house with marvels, arranging Savonnerie tapestries, marble statues and orange trees in silver tubs among the trees. Following a collation of candied fruits set amid miniature palaces of pastry and marzipan served in the grove of the Etoile, the King led his guests by carriage to admire the Bassin des Cygnes, after which they repaired to the outdoor theater constructed by the Duc de Créqui, where they watched Molière's *Georges Dandin* and one hundred dancers in Lully's ballet *Le Triomphe de Bacchus.*

Supper was served by the light of 300 candles alongside a model of Mount Parnassus, mythological home to Apollo and the Muses, equipped with real waterfalls. Sixty lucky people sat down with the King to fifty-six dishes, while another forty tried to look graceful about joining the Queen. Louise, who was still official mistress, sat next to Louis, but as the sound of the violins mingled with the rustle of the fountains, he could barely pull his eyes away from Athénaïs, shrieking with laughter among her friends — one of whom was Mme. Scarron. After supper, 3,000 guests danced outside the old château in an octagonal ballroom, specially created for the occasion by the royal architect, Le Vau, and adorned with great swaths of flowers. As once before, the fête concluded with magnificent fireworks, illuminated 1,000 at a time. When the rockets formed the King's insignia in the sky, it was as though he had brought back the daylight for the delight of his secret love.

This fête, the second of the three great divertissements given at Versailles, opens a new era in Louis's reign. In the plans for the entertainment, Louis rehearsed the dominance over nature that was to characterize his project for Versailles, intended to show his mastery over his realm. It pleased him to ride roughshod over nature using his wealth, his will and his imagination to subdue it to his desires. In thus humanizing the landscape, he made himself master of it, showing his power to modify and even enhance what God had created. In fact, the three great fêtes of 1664, 1668 and 1674 might be interpreted as three "pagan Masses," celebrating Louis's omniscience as monarch. The world of the fête was one of constant mutation, of metamorphosis, the bright lights turning the Grand Bassin into a sea of fire beneath fountains of cascading fireworks. Statues became dancers; courtiers reappeared as shepherds, warriors, medieval troubadours; the very trees seem to uproot themselves to follow the King's progress. In this shifting, shimmering world of illusions, the one constant was the King himself, the fixed point around which the universe of his ingenuity revolved. Everything — fire, water, night, day — was subjected to his will.

This sense of Louis presenting himself as the locus of a fluctuating world is connected with his cultivation of the cult of the sun god, the theme that would dominate the decoration scheme of Versailles. Copernicus had compared the sun to a monarch, with a family of stars revolving around his throne, and Louis adopted the idea enthusiastically in his desire to establish himself symbolically as the center of the French world. The stars, in Louis's own words, reflect the light of the sun "like a kind of court." His chief designer, Le Brun, conceived the allegorical pattern of the statuary in the garden of Versailles to illustrate the union or linkage which composes the universe, the same "chain of being" ordained by God that was expressed in the monarchical hierarchy of the nation. It was natural, then, that in selecting a symbolic persona for himself, Louis would choose Apollo, traditionally associated, in his incarnation as Phoebus, with the sun. "Since the sun was the emblem of Louis XIV and the poets link the sun and Apollo, everything at Versailles was related to that Greek god," explained Felibien in his guide to Versailles in 1671. Apollo is the god of the bow and the lyre. He punishes as he cures. He is the incarnation of rational order, the triumph of the human will to civilize against the natural anarchy of his rival, Dionysus. As the sun, Apollo Phoebus, he is called the Luminous, the Pure, while in his traditional relationship with the Muses, he becomes the god of the arts and of music. In sculpture, via the Greek *kouros,* Apollo is the ideal of masculine beauty and strength, and his gaze, his objectification of the world, is "sublime, enlarging human power against the tyranny of nature."[9] Many contemporary witnesses of Louis's divertissements commented on how they were dazzled by the brightness that surrounded him, a brightness that seemed superhuman in a world whose darkness, broken only by smoky candlelight, is almost inconceivable to a complacent modern imagination. In a sense, Louis offered more than an identification with Apollo — in the night-made-day of his gardens that night in 1668, le Roi Très Chrétien was inviting his subjects to witness his apotheosis, that moment when a mortal is transformed into a god.

Louis had found as his consort a woman he felt was worthy to support his self-mythologizing. Athena might, after all, make an exception for Apollo. Athénaïs de Montespan was the perfect feminine counterpoint to Louis's conception of himself, which he planned to display in the greatest palace Europe had ever seen. Moreover, she was as hungry for power and splendor as Louis himself. The genius loci of Louis's house seemed somehow to reside in the changing natures of his lovers, and the divertissement was a farewell to the pastoral conceit of Versailles as the King's pleasure house. It was now to become the literal manifestation of the glory of Louis XIV. The transformation began with Athénaïs.

Chapter Five

"Of all the violent passions, the least
unbecoming in women is love."

C ardinal Mazarin left Louis XIV three gifts: his kingdom, his taste
and Jean-Baptiste Colbert. Without Colbert, no less than Le
Brun, Le Vau, Le Notre and Mansart, Europe's greatest baroque
palace could not have been built. While Le Brun and Le Vau designed
the house, Mansart constructed it and Le Notre created the gardens,
Colbert was the money man. Not that Colbert, the merchant's son
from Rheims who became Mazarin's secretary, then minister of
finance and superintendent of buildings to Louis, ever liked Versailles
very much. Like many people, at first he failed to understand Louis's
passion for the place, and repeatedly tried to divert his master's attention to the Louvre, which he considered the proper residence for the
King. Versailles was too flat, too damp, too unhealthy; there was no
proper town or even a water supply. Why did the King insist on retaining the unfashionable little house built by his father as the centerpiece of his palace? The foundations were unsteady, and a new hill
would have to be made to accommodate Louis's plans. Moreover, the
construction costs — one third of all taxes for thirty years — were so
astronomical that Louis could not even bear to look at the accounts.
These were Colbert's headache, and much of the ingenuity he
deployed in improving the French economy was motivated by the
necessity to alleviate it, but he grumbled and fretted, and his prudent
soul was never reconciled to the terrible expense of his master's dream.

Colbert was so cold and impassive that he was nicknamed "the North." His passion was administration — not a prepossessing enthusiasm, but one for which France had reason to be grateful. When Colbert took over, the treasury was meager and agriculture and trade had been severely damaged by the civil wars during Louis's minority. Nevertheless, Louis was determined to continue the project begun in his father's reign by Cardinal Richelieu and developed by Mazarin, to create a strong and united nation with a comprehensive cultural identity. Colbert was an unimaginative man, but he understood his master's ambition for France, and set about providing him with the means to achieve it. In just ten years, he doubled the national revenues, starting with the reform of the tax-collecting authorities to put the treasury in surplus without raising taxes. This money he ploughed back into French manufacture and export, using the court as a showpiece to advertise the best French workmanship. Colbert poked his nose into everything. In addition to sharing the administration of the Academy for Painting and Sculpture with Le Brun, he established and directed the Academy of Architecture, oversaw the building of France's first navy, controlled import tariffs and customs barriers, improved the French West India trading company and encouraged French expansion into Canada. Louis wrote to his son the Dauphin: "Never forget that it is by work that a King rules," but the financial regeneration of France was the product of Colbert's work rather than Louis's. It seems fortunate, though, that the imaginative part of the proceedings was left to the King.

Louis XIV's famous declaration, "Versailles, c'est moi," encapsulates the spirit of the baroque, and Versailles itself became the model, or ideal, for grand architecture throughout Europe in the seventeenth and early eighteenth centuries. The idea of a baroque work, known as the "concettismo," is "the transformation of a thought through the work of different disciplines,"[1] that is, the separate elements of the object are demonstrated by the cumulative, interrelated impact of its constituent elements. At Versailles, architecture, sculpture, painting, decoration and landscaping all worked together to create a symbiotic impact which was greater than that of any element considered separately. Thus the unified appearance of château, gardens, town and roads created a spectacle which was best appreciated if all were examined together. The baroque is the expression of the classical idea of life lived as a spectacle, in which men conduct themselves as "actors" before God and every public gesture becomes ceremonial. It is notable that many seventeenth-century books on religious or public affairs have titles like *Theatrum ceremoniale historico-politicum* or *Theatrum ecclesiasticum*. Louis's genius was to adapt this conception of life as theater for his own political ends. The architecture of Versailles, and the public life of its owner, became, as never before, the theatrical expression of, and the metaphor for, absolute power. Louis and Versailles came to exist in a symbiotic relationship, the one personifying and defining the majesty of the other.

After the divertissement given for Athénaïs in 1668, Louis had his workmen brought in (a total of 30,000 men were needed to complete the château) to create an "envelope" of stone around the original building which would form the core of a new house. The principal artists at Versailles, Le Brun, Le Vau and Le Notre, had worked together at the château of Vaux-le-Vicomte, the residence of Louis's former finance minister, Nicolas Fouquet. In 1661, Fouquet gave a famous fête at Vaux, the splendor of which enraged the King as it was largely funded by money Fouquet had supposedly embezzled from public coffers. Fouquet was condemned to imprisonment, and Louis availed himself of the treasures of Vaux as well as of its creators. Le Vau designed the château at Versailles in collaboration with Le Brun, who was also the King's painter-in-chief and responsible for the interior of the château. When Le Vau died in 1670, his designs were realized and expanded by Mansart.

From 1674 onwards, the court took up a partial residence at Versailles, but it was not until 1682 that the building was ready for a permanent move. The relocation of the court has often been attributed to Louis's dislike of Paris, a city tainted by childhood memories of the development of the wars of the Fronde, but this argument is as unjust as it is often repeated. The last winter Louis spent in Paris was that of 1670, twenty years after the Fronde, and too much emphasis is placed on the idea that he somehow found the town traumatizing. Louis did prefer Versailles, but not because he hated the Louvre. Rather, Versailles provided an appropriate backdrop for his sovereignty in a way that his town palaces, which had developed rather haphazardly from the fortified castles of a more warlike age, never could. His move was not an attempt to punish Paris, on which he lavished a great deal of money throughout his reign.

The construction of the central apartments, on a direct east–west axis, allowed the King's day to reflect the movements of the sun's cycle, and every room in the château was oriented towards this symbol of power. In Le Notre's plans for the park, the water ran from north to south, creating the suggestion that the two contrary elements were harmonized by Louis's presence. The "space" of Versailles, its staircases and diagonal perspectives, opened with movement, so that the rhythms of the King's day corresponded with the rhythmic successions of the rooms. The visitor is guided, as by an orator through a speech, through the "ideas" of the building. Versailles embodies a social hierarchy which has the King at its summit; the favor a courtier enjoyed could be calculated architecturally by how far he was allowed to progress through the rooms and courtyards towards the person of the King. The Cour Royale, the Cour des Ministres and finally the Cour de Marbre, in the heart of the building, were all subject to strict gradations of precedent. Louis was passionate about the aesthetics of his château. When Mansart protested that the chimneys would smoke if their position was not altered, the King replied that he didn't care about the smoke as long as it did not spoil the view. Drafts didn't concern him provided his doors were splendidly symmetrical. If there was no town, then a town would grow where the King was. If there was no water, then the King would force it to flow. And as Louis controlled the structure of his house, so he would control its inhabitants. The etiquette of Versailles mirrored the fact that in its every aspect, the château was a testament to the King's God-given majesty. More practically, the lesson Louis had learned from the Fronde wars — that an independent nobility was a potential source of insurrection — meant that if he intended to keep the nobility permanently under his eyes, he needed a palace big enough to hold them. Quite literally, Louis's house had to contain his aristocracy, and thus, artistically and politically, Versailles represents Louis's personal achievements, the stage for the performance he made of his life.

The apartments assigned to Athénaïs de Montespan after their completion in 1676 are perhaps the greatest indication of her importance to Louis at the time. Her suite comprised twenty rooms adjacent to the King's on the second floor of the château, while the Queen had to make do with eleven. It was in Athénaïs's rooms that she and Louis would closet themselves in the window where Athénaïs made the King laugh until he ached with her remarks about those who passed beneath. The courtiers came to dislike this habit so much that they referred to walking under her windows as "going before the guns." Even the Queen was not safe. Once, during a promenade, her carriage forded a stream and filled with water, and Athénaïs declared that if she had been there, she would have called out, "La Reine boit," punning on the similarity of the verbs "to drink" and "to limp." Louis could not help laughing, but he would sternly remind Athénaïs that Marie-Thérèse was still her mistress. In fact, though Athénaïs's jokes were often cruel, she herself was not really malicious, or *méchante*. She would pour vitriol on bores and flatterers, but once she had made Louis laugh, she forgot her unkindness, as she never really meant to offend anyone, and much as the courtiers hated being the butt of her jokes, they never lost a taste for them.

Athénaïs was sometimes accused of callousness, but her ruthless lack of sentimentality might more accurately be seen as a reflection of an age which was much less compassionate, far more cruel. When Athénaïs's coach ran over a man and killed him, her companions reproached her because she did not burst into tears as they had done, but she accused them of hypocrisy, arguing that they were weeping at their own distress at the terrible sight and not for the victim. After all, people were run over all the time without causing grief among the court ladies. Mme. de Sévigné is equally realistic about the brutalities of the world she inhabited. Writing to her daughter with news of a battle in 1676, she reports cheerfully: "Condé was taken by storm the night of Saturday to Sunday. At first this news makes your heart beat faster; you think we must have paid dearly for this victory. Not at all, my dear, it only cost a few soldiers, and not one with a name." Emotion was saved for family or friends; the misfortunes of others were part of God's will and therefore a waste of feeling. Indeed, delight in cruelty was a disturbing pleasure for people of all classes, and the scaffold at the Place de Grève was as popular an outing as the opera or a good sermon. The master of the future Parisian doctor Noel Falconnet wrote to the boy's father that, as a reward for studying hard, he was treating his pupil to a viewing of a man being broken on the wheel. This was the more barbaric face of the occasionally caustic wit Athénaïs had learned to display in the salons of Paris, a symptom of a world where amusement and pain coexisted in far closer proximity than they do today.

Athénaïs shared Louis's passion for Versailles and had an equal taste for splendor, but like Louis she was not above the practical. The King took great pride in his kitchen garden, with its lettuces, cabbages, peaches and his favorite strawberries, and had no reservations about giving the Doge of Venice or the Siamese ambassador a tour of his vegetable patch. He even wrote and printed his own guidebook to the gardens of Versailles. Athénaïs delighted him with her design for a fountain, built on what is now the Bassin d'Apollon, which was based on a gilded weeping willow with over one hundred jets of water gushing from its branches. The water tree impressed everyone with its ingenuity, as did the exquisite porcelain Trianon which Louis had constructed for Athénaïs in 1670 on the site of a demolished village. This was a series of miniature pavilions made of blue and white Delft tiles enclosed by flower gardens of anemones, Spanish jasmine, tuberoses and orange trees which produced the intoxicating perfumes Louis and Athénaïs loved. It was a toy house, a house to make love in, and it says a good deal about Mme. de Maintenon's character that she later claimed it was too cold and had it pulled down.

Another lesson Louis had absorbed from Mazarin's predecessor, Richelieu, was that the "mythologization" of the monarchy was a powerful instrument for cultural unity and control. The arts could be used to exalt the King and to manipulate the opinion of the educated classes into a consciousness of national glory.

During Louis's adolescence, the dominant influence on culture in Paris was Italian, and the King was anxious to develop an indigenous style of French painting, music and dance which would be unique to his own court. Richelieu had, for example, turned the court ballets into political allegories, with the identification of the monarch with the sun as a prominent motif. As the decoration of Versailles had established, it was an ideal metaphor for the artistic representation of royal power. In 1621, Louis XIII had danced in the ballet *Le Soleil,* taking on the image of the sun with its overtones of divinity. The classical origins of the sun cult were numerous, but one of Louis's favorite incarnations, as we have seen, was that of Apollo, the sun god, and his encouragement of French culture was in some sense a pacific "Apollonian" counterpoint to the other arts his reign celebrated, those of Mars. The sun god is the center of the universe, and the begetter of the arts which glorify his power. Every work of art created in his reign, Louis believed, formed a fragment of his personal glory. Yet while Apollo is a leitmotif in Louis XIV's personal iconography, in Molière's comedy *Amphitryon,* the King took on the role of Jupiter.

In the play the conflict between the King, his mistress and her husband was played out on a literal stage, at the Tuileries on 16 January 1668, and before Athénaïs could enjoy her promising future, she had to await the dénouement of the piece. The stately masque of Versailles was still in the future and for the present, events had a more melodramatic flavor.

> *Un partage avec Jupiter*
> *N'a rien du tout qui déshonoré*
> *Et sans doute il ne peut être que glorieux*
> *De se voir le rival du souverain des dieux.*[2]

Thus Molière has Jupiter console the deceived husband, Amphitryon, who, returning from the wars, discovers that he has been cuckolded by Jupiter, who has taken Amphitryon's shape to spend a night with his wife Alcmène. The play has been categorized as belonging to the "literature of war" which developed as a subgenre following the King's return from his first successful military campaign and which also includes Corneille's *Au Roi de Son Retour de Flandre.* The implications of Molière's account of the returning warrior duped by the king of the gods have proved an irresistible parallel to Louis's affair with Athénaïs, though the play cannot be read as a rigorous allegory; it is, after all, an adaptation from Plautus, and was also adapted by the English poet Dryden. Given the general toleration of a king's extramarital dalliances, Molière could presume that his audience would respond with a degree of sophisticated amusement to any allusions the piece seemed to cast on current events. Jupiter's justification reflected the opinion of the court that to be cuckolded by the King was no disgrace. Conversely, a change of *maîtresse en titre* amounted to an affair of state, and the court cabals would be anxious to learn about the situation so that they could realign their loyalties and know who to cultivate. Thus Molière's reference to the affair would have been apposite. *Amphitryon* is a tempting source of clues to the extent of public knowledge of Louis's relationship with Athénaïs after the 1667 campaign. Did Molière wish to flatter the King by ridiculing the Marquis? Or did Louis take pleasure in seeing his love affair so slyly revealed? Despite the coincidences of life and art, it is best not to see the play as a "key," particularly as Louise de La Vallière was still the official mistress, and some ambiguity still shrouded Athénaïs's position. For example, the Marquis de Saint-Maurice, who had observed Louis's interest in Athénaïs in Flanders, wrote to the Duc de Savoie in February 1668, a month after *Amphitryon* was performed before the court, that despite the King's attentions, Mme. de Montespan "still held firm." At the theater of the court, the drama was just beginning. If the Marquis de Montespan knew of it, he had the sense, for the moment, to hold his tongue.

While his wife had been campaigning with the King, Montespan, hardly a triumphant Amphitryon, had fought a more or less ignominious campaign of his own near another disputed border with Spain at Roussillon. His conduct was passable at first, and he fought in the front line in a brief skirmish with the Spaniards. Louis, occupied in Paris that autumn of 1667, cleverly magnified the incident in order to soften up Montespan. "The King claims to be very satisfied with the bravery and bearing which you have shown in this encounter," ran the dispatches, "and His Majesty will give proof of this when he has occasion."[3] If, perhaps, it turned out that Amphitryon would be content to share his wife with Jupiter.

Delighted to find himself for once in the King's good graces, and too conceited to question the reason, Montespan celebrated with a little romantic dalliance of his own. He kidnapped a serving-girl in Perpignan and spirited her away disguised as a member of his own cavalry. The girl's outraged family had her apprehended by the bailiffs and committed to prison for her own safety. Montespan disgraced himself by fighting with the bailiff to recover her, but he soon grew bored and abandoned the girl with a meager dowry of twenty pistoles for her honor, returning early in 1668 to Paris, where he may have seen or heard about Molière's play. He remained there until 1 March, borrowing yet more money, and appearing to notice nothing odd in his domestic affairs, even though Athénaïs had moved their lodgings from St. Germain to the Rue St. Nicaise on the right bank, supposedly in order to facilitate her attendance on the Queen. Montespan, now in debt to the sum of 48,000 livres, could not stay long in Paris for fear of his creditors. Before setting off with his company back to Roussillon, he signed a document giving Athénaïs power of attorney over his affairs in his absence, demonstrating that at this stage he still had complete trust in his wife, even if he appeared to be indifferent to her welfare. He received notice of leave in June, and spent some time at his château, Bonnefont in Gascony, before returning to Paris at the end of the summer.

In September, the court were at Chambord, the childhood home of Louise de La Vallière, who still remained at court as favorite to shelter Athénaïs from scandal, a bizarre arrangement that continued for a total of six years. Louis made love to her absentmindedly from time to time, but had really lost all interest in her. Louise attempted a symbolic reproach to the King at Chambord, indicating a window which contained a famous couplet, supposedly scratched on the glass by François I: "*Souvent femme varié/Mal habie qui s'y fie*" — Woman is often fickle/Foolish the man who trusts her. Annoyed, Louis had the pane removed. Athénaïs was typically less reticent, complaining to Louis in no uncertain terms about his want of delicacy. Failing to placate her, Louis admitted that the situation had come about "*insensiblement.*" "Insensibly for you, perhaps," sniffed Athénaïs, "but very sensibly for me!"[4] It appears that Louis was dissembling, since something in his character clearly found this "harem" model appealing: it was to be repeated throughout his life. Perhaps he felt that Jupiter had the right to more than one woman at a time.

At the time of the visit to Chambord, Athénaïs discovered to her horror that she was pregnant. She was so anxious that she lost weight and her complexion faded. Mme. de Caylus wrote: "She is so changed that no one would recognize her." Until now, Athénaïs's husband had remained as ignorant as Molière's cuckold of the affair, but now the storm would surely break. No amount of classicized double entendres could conceal the fact that double adultery was a serious and shocking offense. The King's confessors would turn a blind eye to legions of seduced maids-of-honor, but a married man who cohabited with a married woman committed sacrilege in the eyes of the Catholic Church. Moreover, Montespan could legally claim any children his wife bore by the King as his own. Athénaïs was so frightened of this that she even considered asking Louise to pretend that the baby was hers.

Athénaïs was frantic, but she rallied herself and concealed the source of her despair under a new style of dress she had invented, a *robe battante* in loose, flowing chiffon. She was able to remain inconspicuous when the dress, slyly known as *l'Innocente,* immediately became the height of fashion. If Athénaïs suffered from the shame of this first pregnancy, "She consoled herself for the second," wrote Mme. de Caylus, "and carried her impudence about the others as far as possible." Later, everyone at court knew that if Mme. de Montespan was wearing her *robe battante,* she must be pregnant again.

When the time came for Athénaïs to give birth to their first child, Louis took charge of the arrangements personally. He rented a little house in the Rue de l'Echelle, not far from the Tuileries. As Athénaïs's labor began, Clément, the *accoucheur,* was summoned, blindfolded and pushed into a darkened room. When his eyes were uncovered, he saw a masked woman in the bed. The candles were put out. The doctor began to voice his opinion on such an odd arrangement, declaring that he was sure this secrecy must be concealing a scandal. He was silenced by a man's voice from the bed curtains, instructing him that he was there to do a job, and not to deliver a moral discourse. Clément then grumbled that he was hungry, and really couldn't begin until he had eaten. A young man slipped out from the shadows and rummaged around, producing some bread and jam, which the doctor munched appreciatively, adding that a little wine to wash it down wouldn't go amiss. "Have patience," muttered the King, "I can't do everything at once."

"Finally," remarked the doctor as a full glass was produced.

Just as he was about to ask for another, a groan from the bed put an end to the apparently interminable meal, and the doctor rolled up his sleeves. Louis hid once again in the bed curtains and held Athénaïs's hand, constantly asking when it would be over. The child was delivered about an hour later. Louis had to shield his face as he handed the doctor a candle.

This charming (if in part apocryphal) story shows Louis, who had probably never prepared a meal in his life, let alone served a bourgeois with a glass of wine, at his most human. For a while, in the dim candlelight, Louis and Athénaïs could have been any young lovers, he stroking her hair and soothing her as he waited anxiously to see his child. So much secrecy surrounded the birth that there is even dispute as to the baby's gender, but it seems most likely that it was a girl. She was spirited away by one of Athénaïs's maids, a Mlle. des Oeillets. Her name is not known for certain – it is thought to have been Louise-Françoise, a fitting combination of her parents' names — for she died, inconspicuously, three years later. Athénaïs was to give her second daughter by Louis, Mlle. de Nantes, born in 1673, the same name as her mysterious elder sister.

Despite the secrecy surrounding her pregnancy, it could not be long before Montespan discovered Athénaïs's secret, although it is uncertain how exactly he learned of her betrayal. His father, the old Marquis d'Antin, had taken a sanguine view of the matter. When he heard the story, he lifted up his hands and cried "Praise the Lord! Here is Fortune knocking on my door at last!" Athénaïs's own father, the Duc de Mortemart, was unkindly supposed to have taken a similar view of his daughter's moral decline. A court poem describes his reaction to the news of her pregnancy:

> Quand Mortemart eut aperçu
> Que Montespan avait concu
> Il prit son theorbe et chanta
> Alleluia![5]

The Marquis de Montespan, however, would not have his pride insulted even by the King, and resolved to create a scandal. Having ignored far more obvious hints, Montespan finally saw the light when the Duc de Montausier was appointed governor to the eight-year-old Dauphin. The Duc's wife was Athénaïs's friend Julie, who had helped her to arrange rendezvous with the King at Avesnes in the first secretive stages of their affair, and it was suddenly obvious to Montespan that the Duc owed his appointment to Athénaïs's gratitude for this assistance. If this was so, it was a bold demonstration of power on Athénaïs's part. Montespan rampaged through Paris society, recklessly denouncing the King as a second David, a thief and a vile seducer of women (obviously in a different league of wickedness from that of a man who kidnapped only servants). He bored and embarrassed the whole town with his tirades, and when society was not yawning, it was sneering at this ridiculous little Gascon who had the bad taste to complain that the King had seduced his wife. Why not be content to disguise your cuckold's horns with a discreet profit, since there was no disgrace in that? (This level of tolerance was to some degree contingent on the fact that Athénaïs's pregnancy was unknown, as double adultery resulting in children was a much more serious matter.) But Montespan was the opposite of discreet. He showed the King's cousin

Mademoiselle, one of his godparents, a text he claimed to have written which criticized the King in the strongest terms and called down Biblical imprecations on his royal head. Mademoiselle tried to reason with Montespan. "You are mad," she told him. "You must not tell such stories. People will never believe that you wrote this harangue; they'll think it's your uncle, the Archbishop of Sens, who is on bad terms with Mme. de Montespan."[6] But Montespan was too maddened with rage to pay her any attention.

Concerned, Mademoiselle sought out Athénaïs, and they took a private stroll on the terrace at St. Germain. Mademoiselle warned Athénaïs of her husband's fury, adding that if he did not calm down, he ran the risk of ending up in prison. Athénaïs hid her fear with a show of bravado, replying that she was ashamed to see her husband causing as much amusement to the hoi polloi as the vulgarities uttered by her parrot. Just at that moment, Athénaïs received an urgent message that Montespan was actually in the palace, in Mme. de Montausier's apartment. Too late, she rushed to her friend, and discovered Julie prostrate on a sofa, weeping and trembling with fear.

The next time Montespan appeared, he found Athénaïs with Julie. He made an appalling scene, treating both women to "unimaginable insults," according to Mademoiselle, and then disappearing like a stage villain, leaving them hysterical with fear. It would have been funny if it hadn't been real, but as it was, Athénaïs was tormented by his harassment. He stalked her, breaking into her bedroom at night and then vanishing, or lying in wait for her and beating her. Even worse, he was boasting in Paris that he was frequenting the filthiest brothels in town in the hope of contracting syphilis and passing it on to the King via Athénaïs. Terrified, Athénaïs changed her lodgings and moved into Mme. de Montausier's apartment. When he found out, Montespan broke down the door and attempted to rape his wife, who clung to her friend for safety, both of them screaming for help as Montespan tried to wrench them apart. The servants rushed in, and Montespan had to content himself with screaming abuse at Athénaïs. The next rumor was that Montespan was planning to abduct his wife and carry her off to Spain.

It seems curious that the King should allow Montespan to remain at large, but it was difficult for him to intervene. There was no legal reason why a man could not insult, beat or rape his own wife, and beyond providing her with bodyguards, there was little Louis could do without attracting the attention of the Queen. It is depressing that Louis did so little to protect the woman he loved.

Was it love or pride that made Montespan lose his mind? If he truly loved Athénaïs, he had hardly given her cause to believe so, with his debts and extravagance, his voluntary absences and his exploits with camp followers. Having experienced his rage, Athénaïs must have felt more than ever that she was justified in trying to escape from such a man. Insults and assaults were hardly the way to win her back.

Eventually, Louis did act. He produced a lettre de cachet which banished Montespan to the prison at Fort-l'Eveque on the grounds that he had challenged the King's authority with regard to the choice of preceptor for the Dauphin. Lettres de cachet were one of the most objectionable features of the French ancien régime. They enabled the King personally to imprison anyone who displeased him, indefinitely and without trial. A week cooling his heels in an unwholesome strong room seems to have calmed Montespan's temper, and he accepted that the separation from Athénaïs was inevitable. He indicated this acceptance by revoking the power of attorney he had made in his wife's favor the preceding spring. A few days later he was released, with strict orders to remain at his country estate, effectively in exile from society.

At this point, there were rumors that Louis had succeeded in paying off Montespan. Mme. de Sévigné's correspondent Bussy-Rabutin whispered about the sum of 100,000 livres. However, he had his own reasons for making out that Athénaïs was a piece of goods for sale, as he was peeved that one of his own relatives, Mme. de Sévigné's daughter, had not succeeded in turning an earlier flirtation with the King to the good. Both Mme. de Caylus and Monsieur's second wife, the Princesse Palatine, later agreed that Montespan might have been more reasonable if he had been rewarded from the first, but he was either too proud to sell his wife or too obtuse to realize that a quiet, civilized acquiescence was a better means of obtaining such a reward. Whatever the case, his subsequent theatrics suggest that he received no financial satisfaction.

Montespan left Paris with his three-year-old son Louis-Antoine to join his mother and daughter Marie-Christine in Gascony. Athénaïs was not allowed to see her boy again until he was fourteen, and this loss of her legitimate children was the first great sacrifice she had to make for Louis's sake. It seems likely that the anxious and ambitious love she showed for her children by the King was fueled by guilt at her perceived desertion of little Marie-Christine and Louis-Antoine. When Montespan arrived at Bonnefont, he insisted on having the main gates opened, claiming that his cuckold's horns were too tall to pass through the postern. He informed the waiting household that his wife was dead, sarcastically attributing the demise of "his dear and well-loved spouse" to "coquetry and ambition." It is claimed that he invited all the neighbors to a sham funeral in the village church, during which a dummy of Athénaïs was buried, and dressed his family in full mourning. He draped his carriage in black crêpe and rattled about the countryside with a large pair of antlers strapped to the roof. His eccentricities might be confined to the provinces for the present, but it was always possible that the mad Marquis might reappear.

As for Julie de Montausier, her elderly nerves never recovered from the shock of the episode. Her mother may have been a famous *précieuse,* but the rude intervention of real passion was too much for a woman more accustomed to the elegant, casuistical gallantries of the salon. Julie went into a decline and died, begging forgiveness on her deathbed for her involvement in promoting the King's affair with Athénaïs.

For Louis, the next years were happy ones, filled with his favorite activities of fighting, building and lovemaking. Although Athénaïs was now certain of his regard for her, there were still many obstacles in the way of the domination she was coming to crave. Louise de La Vallière was still a lingering, reproachful presence, and Athénaïs's marriage was still a potential barrier to the certainty she sought.

Perhaps she felt rather exhausted at the prospect of all the plotting and intriguing, lovemaking and quarreling, cajoling and charming that lay ahead of her. Louise was so stubbornly entrenched that more than natural means might be necessary to remove her, and traditionally, the Devil had always been a friend to the Rochechouart women. During her childhood at Lussac, Athénaïs may have shivered with fear in the candlelit nursery as her nurse Nounou recounted the family legend of her early sixteenth-century ancestor, Renée Taveau. In 1530 Renée, the young daughter of the Baron de Mortemart, fell ill, and her husband, François Rochechouart, found her dying. She was buried, still in her teens, covered with her jewels, notably a magnificent diamond ring. After the interment, a greedy servant tried to rob her grave and steal the jewel. Unable to force it off her stiff, cold finger, he decided, horribly, to bite the finger off at the joint in order to get the diamond. As he bit into the chilly flesh, the "corpse" suddenly woke up. It was not long, of course, before stories of vampirism and devil worship were added to the tale. Poor Renée — who, presumably, had not died at all but had merely fallen into a coma — was rumored to be a demon, full of supernatural lust, but her husband was so delighted to get her back that, demon or not, he gave her three children, one of whom was Athénaïs's grandfather.

In the seventeenth century, many court ladies still consulted "sorcerers," clattering down in their carriages from St. Germain, masked and giggling, to have a fortune told, a beauty potion made up, or perhaps to purchase a little "powder" to encourage a lover's flagging ardor. Two such practitioners, Mariette and Lesage, operated from the slum district of St. Denis, and offered a variety of devilish products and services, including aphrodisiac potions imbued with special powers from having been passed under the holy chalice used for Mass. Athénaïs and her sister-in-law, Mme. de Vivonne, paid them a visit hoping to acquire a mixture that would put the finishing touch to Athénaïs's plan to replace Louise de La Vallière as *maîtresse en titre*. Mariette recited an incantation over Athénaïs's head and sent her away with a powder, probably composed of Spanish fly, well known for its capacity to excite and harmless enough if administered in small doses. It would not be difficult for her to administer the aphrodisiac, as Louis was in the habit of taking "purges" for his bowels, and was not curious as to their contents. In the 1670s, the royal doctor D'Acquin, who owed his position to Athénaïs's favor, was prepared to turn a blind eye to her ministrations, particularly as he probably knew that such love powders were no more dangerous than the purges he himself prescribed. Maybe Athénaïs did not really believe that she was actually invoking Satan in her cause, but she would nonetheless have known that he is a treacherous ally however tenuous the connection, and generally exacts a price for his services. Much later, she would come to regret her playful visit to the sorcerers as the greatest indiscretion of her life.

Chapter Six

"Greater virtues are needed to bear
good fortune than bad."

Athénaïs did not rely exclusively on spells to affirm her position.
With Montespan still lurking threateningly in the wings, she
decided to attempt a legal separation from her husband, and in July
1670 began proceedings in the Châtelet court in Paris, petitioning for
relief from his "cruelty and improvidence," charges which were reasonable in themselves, regardless of any other motivations for the separation. Athénaïs requested the return of her dowry, which was in
fact still largely unpaid and in any case promised to Montespan's creditors, in order to provide herself with a separate maintenance, and
permission to live officially apart from her husband. This was the
"separation of bed and board" that her mother Diane had obtained
from the Duc de Mortemart, in legal terms the throwing off of the
restrictive "shackles of *couverture*." The case did not progress through
the lumbering leviathan of the French legal system for four years, but
its instigation at this point testifies to an increase in Athénaïs's certainty that she would remain an important part of the King's life.

Indeed, there seemed no question that Athénaïs was firmly established as *maîtresse en titre,* despite the continuing presence of Louise.
The King seemed more in love than ever, and showed his passion more
publicly, taking Athénaïs with him to the famous fête given by the
Prince de Condé at Chantilly to admire the creations of Condé's celebrated maître d'hôtel, Vatel. During the spring of that year, 1671, the
court had progressed through the newly conquered towns of Flanders,

accompanied by 30,000 men under the command of the Comte de Lauzun who were to fortify and man the French garrisons. En route, they deposited Madame Henriette at Dunkirk, where she was to be collected by the English fleet for a visit to her brother Charles II, King of England, in order to negotiate a secret alliance between her native and adoptive countries. Known as the "Wheelbarrow Campaign," this mission prepared the Anglo-French axis for the invasion of Holland in 1672. Athénaïs excitedly described Madame's departure to her brother Vivonne.

Ah, what a beautiful day! Madame was radiant with joy, the Queen too had a joyful air. I think that all the most beautiful women were united to ornament the fête. I have never seen the King so handsome. One would never have dared to think that he was preoccupied by so many important interests, gallant with all the ladies, as respectful as one could be to the Queen, so that all the world had reason to be content . . . The fleet of the King of England was superb. Madame embarked with a great deal of courage. Nevertheless, we believed, all the court and I, that her last interview with the King had been touching because her eyes were full of tears. The Queen held her a long time in an embrace, and only left her when the King said, "It is not an eternal separation, we will see one another again soon." So Madame recovered her composure and embarked with a tranquil air, which imposed silence upon us about the dangers of the sea which we were imagining. The court remained at the port for as long as we could distinguish them. Then the King took the Queen on one arm, and me on the other . . .[1]

It was during this tour, Voltaire writes, that "Mme. de Montespan's triumph shone forth . . . At such times as she rode alone, she had four bodyguards posted at her carriage door . . . It was to Mme. de Montespan that all the court paid homage, all honors were for her save those reserved by tradition and protocol for the Queen."[2] Louis had shown a positive genius for separating affairs of heart from those of the state, since Marie-Thérèse was the only person at court not to guess what was going on. Such blindness seems inconceivable, yet she continued to behave affectionately towards Athénaïs as she went about her service. It is doubtful that Athénaïs felt guilty, and she had the good taste not to pretend to, either. It was during this trip that the King's party was forced to sleep together under the Queen's beady eye. Mademoiselle describes vividly the miserable dinner they made of chickens so tough they could hardly pull their legs off. Mme. de Thianges tried to make the best of it by remarking from her uncomfortable straw pallet that she felt renewed faith in Jesus, as it was so easy, surrounded as they were by lowing cattle, to imagine herself in the stable at Bethlehem. Such voyages were not without other difficulties for Athénaïs. She was once present at a military review at which she was greeted by the King's German soldiers with the cry "Koenig's Hure, Hure!" — "See, see the King's harlot!" She bore it with good grace, refraining from comment save for to answer the King, when he asked how she had found the experience: "Perfectly correct, except that, since I had the German translated, I find they are very naïve to call things by their proper names."[3]

Madame's diplomatic mission was a success, resulting in the 1670 Treaty of Dover, whereby Charles II agreed to provide 6,000 soldiers and fifty ships to aid Louis in his planned war against the Dutch in exchange for an annual subsidy of 3 million livres. Sadly, Henriette did not live to savor the approbation she had earned. By 29 June, just eleven days after her return to St. Germain, she was dead.

Madame's sudden death, occurring as it did so soon after the signature of the sensitive treaty with Charles of England, who had loved "the sweetest princess ever to walk this earth" very dearly, quickly gave rise to ominous rumors. Henriette had expired after drinking a glass of chicory cordial to quench her thirst on a hot day. Shortly afterwards she was complaining of such agony that she declared, "Were I not a Christian, I would kill myself, so violent are my sufferings." She lingered for nine hours, dying, in Voltaire's words, "in the flower of her youth and in the arms of Bossuet."[4]

Louis had loved his sister-in-law, too well in the opinion of her husband Monsieur, and the whole court joined with him in mourning the dizzy, charming, delicate Duchesse d'Orléans. Bishop Bossuet, tutor to the Dauphin, summed up the general mood in his famous funeral oration. "O cruel night, tragic night, night of terror! When there rang out, sudden as a clap of thunder, that shocking report: Madame is dying, Madame is dead!"[5] He compared her to a fragile wild flower, blooming in the morning, desiccated by sunset. Athénaïs and Louise had visited her deathbed together, weeping for

their friend and erstwhile mistress. They had both been plucked by the
King from the beautiful coterie of attendants known as "Madame's
flower garden," and perhaps her death marked for both women, triumphant and vanquished alike, the passing of their youth at the King's
court of love.

The rumors of a fatal poison in the chicory water soon began
to point to Monsieur. Monsieur had led a life of both enviable tranquillity and immense frustration. In his childhood, his mother Anne
had been anxious to prevent the growth of any rivalry between her
sons of the kind that had developed between Louis XIII and his
brother Gaston d'Orléans (the father of Mademoiselle), which might
threaten the security of the nation. Accordingly, Monsieur was deliberately emasculated, dressed in frilly girls' clothes and encouraged to
interest himself only in pictures and dress rather than in politics or
military strategy. The plan succeeded so well that Monsieur became,
in Nancy Mitford's words, "one of history's most famous sodomites,"[6] a vice which he was supposed to have learned from the Duc de
Nevers. (It was likely that Louis XIII, too, had had homosexual lean-
ings.) Despite Louis's personal abhorrence for "the Italian vice," he tol-
erated it in Monsieur, whom he adored so long as he behaved, and
allowed Athénaïs to persuade him to arrange a marriage between
Nevers and her impoverished niece, Mlle. de Thianges. He then
appointed Nevers to so many sinecures that the girl might as well have
been an heiress.

Monsieur flaunted his homosexuality as the only form of distinction permitted him. When young, he had proved himself an able as
well as a highly decorative soldier, arriving on the field hatless (for fear
of crushing his wig) in a splendid get-up complete with powder,
rouge, fluttering ribbons and diamond jewelry. Louis, however, disapproved of his brother distinguishing himself in war, and encouraged
him to retire from the army. Monsieur's château at St. Cloud was celebrated for its beauty, and he was the arbiter elegantiarum for the whole
court, but his love of art could not compensate for his sense of super-
fluity, and he became rather embittered, loving his brother for the distinctions he conferred, but hating him for keeping him in a state of
financial dependence, forced to dance attendance on the royal whims
like all the other courtiers. "Now we are going to work, go and amuse
yourself, brother," Louis would say condescendingly. Monsieur was a
great friend to Athénaïs as well as to her sister, Mme. de Thianges, but

he was influenced by a malign cabal of minions who tried to wheedle favor through exploiting his weakness for a pretty face. Most prominent among them were the Marquis d'Effiat and the Chevalier de Lorraine, Monsieur's lover. Monsieur was completely under the sway of his poisonous little darling, so much so that Louis had exiled Lorraine from the court early in 1670 as a result of Madame's reports of her husband's increasing abandonment to debauchery. It was Lorraine, the rumormongers whispered, who had procured in Rome the fatal poison with which Monsieur had destroyed his wife. There had never been much love lost between them — indeed, their quarrels and sulks were common knowledge — but the part Madame had played in the exile of the Chevalier had put her in danger, and she berated her husband for her murder even as she lay dying. Monsieur, unperturbed, even suggested that the chicory water be tested on a dog. His sanguinity was supported by the autopsy, which confirmed that Henriette had died of natural causes. "Thus," wrote Lord Arlington, the English secretary of state, "were allayed most of our suspicions,"[7] but the qualification testifies to an enduring doubt.

With heartless pragmatism, Louis proposed the vacant position of Duchesse d'Orléans to his cousin Mademoiselle while the previous incumbent's body was barely cold. Mademoiselle was disgusted, though not by her cousin's indelicacy but at the suggestion that she, the greatest heiress in Europe, who had refused the hands of five monarchs and innumerable lesser suitors, should ally herself with this strutting, preening younger son. Impossible! Perhaps her refusal was a deliberate snub to the Bourbons, since in her youth Mademoiselle had set her cap at Louis, but then ruined her chances by taking the opposing side in the Fronde wars.

It might seem surprising that Mademoiselle, a member of the royal family, should have sided against the King, but in essence the Fronde was not antimonarchical so much as anti-Mazarin. During Louis's minority, the Frondeurs had wanted to offer the regency to Gaston d'Orléans instead of to Anne of Austria, who, it was perceived, was entirely ruled by Mazarin. Mazarin was unpopular with the old aristocracy, and though the Prince de Condé had saved the monarchy by riding furiously to Paris with his troops at Mazarin's request when the regency was contested, he soon grew irritated at taking orders from the cardinal. Condé did not seem to understand that he could not oppose the King's minister without opposing the King, and in 1649 he had sent his personal army to aid the Frondeurs in the French provinces. As a result, Mazarin had had him arrested, and in 1650 Condé retaliated by trying to seize Paris. As his troops attempted to storm the town, Mademoiselle tried to rouse her father, Gaston, to come to his aid. Gaston prevaricated, so Mademoiselle, magnificent but misguided, rushed to the Bastille and, claiming that she was acting on his authority, had the cannons turned on the King's troops. "She has killed her husband," remarked Mazarin,[8] watching the battle, as Mademoiselle's hopes of marrying Louis went up in smoke. When order was restored, Mademoiselle had been invited to "retire" for a while, and though both she and Condé were eventually rehabilitated and permitted to return to court, she felt cheated of the crown she was convinced she deserved.

Mademoiselle was suspicious of Monsieur, and believed the rumors that he had poisoned his wife. She expressed a sharp concern for her own safety, remarking tartly to Monsieur: "As it is not likely that I should ever come to terms with your favorites, I shall never be anything else to you but a cousin, and I shall endeavor not to die before the proper time . . . You can repeat this speech to your precious Marquis d'Effiat and M. de Lorraine. They have no access to my kitchens, I am not afraid of them."

Monsieur did marry again, as soon as the official period of mourning was over. The royal house of France needed heirs, and of Louis's children with the Queen, only the Dauphin had lived. The Bourbons were not a lucky family when it came to wives. Like his brother before him, poor little Monsieur turned famously pale when he caught sight of his strapping new spouse for the first time. "How will I be able to sleep with her?" he groaned. The lady in question was Elisabeth-Charlotte of Bavaria, daughter of the Elector Palatine, known as La Palatine or Liselotte to her family. A Valkyrie of a woman, she was large, stout and red-faced, and cheerfully open about her own ugliness. She was passionate about hunting, eating and her brother-in-law, a fascination that Louis returned with uneasy affection. She and Athénaïs never hit it off as Athénaïs was less than kind about the new Madame's appearance, and La Palatine was wary of Athénaïs's quick French wit. They had no sense of humor in common, as Madame's taste in jokes was for the slapstick and lavatorial. She describes in her enormous correspondence one evening chez Orléans during which Monsieur "let off a great long fart. He turned to me and said, 'What was that, Madame?' I turned my behind in his direction, let off one in the same tone and said, 'That, Monsieur.' My son said, 'If it comes to that, I can do as well as Monsieur and Madame,' and let off a good one, too. Then we all laughed."[9] It is hard to imagine Athénaïs deriving much amusement from such horseplay. But La Palatine was not a total boor. She loved the theater, and was a vivid, if not elegant writer. Monsieur did manage to do his duty to France and give her three children, assisted by the attachment of his rosary to a certain part of his body, which resulted in a great deal of rattling under the blankets. Louis allowed the Chevalier de Lorraine to come back as a reward for his brother's good behavior, so Monsieur had good reason to be grateful to Madame. So all in all, this unlikely match was much more successful than his first marriage. Monsieur was particularly pleased that his tomboyish wife cared more for her riding habits than for court finery, as it gave him the freedom to bedeck himself in her jewels as well as his own. "Monsieur is the most foolish woman at court," ran a contemporary joke, "and Madame the most foolish man."

Mademoiselle, meanwhile, had more personal reasons for refusing Monsieur's hand. Her real motivation may have been that, aged forty-three, she had fallen in love for the first time. It was her romance that provided Athénaïs with a definitive opportunity to involve herself in court politics.

The object of Mademoiselle's long-dormant passion was Athénaïs's old friend the Comte de Lauzun. Although Athénaïs had not quite forgiven Lauzun for intimating that he had once been her lover, she was incapable of bearing grudges, and she liked Lauzun's wit as much as she was amused by his strutting, Gascon arrogance. When her second child by Louis, a boy, was born, at St. Germain in the winter of 1670, it was Lauzun who was entrusted with smuggling him out of the palace. Athénaïs barely had time to see the child before he was wrapped up, hidden under Lauzun's coat, and smuggled through the freezing park to a hired carriage waiting at the gate. It was the kind of drama they both enjoyed.

Despite his stunted, flabby body and indifferent title, the lieutenant of the armies enjoyed great success with women, which he had manipulated to elevate himself from a lowly beginning as a simple soldier to his present powerful position. If his ardor was not aroused by Mademoiselle's less-than-beauteous middle-aged charms, then his insatiable ambition certainly was. If he could become Mademoiselle's husband, he would become the Duc de Montpensier, first cousin by marriage to the King, and the richest man in France. Mademoiselle, for her part, was as ridiculously enamored as a convent virgin of fourteen, and so determined to marry her lover that Louis, with great reluctance, gave his consent to the match. "I do not advise it," he said, "but I will not forbid it, though I beg you to be careful — Many people dislike M. de Lauzun." Dazzled by each other, Mademoiselle and Lauzun began to plan an ostentatious state wedding.

The reaction to this engagement is best captured by Mme. de Sévigné in a letter dated 15 December 1670:

> What I am about to communicate to you is the most astonishing thing, the most surprising, the most marvelous, the most miraculous, most triumphant, most baffling, most unheard of, most singular, most extraordinary, most unbelievable, most unforeseen, biggest, tiniest, rarest, commonest, the most talked about, the most secret up to this day, the most brilliant, the most enviable . . . in short a thing that will be done on Sunday.[10]

Such a match was indeed unheard of, but while Mme. de Sévigné and her set considered it a tremendous joke, one faction at court saw it as a serious threat to the King's authority. The Queen, Monsieur, the Prince de Condé and his son M. le Duc, the princesses of the blood and Mademoiselle's sister Mme. de Guise all petitioned the King to undo his consent, terrified of the precedent that would be set if a commoner were allowed to marry into the royal family. This obsessive concern for breeding seems slightly ridiculous today, but it was the dominant social force of the times, and treated with deadly seriousness. Feeling ran so high that the Maréchal de Villeroy threw himself on his knees before Louis, imploring him to prevent a union that would so seriously diminish the royal reputation. Athénaïs, however, found herself in the opposite camp.

Lauzun and Athénaïs had more than the secret of the birth of Athénaïs's child in common, for Lauzun had also been instrumental in facilitating the Nevers marriage for Athénaïs's niece. "Mme. de Montespan does marvels everywhere," wrote Mme. de Sévigné, impressed by the success of the unlikely match that repaired the Thianges fortunes. So it seemed right that Athénaïs, who was also fond of

Mademoiselle, should pursue Lauzun's interest with Louis, and she promised to do all she could to help to counter the appeals against the marriage. Soon, though, she began to doubt the wisdom of her promise, so strong did the opposition seem. She herself received a visit from the Princesse de Carignan, who asked her to use her influence with Louis to prevent it, on the grounds that he had regretted giving his consent from the moment he had done so. Athénaïs, seeing the way the wind was blowing, realized that her own position would be compromised if she found herself on the losing side. And so, with a rather dishonorable motive of self-preservation, she betrayed Lauzun and advised Louis to put an end to the affair. Undoubtedly, hers was the decisive intervention.

On 18 December, Louis summoned his cousin and Lauzun and told them he could not permit the wedding to go ahead. The settlement had already been made, and Lauzun had been the bearer of the name of Montpensier for a whole day, but it was not to be. He could not allow his rage to show, being obliged instead to make a great performance of his broken heart. Mademoiselle's grief was sincere and vociferous. She railed and wept and took to her bed, but breeding conquered in the end, and by 24 December she had collected herself sufficiently to return her duty calls. "So that is that," concludes Mme. de Sévigné bluntly.[11] Lauzun retained the goodwill of the King by exhibiting just the right blend of sadness and stoicism, and Athénaïs was in high favor with those in the know for her good judgment, having remained apparently strong in Louis's moment of weakness, bringing "joy not only [to] the court, but to the whole realm in the rupture of this marriage for which no example can be found in history." Skillfully, Athénaïs concealed her involvement from Mademoiselle, but she had turned her friend Lauzun into an implacable enemy, and he set about plotting his revenge.

In 1671, Athénaïs's position was still sufficiently ambiguous for it to be plausible that the King would return to Louise, and Lauzun planned to precipitate the favorite's downfall by bringing this about. Louise was still hanging on with masochistic tenacity, partly out of concern for the position of her children, and partly in the hope that she would return to favor. Louise's apologists claim that she remained at court in the role of a suffering martyr, publicly expiating her sins, but this is an explanation provided retrospectively by Louise herself. At the time, she showed herself to be weak yet stubborn, and not above attempts to manipulate the King's remaining affection, a tendency which Lauzun hoped to exploit.

Historians are at odds as to the cordiality of the entente between the two women. In the code used by Mme. de Sévigné to avoid censorship of her gossipy letters, she refers to Athénaïs and Louise respectively as "the Torrent" and "the Dew," nicknames that neatly sum up their characters and the inevitable conflicts between them. Publicly, at least, everything went on harmoniously, as is demonstrated by one record of Louis and his two women departing to hunt the wild boar at Fontainebleau in the same carriage. On another occasion, the English envoy the Duke of Buckingham was received by Lauzun while the King was still officially in mourning for Henriette d'Angleterre. After supper, Athénaïs and Louise appeared, led by the hands of a masked cavalier, and all three performed a charming ballet, at the conclusion of which the ladies "chased" Louis (for of course it was he) for his diamond-studded sword. This Louis presented to Buckingham in an elegant piece of diplomacy centered on his knowing play on words: "Since the ladies have disarmed me, I offer you my sword." The gift was worth 16,000 ecus.

To maintain the pretense that Louis was still in love with Louise, she and Athénaïs were always lodged in adjoining rooms, where they shared their meals, their toilette and their leisure time. During the military campaign of 1673, for example, Louis gave Colbert precise instructions, along with a plan, for his ladies' lodgings. Athénaïs's room was to have direct access to his own, while Louise's, next door to Athénaïs's, should be separated from it by a discreet passage.

Louis was scrupulous about appearing fair to the odalisques in his seraglio. In 1669 his architect Jean Marot was commissioned to create four grottos in the rocaille style at a cost of 1,000 livres each, two for the Duchesse de La Vallière and two for Mme. de Montespan. Pointedly, Louise's was decorated with a fresco of Calypso mourning her abandonment by Ulysses. Everyone knew that when the King was "*chez les dames,*" as the polite euphemism ran, he passed through Louise's room only to gain access to Athénaïs's. One spiteful story has it that Louis had a spaniel (named Malice in some versions), which he tossed to Louise as he passed, saying, "Here, Madame, take your company. That will do for you." Given Louis's famous good manners towards women, this seems somewhat unlikely, but it is common to hate those whom we have wronged, and Louis in particular was not a man who was comfortable with the dissonance of guilt. He was intrinsically vastly selfish, and though he was good-mannered because graceful manners pleased him, he was utterly indifferent to the feelings of others if they compromised his own inclinations. Louise's mute, reproachful grieving must have been at once painful and exasperating to the King, and incensing to Athénaïs.

A great deal has been made of Athénaïs's cruelty to the fallen favorite; of how she turned all her capacity for bitchy wit on to poor Louise and forced her to act as a ladies' maid, dressing Athénaïs's hair in preparation for a rendezvous with the King. "The Montespan woman," wrote the Princess Palatine, "derided La Vallière in public, treated her abominably, and obliged the King to do likewise." If Athénaïs really was so unkind (and La Palatine, of course, had her own reasons for disliking Mme. de Montespan), then surely Louise's infuriating lack of dignity provides some excuse? It seems reasonable that Athénaïs should feel just as threatened by Louise's presence as Louise was by hers. Athénaïs was in a position akin to that of a second wife whose wishes are constantly thwarted by her husband's duty to a demanding ex, and her lack of patience, if not the way in which she manifested it, is understandable. As long as Louise was there, Athénaïs could not be certain that the King loved her exclusively. She was quite justified in this doubt. One of the quarrels between the two women erupted over a pot of marvelous rouge which Louise refused to lend to Athénaïs. She agreed to surrender it only when Louis intervened, and even then, only on condition that he distribute his favors equally. The result was that Louise fell pregnant again, and storms raged in the harem. (Presumably Louise lost the child, as no more mention is made of it.) She remained a thorn in Athénaïs's side, making a great fuss of the angelic patience with which she withstood her rival's attempts to drive her out.

It is difficult to find a reason for Louis's desire to keep both women quite so close to him, especially in view of the trouble it occasioned him. Yet this was a model he repeated throughout his life. The current mistress usually presented him to the new, after which both women would be maintained in uneasy cohabitation. This was the case with Madame Henriette and La Vallière (although it is unlikely that in this case Louis actually slept with his sister-in-law), with La Vallière and

Montespan, with Montespan and Mlle. de Fontanges and finally with Montespan and Mme. de Maintenon. Louis was clearly polygamous by temperament, and saw no reason to resist his inclinations.

In addition to putting up with the presence of her disgruntled rival, the mistress of the moment was expected to ignore his numerous transient infidelities. It was quite usual for Louis to take a turn with Athénaïs's ladies' maid as she finished dressing, to tumble into bed with Mme. de Thianges, if her sister was indisposed, or simply to avail himself of a pretty servant he passed in the palace. Although Athénaïs enjoyed sex with Louis, she may have been grateful rather than otherwise that these brief, meaningless liasions deflected his appetite to some extent. In any event she seemed untroubled by quick physical encounters, feeling threatened only when the King's emotions seemed to be engaged, as they still appeared to be with Louise.

Athénaïs's independent, sociable nature was also aggravated by the closeted conditions in which she and Louise lived. The Marquis de Saint-Maurice recalled in his memoirs[12] that Louis "kept his first two declared mistresses in a state of semi-imprisonment, forbidding them visitors for fear of persuasions to intercession." Louis was always infuriated by the idea that his lovers might try to influence him, and though Athénaïs and Louise were not actually confined to their apartments, they did lead a sequestered life, and were not fully at liberty to come and go as they pleased. Moreover, they knew that whatever they did would be reported back to Louis. Perhaps he was jealous, or amused by the conceit of a harem, since they were metaphorically, if not literally, locked up, and "no one dared to look at them."[13] Living together as they did in such a restricted environment must at times have been so intolerable it is hardly surprising that the tension sometimes exploded into quarrels.

Lauzun, believing that Louise's influence was still sufficient to enable him to effect a rapprochement, encouraged her to make a retreat to the convent, in the hope that Louis would gallop after his suffering maiden, as he had done nine years before, and return her to favor, his love reignited by her escape.

The strategy had worked in 1662, when Louise had fallen out with the King over her loyalty to an old friend, Anne-Constance de Montalais. Louis disapproved of Anne-Constance, who was not only an ally of the disgraced Fouquet, but had been acting as a go-between for Mme. Henriette and her alleged lover, the Comte de Guiche. Perhaps Louis was piqued by his sister-in-law's fickle affections, or perhaps he felt that Anne-Constance had gone too far in arranging for De Guiche to visit Henriette in disguise. Whatever his reasons, he forbade Louise from seeing her friend. Never much of a politician, Louise stubbornly remained loyal to Anne-Constance, and the lovers had quarreled. Louise left the Tuileries for Chaillot, where the King found her the same night, shivering and sobbing on the parlor floor. He ordered a coach to return her to court, and afterwards they had seemed more in love than ever.

So, early on Ash Wednesday 1671, while the music and laughter of the great carnival ball continued into the dawn, Louise exchanged her elaborate court dress for a simple gown and once again walked from the Tuileries to the village of Chaillot, where she demanded sanctuary from the nuns at the Visitandine convent. In a suitably dramatic touch, the abbey was consecrated to Mary Magdalene. At Lauzun's suggestion, she left a letter for the King explaining that all she wished was to repent, and that she wanted to abandon the court, her children and her fortune for a life of prayer.

On hearing the news, Louis did not trouble to alter his program for the day, departing for Versailles as planned with Mademoiselle and Athénaïs in his carriage. Athénaïs was exuberant at this display of indifference. On the journey, Louis did at least become rather emotional, and the two women were obliged to squeeze out a few empathetic tears. Athénaïs diplomatically imitated the King's regret, and Lauzun, whose role in the affair, obviously, was unknown, was dispatched to reason with Louise. He rushed to Chaillot, certain that his plan had worked, but Louise told him that she was sincere, and had no desire to return to court. Back dashed Lauzun to Versailles, where he explained this obstinacy so eloquently — Louise, he reported, had said that having given her youth to the King, she wished to dedicate the rest of her life to God — that Louis was moved to tears, and sent Colbert to return her, by force if necessary. Now convinced of the King's sincerity, Louise gave up her vocation with remarkable ease, and was back at Versailles by six o'clock in the evening.

Through this hypocrisy and emotional blackmail, Louise achieved a respite. She was received in tears by the King, and Athénaïs, too, wept and clasped Louise to her bosom like a long-lost sister. Presumably her tears were tears of rage, but at least they seemed appropriate to the general mood. But Lauzun's plan was only half-successful, for although Louise enjoyed a new favor, Athénaïs was by no means repudiated. The opinion of the court was that Louise had made herself ridiculous, but things went on pretty much as before. It was felt that Mme. de La Vallière no longer sighed for the convent and that she was happier because the King had more regard for her than before. Bussy-Rabutin was not convinced. "I maintain that it is for his own interests and from pure politics that the King has recalled Mme. de La Vallière." As Athénaïs's separation bill crawled through the courts, it was still necessary to provide a cover for her presence. Even though no one believed that the King was still sleeping with Louise, she continued to pursue her advantage, succeeding in having all her debts paid on the basis that she would otherwise be unable to afford to accompany the court to Flanders on the usual summer campaign. Athénaïs had to content herself with the King's private passion.

Lauzun, meanwhile, had profited from the disappointment of his canceled marriage. The King had assured him that he would be so favored as not to regret the fortune he had lost, and immediately after the breaking of the engagement, Lauzun had received 500,000 livres in compensation, and the even more valuable *grande entrée,* which had been accorded to Athénaïs's father in the previous reign, an honor reserved for the king's gentlemen of the chamber which allowed access to the royal person at all times. The influence thus granted to Lauzun was immense, and he would also be able to profit from courtiers who would pay him well to put their requests to the King in private moments. Louis also gave Lauzun the governorships of Berry, Bourges and Issoudun, which provided a large rental income, and included his name among the candidates for a *maréchal*'s baton. But none of these rewards appeased Lauzun's rancor against Athénaïs. On the surface, they remained friends, and he concealed his urge for revenge with courtesy, lending Athénaïs his fine horses for the 1671 Flanders trip and sending her beautiful Flemish pictures on a visit to Amsterdam.

When the Maréchal de Gramont resigned his commission, Lauzun asked Athénaïs to solicit the post for him. He knew that Gramont was keen that it should go to his son, the Comte de Guiche, the disappointed lover of poor Madame Henriette, who, as a result of his attentions to that lady, was in low favor at court. Lauzun did not really trust Athénaïs, who had already betrayed him, and he resorted to extraordinary measures to prove her disloyalty in the matter of the commission. With the help of a bribed maid, he managed to conceal himself underneath Athénaïs's bed, where he waited for the King to join her. Among other things, he heard Athénaïs criticizing him to the King, and trying to persuade Louis to give the post he coveted to Guiche. "More happy than wise," Lauzun remained undiscovered as the King got up, dressed and left Athénaïs to make her toilette for a grand ballet that was to be given that evening. The maid pulled Lauzun out and he waited at Athénaïs's door until she emerged. Then he politely inquired after the success of her mission. As soon as she had dissembled that the King was certain to give him the post, thanks to her regard, Lauzun grabbed her roughly and hissed the most terrible insults into her ear, repeating exactly the conversation she had just had with the King. He said she was a lying whore and a fat gutbag on whom he would revenge himself. (This last insult was probably the most hurtful, though Saint-Maurice notes that at the time Athénaïs was not too fat, notwithstanding a little embonpoint.) Unable to understand how Lauzun had overheard her, Athénaïs was speechless with fright. Staggering to the room where the ballet was being rehearsed, she fell down in a faint.

Why was Athénaïs so anxious to alienate her former friend? Perhaps she reasoned that since she had betrayed him once to protect her own reputation, he would remain an enemy, and if he became too powerful he could threaten her again. Lauzun's conduct shows the dangerous extremes to which he was prepared to go to catch her out, so she was certainly correct in her estimation of him as a formidable opponent. At court there was precious little room for loyalty or for mercy. Lauzun had to be disarmed. In the meantime, alarmed by Lauzun's threats, Athénaïs asked the King for an extra bodyguard, though she did not reveal the reason for her request, and was granted four personal attendants.

Athénaïs found an ally in her scheme to displace Lauzun in Louvois, the minister for war. Louvois was one of the four members of the King's Council of State, which met every day at a green velvet table edged with gold. Like Colbert, he was from the middle class, appointed on the basis of Louis's view that men who owed their positions entirely to him, rather than to their family names, would prove more loyal and able servants. The model worked extremely well for fifty-five years, with son succeeding father to the council, but the ministers were not free of their own jealous rivalries. Louvois constantly jockeyed for position with Colbert, with whom Athénaïs was on good terms, but he also hated and feared Lauzun. She affected a friendship for Louvois, who had never trusted her, and together they began to hint to Louis that Lauzun's power was dangerous, that the adoration he inspired in his troops was practically treasonable, and that the planned marriage to Mademoiselle showed how desperate he was to grab royal privileges for himself. This ugly campaign of defamation was designed to make Louis question Lauzun's loyalty and distrust his ambition. Louvois suggested that Lauzun's habit of giving extra money to his officers was a way of trying to buy loyalty due to the King, and that Lauzun was perhaps acting as a double agent for the Dutch. He even hinted that Lauzun was conspiring with his fellow Gascon the Marquis de Montespan to kidnap Athénaïs.

Things came to a head in November, when Athénaïs found herself in public opposition to Lauzun over the appointment of a new lady-in-waiting to the Queen. Athénaïs was pushing her friend Mme. de Richelieu, while Lauzun supported the candidacy of Mme. de Créqui. Athénaïs chose this moment to confide to Louis that as long as Lauzun was at court, she feared for her life. Called upon to explain himself, Lauzun lost control and let loose a torrent of abuse against the mistress, claiming to Louis's face that Monsieur and he himself had slept with Athénaïs. The King was so furious that, in what Saint-Simon called "perhaps the finest action of his life," he broke his cane and threw it out of the window, saying that he would have regretted having struck a gentleman. The King gave Lauzun five days to make a public apology, but instead he produced a document attempting to justify his conduct. This rash behavior, together with the rumors planted by Louvois, were enough to finish him, and on 26 November, following his arrest at St. Germain, Lauzun was conducted by the commander of the musketeers, D'Artagnan, to the fortress of Pignerol to join the former minister Fouquet. Here, in a dreary cell, without even books or writing materials to amuse him, Lauzun was given nearly ten years to reflect on the folly of offending the King's beloved.

Athénaïs had shown her claws. Yet although this display of power would terrify anyone who thought of usurping her, Athénaïs paid for her victory with a growing paranoia about her safety, a fear so strong that she would not even walk from her room at St. Germain to the chapel without her bodyguards. (She did at least remain a confidante of Mademoiselle's, since the King's cousin did not suspect her involvement in Lauzun's disgrace.) It is probably this situation that Mme. de Sévigné is describing in a letter of January 1672 in which she writes of "the continual ravings of Lauzun, the black despondency or miserable troubles of the ladies of St. Germain," suggesting that "perhaps the most envied of them all is not always free of them."[14] However silken the ropes that bound her, Athénaïs was learning that the struggle to maintain control of her life left her, in some ways, no freer than the unfortunate Lauzun.

Chapter Seven

"Virtue would not go so far without
vanity to bear it company."

In the summer of 1665, an eager Italian tourist, the Abbé Locatelli, sneaked into the gardens of St. Germain early one morning to catch a glimpse of the famous grottos whose fountains, with their mythological sculptures, anticipated those of Versailles. Much to Locatelli's discomfort, he was also treated to a surprise view of the King of France taking a clandestine promenade with Louise de La Vallière. The trespasser threw himself to his knees, and then, as Louis beckoned him over, tried in his best French to explain himself, saying that he was visiting from Bologna. "You are from a wicked country," replied the King sternly.

"How so?" asked the brave little abbé, to the horror of his companions. "Is not Bologna the mother of universities, the palace of religion, the birthplace of many saints, among whom we honor the incorruptible body of St. Catherine, at whose feet Catherine de' Medici, Queen of France, laid the scepter of her realm?"

Louis politely raised his hat at the mention of St. Catherine, but he snubbed Locatelli firmly by declaring: "You undertake a difficult thing in wishing to defend a country where men butcher other men." (In the commedia dell'arte, of which Louis was an enthusiast, Bologna was represented as the most brutal of the Italian city states.) Locatelli blushed with mortification, and his party made their escape, but his curiosity about the French monarch remained undimmed, as did his admiration for Louis.[1] Some years later, he contrived to be present as the King heard Mass in Paris, and his account of his emotional reaction is representative of the religious awe Louis inspired.

> The King remained standing, but followed the office with much attention . . . My eyes having encountered his at the moment when I began to look at him, I immediately felt once more within myself that secret force of royal majesty, which inspired me with an insatiable curiosity to gaze at him . . . but I only dared to fix my eyes on him when I was certain that he could not see me. I returned to the hôtel so happy that in wishing to express the joy with which I was transported, I seemed to have lost my reason . . . Forgive me, reader, if this joy seems to make me rave; in my happiness at having seen the King, and having been seen by him, I believe that I have attracted the regard of an Empyrean divinity.[2]

As his conversation with Louis at St. Germain proves, Locatelli was no cringing sycophant. His apparently excessive joy is no more than a reflection of the belief in the semidivinity of the monarchy held by both Louis and his subjects. Not only was the King the arbiter of all temporal power, the focus of all worldly ambition, he was also a living symbol of God's order. No wonder that his doubly adulterous relationship with Athénaïs would come to be seen by some as a blasphemy, a sacrilege visited physically on his holy body. For one woman, possessed of a most worldly piety, the struggle to reform the King's errant soul came to be seen as a religious mission, a vocation to which she would dedicate herself as devotedly as the strictest bride of Christ.

Françoise Scarron, who was to become the Marquise de Maintenon, is an enduringly fascinating and enigmatic character, adored and loathed by the French in equal measure, now as then. Her relationship with Athénaïs de Montespan was lengthy and hugely complicated, encompassing mutual support and mutual hatred, intense sympathy and intense rivalry. Yet it was Athénaïs who originally discerned La Maintenon's talents and brought her from obscurity, a charity she would come bitterly to regret. The birth of Athénaïs's first child by the King in 1669 was swiftly followed by the arrival of the Duc du Maine in 1670, and she found herself in need of a discreet, capable person to raise her children in the requisite secrecy. She could not have kept them with her even if her career as *maîtresse en titre* had allowed her sufficient time to care for them, as the unresolved issue of her marriage meant that neither she nor Louis could publicly acknowledge them. Louise de La Vallière's children had been officially adopted by Mme. Colbert, but Athénaïs's more precarious circumstances demanded someone far removed from court circles. The obvious choice seemed to be Mme. Scarron, that ubiquitous presence in refined Paris society who had dried Marie Mancini's tears as the King's wedding procession rode into town and exchanged witticisms with Athénaïs at the Hôtel d'Albret in the first years of her marriage.

Although she was very poor, and lodged as a lady boarder in a convent, the young widow Scarron had carved a niche for herself in the select world of the Paris salons with her elegant manners and education, allied to a tremendous talent for making herself useful. She nursed her friends through illness, ran errands, assisted them on weary journeys; in short, she acted as an ideal lady companion to half the hostesses in Paris. She was very easy to like, because her rich friends found her truly *sympathique* and at the same time were able to patronize her a little, an excellent combination for social success. Athénaïs was very fond of her, and when her husband, the poet Paul Scarron, died, it was Athénaïs who had seen to it that Mme. Scarron eventually received the pension granted to him by Anne of Austria.

Françoise Scarron began life in 1635 in a prison cell. Her father, Constant d'Aubigné, was a spendthrift who, among other criminal activities, had murdered his first wife by stabbing her seven times with a dagger when he caught her in flagrante delicto. His second wife, Jeanne de Cardilhac, gave birth to Françoise, their third child, in the prison at Niort, where her husband was serving a sentence for espionage. After a few squalid years with her mother in Paris, Françoise was adopted by a Protestant aunt, Mme. de Villette, who began her education. Surprisingly, given what a bigoted Catholic she became in later life, Françoise's family had strong Protestant links: her grandfather, Theodore Agrippa d'Aubigné, who lived in Geneva, was a well-known Huguenot writer.

When Françoise was eight, her father was released from prison. He took the family to the colony of Martinique to try to make his fortune. Hopeless to the last, he promptly died instead, leaving his widow and children penniless again. When she returned to France,

aged twelve, Françoise was taken in by another aunt, Mme. de Neuil-
lant. This one was a fervent Catholic who had obtained a royal order
from Anne of Austria to prevent her niece from being brought up as a
vile Calvinist. She forced Françoise to work like a peasant in ragged
clothes, enduring beatings and starvation designed to purge her of
Protestant devils. For a while, she defiantly turned her back to the
altar when her aunt dragged her to Mass, but unsurprisingly, she was
soon worn down by this miserable existence and agreed to change
her faith. In her correspondence, which forms the bulk of what we
know of her life, Mme. de Maintenon claims she rescinded her vows
to Protestantism only after hearing a learned theological debate at her
Ursuline convent and being reassured that her dear Aunt Villette was
not to be eternally damned. Nothing in Mme. de Maintenon's life, it
seemed, ever occurred for anything but the most worthy reasons.

 . On completion of her convent education, Françoise returned to
her mother, who introduced her to the forty-year-old Paul Scarron,
whom she had met at his rooms in the Hôtel de Troyes with an
acquaintance from Martinique. Scarron's burlesque satires enjoyed
a great deal of popularity in his lifetime. He was patronized by
Anne of Austria and well known in literary circles. He was famously
Z-shaped, a ripple of a man, contorted with rheumatism after a carnival frolic in the Seine, but he held court to a salon of aristocrats,
artists, courtesans and intellectuals as he squatted, rootlike, in his
wheeled chair. He called himself "the Queen's invalid," joking that his
patron had founded a hospital to support him since he had assembled
in his blasted body all the diseases to which the flesh was prey. Scarron
was attracted to Françoise, described at the time as having "a smooth,
beautiful skin, light pretty chestnut hair, a well-shaped nose, a sweet,
modest expression and the finest eyes you could wish to see," and he
nicknamed her "*la belle Indienne,*" with reference to her time in the
tropics.[3] Although she cannot have been physically attracted to him,
Françoise in turn enjoyed his wit and appreciated his kindness. Scarron offered the impoverished girl his protection, giving her the choice
between marriage and enough money to enter a convent.

Mme. de Maintenon may have been an intensely pious Catholic,
but the young Françoise wanted to become a woman of the world,
and she plumped for marriage. Half a man seemed better than no
man at all, especially when the alternative was shivering on one's knees
in the Rue St. Jacques, and however holy she became, at sixteen years

old, Françoise was too pretty for the convent. Indeed, throughout her later career at the court, despite her frequent and conventional professions of a desire to retreat from the world, La Maintenon was untroubled by any conflict between her religious convictions and her worldly ambitions. She was later to interpret the post given to her by Athénaïs as a sign that she ought to enter into court life to recover the soul of the King. All that she cared about was the world's regard, and her religion, although perfectly sincere in terms of her faith, was no more than a tool in her attempts to obtain it.

During her marriage to Scarron, she began to establish herself socially, holding a serious and intellectual salon in their home in the Rue Neuve St. Louis in the Marais. Scarron educated his wife in Latin, Spanish and Italian, taught her to write verse and encouraged her gift for conversation. During their wedding, when the notary had asked him the customary question on the matter of what he would bring to his wife, Scarron answered "Immortality!" His prediction was correct, though Françoise was not to be remembered as the wife of a forgotten poet, but as a very different kind of spouse: the morganatic wife of the King of France.

When Scarron died, his widow showed no desire to relinquish her purchase on the social world, and Athénaïs's offer of the position of secret governess to the royal children was the perfect way to establish herself further. Scarron had left her with very little money, despite her careful management of his earnings, and she was attracted by this prestigious, albeit covert role. She was careful, however, to ensure that her acceptance should not be interpreted as evidence of a desire to advance in the world. She consulted her confessor, and agreed with him that it would be improper to accept the charge of Mme. de Montespan's adulterous offspring, but that if it were the King's children she was to concern herself with, that would be permissible. Very cleverly, she insisted that Louis himself make a formal request to her to take up the post, and did not begin her duties until his commands had been issued in an interview at St. Germain.

At first, the job was not without its disadvantages. "If this step was the beginning of Mme. de Maintenon's singular good fortune, it was likewise the beginning of her difficulties and embarrassments," wrote Mme. de Caylus. Because of the need for absolute discretion while Athénaïs remained technically married and the children's paternity could be claimed by Montespan, the children were living with their nurses in separate houses in Paris. The governess therefore had to shuttle between them without making any obvious changes to her usual lifestyle that might arouse suspicion. Mme. Scarron famously described this awkward arrangement in her memoirs.

> This strange kind of honor caused me endless trouble and difficulty. I was compelled to mount ladders to do the work of upholsterers and mechanics who might not be allowed to enter the house. I did everything myself, for the nurses did not put their hands to a single thing lest they be tired and their milk not good. I would go on foot and in disguise from one nurse to another, carrying linen or food under my arm. I would sometimes spend the whole night with one of the children who was ill in a small house outside Paris. In the morning I would return home by a little back gate and, after dressing myself, would go out at the front door to my coach, and drive to the Hôtels d'Albret or Richelieu, so that my friends might perceive nothing, or even suspect that I had a secret to keep.[4]

So anxious was the royal governess to conceal the existence of her charges that she had herself bled before her social engagements to prevent herself from blushing if she were asked any difficult questions. She grew thin and exhausted, but she executed her stratagems so well that no one suspected the reason — not even the nosey Mme. de Sévigné, with whom she frequently dined. But this complicated arrangement was far from ideal, and when Athénaïs's third child by the King, the Comte de Vexin was born in 1672, it was clear that a proper establishment was needed.

A pretty house (which may still be seen today) was purchased on the Rue Vaugirard, near the Luxembourg Gardens, in what was then a quiet, leafy suburb. It was secluded, with a large walled garden where the children could play in private. After taking up residence here, Mme. Scarron virtually disappeared from society, though she did continue to see a few old friends from the Hôtel d'Albret, including Mme. de Sévigné and Mme. de Lafayette, both of whom remarked on her new carriage and horses, and the magnificent materials of her dresses. Mme. Scarron's wardrobe was as elegantly understated as Athénaïs's was flamboyant: she favored plain, dark dresses and discreet jewelry, but now the dresses were beautifully made in the most sumptuous fabrics.

Paris society was very curious about Mme. Scarron's new lifestyle which, according to one of Mme. de Sévigné's friends, was "astonishing. Not a single soul has any communication with her. I have received a letter from her, but take care not to boast about it, for fear of being overwhelmed with questions."[5] Many of the rumors which circulated were less than flattering to Mme. Scarron's virtue, which must have been particularly galling for such a woman, but she maintained her reserve, even going so far as to take in another little girl, the child of a lady-in-waiting, to allay any suspicions. And soon Athénaïs had two more daughters of her own by Louis, Mlle. de Nantes, born in 1673, and Mlle. de Tours, born in 1674, to join the household.[6]

The eldest child, born in 1669, died during the Vaugirard years. Athénaïs's reaction to the death is not recorded, but it may be imagined from her response to the loss of her three other children who died young. Her daughter by Montespan, Marie-Christine, never reached her teens, and the little Comte de Vexin died aged eleven in 1683, outliving his little sister Mlle. de Tours, who only reached the age of seven, by which time the children had been established at court. Athénaïs wrote movingly to her elder son, the Duc du Maine:

> I do not speak to you of my grief, you are naturally too good not to have experienced it for yourself. As for Mlle. de Nantes, she has felt it as deeply as if she were twenty, and has received the visits which the Queen, Madame la Dauphine and all the court have paid her, with marvelous grace. Everyone admires her, but I confess I have paid too dearly for these praises to derive any pleasure from them. Every place where I have seen that poor little one affects me so deeply that I am very glad to undertake a journey which is in itself the most disagreeable that can be imagined, in the hope that the distraction will diminish to some extent the faintness which has not left me since the loss we have sustained.[7]

In describing her daughter's fortitude, Athénaïs seems to be trying to bolster her own courage. The letter gives the impression of an effort to contain terrible grief in a measured framework of words. Despite the frequency of infant death in the seventeenth century, there is no reason to suppose that such bereavements were experienced with any less pain than they would be today.

Mme. Scarron grieved with Athénaïs. She was extremely attached to her charges, and loved Du Maine in particular as though he were her own son. Indeed, she was an excellent governess and truly devoted to the children, for whom she cared tenderly. Unfortunately, she often found herself disagreeing on childcare matters with Athénaïs who, on her fleeting visits, would spoil her babies with sweets and keep them up late, disrupting their routine and leaving them fretful and overexcited. Mme. de Montespan's detractors often seek to prove that among her other crimes she was a bad mother, which certainly was not the case, but it is true that she lacked the governess's firm patience. Although Athénaïs accepted that her position as mistress, which involved duties as well as perquisites, precluded looking after the children herself, she still felt guilty and frustrated and tended to overcompensate when she did see them. So she often found herself losing her temper with Françoise, whose virtuous reputation seemed like a mute reproach to the immorality of her own life. It must have been hard not to be jealous when the children seemed to respond better to their steady, quiet governess than they did to their distant, glamorous mother, and Athénaïs frequently vented her frustration in passionate tears. She felt the governess's assumed superiority particularly when she was pregnant. "In God's name," she wrote to Françoise of a projected visit to court, "do not make any of your great eyes at me."[8] It is typical of Mme. Scarron's character that she was able to take the moral high ground with Athénaïs, to whose "sin," after all, she owed her good fortune. The King was never included in any of this implied disapproval.

Yet Louis did not take to Mme. Scarron at first. Intimidated by intellectuals, he disliked *précieuses* and bluestockings, and he was put off by Mme. Scarron's frigid reserve. Athénaïs made sure she kept her own displays of intelligence light and amusing, whereas Mme. Scarron seemed serious and, perceived through the prism of the court fashion for mocking the *précieuses,* rather ridiculous. Louis referred to her to Athénaïs as "*votre belle esprit,*" "your learned lady." But gradually, as he got to know his children, he began to appreciate and respect her. Initially he spent very little time with his illegitimate children, but in 1672 the baby boys, the Duc du Maine and the Comte de Vexin, were brought to court for the first time. The nurse came in with them, while Mme. Scarron waited outside.

"Whose children are these?" asked the King.

"They surely belong to the woman who lives with us," replied the nurse, "if one judges by how upset she is when the least harm comes to any of them."

"And who do you believe to be their father?"

"I don't know anything," said the nurse. "But I imagine that it is a duke or a president of the Parlement."

The King found the nurse's ingenuousness hilarious, and he warmed to Mme. Scarron because of the care she took over his children. He came to enjoy her quiet humor and sound good sense, and remarked once that there would be pleasure in being loved by her, as she knew how to love.

It has been argued that Mme. Scarron had laid her plans for the King's soul — and even that she became his lover — at this early stage, but the latter suggestion is ridiculous. Louis was far too much in love with Athénaïs (and still involved in complications with Louise), to consider another serious attachment, and Mme. Scarron would have accepted nothing less. She was far too calculating to believe that she could hold the King on the strength of a one-night stand — Athénaïs would have chased her out in an instant. Moreover, Mme. Scarron loathed sensuality, and had a pious abhorrence for sex, indeed for any kind of passionate feeling: "Her lips were never touched with fire, and no flame, holy or unholy, ever burned in the depths of her heart."[9] She confessed rather sadly that her mother had never kissed her as a child, so she may always have been uneasy with physical affection. And whatever sexual relationship she had had with Scarron must have destroyed any pleasure she might have taken in lovemaking. Although paralyzed, Scarron had retained the use of his right hand, and, it was rumored in Paris, of another member, and salacious gossip abounded as to the unnatural gratifications he demanded from his young wife. The type of satisfaction Scarron required to accommodate his deficiencies might well have disgusted a sixteen-year-old girl.

Perhaps Françoise Scarron offered up her marital sufferings to God, with whom she was always on excellent terms, and if she took any interest in physical matters it may have been that they offered her a taste of the only pleasure she would ever covet, which was power. She was not particularly interested in personal attachments for any other reason; indeed, her own explanation of her emotions was always rather dismally priggish: "I did not desire to be loved in particular by anybody. I wished my name to be uttered with admiration and respect." The governess, then, was quietly concerned with her own advancement, which she interpreted as a service to God. As for the King, it would be a long time before his passion for Athénaïs began to wane.

There is ample proof of this in the fact that, in 1673, Louis legitimized his children by Athénaïs. This was a difficult maneuver, because if Montespan chose to exercise his rights, he could cause a terrible scandal. Given Louis's diplomatic ambitions in Europe, he could hardly be seen to be engaging in litigation against one of his subjects in so delicate a matter. But the King was determined to find a solution, motivated by the desire not only to resolve the legal issue, but to demonstrate his affection for his children and their mother. Athénaïs was equally set on achieving a secure position for her children, and Louis could hardly refuse the reigning mistress what he had already granted the displaced one. Furthermore, Athénaïs knew that the acknowledgment of the children would finally bring her recognition as the official *maîtresse declarée* and, after six years of hiding behind Louise de La Vallière's petticoats, her ambition was no longer prepared to tolerate an ambiguous role.

A legal precedent had to be found to authorize an act of legitimization in which the mother was not named. Louis's grandfather, Henri IV, had legitimized two of his bastards by married women, César de Vendôme, the son of Gabrielle d'Estrées, and Antoine de Moiret, son of Jacqueline de Bueil, but he had been able to name the mothers because their marriages, mere contracts of convenience, had been annulled, and no such judgment had as yet dissolved the sacred and legal union of Athénaïs and her husband. M. de Harlay, Louis's procurer general, suggested a solution. The Duc de Longueville, who had recently perished in battle on the borders of Flanders, had a son from an affair with the wife of the Maréchal de Ferte, and had requested in his will that his mother should pursue the legitimization of this natural grandson, to whom he had left a large fortune. No mention was made of the identity of the child's mother. The dowager duchess, who adored her lost son, accordingly petitioned the King, who was delighted to grant her request.

Longueville's will was most fortuitous, since it allowed Louis to establish the necessary legal precedent while appearing to generously grant the dying wish of a hero. So, on 7 September 1673, letters patent were issued to legitimize the child, giving him the title of Chevalier d'Orléans. On 18 December, Mlle. de Nantes, born at Tournai while Athénaïs was following the campaign of 1673, was baptized Louise-Françoise at St. Sulpice. The register of baptism leaves the names of father and mother blank, mentioning only Louis-Auguste, the baby's elder brother, the Duc du Maine, as godfather, and, extraordinarily, Louise de la Beaume le Blanc, Duchesse de La Vallière, as godmother. The rather brutal use of Louise as a cover to divert attention from the child's maternity is explained by the fact that on 20 December, letters patent were issued to legitimize all three children. Presumably, it was thought necessary to conceal the King's intentions lest Montespan intervene at the eleventh hour.

In the documents, Louis merely announces that "the affection with which Nature inspires Us for our children and many other reasons which serve to considerably augment these sentiments within us compel us to recognize Louis-Auguste, Louis-César and Louise-Françoise." The children were given their official titles, but Athénaïs had to remain disguised by the phrase "many other reasons." It was hardly on a par with the effusive compliments dished out to "our well-beloved Louise de La Vallière." But if her exclusion rankled, Athénaïs still had much to be pleased about. There could be no doubt now that the King regarded her as his official mistress, and her children had had their royal blood acknowledged. As a woman who took delight in the flimsiness of words, she could not have been too distressed by the verbal precautions her lover had taken.

It is interesting to note, given the polygamous model on which Louis established his incoming and outgoing mistresses, that Mme. Scarron did not arrive at court until 1674, the year that Louise de La Vallière finally left it, though of course at the time no one foresaw the role she would come to play in the King's life. The presentation of the children at court was delayed until the Montespan separation bill, which was still creeping through the Châtelet, had been decided in favor of Athénaïs. The Duc du Maine made a discreet appearance on 5 January that year, witnessed by Mme. de Sévigné, but the formal introduction of the children was not made until July, when Du Maine, the Comte de Vexin and Mlle. de Nantes came to live at court under Mme. Scarron's care. Mme. de Sévigné, who had perhaps observed the pattern in Louis's habits, predicted that her arrival would be a source of conflict. "The Dew and the Torrent are bound close together by the need for concealment, and every day they keep company with Fire and Ice [Louis and Mme. Scarron]. This cannot continue long without an explosion."

Louise, meanwhile, had finally realized that the King was never going to return to her, and her conviction that she should devote the rest of her life to God had been growing steadily. Her instinct for dramatic gestures of penitence was still strong, and instead of taking the advice of Louis's cousin Mademoiselle that she enter a convent simply as a lady boarder, Louise decided to apply for admission to the Carmelite order on the Rue St. Jacques. The Carmelites were one of the strictest of the conventual orders, and Louise's desire to be accepted there formed part of her plan for repentance, since the nuns traditionally refused to accept any woman who did not have a spotless reputation. Louise had visited the convent in disguise, but her companion had accidentally addressed her by her real name, whereupon the pleasant demeanor of the nuns had become cold and disapproving. All the more reason, then, for Louise to force her entry, in an ironic display of pride, into a community that would have no truck with such a public sinner. The choice of the Carmelites was a strong reproach to Athénaïs: if Louise deemed her sin so grave as to require incarceration in a silent convent, where she would go barefoot and live on alms to atone for it, how much greater, she seemed to be suggesting, was the sin of the double adulteress?

Louise confided her intentions to Bishop Bossuet, former prelate of Condom who, since 1662, had held a position at court as tutor to the Dauphin. Bossuet, who was to become a great friend of Mme. Scarron, approved her intentions and agreed to discuss the plan with Athénaïs. Athénaïs treated the idea with fearful contempt, retreating as usual into mocking laughter. "La Vallière a Carmelite nun? Insolent and ridiculous!"[10] As well as despising Louise's theatrical excesses, she was wary of the public exposure her predecessor's departure would bring. Undoubtedly, she was also sensitive to the censure implied by the choice of the Carmelites, and perhaps afraid of what Louise's decision might indicate for her own future. Would she, too, be expected to retreat into the harsh, rigorous life of a nun if the King should grow tired of her? To Athénaïs, who thrived on the energy and intrigue of court life, the idea of mortifying her beautiful flesh under a terrible rule of silence was anathema. But her main feeling, of course, was delight at finally being rid of her irritating rival, so she made no objection to Louise's vocation, requesting only that her choice of retreat be a little less extreme.

Louise, however, had already managed to overcome the Carmelites' resistance to her application by talking her friend the Maréchal de Bellefonds into interceding with them via his aunt, a member of the order known as Sister Agnes. By October 1673, this lady had eventually persuaded the nuns to accept Louise, and all that remained was to obtain the permission of the King. Athénaïs, anxious to prevent the scheme, sent Mme. Scarron to try to deter Louise, but even her frightening descriptions of the austerities of convent life failed to change the former favorite's mind. Would it not be wiser to enter the convent as a private benefactress, to give herself time to reflect? persisted Mme. Scarron. And, she might have added, not to cast aspersions on the current favorite. "Would that be penitence?" asked the immovable Louise. She complained to the governess about the way Athénaïs and Louis treated her. "When I suffer at the Carmelites, I shall think of what these persons made me feel," she declared.[11]

The combination of Louise's stubbornness and Bossuet's entreaties eventually succeeded, and 21 April 1674 was fixed as the date for the Duchesse de Vaujours to retire from the world. The court did not really believe in her vocation — they had seen it all before. "Mme. de La Vallière talks no more about retiring," wrote Mme. de Sévigné. "Her waiting woman threw herself at her feet to dissuade her from doing so. Could she resist such an appeal?" Most people thought that Louise was crying wolf again. Later, to suit her own purposes, Mme. de Maintenon, as she had by then become, interpreted Louise's eagerness to embrace the Carmelite order as a wondrous instance of the workings of grace, but at the time she, too, was less than convinced. Only Bossuet recognized the sincerity of the former favorite's decision, and attempted to compensate for the general mood of skepticism. "The whole court is edified and astonished at her tranquillity and cheerfulness," he wrote to the Maréchal de Bellefonds. "The strength and humility which accompany all her thoughts are surely the mark of the Finger of God, the work of the Holy Spirit."[12] Never one to miss out on any praise, Louise let it be known that she had been accustoming herself to Carmelite sacrifices by wearing a hair shirt, fasting and sleeping on the floor.

Before her departure, Louise had herself painted by Mignard with her children, the Comte de Vermandois and Mlle. de Blois. The portrait is a serious, melancholy picture, in which Louise appears to be looking beyond the court trappings — an overflowing jewel box, a purse of gold, a mask for a ball — that surround her. She holds a rose with falling petals, and two books are displayed: Thomas à Kempis's *Imitation of Jesus Christ* and *The Rule of St. Thérèse,* patron of the Carmelites. Engraved on a column is the Latin inscription "*Sic Transit Gloria Mundi.*" Louise never was very original.

Despite the fact that she clearly intended to abandon her children along with her jewelry, no one has ever suggested that Louise de La Vallière was a bad mother. Unlike Athénaïs, she did not seem passionately attached to her offspring. She and her daughter, the first Mlle. de Blois, had been a pretty sight at court, addressing one another as "Mademoiselle" and "Belle Madame," and Louise was farsighted enough to ensure that a good match be arranged for the little girl, who became the beautiful and popular Princesse de Conti. Louise's son, the Comte de Vermandois, did not do so well. He was involved in a homosexual scandal at the age of thirteen, and Louis showed far less tolerance to his son than he extended to his brother Monsieur. In 1680 the boy was banished from court, and he died three years later in obscurity. Bossuet reports (approvingly) that the reformed sinner did not shed a single tear of sympathy or regret for her wayward son. On her retirement into the convent, Louise left the jewels she had received from the King to raise the funds for her children's care, along with her estate at Vaujours, but she appears to have had no qualms about locking herself away from the children themselves forever.

Louise's choice of date for her admission into religious orders was symbolic, for in April the court was to be at Fontainebleau, where she had originally become Louis's mistress. When the time came, she made a round of farewell visits like "a princess taking leave of a foreign court."[13] She took a formal leave of Louis, who shed a few sentimental tears, and then publicly prostrated herself at the feet of Marie-Thérèse and begged her forgiveness. "As my crimes have been public, it is right that my penitence be equally so,"[14] she declared. The Queen pardoned her. Annoyed by the light this apology cast on her own position, Athénaïs invited Louise to take her last meal in her private lodgings, away from the sneers of the courtiers. The next day

Louise appeared at Mass before setting off in her coach for Paris, attired in a splendid gown, bidding goodbye to all the courtiers crowded around her coach for all the world as if she was departing on a journey to her estate rather than to what many around her considered a prison.

Nothing so became Louise's life at court as her leaving of it. On arrival at the convent, she immediately adopted the nuns' coarse habit and sheared off her beautiful blond hair. "I have made all my life such a bad use of my will that I am come to surrender it into your hands once and for all," she announced to the Mother Superior. A year later, when her novitiate was completed, a crowd of courtiers — which included the Queen, but not the King or Mme. de Montespan — attended the ceremony of vows in the Rue St. Jacques. Bossuet preached a moving sermon and Louise was enveloped in the black veil which represented her death to the world. All the wicked society ladies had a good cry, and then tripped back to court to resume their gambling and gallantries. "After all," sniffed Mademoiselle, "she was not the first sinner to be converted." Louis gave no indication that he thought any longer of his old love, even though she lived, under her new name of Sister Louise de la Miséricorde, until 1710. Athénaïs, on the other hand, paid her at least two visits, the first being the occasion where she famously organized a lottery and cooked her own sauce, which she ate with a hearty appetite. Whether her motive was to gloat or to commiserate it is hard to know.

Chapter Eight

"Moderation has been declared a virtue so as to
curb the ambition of the great and console
lesser folk for their lack of fortune and merit."

It could never be said that the relationship between Athénaïs de Montespan and Louis XIV was a peaceful one, but the years between 1674 and 1678 were probably their happiest time. Mme. de Sévigné's nickname for Athénaïs, "the Torrent," was an apt one, for her passionate nature seemed to swell as her status and power increased, engulfing everyone around her in her tantrums and rages as well as her delights. Mme. de Sévigné's letters attest to the fascination Athénaïs's beauty and temperament held for the aristocracy, and this zealous gossip chronicles every quarrel and rapprochement of the lovers during these turbulent, exciting years. At last Athénaïs was free to embrace the role which she had for so long believed to be her destiny, and for which she had endured public censure and six years of private frustration. Her rival was safely incarcerated in the convent, her children were legitimized, she was pregnant with another of the King's children, Mlle. de Tours, born in 1674, and she was finally able to revel in her new public persona as the separation from her husband she had longed for had been achieved.

Until April 1674, Montespan had been kicking his heels in the provinces, but the separation proceedings were resumed as soon as Athénaïs, who had let her application lapse, received notice that he was pursuing his inheritance from his mother, which would perhaps render him solvent enough to agree to the "separation of body and goods" on friendly terms. In defiance of the order that he remain in exile, Montespan installed himself in Paris when the case began again, in gloomy lodgings close to the convent on the Rue St. Jacques where Louise de La Vallière was expiating the sin he was expected to authorize his wife to continue committing. Louis was disconcerted by his presence, and wrote to Colbert from the front for an explanation. Colbert's response, that it was necessary that Montespan remain in situ for the two weeks or so it would take to resolve the case, prompted the King to insist that the action be expedited promptly. Recalling the scandal Montespan had tried to create before, Louis was anxious that his presence do nothing to harm Athénaïs, or to attract publicity to the case.

Any hopes Athénaïs might have had for an amicable settlement were dashed when Montespan announced, through the intermediary of his lawyer, Claude-François Brierre, that he wished to be reimbursed for the whole of his wife's dowry. Even if the impecunious Duc de Mortemart had been able to pay, this was hardly reasonable given that Montespan had already squandered most of the money himself. The case was then put before a judge, and Athénaïs, who was represented by her friend the King's counsel Gaspard de Fieubert, was given the unheard-of advantage of being able to prosecute her suit, that is, to bring proof of her husband's cruelty, while Montespan had to prove the contrary. Normally, it was impossible for a wife to achieve a separation without the cooperation of her husband. The witnesses for each claimant were heard on 19 and 20 June, and the separation of "goods" was passed three days later, preceding the final judgment, which was made by six judges on 7 July. Unsurprisingly, they found overwhelmingly in Athénaïs's favor, although the grounds on which they did so were all acceptable evidence for a separation regardless of the power of the wife's lover. The judges accepted Athénaïs's complaint of cruelty against her person, disorderly conduct and the dissipation of her resources. However, Montespan's lawyer was so shocked by the pronouncement against his client that he could not bring himself to read it. Montespan was ordered to pay back the 60,000 livres of his wife's dowry that he had already received and to pay her an additional 4,000 livres annual alimony, as well as to settle any debts she had contracted during their communal life. He was forbidden to come near Athénaïs, and served with a formal petition to this effect on 16 July.

The ardor with which Athénaïs initially prosecuted her rights was hardly charitable. True, Montespan had beaten her, used her to obtain money dishonestly, been unfaithful to her and refused to allow her to see her children, yet it is surprising, for their sake if not for his, that she was not more lenient, given that she was hardly a blameless wife. Perhaps she was paying her husband back for the humiliations of their years together, or taking revenge for the scandal he had caused at court in 1669. As the mistress of the King, Athénaïs could have afforded to be generous, but instead she proceeded immediately to have the furniture from Montespan's poor lodgings seized, and threatened to do the same with his property holdings to raise the 60,000 livres he owed her.

Montespan was outraged at his wife's apparent intention to ruin him and their children's patrimony. He claimed that he owed her nothing, and counterattacked by demanding the interest Athénaïs would theoretically have received on the unpaid portion of her dowry. Perhaps it was the pathetic inventory of the Marquis's Parisian possessions that brought Athénaïs to her senses. His goods amounted to the value of a mere 950 livres, comprising in total a Flanders tapestry in seven pieces, a walnut bed, four curtains, two wool blankets, eight folding chairs and four dining chairs decorated with embroidery, twelve carved chairs, a Venetian mirror and a walnut cabinet with two cupboards and several drawers. Athénaïs was often criticized for being avaricious and grasping, but she was as generous with money as she was fond of it, and she was moved to a wry pity by the evidence of her husband's poverty.

And so, having won her case, Athénaïs decided she was prepared to be magnanimous. She claimed via her lawyer that she had never wished to bring about the ruin of "the house of the said Seigneur her husband, nor to prejudice his children" and, with the exception of the value of his Paris goods, she accepted that her annual pension should be devoted to the education and care of the children. She also postponed her claim for the 60,000 livres of her dowry until the Marquis came into his father's estates, and undertook to discharge 90,000 livres' worth of debts. Montespan accepted the deed of separation without demur, and the settlement was signed by "the high and mighty lady Françoise de Rochechouart" at Versailles on 23 July. In this document, Athénaïs asserted that she wished as far as possible to contribute to "the luster of the house of Montespan" (she certainly did that) and to ensure that her children were provided with the means to be brought up according to their rank and station. Montespan talked of mending his ways and rejoining the military, and seemed now to accept the separation calmly. Athénaïs had, in the end, acted with a commendable generosity, and she was now to an extent relieved of the taint of double adultery which had so far clouded her relations with the King. She was ready to give her name to an age.

That year, 1674, was also a watershed for Louis. France had declared war on Spain once again in October 1673, and the French armies had conquered the disputed region of the Franche-Comté after a difficult yet gloriously brief four-month campaign. France stood alone in Europe, and Louis was determined that his ambitions would not be cowed, even if he had to make war on Spain and Holland at the same time. Now he faced the greatest challenge to his aspiration for European dominance, which would eventually be achieved in 1678 with the Peace of Nijmegen. That year marked the turning point in a policy he and his ministers had been attempting to realize since the outbreak of the wars with Holland in 1667.

The first Flanders campaign, fought in the name of Queen Marie-Thérèse and during which Louis and Athénaïs had become lovers, had ended with the successful cessation of the Franche-Comté to Louis by treaty. However, anxiety about France's expansionist tendencies provoked Sweden, Holland and England to sign a treaty of alliance in order to contain them. Louis was forced into a coalition with his former enemy Spain, and re-ceded the Franche-Comté in exchange for Spain's acceptance of his conquests in the Spanish Netherlands. This was confirmed by the Peace of Aix-la-Chapelle of May 1668. So Holland now faced the French armies without the barrier of the Spanish territories in Flanders. The next four years were a frenzy of diplomatic maneuvering. Thanks to the efforts of his sister-in-law Madame Henriette, Louis had effectively bribed the English into abandoning their former alliance and entering into a new war with Holland on the French side, a move which was hugely unpopular in England. Dutifully, though, the English had begun the campaign with an attack on a Dutch convoy off the Isle of Wight in March 1672. In May, Louis joined his army, now a force of 120,000 men, at Charleroi.

The French army seemed unbeatable. After the practically simultaneous conquest of four important strongholds — Weinberg, Wesel, Burick and Orsai — Louis set his sights on Amsterdam. The Dutch, commanded by William of Orange, whom they had elected as stadtholder, had destroyed the bridges across the Rhine, but the French, in a particularly bloody battle, swam their horses defiantly into the river. The crossing of the Rhine was probably the greatest moment of Louis's personal military history, and it brought him to within two leagues of Amsterdam. In desperation, William issued an order for the sluices on the flat polders of the Zuider Zee to be opened, and the Dutch valiantly flooded their own country rather than let Louis take its capital. The same day, they sued for peace.

The Dutch were prepared to concede 10 million livres, Maastricht, Brabant and the Rhine towns as well as Dutch Flanders, but Louis wanted more. Beyond these concessions, he demanded another 14 million livres, the towns of Nijmegen, Grave and Moers, a trade agreement favorable to the French, freedom of religion for the cruelly oppressed Dutch Catholics and, in a rather nasty piece of pomposity, a tributary medal to be presented to him annually by the Dutch ambassador in thanks for the peace. Despite his victories, Louis's exigency with the Dutch now threatened him with a European war. In 1673, he left again for the front, accompanied famously by those three "Queens of France" — Athénaïs, Louise and, of course, Marie-Thérèse — whom the populace were astonished to see in the same carriage. Athénaïs was pregnant at the time, and her baby, Mlle. de Nantes, was born at Tournai. The siege of Maastricht began, during which D'Artagnan, the famous musketeer, was killed. The siege is recorded in one of the fourteen canvases devoted to the campaign by the artist Van der Meulen, commissioned years later for the royal pavilion at the house Louis built at Marly. The pictures have a curious quality of stillness to them, their wide plains and chill northern skies reflecting a more disciplined composition than the crowded, sprawling epics painted by Le Brun. Louis seems to glow in the paintings, always the central figure and slightly larger than life, as though his presence drains the color from the muted tones of the surrounding Flemish landscape. On his white horse, the walls of Maastricht before him, the young hero of the painting is the ideal of the warrior prince. Yet in reality, Louis was increasingly beleaguered. In September 1673, the Hapsburg emperor Leopold declared war on France, as did Denmark and the electors of Cologne and Münster. Spain joined in October, while the English concluded a separate peace with Holland in February of the next year.

In July and August of 1674, Louis staged the last and the most extravagant of his three grands divertissements, designed to display his strength and his mistress to the world. It was a gesture of political defiance, as well as one of love; proof that neither Louis's armies nor his coffers were exhausted. To dance through his gardens with his lover while the whole of Europe schemed against him was entirely typical of Louis's majestic insouciance. As the separation from Montespan was practically completed, Athénaïs could now be publicly acknowledged for the first time as Queen of the new Versailles. Over six days, Louis choreographed the familiar but still breathtaking range of entertainments — operas, ballets, collations, fireworks — around the sections of the palace which had just been completed. The first event, a performance of Lully and Quinault's new opera *Alceste,* showed off the Cour de Marbre; the second, a pastoral ballet entitled the *Eclogue de Versailles,* used the new gardens of the Trianon as scenery. *Les Fêtes de l'Amour et Bacchus,* inspired by the beginning of Louis's love affair with Athénaïs six years before, was performed in the Allée du Dragon. A feast was served in the new suite of *"grands appartements,"* and the highlight was an illuminated promenade by gondola on the canal, with a light display by Le Brun. For the King, this magnificent homage to his love was a complementary aspect of his increasing martial power, since at Versailles, politics and aesthetics moved in a constant symbiosis.

While the cost of Versailles was one of the trials of Colbert's existence, Louis always knew how his expenditure would demonstrate his power internationally. One awed envoy from Brandenburg estimated that the house, gardens, fountains, lakes and orangery alone must have cost at least 24 million livres, leaving out the expense of stables, works of art, decoration and domestics. Versailles became a barometer of the political climate of Europe, and when the works paused, the continent worried, since it meant that money was being diverted for the King of France to go to war again. For the court and the ambassadors, Versailles was a book as much as a palace, the means by which the Sun King used all available symbols to create and impose his power. Nothing in the design of Versailles was without its symbolism, from the statues — Apollo in his chariot, or the giant Encelade being crushed by rocks for his defiance of Zeus — to the fountains, whose choreography was minutely devised by Colbert and the master of the fountains in a ten-page manual, so that when the King walked in his garden, they would spring to life in order — the Couronnes, the Pyramide, the Dragon, the grotto of Ceres, the Dosme, the Apollon, the horses, the Latone, the Aigrettes, the bosquets, the Cinq Jets — the music of the water coming alive with Louis's step and fading with his retreat, as though the rainbow cascades were activated merely by his presence. The legions of undergardeners sprinting between the fountains, struggling at the taps with damp hands and rasping lungs, were invisible, and where the King walked, the music of the water followed him.

"Life," Louis wrote in his memoirs, "is a mixture of pleasure and greatness." No one understood this better than Athénaïs de Montespan. One of her chief attractions for Louis was her enthusiasm for and grasp of the crucial seventeenth-century concept of *gloire*. The literal translation of the word, "glory," seems too vague a term for an idea which, if not entirely coherent, certainly had meaning for the King and his contemporaries. *Gloire* encompassed everything that was done to magnify the King's power and splendor on earth, and all that would contribute to the greatness of his posterity. In the "memoirs" written (or, more probably, ghosted) as an instruction to his son the Grand Dauphin, Louis uses the word repeatedly, and his tone is picked up by other correspondents, most notably Colbert, in relation to him. No action of a monarch's life, teaches Louis, can be committed without reference to the idea of *la gloire*, which thus encompasses the monarch's constant awareness of his own condition as a prince. Even recalling his powerful emotions of grief on the death of his mother Anne, Louis is unable to neglect the opportunity to remind his son of the obligations of kingship: "This event . . . did not fail to affect me so deeply that for several days it made me incapable of giving my mind to any other consideration than the loss I was sustaining. For, although I have told you continually that a prince must sacrifice all his private emotions for the glory of his empire, there are occasions when this principle cannot be put into practice just at first."

Elsewhere, the King writes to the members of the Petite Académie in 1663: "You may judge, Messieurs, the esteem which I have for you, because I am entrusting to you the thing which is the most precious in the world, my glory."[1] *Gloire* embraced not only political or military achievements, but cultural and romantic ones, too. Louis saw it as an obligation to encourage the very best painters, sculptors, architects and writers to beautify his reign for eternity — "Nothing contributes more to the glory of the prince than these immortal works which the painters and sculptors leave for posterity."[2] Equally, the love of the most desirable, beautiful women was an essential component of *la gloire*.

Athénaïs perfectly understood her lover's equation of glory and seduction, knowing that his love for her was the necessary complement to his political power. "Glory," Louis wrote, "is an exacting mistress . . . In the love of glory, one must display the same refinements — nay, even the same restraint — as in the tenderest passions." According to the gallant psychology of the times, a love affair was prestigious or glorious in proportion to the qualities of the beloved, and if Athénaïs occasionally accused the King of loving her only because he judged it his duty to have the finest woman in France as his mistress, she nevertheless agreed with his estimation of her. Whether Louis loved her for herself, or for the fact that her beauty, her wit and her blood made her the most desirable woman in his kingdom, Athénaïs was prepared to live the glorious symbolism of her role superbly.

Perhaps in some ways, Louis did choose Athénaïs as *maîtresse en titre* because he owed it to his "image." Neither Marie-Thérèse nor Louise de La Vallière were fitting consorts for a man of Louis's ambitions. Yet Athénaïs enraptured him in private as much as she flattered him in public. "Her mettle, her spirit, her beauty which surpassed everything seen at the court, flattered the pride of the King, who showed her off like a treasure. He was proud of his mistress, and even when he was unfaithful to her he returned quickly because she was more gratifying to his vanity."[3] Athénaïs's sense of her own worth proved a powerful attraction to Louis, as she seemed to be the only person in his world who was not afraid of him. She teased and scolded him, delighted him with her jokes and terrified him with her tantrums; she loved him as an equal because, as a Mortemart, she believed herself to be so. A Mortemart was a prize even to a King of France. If La Vallière had claimed to prefer the man to the King, then Athénaïs, uniquely, was able to love the King simply as a man, a quality which commanded not only a twelve-year passion, but a powerful respect.

Athénaïs's faith in her own breeding was the principal basis for her belief in her value. She once wrote to her son, the Duc du Maine: "You are the son of a hero . . . It is well that you should know that you are fortunately spared any admixture of blood less noble — as is

A Baroque Venus. Behind Athénaïs is the famous gallery of her house at Clagny.

Louis XIV as the young soldier who fell in love with Athénaïs.

"One of history's most famous sodomites": Louis's dandyish brother, Monsieur, the Duc d'Orléans.

Louise de la Vallière was Louis's first mistress, but she was shy and unpopular.

Henriette, Duchesse d'Orléans, Monsieur's first wife, who died suspiciously young.

Anne of Austria, the King's mother, and her Spanish niece Marie-Thérèse, his wife.
Anne was Louis's model for a queen, but Marie-Thérèse was never able to live up to it.

Louis's greatest and most enduring passion. The gardens and château of Versailles seen
from the Paris Avenue, 1668.

Parrocel's depiction of the crossing of the Rhine (left) and Van der Meulen's "Siege of a Flemish Town" (below) illustrate Louis's obsession with military glory.

The Trianon: a playhouse and hiding place for Louis and Athénaïs.

Athénaïs surrounded by her legitimized children. The Duc du Maine, who betrayed his mother for Mme. de Maintenon, is on the right of the picture.

MARIE ANGELIQVE D'ESCORAILLES
DE ROVSSILLE DVCHESSE DE
FONTANGE

Louis's last mistress, Marie-Angélique,
Duchesse de Fontanges. "As beautiful as
an angel and as stupid as a basket."

Ie fus du Genre humain la mortelle Ennemie,
Par l'horreur de mes jours, on vit regner la mort,
Et mon Crime partout, portant son Infamie,
Fit la guerre aux Mortels, et termina mon sort.
LE PORTRAIT DE LA VOISIN
Bruslée vive à Paris le Ieudy 22.e Fevrier 1680

Madame de Voisin, "the empress of poisoners."
Was Athénaïs a customer?

Monsieur's second wife, the Princess Palatine,
Duchesse d'Orléans, adored Louis but
loathed Athénaïs.

Françoise Scarron, born in a prison,
became the secret royal bride.

Louis and his son, the Grand Dauphin, grandson the Duc de Bourgogne
and great-grandson the Duc de Bretagne, with Madame de Ventadour,
the infant Duc's governess.

Françoise-Marie de Bourbon and Louise-Françoise de Bourbon.
Spoiled and mischievous, Athénaïs's daughters became the leaders
of the new generation at Versailles.

The château at Oiron. Athénaïs filled her last home with portraits of Louis, but he never slept in the King's bedroom there.

Giovanni Lorenzo Bernini's bust of Louis XIV. The seventeenth century's greatest portrait of its greatest monarch.

often the case with people of your kind [royal bastards] . . . You are the exception to the rule, in that in both bloodlines you can count courage, nobility, wit. While this gives you a singular advantage, to be sure, it still imposes an obligation to live up to both."[4]

Du Maine's Mortemart blood, then, imposed as much responsibility as his Bourbon lineage. In enacting the role of Louis's mistress with maximum splendor, Athénaïs, too, was doing her duty to her great family name.

"Mme. de Montespan was imbued with the same sense of glory as the King," wrote Mme. de Caylus, and indeed, Athénaïs's pride was exceeded only by his. She established this mutual goal publicly in 1670 with her selection of the King's protégé Molière to create a five-act comedy with music and ballets in which the King would dance as Apollo. She entitled it *The Magnificent Lovers,* as much for herself and the King as for any imaginary protagonists. Athénaïs and Louis, the title implies, were the most beautiful, most splendid, most imperious lovers in the world. Appropriately, this was the last time the thirty-two-year-old King was to dance in public, and it was the perfect swan song for his balletic career.

The art of ballet owes a great deal to Athénaïs, since it was as a result of the enthusiasm for dance she shared with the King that choreographic sequences and different balletic movements began to be categorized and recorded for posterity. Ballet might be seen as the art which most profoundly reflects the beliefs and ambitions of the seventeenth century. To dance well was to demonstrate the perfectibility of human nature, the harmonious expression of the civilized as opposed to the natural. In the ballet, wrote the Abbé de Pure, "you appear as you are, and all your actions are dependent on the eyes of the spectators, exposing to them the good and the bad with which Art and nature have favored or disgraced your person."[5] Louis took the ballet extremely seriously, rehearsing until he made himself ill, as though to be the finest dancer in the realm was yet another manifestation of his kingship. Ballet was the most civilized of fantasies, illustrating the aspiration to transcend, or at least to seem to transcend, the reality of a world which was often harsh and cruel. Even at Versailles, the glittering apex of the social structure, it was impossible to ignore the poverty and misery of most of the world; even at Versailles, justice was arbitrary, hard and increasingly tyrannical — indeed, Versailles imposed its own cruelties, its own humiliations, on those who were not sufficiently beautiful or well born. Hence the ballet became the ultimate manifestation of the need to appear graceful, suggesting that masked, on a stage, a pastoral idyll or a classicized love, untainted by the vulgarity of life, was attainable.

Appearances, then, were all, and Athénaïs was determined that her personal *gloire* should match that of the King. From 1674 onwards, she pursued material ambition assiduously. Mme. de Sévigné now gives her another private nickname — "Quanto," from the Italian card game Quantova — meaning "how much?" If Athénaïs's desires seemed insatiable, so, too, was the King's eagerness to gratify them, and he encouraged her extravagance, giving her access to his treasury for her needs, for her spending was yet another indication of his power. But Athénaïs was always too clever to show any sign of covetousness or to turn a hint into a demand. Knowing, for example, that Louis disliked being asked for jewelry — so generous with everything else, he was niggardly when it came to jewels — she never accepted it as a gift from him, preferring to borrow what she wished to wear. This demonstrates a perceptiveness about Louis's psychology, for he had a peculiarly uneasy relationship with jewelry, probably rooted in the humiliating sale of so many of the crown jewels during the Fronde, and at the time of his marriage he had been mortified by the discrepancy between the dazzling diamonds of his wife's retinue and the relatively poor adornments of his own. The King was enchanted by Athénaïs's reticence, and it prompted him to be more generous to her than he had ever been to Louise. In 1674, he wrote to Colbert from the front near Dole, instructing him to have a beautiful casket made for the jewels that Athénaïs might "borrow."

The casket must contain a pearl necklace, and I wish it to be of fine quality; two pairs of earrings; one of diamonds, which must be fine ones, and one of other stones; a case with diamond fastenings; a case with fastenings of different kinds of stones, which must be removable two at a time. I require stones of different colors, so as to allow of them being changed. I shall also want a pair of pearl earrings. You must also procure four dozen studs, in which the central stones must be removable, while the outer circle must consist of small diamonds . . . It will be necessary to go to some expense over this; but I am quite prepared for it, and it is my wish that the work should not be done hurriedly.[6]

The pearls in question turned out to be larger than the Queen's.

Athénaïs extended her influence far beyond personal ornament. She was anxious that her Mortemart relations should share in her good fortune. Despite the unkind jokes speculating that the Duc de Mortemart had greeted his daughter's disgrace with avaricious delight, the family had not initially reacted well to her scandalous ascent to the position of royal mistress. Any paternal misgivings may have been eased by the Duc de Mortemart's appointment as governor of Paris and Ile de France in 1669. In accepting this prestigious post, the impecunious Duc was also released from his ceremonial duties for which, at sixty-nine, he considered himself too old. In 1668, however, her brother Vivonne had gone so far as to renounce his right to succeed his father as first gentleman of the chamber as a gesture of protest.

Yet Vivonne, who was, after all, a great friend of the King's, ended up doing extremely well out of his sister's disgrace, though perhaps he may have found the charges of nepotism hard to take since, like all the Mortemarts, he was extremely able and talented in his own right. Louis certainly loved him, and never tired of telling hilarious stories about Vivonne's adventures. Like his father, Vivonne fancied himself as a gallant, but he did not have his father's way with the ladies; indeed Bussy-Rabutin claimed that Vivonne failed even "with women who until that moment had refused nobody." Following another family tradition, the tendency of the Mortemarts to ruin themselves and then save the day with a fortuitous marriage, Vivonne had repaired his father's squandered fortune by marrying a tremendous heiress, Antoinette-Louise de Roisy, who brought with her a dowry of 800,000 livres. Further resources were provided by the King, who paid off 300,000 livres of debts (sadly, less than a fifth of the astronomical family total) and provided another half a million to release the ancient family title of Maréchal de Créqui. By way of further compensation to his friend for the theft of his sister's virtue, Louis named Vivonne captain-general of the galleys, with charge over the French Mediterranean fleet; vice-admiral of the Levant; viceroy of Sicily and governor of Brie and Champagne — the latter no doubt prompting many jokes at the gourmand governor's expense.

Yet of all these honors, the only one that is known to have been bestowed as a direct result of Athénaïs's influence was the *maréchal's* baton. She had searched through the King's pockets for the list of

newly appointed *maréchals,* and treated him to a violent tantrum
when she discovered that Vivonne's name was absent. Louis, who was
never able to refuse Athénaïs to her face, explained the omission as an
error by Louvois. "Send for him at once," Athénaïs demanded, and
gave Louis a good scolding until the minister appeared. Louvois
quickly grasped the situation, apologized and added Vivonne's name
to the list. Nepotism may have been a way of life at court, but for
Athénaïs to proclaim her rights so stridently was evidence of either
tremendous courage or tremendous arrogance when a few offensive
words might have been enough to have a lesser woman whisked off
to a convent. Luckily for her, the King enjoyed being berated by the
woman he loved, and luckily for the fleet, Vivonne was a brave admiral who distinguished himself throughout the 1670s.

Athénaïs enjoyed a close relationship with both of the sisters who
still maintained some contact with the world, the Marquise de Thianges and Marie-Madeleine, who became Abbesse de Fontrevault.
Mme. de Thianges, bored by her husband's country tastes, spent most
of her time at court, cultivating her interests in music, theater and
opera. She had been a prominent member of the salon established
privately by Mademoiselle at the Palais du Luxembourg during the
years of her disgrace after the Fronde. It was here that the vogue for
pen portraits was introduced, with Mademoiselle extemporizing
those of the King and Monsieur for the amusement of her guests.
The genre was later mastered by La Bruyère in his *Caractères* of 1688.
Louis would often accompany Mme. de Thianges to hear lectures by
the writers Racine and Boileau, and as has been stated, she occasionally substituted for Athénaïs in other respects, though, surprisingly,
without arousing her sister's jealousy. Athénaïs looked after Mme. de
Thianges's family well. She shared with her sister the percentage on all
sales of meat and tobacco in Paris that she had been granted, and was
also, of course, responsible for arranging her niece's lucrative marriage. The Marquis de Thianges benefited, too: he was appointed a
lieutenant in the Duc d'Anjou's household cavalry.

The Abbesse de Fontrevault was perhaps the most beautiful of the
three sisters described by Voltaire as "the three most beautiful women
of their age," and also the cleverest scholar. She had taken up her
vocation, rather sadly, under pressure from her father, but resigned
herself most successfully to a religious and academic life. She knew

Spanish, Italian, Latin, Greek and Hebrew and was a prolific translator of the classics and writer of verses, religious tracts and moral treatises, one of which, on manners, remained in print well into the eighteenth century, and she was as successful in her religious life as she was in her worldly studies. Marie-Madeleine, a true *femme savante* in the intellectual tradition of the salons, was greatly admired by serious thinkers, including Athénaïs's enemy Bishop Bossuet. Her elevation in 1670 to abbesse of Fontrevault, a great twelfth-century Benedictine convent, was a somewhat controversial measure of Louis's respect for his mistress's family, since the post, which carried the responsibility for sixty convents, had traditionally been reserved for women of the blood royal.

When the Abbesse visited Paris in 1675 to tend the Duc de Mortemart, who had suffered a stroke, the Queen invited her to dinner and presented her with a diamond worth 3,000 louis. Marie-Madeleine had the Mortemart gift for conversation, with a sharper intellectual edge: "Mme. de Thianges talks like a woman who reads," it was said, "Mme. de Montespan like a woman who dreams, and Mme. de Fontrevault like a woman who talks."[7] Although she did not appear at large court functions, Louis was so captivated by her conversation that he tried to persuade her to stay at court. It was to no avail — she was committed to her abbey — but she did continue to make brief excursions to Versailles to visit her sisters. It is typical of the rather flexible religious sensibility of the early decades of Louis's reign that the nuns apparently made no objection to their abbesse paying calls to a woman considered by the *dévots* to be the disgrace of the nation. The Abbesse was certainly no prig. When she was in Paris, for instance, she would accompany Athénaïs to hear the sermons of a plump Jesuit priest who was the double of Vivonne. The ladies were greatly diverted by hearing worthy sentiments and religious homilies delivered by what appeared to be their roué of a brother got up in a surplice.

Athénaïs's main family priority was the welfare of her children by the King. Now that, to her delight, they were established with Mme. Scarron at court, and she herself was officially recognized as the *maîtresse en titre,* she wanted a proper residence of her own. She already had a little pleasure house, the exquisite porcelain palace of Trianon, which Louis had had built for her in 1670 in the grounds of Versailles, and in the evenings, she and Louis would sail down the Versailles canal, perhaps in one of the two magnificent gondolas presented to the King by the Doge of Venice, to enjoy its superb flower gardens.

Trianon, an ensemble of four pavilions enclosing a central salon, had been inspired by the discovery of the Tour de Porcelaine at the Imperial Palace of Nanking in 1664 and constructed by Le Vau in the chinoiserie (more properly *lachinage*) style first popularized by Mazarin. Blue and white Delft tiles covered the walls, while the interior was of polished white stucco ornamented with azure (in a neat dramatic irony, this décor was created by a duo of Carmelite monks). Externally, the miniature palace presented a charming mélange of classical and approximately oriental styles. Aside from the salon, which was designed for more formal entertainments, the main feature of Trianon was the bedroom, named, of course, "*La Chambre des Amours*," which was decorated in white, silver and blue and boasted a huge, mirrored bed trimmed with gold and silver lace, tasseled fringes and gold and silver braid. Here, if anywhere, snug inside the gilded canopy and flounced curtains, the King and his love could make a secret world.

The pavilions were largely given over to the preparation of food, evincing the lovers' shared delight in gastronomic pleasures, but the great joy of Trianon was the gardens. The little house was surrounded by anemones, Spanish jasmine, tuberoses and orange trees, emitting the heady perfumes both Louis and Athénaïs loved. Here, too, Louis's *gloire* appeared to triumph over nature: even in the depths of winter, guests could promenade in a spring garden, thanks to the millions of hothouse flowers that were planted out every day. Like the fountains, fresh flowers seemed to spring up wherever Louis walked — though Le Bouteux, the head florist, had to keep a staggering 2 million flowerpots in constant circulation in order to achieve this effect.

Trianon, then, was a delightful place for moonlit meetings and private games, but Athénaïs wanted a real château that would display her taste and status. Together, the lovers decided to engage the young architect Jules-Hardouin Mansart, who had taken over the construction of Versailles after Le Vau's death in 1670, to design a house at Clagny, an estate that Louis had purchased in 1665 to enlarge the parkland of Versailles. The King had originally decided on another little pleasure house, but Athénaïs was tired of trinkets, and when she saw the plans she remarked with audacious contempt that it was the sort of thing one gave to chorus girls. Chastened, Louis gave her one of the most beautiful buildings in Europe.

Of all the spectacular gifts Athénaïs received, Clagny was the most impressive. It took 1,200 men to build the house which cost 2,074,592 livres (more than $11 million in today's values). Until the house was completed, Athénaïs lodged in the old manor house on the estate, which was pulled down in 1677, and was involved at every stage — in 1674 Louis wrote to Colbert from the front: "[As to] the plan for the house at Clagny, I have no answer to send to you at present, as I wish to ascertain what Mme. de Montespan thinks about it."[8] Mansart constructed the house on similar lines to Versailles: east to west, with two wings perpendicular to the main façade, which had nineteen windows facing west. At either end of the wings were an orangery and a painted chapel, and in between stretched the gallery, 210 feet long by 25 feet wide, and ornamented with bas-relief sculptures and huge paintings from the *Aeneid*. Above the entablement hovered allegorical divinities of the seasons, the elements and the four corners of the earth. The dome in the center of the house formed the roof of Athénaïs's salon, which was reached by five marble steps and surrounded by huge corinthian columns, and had an anteroom in black and white marble on each side. The court was fascinated by Athénaïs's new palace — even Queen Marie-Thérèse could not resist paying a visit to the works.

Since both Louis and Athénaïs were passionate about gardens, the garden at Clagny became a wonder. Louis writes again to Colbert: "Mme. de Montespan is most anxious that the garden should be planted this autumn. Do everything that will be necessary to oblige her in this matter."[9] After a second estate had been bought to give the gardeners the scope they needed, Clagny's park extended to 429 acres. André le Notre, the most celebrated gardener in France, who had created the "miracle" of the Versailles gardens as well as those of Sceaux, St. Cloud, Fontainebleau, Chantilly and the Tuileries, was employed to design the grounds, and remarkably, Athénaïs's gardens were finished by 1675. Mme. de Sévigné, that ardent gossip, was prompt in paying them a visit. She was delighted by them, and commented on how triumphant Athénaïs appeared amid her workmen. "You know Le Notre," she gushed. "He has left a little, dark wood which makes a perfect effect; there's a forest of orange trees in large tubs, on both sides of them are palisades covered with tuberoses, roses,

jasmine and carnations; a beautiful, surprising, enchanting idea —
everybody adores this spot."

A charming conceit was the model farm Athénaïs created, prefiguring the vogue for mock rusticity that took off in the following century. This little caprice cost 2,000 ecus, which were spent, in Mme. de
Sévigné's words, on "the most passionate turtle doves, the fattest sows,
the fullest cows, the frizziest sheep and the goosiest geese." Athénaïs,
then, was playing at milkmaids long before Marie Antoinette thought
of it.

Clagny has been described as "perhaps the most regularly beautiful
house in France,"[10] and while it lacked the awesome scale of Versailles, many contemporaries considered it far lovelier.

Little is known about the interior of Clagny, aside from the famous
gallery which forms the background for the seductive portrait of its
mistress. The décor would have imitated that of the interiors of Versailles, where Le Brun and Hardouin-Mansart replaced the gilded
paneling popular under Louis XIII with an Italian scheme of pictures
inset in multicolored marbles and gilded bronze. Furniture at the time
was magnificent but generally rather sparse. However, as the idea that
it should provide comfort gained ground, it was becoming more
diverse. Moreover, with the stability and refinement of the social life
at Louis's court, it was beginning to be positioned more naturally,
grouped for conversation rather than placed standing stiffly against
the walls. Appropriately, the "commode" became popular at this
time, and although French furniture did not reach the zenith of its
beauty and ingeniousness until the eighteenth century, artists like
Boulle were already creating pieces which reflected a new style of
domestic arrangement, more private and relaxed.

Athénaïs certainly possessed some of the tapestries that were being
produced at the Gobelins manufactory, reorganized by Colbert in
1662 and immortalized in Le Brun's painting of Louis's visit there.
Many of the images on these tapestries were created from cartoons by
Le Brun, some of them, such as the *Histoire du Roi* or the *Histoire
d'Alexandre,* featuring the King's personal iconography and others
reflecting contemporary fashions such as interest in the exotic East.

Clagny was very much a baroque house, like Versailles engaging in
the heterogeneous dialogue of styles promoted by the ease of intellectual exchange in seventeenth-century Europe. It anticipated, but

was not of, the neoclassical age; rather it represented an interaction of the baroque and the classic, the simpler, more contained, classical design of the house being enlivened by the baroque decorations, whose richness and variety formed a contrast to the static lines of the structure. In a sense, Athénaïs herself was very much a "baroque" personality: mercurial, emotional, capricious, excessive. One writer describes her *"galanterie,"* at once proud and disturbing, ambitious and eccentric, as quintessentially baroque. Her taste combined an exquisite refinement with a liking for the bizarre, almost the brutal, the one exemplified by the delicate silver filigree carriage drawn by white mice she devised to amuse Louis; the other by pet bears she was to keep in her private menagerie at Versailles. The characters of Louis and Athénaïs were drawn to each other not only by their love of magnificence, but by their delight in the fantastic, the theater they could make of their lives; yet this delight might be labeled "classical" for the paganism inherent in the elevation of Louis the Sun King over His Most Christian Majesty. Thus in the personalities of the *amants magnifiques* was reflected their location at the cusp of a fluid, contrasting interaction between the dominant and the emerging artistic forms of the day.

One of Louis XIV's finer qualities as a king was his extraordinary capacity for *le détail de tout,* which probably stemmed from his great need for control through knowledge. He was interested in everything, and never too concerned with great matters of state to neglect domestic niceties. His letters to Colbert regarding his plans for Athénaïs's house or her jewelry demonstrate just how intimately she was involved with his life, and the extent to which he consulted her taste in artistic, if not political matters. At St. Germain, for example, which Athénaïs found tired and old-fashioned, Louis directed Colbert to redesign her apartments. "How is it," he wrote to his minister, "that you have inquired nothing concerning the work that must be done at St. Germain on the terraces of the apartment of Mme. de Montespan?"[11] Athénaïs was to have new decorations, a fountain, a birdbath, a little garden, and Colbert was expected to find the time to see to them, in between dealing with small matters such as the government and the economy. Louis always tried to anticipate Athénaïs's responses. His constant questions were, "What will she say?" and "Will this please her?" If it is allowed that the greatest years of the Great Century were between 1668 and 1680, this greatness must be seen as involving Athénaïs to a significant degree, since Louis was as concerned with and influenced by her taste and her appreciation as he was with his own.

It was Primi Visconti who christened Athénaïs the Real Queen of France, a role in which she was recognized by at least one ambassador. She was, after all, internationally famous. An African embassy respectfully presented gifts of a tiger, a panther and two lions to Louis, for his new menagerie; a golden pheasant and a Moorish dwarf to Marie-Thérèse, and a selection of pearls and sapphires to the King's "second wife" (presumably a commonplace for the ambassadors). Athénaïs's status was such that Saint-Simon describes her salon as "the center of court life — the center of pleasures, of fortunes, of hopes, the terror of ministers" (though as Saint-Simon could not for long contain his loathing for the legitimized royal bastards, he added that it was also "the humiliation of all France"). In later years, the cachet of a royal mistress was such that the eminently chaste Elector Frederick III of Brandenburg selected a lady to whom he gave the title and court functions of being a mistress, though not the more intimate favors the position usually merited.

The extent of Athénaïs's political influence was, however, negligible. Despite Mme. de Caylus's estimation that "Mme. de Montespan had an ambition to govern and to make her authority felt," it was really only Mme. de Maintenon who secured any purchase on the King's political direction. Athénaïs was able, of course, to secure powerful and lucrative positions for herself and for her family, and she had some influence on other appointments (her admiration for the oratory of Bishop Bossuet, for example, had led to his appointment as preceptor to the Grand Dauphin, a piece of discernment which, as in the case of Mme. Scarron, Athénaïs would come to regret), but Louis adhered adamantly to the principle that love should not be allowed to interfere in politics. Early in his reign, he had asked his councillors to inform him if they suspected that any woman was exerting undue influence on his decisions, and promised that in such a case he would be rid of her in three days. In his "memoirs," he expressed his conviction that "time given up to love affairs must never be allowed to prejudice affairs of state . . . And if we yield our heart, we must never yield our mind or will . . . We must maintain a rigorous distinction between a lover's tenderness and a sovereign's resolution . . . and we must make sure that the beauty who is the source of our delight never takes the liberty of interfering in political affairs." Louis's rhetoric had certainly collapsed by the time of the ascendancy of Mme. de Maintenon, but perhaps this motivated him all the more strongly to assert the principle.

This political mistrust of women was not confined to the King's lovers. After Mazarin's death, Louis had effectively banned his mother Anne from politics, despite her obvious capability, while Marie-Thérèse was barred from attending councils, traditionally a prerogative of the Queen Regnant. Athénaïs may have been disinclined to meddle when she recalled the fate of Marie de Hautfort and Louise de Lafayette, the only two women who had held any sway over Louis's father: Cardinal Richelieu had swiftly dispatched them respectively into exile and a convent. Indeed, with the exception of Anne of Austria, the period is notable for its lack of politically influential women. Louis's attitude may have been fueled by the brief resurgence of feminine power that had taken place during the hated Fronde, in which the Duchesse de Longueville and his own cousin, Mademoiselle, had played an active part. Women were generally considered dangerous, meddling and too light-minded to comprehend the magnitude of military or diplomatic strategy. It is a pity that neither Mme. de Maintenon in Louis XIV's reign or Mme. de Pompadour in Louis XV's, both of whom were women of tremendous intelligence, did nothing to disprove the theory.

Louis also made it clear that he was bored by too much demanding political discussion, and Athénaïs understood that it was her role to amuse rather than to advise. Still, she created a private sphere of influence through her intimate circle. As well as the advantages she obtained for her immediate family, she was instrumental in the selection of the Duc de Montausier as the Dauphin's tutor (the appointment that originally alerted her husband to her infidelity), and the gift of the governorship of Guyenne to her old friend the Maréchal d'Albret, in whose salon she had first met Mme. Scarron. Her allies the Duchesse de Richelieu and Louvois's mistress Mme. du Fresnoy were given positions in the Queen's household, and she encouraged the King to make the Queen's doctor, Antoine d'Acquin, his own *premier médecin* (a favor that D'Acquin returned by turning a blind eye to those little "love potions" Athénaïs purchased in Paris). Rather eccentrically, Athénaïs chose La Vienne, a famous Parisian swimmer, as the King's first valet of the chamber. To have power over such a person, even though he was officially only a servant, would have been extremely useful to a royal mistress, for Vienne became one of Louis's closest confidants. Finally, in addition to the Thianges–Nevers marriage, Athénaïs arranged matches between her nephew Louis de Rochechouart and Colbert's third daughter, and her niece Gabrielle-Victoire de Rochechouart and the elderly, but very rich, Marquis de Canaples. It was in the marriages of her own children, though, that the extent of Athénaïs's power was eventually demonstrated. By conferring such favors and obligations, Athénaïs profited from the negative example of the friendless Louise de La Vallière by surrounding herself with powerful supporters, thus ensuring that it was in the interests of many courtiers that she remain *maîtresse en titre.*

If Athénaïs's political power was concerned merely with her immediate circle, her influence on the culture of the court, and hence that of the nation, was highly significant, prefiguring that of Mme. de Pompadour in the eighteenth century. Louis was determined that the artistic grandeur of his reign should match its military triumphs, to which end Colbert founded four academies between 1666 and 1672 for the encouragement and perfection of the arts. To the Académie Française, founded by Richelieu in 1635, and the Petite Académie de Peinture et de la Sculpture, founded by Mazarin in 1648, were added the Académie de France à Rome (1666), the Académie des Sciences (1666), the Académie d'Architecture (1671) and the Académie de Musique (1672). "His Majesty," explained Colbert, "loving the fine arts as he does, will cultivate them with all the more care since they could serve to eternalize his great and glorious actions."[12] All such egotism perhaps seems petty, but Louis's was at least a glorious ego, and it was matched by that of his mistress. Athénaïs, too, used her new power of patronage and her exquisite taste to promote the grandeur of her lover and of France.

The Mortemarts were all discerning *amateurs* of the arts. Athénaïs's brother Vivonne was one of the first great noblemen to allow that artists and writers might be treated as social equals, on one occasion hauling himself up three flights of stairs to pay a call on the eminent writer Boileau, as the latter proudly records. Athénaïs shared her brother's appreciation of literature, and was among the first to promote the talents of the "four friends," the writers Molière, Racine, La Fontaine and Boileau. It was she who selected Racine and Boileau as the official historians of Louis XIV's reign, and she and the King enjoyed listening to readings of the manuscripts describing the progress of the Dutch wars immediately as they were written, and discussing them afterwards.

Molière, whose delight in audacious comedy and hatred of hypocrisy appealed to Athénaïs, could not fail to become a favorite of hers, and perhaps she had an additional private affection because it was she who had to some extent inspired him to write *Amphitryon*. Athénaïs once complained to Louis that his gardens lacked *fantaisie,* that appearance of enchantment which was so essential in the ballet, and which was to become such a feature of the divertissements at Versailles. Such *fantaisie* was lavishly orchestrated in Molière's productions. Thanks to his royal sponsor, he was able to stage extravaganzas such as *Psyche,* which cost 170,000 livres and boasted a chorus of 300 divinities floating on clouds, as well as a wave machine, flying zephyrs and furies and a troop of imps.

La Fontaine, author of the famous fables, paid a fulsome compliment to Athénaïs's taste in his 1678 dedication to Book Seven:

> *Le Temps, qui detruit tout, respectant votre appui*
> *Me laissera franchir les ans de cet ouvrage:*
> *Tout auteur qui voudra vivre encore après lui*
> *Doit s'acquerir votre suffrage*
> *C'est de vous que mes vers attendaient tout leur prix*
> *Il n'est beauté dans mes écrits*
> *Dont vous ne connaissez jusques aux moindres traces*
> *Eh! qui connait mieux que vous les beautés et les grâces?*
> *Paroles et regards, tout est charme dans vous.*[13]

Racine's response to the relationship between Louis and Athénaïs in the early 1670s was much darker and more complex than the conventional flatteries of La Fontaine. Louis liked Racine: he granted the playwright the post of gentleman-in-ordinary, and the two men were close for many years. Racine would read aloud to Louis when he was ill, translating Plutarch from the Latin straight from the page. Although Racine had had a strict Jansenist upbringing, which had instilled in him beliefs to which he would eventually return, he was seduced by the glamor of court life. Seeing him walking with the Marquis de Cavoye, Louis observed, "I often see those two together and I'm sure I know why. Cavoye likes to think he is an intellectual, and Racine fancies himself as a courtier." The success of Racine's early drama was largely due first to Athénaïs's backing, and then to Louis's, and has been interpreted as implicitly supporting the absolutist statecraft Louis was attempting to impose. Derived from Machiavelli, Racine's political views at the time accorded with the King's idea that the interest of the state has primacy over that of the individual; that decisiveness and ruthlessness, rather than generosity, are the prerequisites of stable rule. Racine's kings are majestic autocrats, but he also explores the effects of their rule on their subjects.

Bajazet (1672) takes place in a seraglio whose occupants are obsessed with their bloodthirsty, sexually rapacious ruler, Amurat. The erotic potency of the piece is generated by the interplay of power and subjection, the oppression of Amurat's subjects being the predicate of their capacity for pleasure. Amurat is the center of their universe, but they are emasculated by their need for his authority, a precise dramatization of the dynamics of power as they would come to be enacted at Versailles. The necessity of pleasing the King's mistress is another aspect of the courtier's impotence. Even though the mistress's status would be lower than a man's, the King's power becomes hers, elevating her above her sex and emasculating the male courtiers, demoting them to feminized supplicants. Louis's political project shared the same logic of absolute power as Racine's theater, its workings "imprisoning the world in its marvel . . . according to the will of the King."[14] The courtiers in *Bajazet* are frightened by their inability to "see" Amurat, for only his presence illuminates the labyrinth they inhabit. Sense, like flowers or fountains, springs up where he walks. The obsession with vision in Racine's play accords with the emphasis Louis himself placed on the visual, performative aspect of his monarchy. Not to be seen by the King was simply to not exist. In his "memoirs," Louis wrote that "the sons of France . . . for the good of the State, must never have another retreat than the court, nor any other place of security than in the heart of their brother." This heart was Louis himself, and it was a grave offense not to appear frequently at court, to be looked at by the King. Those who transgressed were rewarded with the phrase "I do not know him," or, even more dreadfully, "He is a man that I never see." Remember the delirious joy of the Abbé Locatelli at having been "seen" by the King. Not to be passed over for places, pensions, promotions, meant literally to be visible, to be seen, and the neuroses of the seraglio of

Bajazet are precisely those of the enclosed world of Versailles, where a lifetime could be devoted to catching the trajectory of the royal gaze. If it paused, success; if it traversed, darkness.

Racine's play suggests that pleasing the mistress, then, was a step towards pleasing the eye of the king, and in some respects, Athénaïs's taste was more advanced than Louis's, which tended towards a rather rigid and grandiose style, as exemplified by the highly competent but unoriginal works produced by the Académie under the direction of Le Brun. These mostly took flattering classical analogies of the King's life as their subjects, such as the *Histoire d'Alexandre,* which followed the story from Louis's favorite Plutarch and flattered his imperialist ambitions. Athénaïs, by contrast, admired the works of Dutch masters such as Vermeer, which Louis found inexplicably — or perhaps perfectly explicably — quotidian. Perhaps he was less interested in art that did not flatter his personal glory. The relationship between aesthetics and vanity is indeed vexed when it comes to the question of patronage. Did complicity in their mutual project of self-aggrandizement mean that Athénaïs and Louis appreciated only art as an accessory to self-promotion? The question might equally be posed of a Borghese or a Medici, and perhaps what matters ultimately is that the works of art were commissioned and executed, whatever the motives of their owners. Even if Athénaïs patronized painters or architects merely out of vanity, her taste transcended the conventional limitations of her time, and her use of her fortune to buy art therefore made a valuable contribution to the cultural ebullience of the Grand Siècle.

Athénaïs, like Louis, loved music. Concerts were held in her apartments, and she herself played the harpsichord. Her daughter Mlle. de Nantes was a notable dancer and musician, and Athénaïs encouraged her to learn the guitar, which Louis had brought into fashion by taking lessons in his youth. She also patronized a female musician, Elisabeth Jacquet de la Guerre, who composed cantatas to Old Testament texts and was an accomplished harpsichord player, going on to compose a lyric tragedy, *Cephile et Procris,* about the Nine Years war, performed in Paris in 1694. Athénaïs shared her enthusiasm for music with Mademoiselle, who employed her own troop of violinists and also patronized women artists, most notably the popular singer Hilaire Dupuy. The Vivonnes, too, were keen musicians: one librettist, Isaac de Bensérade, dedicated to the Duchesse de Vivonne a poem which played on the family connection with the navy, as well as on its tendency to corpulence. The Duchesse recited it in her role as a nereid in a ballet in 1665. "I expect him to appear at any moment," she sang, referring to her lover, played by Vivonne, "and every whale I see reminds me!"

Athénaïs also took an interest in the career of her Poitou countryman Michel Lambert who, since 1661, had been master of the King's chamber music. A singer, composer and lutenist, he created many of the ballets in which Athénaïs performed. Lully, the superintendent of music, was also a friend, as was the librettist Quinault. Athénaïs's taste did not always overcome her vanity, and in 1677 she quarreled with Quinault when the opera *Isis* was performed at St. Germain. The heroine of *Amphitryon* did not take kindly to the inclusion of the character of Juno, Jupiter's wife, traditionally portrayed as jealous and vengeful, implying that her role had changed from seductive lover to nagging wife. Athénaïs was so furious that she had Quinault banned from the theater for two years. She asked Racine and Boileau to compose a more flattering opera on the theme of *la chute de Phaeton,* but the result was not a success, and Quinault was reinstated to create *Proserpine* and *Perseus.*

Athénaïs has been compared to a minister for culture by French historians, and she extended her enthusiasm for pleasure and *gloire* to every aspect of her life with Louis, setting the tone for a court which has been described as a paradox of brilliance and uselessness, a dazzling absurdity. Whether or not the King's concentration of aristocratic power at Versailles was inspired or disastrous is a moot point, but to say that the court of France between 1668 and 1680 was "useless" seems ill-judged. These were the greatest years of Louis's reign, the zenith of his personal triumphs and of French dominance in Europe. He established himself through his victories in Flanders and the Franche-Comte as the most powerful monarch on the continent, holding the balance of war and peace between his elegantly gloved hands, but the legacy France left to the art of living endured long after the Bourbon armies were disbanded.

"French" is still an adjective suggestive of elegance, and well into the twentieth century, civilization spoke with a French accent, savored French cuisine, dressed in French fashions, doused itself in French perfumes, admired French artists and poets, imitated French etiquette, attributed all that was associated with refined living to the influence of France. The aristocrat of Louis's court was ideally an intelligent amateur in every form of activity, a specialist only in the complex art of living. "Wisdom," wrote the contemporary philosopher Saint-Evremond, "has been granted to us principally that we may know how to handle our pleasures."[15] Athénaïs has been called "the most splendid ornament of this splendid century,"[16] the decade or so of her dominance *l'Age Montespan,* and indeed it was she who taught Louis the art of pleasure, who refined his sensuality, who shared her genius for delight with the King and attracted the admiring gaze of all Europe as she did so. Louis had a predisposition to seek *la gloire,* but in his enslavement to Athénaïs's body and his captivation by her spirit he discovered the desire to *paraître aux yeux de la Montespan;* to be seen by her, to amaze as he was himself amazed. Appearance again. If Athénaïs's reign corresponds with the greatest years of Louis's, it is because she was in a great measure his inspiration.

Chapter Nine

"Self-interest speaks all manner of tongues
and plays all manner of parts, even that of
disinterestedness."

The year 1675 proved to Athénaïs that, despite the security she appeared to have achieved, many enemies surrounded her. On 11 April that year, when she went to make her Easter confession at Versailles, the curate, Father Lécuyer, refused in no uncertain terms to grant her absolution. "Is that the Mme. de Montespan who scandalizes the whole of France?" he shrieked through the grille of the confessional. "Well, Madame, cease your scandals and come and throw yourself at the feet of Jesus Christ!"[1] Horrified, Athénaïs appealed to his superior, the local priest Father Thibout, but he, too, refused her the sacrament. For a devout Catholic such as Athénaïs, this was extremely distressing, since without absolution she could not receive Holy Communion at the Easter Mass, an essential obligation in the Church. She asked the King to find some senior churchman who could resolve the problem, but Louis rather misguidedly selected Bossuet to settle the dispute.

Bossuet had impressed both Louis and his mother with the power of his sermons, preached extempore from brief notes. His eloquence, both in the pulpit and in his theological writings, was deservedly famous: his first work, *Exposition of Catholic Doctrine on Matters of Controversy,* had succeeded in converting the roistering general Maréchal de Turenne. Athénaïs, too, had admired him sufficiently to recommend his appointment as the heir's tutor. Immensely learned, and full of integrity, Bossuet was not a wicked man, though the glee he took in thrashing the poor Dauphin shows an unpleasant side to his character, but his piety was rigid and absolutely inflexible. The true Church, in his view, had never altered, and Bossuet would never alter either. He saw his role at court as the prevention of scandal, rather than its toleration, and he was genuinely appalled by Louis's relationship with Athénaïs. So Bossuet's arbitration in the matter of Athénaïs's confession took the form of delivering a lecture on adultery to the King. It was courageous of the Bishop to attempt to reform the King at the risk of incurring his displeasure, even though this courage extended only as far as to attack Louis's mistress rather than the morals of Louis himself. So forceful was his peroration that Louis was overwhelmed, and promised the Bishop that he would see Athénaïs no more. When Athénaïs heard about this, she flew into an hysterical tantrum and took to her bed for two days, seeing no one and tearing the bed linen with her teeth as she slept.

This sudden crisis represents the culmination of a plan hatched between the Bishop and his new friend Mme. de Maintenon. At the end of the previous year, the humble Mme. Scarron had ascended the next rung on the ladder of power by becoming the Marquise de Maintenon. Since her arrival at court, her quarrels with Athénaïs had increased in proportion to the favor she enjoyed. Able to see her children only infrequently, Athénaïs had grown more and more jealous of their sober, reliable governess, and vented her frustration in furious attacks on Mme. Scarron whenever that lady dared to suggest that sweets and late nights were not good for her charges. Whenever they fell out over the children, Athénaïs would imperiously remind the governess of her inferior status as a dependant. "'We' consult us only after their opinion is decided," complained Mme. Scarron to Mme. de Saint-Géran. "'We' demand that I should approve and not give my opinion, I am credited only with good sense, and 'we' make use of me only in order to rule all the better."[2]

Following the strategy of Louise de La Vallière, Mme. Scarron began to put it about that she was no longer able to bear the indignities of her position and that she wished to leave the court to become a nun. In her letters to her confessor, the Abbé Gobelin, she describes the ferocious arguments that beset her throughout 1674. It would seem that even Athénaïs was appalled by her own tendency to violence, for her rages, from which, famously, not even the King was

spared, were always succeeded by fits of exhausted, repentant sobbing. Nevertheless, Mme. Scarron was not inclined to empathy with
her employer's frustrations. As always, she referred her plight to God.

> Mme. de Montespan and I had a violent quarrel today, and as I
> am the injured party, I wept a great deal and she took her
> account of it to the King; I swear that I suffer a good deal by
> remaining in a state where I will have such experiences every
> day, and it would be kind to me to let me have my freedom. I
> have wished a thousand times to become a nun . . . I cannot
> understand that it is God's will that I suffer Mme. de Montespan.
> She is incapable of friendship, and I cannot bring myself to it;
> she does not know how to encounter the oppositions in me
> which she finds there without hating me, she speaks of me as
> she likes to the King, and causes me to lose esteem . . . I do not
> dare to speak to him directly because she would never forgive me.

She adds, hypocritically, that even if she were to speak to Louis, her
debt of gratitude to Mme. de Montespan would not permit her to
utter a word against her.

Of course, Mme. Scarron had no real intention of becoming a
nun, particularly as the King had shown his esteem for her by increasing her annual pension to 2,000 ecus, and making her an additional
gift of 100,000 livres. The poor widow began to dream of buying a
country estate, that great mark of aristocratic prestige, and Athénaïs
became yet more nervous about Louis's increasing fondness for her
former friend, probably recalling her own tactics with La Vallière. It is
a measure of Athénaïs's anxiety that the only way she felt she could
get rid of Mme. Scarron was by securing for her what she herself
coveted: a duchess's *tabouret,* or stool, denied to her because of her
husband's refusal to be made a duc. Athénaïs and her sister, Mme. de
Thianges, decided to arrange a marriage between Françoise Scarron
and the Duc de Villars-Brancas. He was hardly an attractive suitor.
Already widowed twice, he was elderly, smelly and hunchbacked (one
can imagine Athénaïs dismissing this airily, as it would make the governess feel at home), and, even worse, had a reputation for being dis-
honest and villainous. Still, a duc of any kind was an extraordinary
match for a woman who had begun life as a charity orphan. The fact
that Mme. Scarron refused it suggests that she had already conceived a

greater idea of her own future than would be satisfied by a second marriage of convenience. She was determined, quite clearly, to make her fortune at court.

Frustrated, Athénaïs must have complained directly to Louis, for Mme. Scarron's letters now describe her concern at the King's sudden coldness towards her. "My friends have perceived it," she told the Abbé, "and have made their compliments on my disgrace." She decided to preserve her dignity by resigning before she was dismissed, but before she could act on her resolution, Louis made the surprising gift of a further 100,000 livres and permission to acquire the estate and manor of Maintenon. Unsurprisingly, the new Marquise de Maintenon abandoned her plans for the convent.

Why did Louis elevate his children's governess to such a position? It seems that he was reluctant to lose the company of a woman whose conversation and calm temperament he increasingly appreciated, and that he offered her Maintenon to compensate her for her claims of injustice. Throughout their disputes, the new Marquise had made sure that everyone knew just what she suffered at the hands of Mme. de Montespan, and perhaps the King was concerned for his mistress's popularity. Unconsciously, though, Louis was comfortable with a domestic set-up involving two women — the pattern he had established with Athénaïs and Louise — and it probably flattered his pride that Athénaïs should have a rival of sorts to keep her on her toes. Moreover, Louis genuinely enjoyed spending time with his children and their governess, a pleasure that Athénaïs jealously affected to despise as a bourgeois trait, and he was anxious that the children's welfare should not be compromised. He dispatched Louvois to effect a reconciliation between the two marquises and, for a while, cordiality reigned again, though the intermittent friendship between them continually flared up into rows.

It was now that Mme. de Maintenon began to see her presence at court as a mission to save the King's soul, and the first obstacle to her goal was Athénaïs. Mme. de Maintenon knew that Bishop Bossuet had some influence over the King. Although he had no official justification for meddling with the monarch's conscience, he had made himself popular with Louis by performing such delicate services as supporting Madame Henriette on her deathbed and conveying the news of her demise. He had also been the one to tell Louis of the death of his three-year-old son by Marie-Thérèse, the Duc d'Anjou, in 1671. La Maintenon now worked to establish a friendship with Bossuet, who represented, along with his colleague the Duc de Montausier, the devout faction at court, the "*dévot* party." Despite the assistance he had given the King in his first meetings with Athénaïs, the Duc had become rather a puritan since the death of his wife, and these two men saw Mme. de Maintenon as a potential female missionary who could use her still-evident beauty to persuade where reason failed in dismantling Athénaïs's empire. A new tone now enters Mme. Maintenon's letters to the Abbé Gobelin. "I beg you to ask God to guide my project for His glory and my salvation," she asks. This project was being hatched with Bossuet, and together he and the Marquise plotted to terrify the King into abandoning his love.

The *dévot* party launched their battle for the King's soul at Lent in 1675, when the celebrated orator Père Louis Bourdaloue preached his powerful sermon on adultery for the third time. His text was daring in its condemnation of Louis's adultery in particular, and exhorted the King to set an example to his subjects by abandoning debauchery and returning to a godly life. The following preacher, Jules de Mascaron, went even further, condemning Louis's quest for military glory by comparing a hero to a thief who merely performed at the head of his armies the robberies that petty criminals could carry out alone. With obvious pleasure, Mme. de Maintenon reported the King's discomfort to her confessor, and though Louis was irritated, he was also troubled.

Bossuet's strategy was the delivery of a long explication of Christian humility from which the King could infer that the basis of a Christian life was not mere adherence to the outward forms of the Church, but a loving submission to God's will. His Most Christian Majesty responded peevishly that no one had told him any such thing. Bossuet was not able to persuade Louis that repudiating his mistress was the only route to salvation until she was refused absolution by the Versailles priests at the end of Lent. Had Bossuet himself prompted this refusal? By playing on Louis's superstitious nature, the bishop convinced him that this unrelated incident was a sign from God that he should change his ways. Louis broke down and conceded that he would break with Athénaïs. "I do not require, sire, that you should extinguish in a single moment a flame so violent," wheedled Bossuet, "but, sire, try, little by little, to diminish it; beware of entertaining it." What seems particularly harsh in all this is that Athénaïs was far more pious than her lover, who was never actually refused communion, though he did have enough scruples not to take it. Essentially, Louis was a nominal believer, following, as did almost everyone in France, the observances of the Catholic Church, attending Mass and reading his breviary, but without ever searching his arrogant heart for true belief or repentance. This early cohabitation of faith and sin was perhaps the explanation for the acceptance of His Most Christian Majesty's *"maîtresse declarée,"* a position which appears heavily ironic at a Catholic court. In a letter discussing the King as late as 1694, after his "conversion," the educational writer Fénélon accused him of being superficial in his religion, of loving only his own glory and convenience and of conforming to Christian practice only through fear of hell. It is unlikely that Louis even believed that kings went to hell, but he was nonetheless superstitious as well as sentimental, and Bossuet played on both his pride as a king and his susceptible emotions. Athénaïs, on the other hand, was a devout believer who wished to repent sincerely, at least each time she went to confession, and who undoubtedly struggled with her conscience throughout her career as the national scarlet woman.

After her two-day fit of hysterics, Athénaïs rallied herself and prepared to retaliate. It is likely that she judged that Bossuet and La Maintenon were much less interested in the King's soul than in having power over his judgment, and sinner though she might be, Athénaïs despised such self-righteousness. She treated Bossuet to a splendid display of anger, accusing him of wanting to dominate the King to feed his own pride, and of plotting to remove her because she stood in his way. Bossuet responded with infuriating smugness that if Athénaïs refused to convert and save her soul, then it was her own choice, but that she should not try to block the King's path to salvation. Grinding salt into the wound, Mme. de Maintenon described the mistress's distress to Gobelin, adding sententiously: "Her state moves me to pity. No one cares for her, even though she has done good to many people." Including the gloating governess.

Having failed to terrify Bossuet with her fury, Athénaïs considered blackmail. She investigated his background to see if there was a skeleton in his closet she could rattle before him, but Bossuet's habits were irritatingly free of scandal. Bribery was the next option, and Athénaïs tried to wheedle the prelate into relaxing his severity with the promise of a cardinal's hat. But he was not to be tempted, and Louis made his Easter communion chastely. Humiliated at the failure of her strategies and by the furious gossip of the court, Athénaïs retreated to Clagny to plan her next attack. "The King and Mme. de Montespan have left one another," reported Mlle. de Scudéry excitedly, "loving one another more than life, purely on a principle of religion. It is said that she will return to court without being lodged there, never seeing the King except in the presence of the Queen."[3]

For the next month, Louis kept to himself, seeing his ministers only briefly and spending hours every day with Bossuet, who delivered endless advice on conversion, all centered on the necessity of giving up Athénaïs. Louis suffered a great deal from this conflict of love and duty, conceding only painfully to each of Bossuet's demands. He agreed to live an honest life, and never to fall into sin again. Desperately, Louis asked Bossuet to permit a final interview with Athénaïs, but the prelate claimed that this was not a sign of true repentance, since the good Christian sought to avoid temptation wherever possible. Never at ease with internal conflict, Louis even went as far as to proclaim in a trembling voice to the Dauphin that the boy should follow his father's example in never giving himself up to "guilty attachments."

Yet the final interview was eventually granted, just before Louis's departure for the front for the summer campaign, in a glass-walled room and under the watchful eyes of selected pious courtiers. "They could be seen from head to foot. The conversations were long and sad," Mme. de Caylus reported. Most courtiers, however, did not believe that the separation would last. Mme. de Sévigné had her money on Athénaïs. Athénaïs was improving Clagny as Dido built Carthage, she remarked, but the story would have a different end from the abandonment of Dido by her lover, Aeneas, depicted in the Clagny murals. Even Père Bourdaloue was skeptical, answering Louis's self-congratulatory question, "Father, you must be happy with me?" with: "Yes, sire, but God would be more satisfied if Clagny were forty leagues from Versailles!" Athénaïs said nothing when asked if she would return to court, but she laughed a good deal, and continued receiving visitors as though nothing had happened.

Mindful of these cynical omens, Bossuet delivered his strongest homily yet to the King just before Pentecost. Once more, he emphasized that Louis must banish Athénaïs completely from his life. "Sire," he wrote, "you must know that you cannot be truly converted unless you work to remove from your heart not only the sin, but the cause of it."[4] Louis not only had to leave Athénaïs, but to cease even to love her. A copy of this lesson was sent to Clagny, where it moved Athénaïs to tears, perhaps of repentance, perhaps of regret. Moreover, Bossuet insisted to Louis that political and moral good were inextricably entwined, and that a return to his mistress would be the ruin of France. "The profession Your Majesty has made to change His life has filled the people with consolation, it persuades them that Your Majesty's giving himself to God will render you more than ever attentive to the obligation imposed on you to watch over their misery, and it is from this that they hope for the ease of their cares of which they have great need."[5] Bossuet may have cared that the majority of Louis's people still lived in miserable poverty, but even so he was mainly concerned with the dismissal of Athénaïs.

During her lover's absence at the front, Athénaïs appeared to have accepted the separation and even to have "converted" herself. Both she and Louis took communion at Pentecost. Louis had ordered Bossuet to visit her, and the Bishop reported that she was calm, and occupying herself with works of charity. So many tears, so much violence, so much effort, he believed, were signs that God was working in both their hearts.

Queen Marie-Thérèse was of course delighted by Bossuet's efforts, and attempted to assist him by showing friendship towards Athénaïs, from whom she had inevitably become estranged. Together they visited Trianon, a rather curious choice of excursion, and paid visits to convents (perhaps the Queen was hinting that it was time Athénaïs followed Louise's example). All the court ladies, headed by the Queen, visited Clagny, where the work continued regardless of the interference of bishops. Athénaïs had lost none of her magnificent airs and displayed a confidence she must have been far from feeling. Perhaps she knew in her heart that if only Louis could see her again, all would be well. Separation might kill their love, but "friendship," as all lovers know, was impossible.

In fact, distance seemed to have heightened Louis's ardor. Even amid the excitement and confusion of the Dutch battlefields, he found time to write to Colbert with minute instructions for the improvement of Clagny. "I am much relieved that you have bought the orange trees for Clagny. Continue to take the most beautiful, if Mme. de Montespan wishes it," he wrote on 15 May. If Louis was sending her orange trees, in which they had both delighted at Trianon, it must have seemed to Athénaïs that their love was not over. In total Louis indulged Athénaïs's love of orange trees to the tune of 22,738 livres during his absence in the summer of 1675. "The expense is excessive," wrote the besotted King, "and I see by that that nothing is impossible for you in order to please me." He instructed Colbert to continue to satisfy any wish Athénaïs might express.

Having successfully besieged Maastricht, Louis returned determined to see Athénaïs again. Perhaps his new conquests had recalled to him the beginnings of their own affair. Perhaps the freshness of the orange trees he had lovingly ordered was too enticing after the mud and sweat of the battlefield. There is no discernible reason for precisely why Louis changed his mind, but the casuistical argument current at court was that if both lovers had renounced their relationship, there was no reason why they should not meet in the harmony of friendship. The Duchesse de Richelieu, one of those friends whom Athénaïs had taken care to cultivate, skillfully championed the idea that the sinner had repented and that she was content merely to take her rightful place at court. After all, as Mme. de Caylus conceded, "Why not? . . . Mme. de Montespan ought to be there because of her birth and her duties; she can live as a Christian as well there as anywhere else." So when Louis set off for Versailles in July, the court, the world, were agog to see whether his passion for the beautiful marquise would conquer the fear of God Himself.

It appeared that Athénaïs had won. Her apartments at Versailles were prepared as usual, and Louis, alarmed by Bossuet's exigency, turned the problem of his conscience over to his confessor, Père la Chaise, giving his word of honor that he would "do nothing but what was right." La Chaise, who had a mistress of his own, one Mme. de Bretonvilliers (nicknamed "La Cathédrale" by Parisians), unsurprisingly supported the King in his wish that Athénaïs be permitted to appear at court. Louvois and Colbert were in agreement for once in their hope that the King would return to her, as they feared that in the absence of a *maîtresse en titre,* Bossuet might become too intimate with Louis and threaten their own power. Seeing that Athénaïs had influential allies, Bossuet, terrified that all his work had come to nothing, set off to meet the King at Luzarches in a final effort to dissuade him from falling into sin. He was too overcome to speak, but threw himself on his knees, weeping pathetically. Louis ignored his tears, merely remarking, "Say nothing to me, Monsieur. I have given my orders."

Chapter Ten

"Love, like fire, cannot survive without
continual movement, and it ceases to
live as soon as it ceases to hope or fear."

Athénaïs had to wait one whole miserable year before her lover returned to her. When Louis arrived at Versailles in that summer of 1675, he announced to the Queen and the Dauphin that he planned to keep the vows he had made before his departure, and that they ought to inform anyone who was curious of this fact. Athénaïs had to content herself with a courteous public salutation and no more. Louis insisted on seeing her only in company, and she was forced to keep her anger and frustration to herself. Nothing could more clearly emphasize the ultimate imbalance of power between the lovers than this fact that, unless Louis wished otherwise, he could use the stringent demands of etiquette to avoid any private scene with his suffering mistress, who had no right, even by virtue of their intimacy, to demand an explanation.

Ever the accomplished courtier, Athénaïs once again made a tremendous effort to keep to herself the pain she must have been feeling. If Louis no longer shared her bed, her public position was as strong as ever, since she had not been replaced, and she took care to demonstrate to the court that her social, if not her sexual standing was unaffected. On the surface, she appeared to agree that the King's conversion was a splendid improvement, and one that she shared herself. She maintained her disdainful superiority over the other court ladies, giving splendid suppers and queening it over the Queen. She

exploited her privilege as far as to ignore etiquette by taking precedence over the duchesses, who by rights ought to have preceded her.
If Louis was angered by these liberties, he did nothing to prevent
them, feeling perhaps that he had no right to do so, and the King's
approach set the tone for the court. If Athénaïs was no longer
maîtresse in anything but name, her actions did nothing to suggest it
and, publicly, at least, she managed things so skillfully that after a
while everyone forgot that a rupture had ever occurred.

Everyone that is, except Bossuet. Furious that Athénaïs was, to all
appearances, reestablished, he persecuted her in a most un-Christian
manner. In September, while the court was at Fontainebleau, Athénaïs sent her friend the Duchesse de Richelieu to ask the curate if he
would hear her confession. Despite the fact that her conduct had
been irreproachable for months, the priest reported proudly to
Bossuet that he had refused her on the grounds that although she had
mended her conduct, she had not repented in her heart. The fact that
this was undoubtedly true does nothing to excuse Bossuet's
hypocrisy, since he was perfectly prepared to believe in such a repentance on the part of the King. Bossuet also encouraged Mme. de
Maintenon to aggravate Athénaïs while remaining in good favor with
Louis — not that she needed much encouragement in this endeavor.

Mme. de Sévigné guessed that Bossuet had good cause to worry,
but she was also perspicacious enough to imagine how difficult the
situation was for Athénaïs. Of the visit to Fontainebleau she writes:
"Everything was ready when a bolt fell from the blue that shattered
the joy. The populace says it is on account of Quantova, the attachment is still intense. Enough fuss is being made to upset the curé
[Bossuet] and everybody else, but perhaps not enough for her, for in
her visible triumph there is an underlying sadness."[1]

After months of this strain, even Athénaïs's courage failed, and in
May 1676, while Louis was again away in Holland, she decided to
take the cure at Bourbon, ostensibly because she was suffering from
rheumatism in the knee, but probably to get away from the unholy
alliance of Bossuet and Maintenon. The trip might also have been
something of a public-relations exercise to demonstrate to the provinces that she was still the King's favorite. Bourbon at the time had a
similar status and function as eighteenth-century Bath as a watering
place and social center for the upper classes. The waters were reputed

to cure every ailment from laryngitis, nervousness and rheumatism, to infertility.

Athénaïs was accompanied by her niece and her sister, Mme. de Thianges, and they traveled in typical style, in a barouche drawn by six splendid horses. Behind followed a coach containing six maids, two wagons, six pack mules, Athénaïs's bodyguards and a dozen outriders. In total, the party numbered forty-five. Mme. de Sévigné was following the same route as the royal mistress, a fussy tugboat in the wake of a stately liner, and she avidly reports every detail she was able to glean about the splendid procession. Mme. de Montespan arrives at each staging post to find her room and bed prepared; she dines heartily and then retires. Mme. de Montespan showers gracious streams of gold on every church and convent she passes. Mme. de Montespan receives letters from the army every single day . . .

Athénaïs paused at Nevers, where she was given an official welcome at the château, and thence proceeded to Bourbon, where none other than Louise de La Vallière's brother, the Marquis de La Vallière who governed the province, had laid on a formal reception, which she tactfully declined. The cure at Bourbon lasted thirty days, and consisted of a combination of drinking the waters, therapeutic thermal baths, "medicines" such as bleeding and purges, and bed rest. Mme. de Sévigné was enthusiastic about the results, though her modesty was rather tried by the outdoor baths, and she did not venture into the mud pits. She comments on the excellent mix of Vichy and Bourbon water on offer: "These two rivals are accommodated together, it is no more than one heart and one soul. Vichy rests in the breast of Bourbon and warms itself at her fire, that is to say in the boiling of her fountains." If only the same could have been said of the two marquises.

From Bourbon, Athénaïs and her party set off for Moulins aboard a magnificent barge, painted and gilded, and furnished, as the indefatigable de Sévigné reports, "in red damask . . . with quantities of devices and streamers in the colors of France and Navarre; there never was anything more romantic."[2] Athénaïs had obtained this magnificent equipage from Gilbert Bourdier de Roche, the intendant of the baths, who considered himself amply reimbursed for the enormous expense by the letter Athénaïs reported she had written to the King, full of praise for his attentiveness. So, as far as the provinces were concerned, Athénaïs's status clearly remained intact.

This status was reinforced by the charity she dispensed during her voyage, displaying an inclination towards good works that continued to develop throughout her life. She created twelve new hospital beds, and made a large donation to the Capuchin order. She also engaged in a little sensitive politics. The family of the embezzler Nicolas Fouquet, the disgraced superintendent of finances, at that time incarcerated at Pignerol with Athénaïs's old friend Lauzun, were also taking the waters at Bourbon. They visited Athénaïs on two consecutive days, discussing "the most delicate subject" at length. Mme. Fouquet earnestly wished to be allowed to join her husband in prison, and she pleaded her case with a good deal of modesty and tact. Athénaïs listened compassionately, and promised to make a report to the King. In fact, the first ameliorations of Fouquet's imprisonment were put into practice the following year. Athénaïs's compassion may have been motivated by the fact that her legitimate son, the ten-year-old Marquis d'Antin, was to pay a visit to Mme. Fouquet in the country. Mme. de Sévigné, a champion of the Fouquet family, visited her friend and found the boy good-looking and amusing. It is uncertain whether Athénaïs was able to meet her estranged son in Mme. Fouquet's company, but perhaps this connection created an empathy between the two women that gave Athénaïs the courage to defend the unfashionable Fouquet cause.

In July, the King returned. During the celebratory reception given by the Queen at St. Germain, the Marquise de Montespan was suddenly announced. Louis, the stately monarch who struck ambassadors dumb with awe, who surrounded himself with the strictest etiquette, actually ran across the great salon to greet her, and only just held back from taking her in his arms. Naturally, the *dévot* party were horrified. They managed to keep Athénaïs away from her lover that night, and Mme. de Maintenon hurriedly volunteered to act as a chaperone for the next day's journey to Versailles. When Louis announced that he intended to visit Athénaïs in her apartments at Clagny, the *dévots* assembled a party of worthy ladies to supervise the meeting and bear witness to the "pure and simple friendship" the lovers had sworn.

Athénaïs must have known that this was her last chance. All the witnesses agreed that she looked more beautiful than ever, like a blushing virgin. Louis crossed the room and drew her towards the window. He began to speak pompously, sounding just like Bossuet, but Athénaïs cut him short, murmuring, "It's useless to read me a sermon. I understand that my time is over." He wept; she wept. Athénaïs, who never cried in public, knew that day how to use her tears. "You are mad," she said, smiling sadly.

"Yes, I am mad, since I still love you," he replied.

Then they made an elegant bow to the company and withdrew to Athénaïs's bedroom.

"And thus," said Mme. de Caylus with a sniff, "came the arrival of Mme. la Duchesse d'Orléans and M. le Comte de Toulouse." The King's soul, it appeared, would have to take care of itself.

The *dévots* had prevailed briefly, but in the glorious flesh, Athénaïs was too much for them. Her rare combination of great beauty and superb wit were incomparable. When she entered a room she made other women invisible; when she talked, she rendered them dumb. Louis's sensual attraction to her was simply too strong for him to resist. The sense of provocation, of competition even, that he felt with her meant that she always excited him, that she was always a challenge to be freshly overcome.

The priests in their black gowns retired to mutter like disgruntled crows, and with the reconciliation of the lovers, happiness returned to Versailles.

"Joy has returned and all jealous airs have vanished," commented Mme. de Sévigné. Athénaïs had never been more fêted, more adored; the King seemed to be in love twice over, and as usual everyone ignored the Queen's tears. Everything was done to please the triumphant favorite: there were balls, concerts, ballets every day. Bossuet claimed that the death that year of the great general Maréchal de Turenne was a punishment from God for the King's wickedness, but although Turenne was deeply mourned, no one took much notice of Bossuet's dire predictions. Mme. de Maintenon was peeved at the mishandling of the affair, declaring that holiness was all very well, but Bossuet was not enough of a courtier. If Athénaïs was ever to be ousted, it would have to be through the wiles of the salon rather than the imprecations of the pulpit.

The court was anxious to prove itself as friendly to Athénaïs as it had previously been hostile, and Athénaïs celebrated her victory as publicly as she had disguised her defeat, returning the King to his people in a series of glittering entertainments. She was referred to as the *maîtresse regnante,* a title always conspicuously denied to its proper bearer, the Queen, who stayed often alone in her apartments, solitary and uncourted. Occasionally, Marie-Thérèse amused herself with a Spanish play, to the discomfort of her few unlucky guests, who shivered in the almost empty, cavernous rooms, the majority of the court having made their excuses to join in whatever amusement was being offered by the "real Queen." It was Athénaïs's favor that everyone sought, and the vanity that had supported her dignity throughout the period of her humiliation now blazed forth in a determination to subdue Versailles to her will.

From one aspiring ally, a courtier named Langlée, Athénaïs received a marvelous dress "of gold on gold," reports Mme. de Sévigné, "all embroidered with gold, all edged with gold, and on top of that a sort of gold pile stitched with gold mixed with a certain gold, which makes the most divine stuff ever imagined. The fairies have secretly devised this work, no living soul knew anything about it."[3] It was delivered as a surprise. When Athénaïs's dressmaker arrived, he at first showed her a different dress which did not fit. Having recovered all her imperious airs, Athénaïs terrified the poor man with a tantrum, after which he timidly inquired as to whether, since time was short, another dress might do instead, and produced the gold marvel which, of course, fitted beautifully. Louis arrived to admire it, but wondered who it was from. "Langlée," answered Athénaïs. "No one else but Langlée could have imagined such magnificence." For days, Langlée was the name on all the fashionable lips at Versailles.

Athénaïs's taste was paramount in sartorial matters. French court fashion is divided into three distinct periods during the reign of Louis XIV, of which the second, and most magnificent, is directly attributed to the influence of Mme. de Montespan. She had already introduced the *hurluberlu* hairstyle, as copied by Marie-Thérèse, and, as her delight in Langlée's gift shows, Athénaïs had a taste for sumptuous fabrics. The richness and overdecoration of the fashions of the 1670s bears witness to her love of lace, shimmering fabrics and gold embroidery. Formal dresses were tightly corseted beneath a low boat neck, with an underskirt and an overskirt, or *manteau*. The first was often made of embroidered taffeta, with the *manteau* looped up on either side of the hips like a pair of curtains, descending into a train behind, whose length varied according to the social rank of the wearer. In 1676, two new fashions appeared: *falbalas,* flounces of fabric ornamenting the bodice of the dress, and painted gauzes or *transparents,* translucent colored materials embroidered with lace or velvet and worn over a plain black gown. Predictably, the Prince de Condé addressed a letter to the court ladies from Chantilly suggesting that the transparents would be more beautiful if worn over bare skin, but Mme. de Sévigné doubted it. Another fashion introduced by Athénaïs was the less formal *déshabillé,* a style prefigured by the *robe battante* she had devised to conceal (or announce) her pregnancies. This was a more relaxed, indoor ensemble consisting of a tunic worn over the skirt, and a taffeta scarf to cover the hair. The *déshabillé* was comfortable as well as being loose and seductive, and Athénaïs adopted it for entertaining in her own apartments. Ever conscious of Louis's pleasure, she realized that the *déshabillé* was also easy to remove in private, and made her body more accessible than the complicated petticoats and lacings that took the help of a maid to get in and out of.

The enduring role of fashion in French culture began to take shape at Versailles, where it represented a symbolic weapon in the battle of etiquette and appearances to which the old aristocracy was being systematically reduced. A longer train or a deeper lace cuff could signify success in the microcosm of the court, where the traditional diffusion of wealth and power was giving way to the King's new order of autocratic government assisted by men whose families were not drawn from the ancient nobility. The stays worn by an aristocratic woman beneath her heavy court dress were tighter and stiffer than those of a middle-class woman, creating "a proud, imposing, theatrical form, manifesting the qualities of a soul and the virtues of a state."[4] One reason why Athénaïs's *déshabillés* were found rather racy was the impression given by such an "undress" of the morals of its wearer. La Palatine was to complain that her daughter-in-law, the Duchesse de Chartres, demonstrated her lazy and dissolute character by refusing to have herself laced up tightly enough. The corset represented the cultivated as opposed to the natural, social control as opposed to permissiveness. For the *dévot* party, Athénaïs's languorous silks were the outward manifestation of her sexual power over Louis, and it is no accident that during the subsequent reign of La Maintenon, fashion became more sober, monochrome and buttoned up.

For both men and women, footwear was symmetrical, pointed and high-heeled, emphasizing the refined idleness of the aristocrat, since any form of real walking was considered rather déclassé. For women, then as now, the high-heeled shoe was an erotic accessory rather than a practical item, and contorted the gait and posture so that only tiny steps were possible beneath their skirts. As a result the ladies of the court glided through the salons of Versailles looking like dolls on wheels. Although Louis was often to be found in his hunting boots, he also favored high-heeled shoes, to boost his height, while Athénaïs, despite the hours she spent in her gardens, showed no interest in outdoor exercise. Monsieur's hearty German wife, the Princess Palatine, declared to a correspondent that only three people in France — the King, herself and a Mme. de Chevreuse — could walk twenty paces without puffing and sweating. Indeed, to get themselves about the courtiers were obliged to set up a private company of sedan chair-carriers who operated like taxis, stuffing their plump and befrilled cargo into the boxes and laboring in the King's wake as he made his ritualistic progress around Versailles.

The uniformity of dress among the upper classes suggests that, for the "quality," appearance and culture were strongly interconnected. This is demonstrated in Molière's *Bourgeois Gentilhomme,* which made its debut at Chambord in 1670, when the protagonist, the parvenu M. Jourdain, is ridiculed for his desire to emulate the élite in his clothes. Frivolous though such minute concerns might seem, the court fashions aided the growth of an industry in France. In 1672, the gossipy *Mercure Galant* commented on the importance of Versailles for disseminating the fashions to Paris and thence to the provinces. Middle-class women began shopping to keep up. "The most beautiful silk fabrics, made up in the best of taste, are used for their clothes . . . They must have elegant *déshabillés* and mantillas of every type and color . . . To this are added earrings, necklaces, bracelets, rings, diamond buckles, a gold watch hanging from a clasp, a gold snuff box, a muff and a fan; this is on the outside!"[5] wrote one despairing father in Montpellier. Fashions were illustrated in engravings, and also by dolls in wax, wood or porcelain, often so beautiful themselves that the Parisian *précieuses* made exhibitions of them. So important did these dolls become to the French clothing economy that by the eighteenth century they were granted diplomatic immunity in order to travel and advertise abroad. As well as originating many of the fashions, Athénaïs also acted as a model for the finest work French couturiers could produce. Whatever she wore was discussed, copied and purchased, and her taste was a central part of the culture that was so influentially spread from Versailles.

"Versailles" is often seen as synonymous with the court of Louis XIV, yet the long period of Louis's residence there sometimes disguises the fact that it did not become the permanent location of the court until 1682. Until this date, the King continued his peripatetic existence to a great extent, moving between the Louvre, St. Germain, Fontainebleau, Chambord, Vincennes and Versailles, partly to avoid the inconveniences of the building works continually in progress in the palaces, and partly to accommodate his love of hunting. Between 1672 and 1678, owing to the Dutch wars, a large proportion of the male courtiers were also absent in the spring. Nevertheless, Louis's great love for Versailles led him to spend as much time as possible there, and many of the customs and rituals that later gave the palace its stately, balletic character were inaugurated in the 1670s. Louis announced the permanent move in 1677, although five more years of furious building were needed before the relocation could take place.

Athénaïs de Montespan does not really belong to the glacial, mechanical Versailles of the latter half of Louis's reign, when Europe could set its watches by the King of France's breakfast time, but to a lighter, more spontaneous period when courtiers who had danced all night in unimaginably sumptuous rooms squabbled over the privilege of a corner of a tiny, freezing garret to sleep in. The accommodation could be so haphazard that many aristocrats began to build their own homes at Versailles, encouraged by the King's grant of free land in the new town in 1671 — Louvois had a house there, as did the Ducs de Guise, d'Aumont, de Noailles, de Créqui and de Luxembourg — and the appearance of Louis's father's old hunting park changed daily, though as ever, the King made sure he had architectural control over the buildings. Versailles in the 1670s, then, was a kaleidoscope palace, its vistas changing as often as the scenes of a theater set. The bedroom one slept in on one visit might not be there the next, it was easy to get lost, and one was as likely to glimpse the King returning from inspecting his gardens with mud on the royal boots as holding court in his robes of state.

While some of Versailles's most famous rooms, such as the Galérie des Glaces and the Salon de la Guerre, were not begun until 1678, Louis was able to occupy his own apartments, where much of the court ceremonial took place, from 1673. Their interior décor was inspired by the style developed by Le Brun and perfected in the

Gallery of Apollo he decorated at the Louvre in 1663. The scheme, which originally encompassed much of the palace but which may now only be seen, much diminished, in the state apartments of the King and Queen, was based upon ceilings of ornamental stuccos integrated with painted panels on a larger, richer and more imposing scale than anything that had been attempted before. Mythological spectators seemed to gaze down upon the visitor, leaning on trompe l'oeil balustrades, an effect designed by Veronese for the Villa Maser in Italy. The walls were decorated with panels or tapestries from the royal collections, some, such as the Salon de Vénus, covered with designs of colored marbles repeated in the floors.

The King's apartments consisted of seven rooms, the Chambre des Gardes, an antechamber; the state room; the Grand Cabinet, or study; a smaller drawing room and a more private Petit Cabinet. In these rooms Louis displayed more than thirty of his favorite pictures, including works by Leonardo (among them the *Mona Lisa* and *San Giovanni*), Titian, Veronese, Andrea del Sarto, Raphael, Poussin and Rubens.

The most important was the great state chamber, the Salon d'Apollon, which was the throne room. The others were all named after Olympian deities that orbited the sun, each satellite representing the influence of its god on the lives of the great kings. Thus Venus was decorated with allegories of love, while Mars depicted the great warrior kings of classical history and Mercury, the King's state bedroom, the wisdom of monarchs. Mercury, also known as the Chambre de Parade, was really only used for ceremonial purposes, since the King had a more private bedroom for actually sleeping in. Its furniture — a balustrade enclosing the bed alcove, eight two-foot candelabra, three three-foot basins, two pedestals holding incense burners, a pair of fire irons and a chandelier — was made entirely of silver. At some point, the room also contained a state bed with a portrait of Athénaïs, in a ravishing *déshabillé,* inserted into the canopy. The silver furniture did not last long — it had to be sent to the mint to be turned into coin during the war of the League of Augsburg in 1689 — but the bed was the one in which Louis XIV's mortal remains were displayed to the world.

To reach the King's rooms, Athénaïs would have climbed the Escalier des Ambassadeurs, possibly the greatest architectural effect so far created at Versailles. It was realized after Le Vau's design, following his death in 1670, by François d'Orbay, who had previously created an apartment for Athénaïs at St. Germain which included a balcony garden and a fountain, where she loved to play. D'Orbay had played a significant role in Le Vau's team when work on Versailles had begun. The staircase, decorated by Le Brun, was Le Vau's last, posthumous collaboration with his old colleague; from now on his place was taken by Hardouin-Mansart, also engaged in constructing Clagny for Athénaïs.

The court met in the King's apartments every morning before processing to Mass, and they were the location for the other main court gathering, which took place three times a week and was known as Appartement. Mme. de Sévigné attended Appartement on Saturday, 25 July 1676, and leaves a detailed description of her pleasure in the entertainment. Everything was divinely furnished, she wrote to her daughter; everything was magnificent. The renewed love between Athénaïs and the King made everything easy. "You wouldn't believe the joy this gives everybody, and how lovely this makes the court." The warring factions were reunited, and everyone was friendly — even Mme. de Maintenon and Athénaïs's sister Mme. de Thianges.

Appartement began at three in the afternoon, after the Queen's public toilette, Mass and the royal dinner. There was plenty of room for the entire court, so no one was crushed or hot, as was common at other large entertainments. Mme. de Sévigné strolled with delight through the marvelous rooms of "confusion without confusion," bowing carefully to the King and reveling in the fact that he returned her bow just as though she were young and beautiful. To the background of the King's musicians she chatted with Athénaïs, remarking on her elegant poise, and the diamonds in her uncovered hair. Athénaïs inquired after the Marquise's visit to the spa at Vichy, and described her own visit to Bourbon, joking that the waters had given her toothache instead of curing a bad knee. Between three and six, everyone was seated at the gaming tables, although Louis popped out from time to time to receive his correspondence. Marie-Thérèse was mad on gambling, and a popular opponent, since she never got the hang of cards and always lost a fortune. The stakes were very high, with anything from 500 to 1,200 louis risked on the turn of a card. So possessed was the Queen by the gaming frenzy that she once missed Mass in order to play, one of the few sins she ever committed. At six, the court set out in a caravan of barouches, with Louis and Athénaïs in the first, accompanied by Monsieur and Mme. de Thianges, followed by the Queen. They drove through the park to the canal, where they took a gondola ride, the musicians still in attendance, returning at ten to watch a play before taking *medianoche* by the light of thousands of candles.

The gambling that was such a feature of Appartement had a crucial role in the court system Louis was in the process of establishing at Versailles. In fact, it increased so much during his reign that Bourdaloue devoted a sermon, *"Sur les Divertissements du Monde,"* to its evils, although his predictable disapproval placed him in a minority, for clergymen from Cardinal Mazarin onwards had gambled and cheated with as much enthusiasm as everybody else. Versailles was nicknamed *Ce Tripot,* this gambling den, and the furious gamesters "howled, blasphemed, made dreadful faces, pulled out their hair and wept"[6] with the zeal of the most miserable addicts on the Rue St. Denis. Cheating was all part of the fun. Louis himself was not particularly devoted to gambling, being too energetic to sit still for long periods, but he enjoyed it enough to permit Hocca, a form of roulette considered so dissolute that it was banned by two Popes and the chief of police in Paris, to be played. His favorite card game was Reversi (in which it was a standing joke that Athénaïs always held the King), among ten or so other games including Vingt-et-Un, Piquet, Quadrille, Cavagnole and Papillon. But more often than not he would retreat restlessly to the billiard table he had installed in the Salle de Diane, leaving the field to the far greater prowess of his mistress.

If Athénaïs had been put off gambling by the extravagancies of M. de Montespan, she gave no sign of it. Indeed, she was one of the most famous, brilliant and reckless players at court. One Christmas night she lost 700,000 ecus at a sitting and then staked 150,000 pistoles on three cards and won her money back. On another occasion, she lost 400,000 ecus at the beginning of the evening, and stayed up until eight in the morning to make good her losses. She insisted on continuing until she had won another 100,000 to settle the debts of some fellow players who had lost all their resources. Athénaïs was not, of course, always so lucky, but Louis always paid her immense debts, along with those of the Queen, without a murmur, although he personally rather disapproved of high play. Sometimes she would run out of stakes, and a messenger would be sent to find the King so that she could carry on. Her losses, and hence those to the treasury, became notorious.

Why was such a ruinously expensive activity so popular? Not to gamble at all was seen as something of a faux pas, and the King's half-hearted rulings against it (army officers, for example, were forbidden to play in 1691) were largely ignored. One obvious attraction may have been the welcome opportunity to sit down. Along with privileges such as dining with the King, or the right to travel in his coach, seating was an important indication of status — though not necessarily of power, given Louis's preference for selecting his ministers from the *noblesse de robe* — and the average courtier could expect to spend most of the day on his feet. Grades of seating progressed from no seat at all through a stool, a chair with a back and an armchair, to a sofa — and which could be taken in front of whom was subject to endless, complicated permutations. A mere gentleman of quality, for example, had the right to a stool only before the princes and princesses of the blood, whereas a cardinal could sit on a sofa before the princes of the blood but only on a stool before the Queen. The King's own children were restricted to a stool in his presence, whereas a duchess was allowed a chair before a grandchild of France.

The court was hypersensitive to such minute distinctions of rank, which were designed to separate as far as possible the pride of blood from the gratification of power, and for the old aristocracy, many of whom were deprived of any meaningful function in government, blood was all. So privilege, in all its minute degrees, was guarded jealously and there were many disputes of the kind described here by the Princess Palatine.

> The Duc de Lorraine aimed to have an armchair before Monsieur and myself, because the Emperor had accorded him one. The King replied that the Emperor had his own etiquette, and he his own, inasmuch as the Emperor granted an armchair to cardinals, although they were not allowed a seat before the King . . . Monsieur wanted to grant a chair with a back, and the King agreed to it, but the Duc wanted to be treated like an elector, and this the King would not admit. Monsieur proposed to do as the King of England did. He does not wish to give us a chair, for our part we claim one, this is why he only sits on a

stool when we are there . . . But the King did not wish to hear this spoken of, and so as not to make an incident out of affronting the Duc, we were obliged to renounce our visit to Bar.

It was not only in the matter of seating that the courtiers had to be aware of tiny gradations of precedence. The later court at Versailles has been compared by one historian to an English public school, having "the same complex unwritten law, the same struggle for trivial distinctions, an intricate and illogical code of privilege, with public shame and biting rebuke for the man who transgressed against its provisions."[7] No one who was anyone knocked on doors at Versailles. The form was to scratch with the little fingernail of the left hand, which was kept long specifically for the purpose. The familiar *tu* address was never to be used in the King's presence. If a message was brought by the servant of a social superior, it was to be received standing and bareheaded. If you passed the service for the King's dinner proceeding to the table, you had to make a formal bow to "the King's meat," and on and on. Etiquette inevitably became a time bomb, guaranteed to explode periodically at weddings, funerals, births and even entertainments.

Amid such a plethora of shibboleths, it was much better to give up a journey than to cause a diplomatic incident over a chair. Athénaïs was herself furious for years because her husband's refusal to be made a Duc denied her the right to a duchesse's *tabouret,* or stool, which had been granted to Louise de La Vallière. Consequently she had to remain standing for much of the time, even though she was the most important woman at court. No wonder everyone was grateful for the relative equality of the gaming table.

It is possible to posit another explanation for the popularity of gambling at Versailles. "There is no harder work," wrote Louis XIV to his son, "than idleness." As power was centralized in the King's person, there may have been an awareness among the aristocracy that their influence was a poor imitation of the real power wielded by their ancestors. Politics and war service offered a minority (from which all women were obviously excluded) the chance of distinction, but many were plagued by ennui, particularly since, in order to find some sort of occupation for the huge court at Versailles, many posts had been subdivided, so that even nominal functions of servitude, such as removing the King's hunting boots, left their holders with practically nothing to do. Gambling must have offered relief from the monotony of the court routine, a chance to behave competitively and to provide a proof, in a sense, of character. This is not to suggest that either gambling or etiquette were consciously invoked by the King as a means of keeping the post-Fronde aristocracy distracted, but when the opportunity to show one's mettle socially through power or skill is removed, it is plausible that energy would be channeled into aleatory, or chance-dependent activities.

An economic reason is equally sustainable. Since aristocrats were expected to maintain an enormously expensive standard of living, of which a sumptuous wardrobe was but one example, many were constantly strapped for cash, and with no prospect of adding to their coffers, for there was no honorable way in which to earn money. They were forbidden to engage in most trades or business, with the exception of wholesale overseas trade, which Louis attempted to encourage, nor were they permitted to work their land on anything but a limited scale. The Church and the army were the only professions it was possible to embrace. Gambling thus became a way of life, the resultant debt often relieved by marriage to rich commoners which served only to further dissolve the aristocrat's grasp on power. Gaming on such a scale, though, could not be wholly justified on the grounds of economy, as there was clearly a good deal of pleasure to be had from it, not least the opportunity to demonstrate the gambler's superiority to worldly fortune.

Just as social status was manifested in conspicuous consumption, so too was it demonstrated by conspicuous waste. Stoicism in the face of loss was the mark of a gentleman, as shown by the Marquis de Beaumont, who calmly gambled away his entire fortune at one sitting without uttering a single remark on the matter. D'Antin, Athénaïs's son by Montespan, inherited his mother's passion with rather more success, winning the equivalent of over a million dollars in today's money at cards.

After Athénaïs, the most famous gambler at court was the Marquis de Dangeau, one of her most skillful gaming cronies, who was able to exist entirely on his winnings. His impassive features made a major contribution to his success. Mme. de Sévigné observed that he played so well amid the distracted chatter of his partners that he could win as much as 200,000 francs a month. Athénaïs was so fond of the Marquis that she persuaded Louis to give him the coveted *brevet,* the right of entry to the King's chamber that her father and brother enjoyed, and later a position in the Grand Dauphin's household. Since his enormous winnings often permitted him to act as Athénaïs's banker, she also obtained an apartment at Versailles for Dangeau, on condition that he created a poem from a series of rhymes dreamed up by the King.

Whether or not she had a right to a stool in other situations, the freedom of the royal purse made Athénaïs queen of the tables, and the gold with which she strewed them was yet another public symbol of her status. But gambling also seems to have answered a need in her character and provided her with a release from the strains imposed by her position. Psychologically, gambling can be seen as a rebellion against logic, intelligence, moderation and renunciation, amorally appealing to those who experience their lives as in some way constricted, and yet containing its own penance in the guilt it provokes from the losses it entails. "The tension of gambling . . . is logically inexplicable . . . The craving for this strange thrill frequently overshadows the desire to win . . . The element of insecurity, win or lose, is of prime importance, and one of the prerequisites for that strange thrill."[8]

Had not Athénaïs, in some sense, staked her career, her reputation, her status at court on the chance of Louis's affections? Recalling the sequestered life she had led behind the screen of Louise de La Vallière, the fear instilled in her by her husband and Lauzun, the sniping of La Maintenon and the threat of transient rivals, it seems likely that the tables offered her an outlet for the expression of the gamble upon which her life as *maîtresse en titre* was founded. Unlike everyone else, Athénaïs might not have been afraid of Louis, but she was always afraid of losing him. Mme. de Caylus observed that Louis loved her because she always needed to be reconquered, but the strain of maintaining her enticing aloofness, even as her vanity recoiled from the humiliations to which she was obliged to subject it, must have been intense. Athénaïs's notorious tempers, and the days she spent alone in bed, tortured with migraine, could be interpreted as the negative symptoms of such strain, while careless, flamboyant gambling represented a stimulating catharsis.

Athénaïs's experience as favorite was an extreme case of the tensions felt by many women at court, obsessed as they were with precedence and dependent on the goodwill of their husbands. Gambling mania in women seemed even more desperate. Unlike their husbands, female courtiers had not even the pretense of estate management or military activity to distract them, and as the aristocracy settled permanently into Versailles, many of the traditional occupations of the chatelaine — caring for the poor and sick, managing the household accounts, supervising the domestic functions of a great estate — became superfluous, if not a downright embarrassment, since a quiet, busy life on one's provincial estate was viewed as a disgrace. Hence gambling, along with dress, gallantry and squabbles about the privileges of rank, was the only recourse of those who were not inclined to join Queen Marie-Thérèse in her endless and gloomy devotions. The financial and moral consequences of gambling were just as detrimental for women. It was not uncommon for them to pawn their jewels, accept bribes to influence their husbands or even to prostitute themselves to settle their debts. La Palatine described a scandalous incident in which two ladies gambling in Paris accused one another of cheating and asked a captain of dragoons to settle the dispute. The lady he found against was so incensed that she slapped the officer in the face, whereupon he turned her skirts over her head, in order, he claimed, to ascertain whether the insult should be avenged with a duel or a kiss. As the cards turned, it seemed that ladies' manners were in as great a peril as their purses.

In fact, as the century progressed, the dissolute behavior of women became a common theme among contemporary commentators. The tongues and morals of womanhood appeared to have become as loose as their *déshabillés.* The Princesse de Monaco, who was generous with her favors, was heard to remark gaily of Louis's penis that, although his power was great, his scepter was very small, unlike that of his cousin Charles of England. Hardly a joke for a lady. Another of Louis's casual flings, the Princesse de Soubise, who maintained her delicate, red-haired good looks with a diet of chicken, fish and salad, outraged her friends by contriving to have her husband sent away from court so that she was able to pursue the King. Louis, predictably, surrendered, but La Soubise was furious when she learned that, although he would increase her pension, he would not offer her the court position that had been the object of the exercise. Mme. de Sévigné commented, in a loyal double entendre, that her friend "has too much good advice to raise the standard of such perfidy with so little prospect of enjoying it for long," but when La Soubise had the

poor judgment to complain of the shabby rewards of her prostitu-
tion, Mme. de Sévigné, along with everyone else in society, cut her.
The Princesse consoled herself by building the Hôtel de Soubise, still
one of the loveliest houses in Paris.

Not all French ladies were as frugal in their diet as the Princesse de
Soubise. The English traveler Robert Dallington had remarked upon
the prodigious greed of Frenchwomen as early as 1604, in his *View of
France;* by Louis XIV's reign their appetites were positively scandalous. A magistrate attending a court ball in 1667 was disappointed
when the lovely dancers appeared to do nothing but eat. Queen
Marie-Thérèse was notoriously greedy, and addicted to her Spanish
chocolate. She complained that no one enjoyed the spicy Castilian
food she prepared in her own apartments, but when she dined in
company she gobbled busily, complaining that everyone would eat
her food and leave her nothing, which the King thought was very
funny. Louis's own appetite was terrifying, as evinced by the veritable
ordeal of refreshments ladies had to endure on journeys with him.

Perhaps his insistence that women did not refuse food was a polite
way of disguising his own greed. The King dined twice a day, and a
typical meal might consist of four plates of soup, one pheasant, one
partridge, stewed mutton with garlic, ham and salad, pastries, fruit
and hard-boiled eggs. In case he was peckish during the night, the
royal chamber was provided with the *en cas de nuit:* three loaves, three
cold dishes, two bottles of wine and a decanter of water. Louis's
bulimic eating was of a piece with his other traits — his building
mania, his love of the vast, grandiloquent paintings of Le Brun, his
love of accumulation and opulent décor, his sexual voracity. He ate as
he was determined to do everything else, like a god. Although the
fork had been in use since 1648, the King, and most of the court,
continued to eat with their fingers. Molière once complained that
some of the King's officers had said he was not good enough to eat
with them, and Louis punished their snobbishness by making a midnight feast of his *en cas de nuit,* sharing it with Molière in his bedroom. The King had dipped his fingers into the same dish as the
playwright, and no one snubbed Molière after that.

Louis also used food to express the gentler side of his nature. He kept
his pockets full of sweets, with which he loved to feed Athénaïs and his
children. Twice a day, he fed his beloved hunting dogs, seven or eight
of which were always to be found in his rooms, with his own hands.

He himself had a penchant for sweet biscuits dipped in Burgundy, his favorite wine. Champagne wine was also popular, though at that time the region produced a flat, sweet red wine rather than the sparkling white for which it was to become famous. Claret Louis pronounced "surprisingly drinkable" when he tasted it for the first time. A true Frenchman, Louis was interested in the quality and freshness of all his food and drink. He was most solicitous of the turkeys bred at Versailles (which, it must be said, he rather resembled in later life), bestowing on their keeper the grandiose title of Captain of the Royal Turkeys. Louis was also proud of the greenhouses at Versailles, which provided exotic fruits such as pineapple for dessert courses.

One of Athénaïs's few surviving letters, to Daniel Huet, a correspondent of her later years, concerns food. "We take the liberty of presenting you with these little *étrennes* [New Year gifts] which accompany the wishes we are making for your health and prosperity," she wrote. "That God increases your courage, that He conserves your good humor, maintains the freshness of your color, that He makes your water purgative, the sweets abundant, the strawberries refreshing and the peas more easily digestible."[9]

Various fads stimulated the appetite of the court. The craze for green peas began in 1660, when one M. Audiger, who had been entrusted with the important diplomatic mission of collecting recipes for liqueurs in Genoa, returned from Italy with a hamperful. They were ceremoniously shelled by the Comte de Soissons — "a name of good omen for leguminous vegetables,"[10] since Soissons was particularly famous for its green beans — and the cooking of the peas was entrusted to one Sieur Baudoin. "All declared with one voice that nothing could be better or more of a novelty," reported Audiger proudly,[11] and Mme. de Sévigné immediately dispatched the news of this latest trend to her daughter in the provinces. Everyone at court soon became ill from a surfeit of green peas. Louis was not keen on the only sad little passion of his wife's life until about 1671, when Mme. de Maintenon began to extol the benefits of chocolate (it was impossible for her to enjoy anything unless she believed it had improving qualities). The humble cauliflower, stewed in stock and served with butter and nutmeg, had its day as a fashionable dish, while white bread and meat were consistent symbols of wealth.

M. Audiger had also picked up the Italian skill of ice-making during his Italian mission, and he introduced to France the new luxury of water ices flavored with fruit, musk, amber and spices. Louis enthusi-astically built two ice houses at Versailles, and ice pyramids two or three feet high, filled with fruit and flowers, became the centerpiece of royal banquets. The appearance of ice in summer lent a miraculous air to the delicate, scented flavors, and Louis, of course, loved any-thing that suggested his power over nature. At summer picnics, guests were served fruit and wine in bowls and goblets cast from ice.

Athénaïs herself had good taste in chefs. Her personal cook, Mouthier l'Aine, was a member of a dynasty of royal chefs: his father had cooked for the Grand Condé, the head of the aristocratic Condé family, and his son, Mouthier Le Jeune, was to become chef to another royal mistress, Mme. de Pompadour. It is not surprising, given her love of food, the effects of her pregnancies and the general culture of gluttony, that Athénaïs struggled to maintain a slim figure. One poem of the 1670s compares her rather Rubenesque physique with that of the skinny Louise de La Vallière.

> L'une boîte et marche en cane
> L'autre est forte et rubican
> L'une est maigre au dernier point
> L'autre crève d'embonpoint.[12]

Most courtiers suffered as a result of their overindulgence, and Louis himself was afflicted by gout. Women seemed to find the vogue for spicy food particularly exciting, although the consequences were all too predictable. An extraordinary example of how unrestrained some women had become occurred when Mmes. de Sceaux and de la Trémoille were caught short in their theater box after a feast of curry. Unable to hold back, they relieved themselves there and then and threw the results into the audience, explaining that they thought this "hygienic." Just how shocking such acts were depends on one's per-ception of standards of hygiene at court.

In the popular imagination, Versailles is sometimes seen as a gilded dung heap where exotic perfumes concealed foul odors and the courtiers relieved themselves cheerfully on staircases or even beneath their clothes. Certainly the world then was generally a much dirtier place, and the elaborate courtesies practiced at Versailles operated to some extent to soften a fundamental grossness of life which had to be ignored rather than concealed. Paris was the dirtiest city in France, and probably in Europe; it could be smelled from two miles outside the city gates, and the narrow, filthy streets of the town, with their streaming open sewers, piles of excrement and rooting pigs made scented gloves and posies a practical remedy against nausea. Versailles was more modern, though lavatories were practically unknown, and the rumor that ladies urinated beneath their skirts probably came about because of the small chamber pots women took to church with them to hear the famous preacher Bourdaloue, whose sermons were hugely popular, but often lasted for over four hours. These little vessels, named for the preacher, saved women from having to miss a word. The King owned an ornamental *chaise percée* on which he was ceremoniously seated during the evening ceremony of Coucher (his formal bedtime), but he considerately used a chamber pot in private, as did most people.

However, his reign might be judged particularly dirty on the evidence of contemporary French conduct manuals, which advised on hygiene as well as manners. In a study of a hundred such manuals from 1500 to 1839,[13] the seventeenth century certainly comes off worst. Only the period 1600–1700 does not specify how frequently the nails, mouth, head, teeth and ears should be cleaned, in comparison with the direction "morning and evening" in 1500–19, or "morning and mealtimes" for 1700–19. Under Louis XIV, then, cleanliness was essentially peripheral and for show, confined in the main to the face, hands and nails.

Bathing, though, was a popular activity during the summer. Henriette d'Angleterre, Monsieur's first wife, frequently held bathing parties at which she and her ladies ventured into a river in their shifts. Queen Marie-Thérèse indulged in long hot baths, using the famous olive oil soap that is still manufactured in Marseilles today. Louis's own personal hygiene is more questionable. A brief dab at the hands and lips with a napkin is thought by some to have sufficed him, while others claim that he and Monsieur were rubbed down with spirits and perfume every morning. Clean linen was certainly important, as it signified status as well as cleanliness, and Louis changed his shirt three times a day. To follow suit, the court engaged laundresses from Paris whose dry-cleaning methods involved oils, bran, alum and lemon juice.

Distressingly, Nancy Mitford has presented Athénaïs to history as a "grubby woman,"[14] but it seems unlikely that someone with such a talent for dress and such concern for her beauty would have been slovenly in her personal habits. There was a bathroom at Clagny with a mosaic floor, modeled on the Appartement des Bains that Louis had designed for Athénaïs at Versailles, and she was fond of perfume and scented creams. As Zola's Nana pointed out, immoral women have a greater stake in hygiene than their dirty but virtuous sisters, and it seems unlikely that the fastidious Louis would have enjoyed sleeping with a sluttish paramour. However, since Athénaïs was so often pregnant, during which time bathing was discouraged, she may not have always been as fragrant as a goddess ought to be.

Louis may have objected to drinking the water prescribed daily by his doctors, but he loved playing with it. In 1669, at St. Germain, he had created a private suite of four rooms, decorated with mirrors, classical frescos and miniature silver fountains. There was a grotto of mirrors with a fountain rising from the floor into a mirrored cupola, refracting an infinity of tiny rainbows across an infinity of Louis. Streams of light, streams of water; the glittering cascades of the first of Louis's private playrooms were quintessentially baroque in their duplicitous realism, their sensuous blurring of the real and the imagined worlds.

The Galérie des Glaces and the famous fountains of Versailles were more formalized, static expressions of this baroque spirit, which was tempered, if not opposed, in much of the architecture of the palace — with the exception of the Appartement des Bains. Here Louis created another voluptuous private space, as much for lovemaking as anything so pragmatic as washing. Situated on the ground floor at Versailles, directly below the King's apartments, the rooms were a secret refuge for Louis and Athénaïs; a hiding place, an erotic retreat. After a suite of anterooms for undressing and changing into special silk robes came the Chambre de Repos, furnished with an enormous bed before a mirror of equal size, and then the bath, an octagonal pool hollowed from a single block of marble, three meters across and one deep, surrounded by couches and fed by a system of hot taps which dispensed perfumed water. The rooms were decorated in sumptuous oriental style for Louis's *reine sultane* with marble columns, polished alabaster and gilding. The bed was embroidered with frolicking pastoral nymphs, suggesting an Eden, a real Sultan's paradise, where Louis could revel in his mistress's opulent nudity in sinless, pagan fantasy.

Such hidden voluptuousness typifies the contrasts of the early years of Versailles — of splendor and squalor, of public elegance in the rigidly stratified etiquette of the public apartments and the private vices of sex, gambling and gluttony. At the height of her fame, Athénaïs was also the heart of the baroque Versailles, its most expressive personality. A description of this period has "the great woman"[15] returning from a gondola party, making a floating, fairylike progress through a summer's night, a naiad in a world composed of endless watery reflections that magnified her beauty even as their tumbling refractions betrayed its exquisite transience. Athénaïs adored the life of the court, and confident at last in the renewal of the King's love, she could afford to dazzle her friends and disregard her enemies. The mirrors of the Appartement des Bains reflected a *grande sultane* whose position appeared, finally, to be unassailable.

Chapter Eleven

"Jealousy feeds on doubts, and as soon
as doubt turns to certainty it becomes
a frenzy, or ceases to exist."

In 1667, soon after their love affair had begun, Athénaïs and Louis,
got up as shepherd and shepherdess, had performed together in the
Ballet des Muses. Flanking them on the stage had been Madame Henriette and Louise de La Vallière, while the Queen, as ever, watched
from the sidelines. So many disguises, opening like Chinese boxes to
reveal even as they concealed. Louis the man who played Louis the
King dancing as Louis the shepherd, with Louise, the official mistress,
who had once been the screen for the King's infatuation with his
sister-in-law and now diverted attention from his new love, who still
appeared, in Marie-Thérèse's eyes at least, as her demure lady-in-
waiting. As Athénaïs attained the height of her success in the 1670s, it
would seem that such disguises had been thrown off, but it was her
ability to negotiate the symbolic theatricality of court culture which
contributed to that success, to her establishment as "the Real Queen
of France."

One reason why it is so difficult to penetrate the true character of
Louis XIV is that his life was entirely given over to the enactment of
his persona as King. Very rarely did any public gesture distinguish his
person from that function, or the function from the person, since
even the most mundane gesture was formalized into a symbolic royal
ritual. True, the awkwardness that had been remarked upon before
the beginning of his affair with Athénaïs had suggested that as a

young man Louis had been uneasy in his role, but it becomes increasingly problematic to differentiate between his public and private personae, or even to claim that such a distinction existed. Primi Visconti observed several times that if Louis was in company and the door opened, he would compose his features differently "as if he had to appear on a stage. Altogether, he knew well how to play the King in everything." No understanding of Louis's relationship with Athénaïs is complete, then, if his lack of a "real Queen," a consort who was capable of fulfilling an equivalent symbolic function, is not taken into account. Early in the 1660s, Louis's attraction to his brother's wife, Henriette, could be explained as much by this unfilled role as by her own personal charms. On one occasion, in 1661, Henriette had even substituted for the Queen in one of the most spiritually resonant of royal roles: the washing of the feet of twelve paupers on Maundy Thursday. This humble ritual, which imitated Christ washing the feet of His disciples, and which was simultaneously enacted by priests and bishops all over France, confirmed the divine aspect of the monarch that formed the sacred justification for his temporal power.

It was an embarrassment to Louis that Marie-Thérèse had failed to do her duty at the church of St. Denis, and her inability to "perform" as Queen continued to humiliate him, though he was too dignified to reveal this in his behavior towards her. As the only time Marie-Thérèse showed any sign of life was at the gaming table (and even then she never managed to win), Louis must have been exasperated that his brilliant court, so carefully managed to display his *gloire* in its every aspect, should have had such a rotund and dreary centerpiece. It was Athénaïs who possessed the innate sense of royalty that Louis required, and by the 1670s, Louis's love for the bewitching shepherdess of the *Ballet des Muses* had developed into a profound reliance on the woman who comprehended so sympathetically his lust for *la gloire* as to execute with élan in the theater of the court the role in which his wife acquitted herself so poorly.

Considered by the court and the ambassadors to be "the Real Queen," Athénaïs could bank on her public importance to Louis in maintaining her position as *maîtresse en titre*. She could not, however, afford to be complacent about the fidelity of his affections. Only two weeks after passing on the news of the Marquise's renewed power, Mme. de Sévigné reported that there was the "smell of fresh meat in Quanto's country." Marie-Elisabeth (called Isabelle) de Ludres was a lay canoness at the aristocratic convent of Poussay in the Vosges mountains. Ten years younger than Athénaïs, she had come to court in 1670, following a broken engagement at the age of fifteen to the Duc de Lorraine, to serve Henriette d'Angleterre, and subsequently Queen Marie-Thérèse. She was in a sense a lesser version of the *maîtresse en titre,* tall, slender and blue-eyed, with a mane of tawny hair, and reputedly as witty as she was pretty. With her strong northern accent, she pronounced a "d" as a "t," which Mme. de Sévigné's daughter Mme. de Grignan laughed at, but the King found it most charming. Louis appeared altogether very interested in the young woman, who bore the honorary title of "Madame" to reflect her status as a canoness, and the court was awash with rumors that Athénaïs was about to be deposed.

It was, of course, not the first time Athénaïs had had to cope with a threat to her position in Louis's heart. Quite apart from the machinations of the *dévot* party, the King was constantly tempted away from fidelity to his mistress by the bevies of ladies only too anxious to surrender their favors. Athénaïs's gracious suppression of her inclinations to jealousy, so long as Louis confined himself to casual flings, had, over the years, proved a wise policy. Louis had no real need to seek satisfaction elsewhere, other than for a little sexual novelty, and in general he treated the women who flung themselves at him "like post horses that one mounts but one time, and that one never sees again," according to the old soldier the Marquis de Saint-Géran, who cheerfully admitted that he would have offered his own daughter for service in the saddle.

Where necessary, Athénaïs used her wit to confound any hussy who looked likely to prove unusually troublesome, and although a French proverb has it that *esprit* may be the weapon of the weak, she deployed it with great success. For her own entourage, she selected women whose virtue was exceeded only by their plainness, although one of them, Mlle. des Oeillets, nonetheless managed to focus the King's roving eye for a moment. Where vigilance failed, rumor, that treacherous ally, could cool Louis's ardor. One pretty rival, Mlle. de Grancey, who resembled La Vallière too closely for comfort, was dealt with by a whisper emanating from Athénaïs's supple tongue that suggested she had a secret child by Monsieur's favorite, the Chevalier de Lorraine. The beautiful princess Marie-Anne de Wurtemburg lost her chance when it appeared that she had prostituted herself to a corrupt Jacobin monk who claimed to have discovered the philosopher's stone. When the King's former lover, Olympe Mancini, now Comtesse de Soissons, vented her spleen on Athénaïs by ensuring that the Queen was surrounded by the most beautiful maids-of-honor she could procure, Athénaïs railed with great self-righteousness against the loose morals of these young ladies, and dispatched the Duchesse de Richelieu to convey this suspicion to the Queen. Alarmed that she should be harboring a potential harem, Marie-Thérèse played straight into Athénaïs's hands by disbanding her maids-of-honor in 1673, replacing them with respectable married ladies.

The Comtesse de Soissons's younger sister Marie Mancini, Louis's first love, had threatened to reappear at court in 1672, on fleeing her unhappy marriage to an Italian prince. Athénaïs knew that Marie was a clever and spirited woman, and that she was certain to try for a reconciliation by playing on Louis's sentimental memories. This time with the approval of the Queen, Athénaïs refused outright to countenance her presence at court. Marie defiantly took up residence at Lys, near Fontainebleau, but Athénaïs succeeded in having her removed to a safer distance. Marie knew when she had met her match, and wisely departed into a compromising asylum with the Duc de Savoie.

Yet the *chambre des filles* was a veritable hydra, and as soon as one pretty head was cut off, another sprang up in its place.[1] However insouciant she appeared, Athénaïs suffered constantly, torn between hope that the latest lover was merely a caprice and fear that this time the King's heart might escape her. And for a time, before and after the religious crisis of 1675, it seemed that Mme. de Sévigné's red-haired friend the Princesse de Soubise might prove more than a passing royal fancy. "Everybody thinks that the King is no longer in love, and that Mme. de Montespan is torn between the consequences that might follow the return of his favors, and the danger of their not doing so, and the fear that he might turn elsewhere," declared La Sévigné.[2]

Athénaïs tried to disgust Louis by hinting that La Soubise was scrofulous, like a beautiful apple rotten inside, but this did not prevent Louis from checking for himself, and La Soubise's son, Armand-Gaston, the Cardinal de Rohan, conceived in 1674 when Athénaïs was heavily pregnant with Mlle. de Nantes, was so much a Bourbon that there was little doubt as to his paternity. Eventually, though, La Soubise overreached herself, and fell into disgrace, as we saw in the previous chapter.

The Soubise skirmish was well won by the time Mme. de Ludres appeared in the King's orbit, and no doubt Athénaïs was sanguine that she could see off this challenge as she had done so many others. Publicly, she appeared confident. "The other day, at play, Quanto had her head resting, with all familiarity, on the shoulder of her friend [Louis], one believed this affectation was to announce, 'I am better off than ever.'" La Ludres, though, seemed ready to match the favorite's cunning. Just as Athénaïs had done in the 1660s, she piqued Louis's interest by maintaining a circle of suitors (which included Athénaïs's brother Vivonne) while keeping herself chaste, angling after a bigger prize. Once again, Athénaïs retaliated by putting about a spiteful rumor: that La Ludres suffered periodically from revolting outbreaks of eczema. But Louis seemed as unconcerned about this as he had been with La Soubise's purported ailments, and by 1677, Mme. de Sévigné's country correspondent Bussy-Rabutin was commenting openly on the new affair, which was confirmed by a poem circulating in Paris.

> *La Vallière était du commun,*
> *La Montespan était de la noblesse*
> *La Ludres était chanoinesse.*
> *Toutes trois ne sont que pour un:*
> *C'est le plus grand de potentats*
> *Qui veut assembler les Etats.*[3]

Athénaïs and Isabelle were now openly at war, each assembling a campful of friends who cut each other in public and sniped viciously in private. Mme. de Thianges was particularly obvious in her defense of her sister, going so far as to strike the new mistress on meeting her and giving her murderous glares when etiquette kept them apart.

A more surprising ally was Mme. de Maintenon. While the engagement of the governess had proved to be a great tactical error on Athénaïs's part, as the war of the King's conscience had shown, the two women were quick to bury their differences when the King was besieged by an outsider. Athénaïs was in the last months of pregnancy, not the best time to press home her advantage with the King, and accepted an invitation to stay at Mme. de Maintenon's country estate. Here Athénaïs gave birth to her sixth child by the King, Mlle. de

Blois, on 4 April. La Maintenon's magnanimity did not extend to caring for the little girl, the fruit of the sin the governess had tried so earnestly to prevent: both she and her brother the Comte de Toulouse, born the next year, were consigned instead to the care of Mme. Colbert, assisted by a Mme. de Jussac.

Meanwhile, Isabelle de Ludres had been profiting by the favorite's absence and insinuating herself with the ladies of the court, who began to show her the same respect they had reserved for Athénaïs, rising in her presence even before the Queen, and sitting down only when she gave the sign. It was this gesture that alerted Marie-Thérèse to the fact that her husband had gone astray yet again, but she declared that she would take no action since, extraordinarily, "that is the affair of Mme. de Montespan." La Ludres even went so far as to fake a pregnancy, convinced that a child would vanquish her rival.

Sadly for Isabelle, she was not nearly as good a psychologist as Athénaïs. Louis's pride would not suffer that he be preempted, and he was furious at the pretentious airs she put on when he had given her no encouragement to act as *maîtresse en titre*. Disgusted by her conceit, he cut her in public and in an instant the court followed suit. All that was accomplished was that he returned penitently to Athénaïs, who was delighted to forgive him, and came back to Versailles as though nothing had happened. Isabelle retreated to the country for a month, then recommenced her service in July. Her time in the sun had been very short. From queening it over the duchesses, she found herself reduced once more to one of Madame's maids. The German princess, who kept her spiteful feelings about Athénaïs for her letters, was less intimidated by the cast-off girl, and remarked, as she played with a pair of compasses, "I ought to scratch out these eyes that have done so much damage!" Isabelle replied mournfully that she couldn't care less, since her beautiful eyes had not secured what she wished for.

La Ludres bore her shame proudly for a while, leaving the room with an absent air when the King appeared and ostentatiously turning her head away from the Queen at Mass. If she had lost all her power, she was determined at least to be respected but, like Louise de La Vallière, she found the daily contact with her victorious rival insupportable, and eventually expressed a desire to retreat to a convent in the Rue du Bac in Paris. There was nothing Louis loathed more than a long face, and he had forgotten his passion for her so completely that when her request was put to him he answered sardonically, "What? Is she still here?" If there was a warning in this, Athénaïs was not inclined to heed it.

Quinault's opera *La Gloire de Niquée* commemorated the love triangle of the year, transforming Isabelle de Ludres into Io, the nymph whose punishment for seducing Jupiter is metamorphosis into a miserable heifer, lowing her inarticulate grief at her abandonment. Although Athénaïs was furious, and everyone else highly amused, to find herself represented as the puffing jealous matriarch Juno rather than the delectable nymph, there was no doubt as to who came off better in the struggle for Jupiter/Louis's affections. Mme. de Sévigné describes the return of "Juno triumphant" to Versailles rather critically: "What triumph at Versailles! What redoubled pride! What certain establishment! What Duchesse de Valentinois![4] . . . What recovered possession! I spent an hour in this chamber, she was in bed, dressed, coiffed, she was resting for the *medianoche* . . . she found in herself all 'the glory of Niquée,' delivering her lines with great superiority over the poor Io, and laughing at those who had the audacity to complain of her. Imagine to yourself all that an ungenerous pride can do and say in triumph, and you will be close to it." Despite this strong disapproval, the Marquise was forced to concede that Athénaïs was quite charming and gracious in her conversation with her.

Mme. de Sévigné also expressed her astonishment that the attachment between Louis and Athénaïs seemed closer than ever; indeed, almost unearthly. As always, Louis spoke his love in gifts, and Athénaïs appeared so covered with diamonds that she seemed to the courtiers like "a brilliant divinity." Her policy of not accepting jewelry made her extremely popular, because Louis circumvented it by organizing a discreet "lottery," in which, for appearances' sake, other ladies, too, could "win" jewels, decorated boxes, or Chinese vases. As ever, the couriers of Europe were kept gratifyingly busy relaying the latest munificence of the Sun King to his *reine sultaine*.

Louis seemed more than ever bound to the sensuality of his mistress. He delighted in her body, in her languorous capacity for pleasure, in the efforts she made to constantly divert, surprise and please him. Even in pregnancy, Louis found her desirable, perhaps more so, as he loved superabundance in everything. It was just as well, for by September, Athénaïs was pregnant yet again. Even so, she went with the King when he departed for what would be the final campaign of the Dutch wars in February 1678. She suffered a good deal from fever on the creeping, freezing journey, but as usual kept her illness to herself, knowing Louis's exigency on the subject. On Valentine's Day, the royal party paused at Vitry-le-François, where the townspeople, in their finest clothes, presented Marie-Thérèse with a gift of sweetmeats and their second Queen with a decorated basket of ripe pears.

This campaign represented the strenuous conclusion of six years of war that were to leave France triumphant as the dominant nation in Europe, but severely damaged financially as a consequence of the vast expenses incurred. After the French conquest of Franche-Comté in 1674, the outlook had been positive for Louis and for France, but the next year, the mood darkened. The Maréchal de Turenne was killed, and the Prince de Condé hung up his spurs and retired to Chantilly. Valenciennes was taken in 1677, by a force commanded by Louis and Monsieur, but the victory was soured for Louis by his jealousy of the popular reaction to his brother's skill. When the brothers rode into Paris, Monsieur was received delightedly, with cries of "*Vive le Roi et Monsieur qui a gagné la bataille,*" the use of the singular implying that it was Monsieur, not Louis, who had won the battle. Needless to say, Monsieur was never allowed to set a dainty, high-heeled foot on a battlefield again. Following the Siege of Ghent, the conflict ended with the Peace of Nijmegen in 1678. Louis renounced some of his conquests, but retained twelve towns which were to be refortified. He also succeeded in retaining control of the Franche-Comté region. Holland, meanwhile, received a favorable trade agreement, but no monetary compensation.

In the provinces, however, the consequences of high taxes and neglected agriculture were already being felt. The Duc de Lésdiguières described a typical situation in a letter to Colbert: "I cannot put off making known to you the misery to which I see this province reduced, commerce here has ceased absolutely, and from everywhere people come to beg me to make known to the King how impossible it is for them to pay the taxes. It is certain . . . that the greatest part of the inhabitants of the said province have lived during the winter on only black bread and roots, and that, presently, one sees them eating the grass in the fields and the bark on the trees."[5] It was a long way from Louis's glamorous warmongering "in lace and feathers."

Athénaïs made her only venture into public politics during the last stages of the war. Rather sweetly, she declared that she was moved by the sufferings of the French people, which she had seen as she followed so many campaigns, and that she wanted to be part of the final effort to gain victory for her ailing country. With the help of Colbert's son Seignelay, she selected a ship, *Le Comté,* which she equipped and manned, from her own private funds, with 200 officers and sailors, mostly recruited from her ancestral estate of Tonnay-Charente, under the command of Captain Louis de la Motte-Grenouille. Colbert's correspondence emphasizes that *Le Comté's* expenses were to be kept separate from those of the rest of the King's fleet, since it was a private enterprise. It was typical of Athénaïs's vanity that she chose such a magnificent, showy way to declare her support for the cause, and in fact *Le Comté* never sailed to war as the Peace of Nijmegen intervened. But it was a bold gesture, and in keeping with the Rochechouart connection with the sea. Of course, such patriotism would also have found approval with Louis, so perhaps Athénaïs's motives, which were never dissociated from her need to please the King, were not entirely altruistic.

Athénaïs's brother Vivonne was involved in the war as admiral of the fleet when the Sicilians, who had formerly been controlled by the Spanish, rose against their overlords with the assistance of the French. Vivonne governed the island for a while, but when the peace treaty was signed it was considered that the presence of French troops in Sicily was prejudicial to the settlement, and he returned to France in 1678.

Despite the strains of the war, the French mood after the Peace of Nijmegen was euphoric, and Louis's popularity reached a height it would never again attain. The birth of another healthy son, Louis-Alexandre, Comte de Toulouse, to Athénaïs at Clagny on 6 June seemed to bestow the final blessing on the apparently semidivine lovers. The year 1678 was perhaps the zenith of the reign, the apogee of the "Age Montespan": Louis appeared invincible; his mistress "stood forth in the full blaze of her shameless glory."[6] Nothing was too good for Athénaïs, and if Louis denied her any political influence, he denied her nothing else. She was the perfect complement to the military might he had established, and "her spirit, her culture, her intellectual and worldly influence must have attracted a great deal of regard to the King."[7] Her train was carried by the Duc de Noailles, a peer of France, while the Queen had to make do with a mere page. Her suite, her toilettes, her soirées were all of a royal magnificence that far outstripped her 6,000-livre salary as a nominal lady-in-waiting. She

received a further 150,000 livres from the King for the care and education of their children, but to assist with her own expenses, including
those streams of gold that tumbled nightly on to the gambling table,
she was given permission to draw on the privy purse.

More than ever, Marie-Thérèse was marginalized among her
priests while Louis spent the best part of his time with Athénaïs, dining with her and their older children, and even conducting meetings
with his ministers in her rooms. Humiliated, the Queen was famously
heard to remark, "This whore will kill me." Although it can hardly be
claimed that Athénaïs spared the Queen's feelings, the numerous historians who resent the significance of Athénaïs's role in the greatest
court France has ever known seem reluctant to acknowledge that she
did perform several practical kind acts for the Queen. For example,
when one of Marie-Thérèse's beloved Spanish waiting women
involved herself in a foolish correspondence with the court of her
native country, at that time allied with Holland against France, Louis
furiously declared that he would send the maid away. The Queen
begged Athénaïs to intercede to change his mind. The maid was permitted to remain, and Mme. de Sévigné records that the Queen was
overjoyed "and declares that she will never forget the obligation
under which Mme. de Montespan has placed her."

The degree of respect in which Athénaïs was held by the entire
court was demonstrated by the sensation of the New Year gifts she
received in 1679. Marie-Thérèse and all her ladies-in-waiting produced presents, but the most magnificent was Monsieur's, who defied
his wife in favor of his old friendship for Athénaïs, which dated from
her début at the Louvre. He gave her a chiseled gold salver with a
border of emeralds and diamonds and two golden goblets decorated
in the same fashion. This sumptuous present was estimated by the
sharp eyes of the court to be worth 10,000 ecus. From the Marquise
de Maintenon, Athénaïs received a little emerald-encrusted book entitled *Les Oeuvres de M. le Duc du Maine,* a charming collection of letters purportedly written by her nine-year-old son, with a preface
scripted by Racine. On the surface, the book was a costly and engaging mark of the respect of the governess for her mistress, suggesting
that at this point, La Maintenon accorded with the general perception
of Athénaïs as invulnerable, and thought it prudent to maintain some
vestige of her former subservient position. But the contents of the
book give a telling insight into the depths to which La Maintenon

was prepared to stoop in her ongoing pursuit of the King's soul, and it was to prove a most effective weapon.

The general view of the strength of Athénaïs's position was, however, misjudged, for it was in 1679 that the *maîtresse en titre* finally began to lose her hold over the King. The Ludres alliance had been disbanded as soon as poor Io mooed her way into obscurity, and the two marquises were once again at daggers drawn. Athénaïs was irritated at the way the governess used her relationship with the little Duc du Maine to make demands on Louis's attention. All Athénaïs's children by Louis were rather fragile (unlike her legitimate children, which is another indication of the weakness of the overbred Bourbon bloodline), but Du Maine gave cause for particular concern. Aged three, as the last of his milk teeth developed, he had suffered a debilitating fever that left him with one leg shorter than the other and a most pathetic limp. After various remedies had failed, Mme. de Maintenon, under the pseudonym of Mme. de Surgères, took him for a cure at Anvers and then to Barèges in the Pyrenees, where a fistula which had developed on the little boy's thigh was treated, and he returned in better health. Although in later life he proved, to his father's great distress, to be a coward on the battlefield, he bore the various horrible treatments to which he was subjected, such as being stretched on a rack, with admirable courage. In 1676, the cure was successfully repeated, to the delight of his mother and aunts, Mme. de Thianges and the Abbesse de Fontrevault, who went to meet him on the road. Despite her pleasure in Du Maine's recovery, Athénaïs was jealous and frustrated that she had not been permitted to accompany her son on this and subsequent visits.

Du Maine was Louis's favorite child, far more attractive and appealing than the lumpen Grand Dauphin, who had inherited all his mother's charm, and La Maintenon was shrewd enough to exploit her proximity to the boy to improve her standing with his father. Athénaïs was by no means a neglectful or disinterested mother, but as we have seen, her court duties left her little time for childcare, and Louis was selfish enough to insist that he always come first. It must have seemed very unfair that he was then so pleased to discuss Du Maine with La Maintenon. She seems to have loved the child for his own sake, and was a painstaking and encouraging tutor, improving Du Maine's confidence so that he was easy and funny with adults, unlike his legitimate half-brother, who had had any natural vivacity he may have possessed whacked out of him by Bossuet. Louis was proud of Du Maine, and La Maintenon lost no opportunity to lavish delicate flatteries on this small extension of the King's person.

Of these, one of the most effective was the little book of Du Maine's letters presented to Athénaïs as a New Year gift. It is hard to believe that such an intelligent man as Louis was fooled by such a crass attempt at manipulation, but then, literary criticism was never his strong point. Mme. de Maintenon had schooled her pupil well in damning his mother with faint praise, while at the same time emphasizing her own good influence. The little boy was forbidden to address the King as "Papa," although on one occasion at a boating party he was given too much red wine, and had his gondolier row up to Louis, whereupon he shouted: "Long live the King my father!" before collapsing in giggles into his governess's arms. His affection for this distant, awe-inspiring man is certainly touching: "I was jealous, Sire, of the letter you did Mme. de Maintenon the honor of writing to her; I so long for signs of your friendship that I can't bear you to give them to other people" (Barèges, 1677), but he also reports disingenuously on his mother's peccadillos: "I have received a letter from the King which fills me with transports of joy, nothing could be more obliging. I shall not do as you did when at Maintenon [during the brief reign of La Ludres] you burnt one from him" (Barèges, 1677). Again, to Athénaïs: "I was inconsolable to see you depart today [for the siege of Ghent]. The King did me the honor to look at me, as he left the chapel, I was delighted with the little sign he made with his head, but afflicted by his departure, and for you, Madame, very unhappy that you seemed to me to be hardly bothered." On one occasion, when Louis was questioning the child on his lessons, and well satisfied with his answers, he praised his son's good sense. "I ought to be reasonable," answered the little Duc studiedly, "since I have a lady around me who is reason itself."[8] Louis was pleased enough to give Du Maine 1,000 francs as a gift for his wise teacher.

To make matters worse as far as Athénaïs was concerned, La Maintenon remained infuriatingly attractive, whereas Athénaïs, at thirty-nine, was beginning to lose her looks. In fact, since the birth of the Comte de Toulouse, the sexual passion between her and the King — that powerful, anarchic constant in their relationship — had been dying. Nine pregnancies had taken their toll on Athénaïs's figure, and her natural tendency to greed led her to overeat to console herself for his waning interest. She put on a lot of weight, which La Maintenon was quick to remark upon: "Mme. de Montespan has fattened by a foot since you saw her, she is astonishing," she reported spitefully to a correspondent. The governess was not alone in her derogatory observations on the favorite's Junoesque curves. On seeing Athénaïs getting out of her carriage, Primi Visconti reported that her legs were so fat, one of them was the size of his torso (to be fair, he added gallantly, "I have recently lost weight").

Mme. de Maintenon, too, was plumper, but a little extra weight suited her full bosom and beautiful vellum skin. Though five years older than Athénaïs, she had retained a fresh, serene beauty, and her eyes were as bright and clear as ever. Athénaïs, by contrast, exhausted herself with the frenzied distractions of the *bassette* table, and, for the first time, appeared to be drinking as well as eating too much. She was under strain, and it was manifest in her looks that her confidence and her energy were evaporating.

If alcoholism is a family trait, it may well have been that Athénaïs struggled with the affliction, for her daughters, and particularly her granddaughter the Duchesse de Berry, scandalized polite society with their drinking. The Duchesse, the daughter of the former Mlle. de Blois, "resembled her grandmother Mme. de Montespan in her eloquence, her embonpoint, her drinking, her sexuality,"[9] and was the black sheep of the royal family, dying aged twenty-four after a life of alcohol, gluttony and promiscuity (the latter most notoriously, it was rumored, involving her own father). Only six weeks after her wedding to the youngest son of the Grand Dauphin, she had to be carried speechless and incontinent with drink from a party at St. Cloud. Both of her aunts, Athénaïs's other daughters, were known to be hard drinkers, "as drunk as a bellringer" three or four times a week in their teens, and they often interrupted their endless competitive sniping to carouse together.[10] Athénaïs herself gave up alcohol at the end of her life, but in this difficult period, she may well have turned to the bottle, which would explain the increased ferocity of her temper, as well perhaps, as the fits of "vapors" which kept her to her rooms for days. Alcohol may also have contributed to the sad ruination of her figure. Mme. de Maintenon's charm might have been quieter than Athénaïs's once-radiant beauty, but it seemed to be more enduring. "It was difficult to see her often without developing an inclination for her," wrote the Abbé de Choisy,[11] while the diarist Saint-Simon commented on her "incomparable grace."

Louis was still so attached to Athénaïs, so proud of her, and so accustomed to her presence at the center of the court, that she perhaps had less need than she perceived to feel threatened. But sadly, along with her looks, Athénaïs seemed to be losing her judgment, and with it her temper. As 1679 drew on without any sign of the King returning to her bed, she began to punish him with furious tantrums, allowing herself to forget that he hated scenes of any kind. Louis continued to spend a good deal of time in her rooms, but rather than being amused by her conversation he had to endure nagging, screaming and fits of tears. When he withdrew to the tranquillity of La Maintenon's apartment, Athénaïs felt neglected and wronged and redoubled her fury, succeeding only in driving him further away. She was mystified by the appeal of this quiet, secretive woman, and her bemusement was shared by the courtiers, who put about rumors that La Maintenon was taking dictation of the King's memoirs, or even that she was a secret procuress who obtained young girls for him. The more perceptive among them, though, had taken to calling her Mme. de Maintenant.[12]

Whatever the attraction, Mme. de Maintenon seemed to be steadily displacing the *maîtresse en titre*. "We are talking of changes in love at court," wrote one of Bussy-Rabutin's correspondents. "Time will make things clear."[13]

Clarification came in the form of Marie-Angélique de Scorailles de Roussille, Demoiselle de Fontanges. "*Belle comme une ange*" was the obvious, and apposite, pun on her name, since she was the most beautiful creature the court had ever seen. The stand-off between Athénaïs and La Maintenon was suddenly eclipsed by a new passion which appeared to threaten them equally.

Angélique, like most of Louis's women, was a gorgeous blond, eighteen years old, slender and delicate with huge grey eyes and a beautiful set of teeth (in itself a sufficient qualification for beauty at the time). "One could see nothing more marvelous," conceded Madame, who had no patience for pretty women. Like Louise de La Vallière, Angélique came from the *petite noblesse*. Her family, who lived in Auvergne, realizing that their beautiful daughter was a great asset, had raised enough money to send her to court with the unspoken yet precise aim of replenishing the family coffers from the royal bed. Angélique made her ambition quite clear in recounting a dream to her new mistress, Madame. She dreamed that she climbed a high mountain, and when she reached the summit, she was dazzled by a brilliant cloud, then she found herself in such profound darkness that she awoke in fear. The dream was interpreted by a monk, who warned Angélique that the mountain represented the court, where she would arrive in great but short-lived state. "If you abandon God," he told her, "He will abandon you, and you will live in shadow forever." This monk was not the only religious soul to be alarmed by Angélique's dazzling vision. On 17 March 1679, Mme. de Maintenon wrote to her confessor, the Abbé Gobelin, using remarkably similar imagery: "I beg you to pray for the King, who is on the brink of a great precipice." It was Athénaïs who, in a terrible error of judgment, pushed him over the edge.

Desperate to distract Louis from his increasing interest in Mme. de Maintenon, Athénaïs drew his attention towards the beautiful young Fontanges girl. She believed that this foolish little provincial would be another Mme. de Ludres, a passing fancy easily controlled and easily disposed of. One evening she pointed the girl out to Louis at Appartement, remarking casually, "Look, Sire, here is a beautiful statue; seeing her I asked myself lately if she came from the chisel of Girardon, and I was surprised when I was told that she is living!"

"A statue, perhaps," replied Louis, "but Good God, what a beautiful creature!"

At first, the King seemed almost shy of expressing his admiration for La Fontanges, joking that here was a wolf who would not eat him, but before long he had given the Duc de la Rochefoucauld a pearl necklace and earrings to present to her, a clear indication that he planned to make her his mistress. Athénaïs had calculated badly. Louis was no longer the handsome, shy young man she had drawn out and encouraged, but a mature monarch of forty-six who, like many middle-aged men, was all too ready to fall head over heels for an exquisite young girl. The very security of Athénaïs's position, and the splendid domesticity she had established with her children at Clagny, diluted some of her erotic appeal, and as Louis moved into middle age, he was anxious to test his virility on younger, more quiescent flesh. One autumn evening, while Athénaïs was safely occupied at the *bassette* table, he retired discreetly to his carriage, accompanied only by his bodyguards, and drove to the Palais Royal, Monsieur's Paris residence, where an accomplice named Mlle. des Adrets showed him to Angélique's room. For all her apparent innocence, it appears that Angélique was not without a few erotic wiles of her own. She knew to resist just enough to make the conquest more delicious, how to abandon herself with a reluctance at once charmingly modest and thrilling. Indeed, the Paris pamphleteers were not slow to detail the King's latest conquest in terms of a military surrender: "This important place, having been reconnoitered, was attacked in all its curvaceousness. The way was cleared, the outskirts were seized, and with much sweat and fatigue, and spilt blood, the King entered in victorious. We can say that no conquest gave him greater difficulty. There were many cries and tears spilt on one side, and never did a dying virginity release such gentle sighs."[14]

At first, Louis installed his new love in a little villa at Château Neuf de St. Germain, but before long she was given her own apartment at court. Angélique probably became Louis's mistress only two months after her arrival in late 1678; in any event, the secret was clearly out early in the new year. Athénaïs was initially complacent, unaware that Louis had any serious interest in the girl, and it was not for several months that she knew herself abandoned. In March, La Maintenon described Athénaïs's state in a letter. "Mme. de Montespan complains of her last *accouchement,* she says that this girl has caused her to lose the King's heart; she blames me, as if I hadn't told her often to have no more children . . . I pity Mme. de Montespan at the same time as I blame her: what would she be if she knew all her misfortunes? She is far from believing the King unfaithful, she accuses him only of coldness. We don't dare to tell her of this new passion."

In May, the governess witnessed a violent quarrel between Louis and Athénaïs, who had finally learned the secret the whole court had been whispering behind her back for months. Louis was unmoved by his lover's fury. "I have already told you, Madame, that I do not wish to be bothered," he said coldly. Athénaïs whipped herself into a fury of denunciation, slandering La Fontanges with all the vitriol she could muster, and then departed to Clagny for a few days to recover herself.

Suddenly, there was a whirlwind of change, and all the regard of the court, all the entertainments it held, were for the aspiring mistress. Athénaïs was still *maîtresse en titre* (and indeed La Fontanges was never completely declared so), but from the King's actions, it was clear that, informal though her position was as yet, Angélique was well on the way to becoming favorite. Louis abandoned the plain, sober style of dress he had affected in recent years and bedecked himself rather pathetically in the silks and ribbons of his youth. Athénaïs was hoist with her own petard. The King was deliriously in love. La Fontanges gave herself tremendous airs, and the malleable loyalties of the court were only too ready to do homage to the King's new passion at the expense of the old. Athénaïs found herself shunned, ignored, eclipsed, as once she had herself eclipsed Louise de La Vallière. "The violence of the King's passion for Mme. de Montespan is no more," wrote Mme. de Montmorency, "and it is said that there are times when she weeps bitterly after the conversations she has with the King."

"Really," complained Athénaïs. "A stupid girl without education, a beautiful painting and that's all. The King is hardly delicate to love such a person, who had affairs back in her province."

Although Athénaïs was spared the final indignity of seeing her rival declared *maîtresse en titre,* she had to tolerate the affair until 1680. For some time, it appeared that La Fontanges was to become a permanent favorite. She flaunted herself before the Queen, appearing at Mass in a coat made from the same azure cloth as Louis's; her carriage was drawn by eight fine white horses; she demanded a position as abbesse of Chelles for her sister Catherine; just like Mme. de Montespan, she spent 25,000 ecus a week on trinkets. The new favorite's portrait was taken by Mignard, and La Fontaine, who had benefited so much from Athénaïs's patronage, treacherously dedicated a flattering poem to La Fontanges, with the inscription:

> *Charmant objet, digne present des cieux*
> *(Et n'est ce point image du Parnasse)*
> *Votre beauté vient de la main des dieux*
> *Vous l'allez voir au recit que je trace.*
> *Puisse mes vers presenter tant de grâce*
> *Que d'être offerts au dompteur des humains,*
> *Accompagnés d'un mot de votre bouche*
> *Et presentés par vos divins mains.*[15]

That La Fontaine, with whom Athénaïs had enjoyed a stimulating relationship of mutual admiration, should prove so fickle, so ready to prostitute his genius in the service of a mere doll, was intolerable. To defer to this uneducated provincial was more than Athénaïs's pride could bear, and she railed at the King's confessor, Père la Chaise, who seemed perfectly complacent at this new romantic peccadillo, since it did not involve double adultery. "*Ce Père la Chaise,*" she punned, "is a real *chaise de commodité.*"[16] She had clearly chosen to forget that she herself had made use of La Chaise's complacency during the religious crisis of 1675. Louis was besotted, and ignored both the rants of his discarded mistress and the querulous mutterings of the *dévots*. One bishop who dared to try to remonstrate with the King about this too-public display of his affection was given the tart reply, "You will do me the pleasure, Monsieur, of conserving your zeal for your diocese!"

Initially, Athénaïs allowed her anger to draw her into open rivalry with Angélique. Comically, the two appeared side by side at the King's Mass, both trying to outdo one another in their demonstrations of piety, clutching their chaplets in two plump white hands and rolling four great blue eyes to heaven like beautiful saints. "It's the greatest comedy in the world," scoffed Primi Visconti. One story has it that the two pet bears Athénaïs kept for her amusement in a little menagerie Louis had given her in the grounds of the palace "accidentally" escaped and destroyed Mlle. de Fontanges's apartment. It is likely to be apocryphal, but it would not have been beyond Athénaïs's enormous capacity for fury to release the ravening beasts into her rival's rooms. If the story is true, it was the last service the bears performed for Athénaïs, for in 1681 she sold them to the Duc du Maine's valet.

In February 1680, the whole court set off to meet the future Dauphine, Anne-Marie of Bavaria, betrothed to Louis's only living legitimate son. At a ball at Villers-Cotterets, Athénaïs showed that she could still outshine her conceited little rival in grace and style. Angélique danced badly, and disgraced herself in the minuet, Mme. de Sévigné commenting that her legs seemed unable to arrive where they ought, and that she managed barely more than a bow. Athénaïs, on the other hand, knew that she danced superbly, and obliged Angélique to retire blushing from the floor. It was this very awkwardness, however, that seemed to enchant the King. In contrast with the tempestuous Athénaïs, La Fontanges seemed all simplicity and admiration, flattering Louis's huge ego with her naïveté and ignorance. Just as Athénaïs had done ten years before, she introduced a new hairstyle, this one created on the hunting field rather than in the boudoir. One day, as the hunt galloped in pursuit of the stag, a branch whipped Angélique's hat from her head so that she appeared before the King with her hair loosely tied in a ribbon, tumbling in curls to her shoulders. Louis found this "rustic" style delightful, and the coiffure *à la Fontanges* became the latest craze.

Realizing at last that anger was useless, Athénaïs tried the tactic of friendship she had employed so successfully with La Vallière, feigning a great affection for the girl, who was so intoxicated with conceit at her own success that she was flattered to have the former favorite attend upon her. Athénaïs dressed La Fontanges for court entertainments, styling her hair with her own hands, as once La Vallière had wound ribbons through her own golden locks, and presented her with a New Year gift of a jeweled almanac containing predictions for the four seasons by La Fontaine. Now believing herself to be secure, Angélique allowed her passion for the king to become ever more obvious, boasting of the advancements she would achieve for her family and flaunting her jewels like a goddess. She showed off her new wealth by giving 20,000 ecus to her former companions in Madame's train. As Athénaïs had guessed it would, this presumption began to irk Louis, especially when La Fontanges had the audacity to order him about in public. Athénaïs maintained a calm façade, writing to the Duc de Noailles about some green velvet to line her coach and remarking casually that the King visited her only twice a day, but that this was better than more frequent and quarrelsome meetings.

If Athénaïs derived any amusement from the situation, it was from the distress of Mme. de Maintenon, who was obviously furious to have her good work on the King's soul undone all over again. Athénaïs teased the governess by suggesting that the King now had three mistresses: herself in name, La Fontanges in bed and La Maintenon in his heart. La Maintenon attempted to persuade the *maîtresse de corps* to give up the king for the good of her soul, but Angélique laughed in her face and asked if she should rid herself of a grand passion as easily as a used chemise. Nonetheless, the governess continued to enjoy the King's high favor, which further wounded Athénaïs's pride. Louis seemed to feel no embarrassment at continuing to spend much of his time with a lady who had remonstrated so openly with him on the subject of his amours. Indeed, caught between the tantrums of the old mistress and the vacuous chatter of the new, he took increasing pleasure in the engaging and easy conversation of the Marquise de Maintenon. For the first time in his life, he was experiencing the comfort of a woman's friendship.

At the end of 1679, La Fontanges gave birth to a baby boy who, despite or perhaps because of the efforts of the surgeons, failed to survive. The difficult birth coupled with the distress of losing her child began to diminish Angélique's ravishing beauty. She suffered from the loss of blood and fits of fever, and her fine features were blurred with swelling. Since she had little else to recommend her, intelligence never having been her strongest asset (she may have been as beautiful as an angel, but she was also, in the court parlance, "as stupid as a basket"), Louis began to tire of her. The vivacious, invigorating young girl had been replaced by a whining, clingy woman whose pretensions irritated him and whose vapidity bored him. In April 1680, he granted her her Duchess's *tabouret* and a pension of 80,000 livres, and though she received the congratulations of the court from her bed, everyone knew that the elevation was a valedictory gesture.

And although she remained at court for some months, Angélique's star was definitely on the wane. Louis was kind to her, since she had received her illness "in his service," as Mme. de Sévigné joked, but he was no longer in love with her. In July the royal family set off on yet another progress in Flanders. Both marquises were included in the party, but Angélique was too ill to travel, and spent the summer languishing in her sister's new convent at Chelles. Four coaches and six and her famous coach and eight were no compensation for her ruined health, and a duchess's pension no consolation for the loss of her lover. Too silly to recognize that beauty, in any case now little more than a memory, was enough to attract the King, but not to hold him, Angélique learned too late that she was no match for Athénaïs's wit or La Maintenon's charm. During the dolorous hours in the abbey, she formed the view that her continuing ill health had a sinister cause. When she returned to court in August, to universal indifference, strange stories began to circulate of her visit to Chelles. Her doctor had ordered mineral water for her, and a servant had brought her six bottles which, fortunately, she had not touched, for when they were examined the next day, they were found to contain poison. "People are saying," wrote Mme. de Sévigné in September, "that the beauty believes herself to have been poisoned, and that she has demanded bodyguards." Easier, perhaps, for Angélique to believe in a conspiracy than to accept that the King no longer loved her.

In March 1681, La Fontanges gave up all hope of reconquering Louis's heart, and, as was now traditional, retired with her household to a convent, Port-Royale in Paris. She was now suffering from a pulmonary abscess. Louis sent the Ducs de Noailles and la Feuillade three times a week to ask for news of her, but he did not visit her himself until it became clear that she would not survive. The Duchesse de Fontanges died on 28 June, vomiting horrible pus. She was twenty years old. Posterity has given her a splendid curtain line, thanks to the eighteenth-century writer Sautereau de Mary. "I die content, having seen my King weep for me." "*Sic transit gloria mundi,*" commented the Marquise de Sévigné sententiously.

Angélique de Fontanges's short life and tragic death lent her a romantic appeal, and the pens of Paris were quick with their eulogies.

> *Autrefois a la cour, on me vit égal*
> *Maîtresse de mon roi, je défis une rivale.*
> *Jamais un temps si court ne fit un sort si beau*
> *Jamais fortune aussi ne fut sitôt détruite.*
> *Ah! que la distance est petite*
> *Du comble des grandeurs a l'horreur du tombeau.*[17]

Angélique was buried in the abbey of Port-Royale, where Louis was represented by the Duc de Noailles. Her heart was taken to her sister Catherine at Chelles, after the delivery of a short sermon by the priest at St. Severin which recalled the warning of her dream. "This heart was God's in the beginning, it was won by the world. God finally took back to Him what was His own, but it was not returned to Him without suffering."[18] It is hard to believe that Angélique would have chosen to be dispatched to salvation quite so expeditiously.

That she had been assisted in this process by the evil machinations of Athénaïs was a juicy rumor that quickly gained currency. After all, had not the poor Duchess complained that she was the victim of a poisoning plot? Gossip sold better than eulogies, and the pamphleteers soon released melodramatic accounts of La Fontanges's demise such as *The Familiar Spirit of Trianon, or the Phantom of the Duchesse de*

Fontanges, recounting the Secrets of her Loves, the Particulars of her Poisoning, and her Death. The quarrels between Athénaïs and Angélique had been well known, and although Athénaïs was popular with *le peuple,* the temptation to create a scandal was irresistible. But what the Parisian hacks did not know was that a far more outrageous drama was waiting to explode on the public stage.

Chapter Twelve

"The passions set aside justice and work for
their own ends, and it is therefore dangerous to
follow them and necessary to treat them with
caution even when they seem most reasonable."

L ate in 1669, Louise de La Vallière, still officially *maîtresse en titre,* had
fallen violently ill. In her meditations on her life, *Reflections on the
Mercy of God,* composed in the seclusion of her convent, she remembered feeling "like a poor criminal on the scaffold, waiting until the
preparations for his execution had been completed." When she recovered, she claimed that her brush with death caused her to begin the
process of atonement that ultimately led her to the Carmelites.

In 1668, the Président de Mesmes, father-in-law to the Duc de
Vivonne, found himself dealing with a rather embarrassing case in the
court of the Châtelet. A pair of charlatans named Adam Coueret
(who went by the alias of Lesage) and the Abbé Mariette were on trial
for sorcery. Although the offense was extremely serious, it was hard to
believe these two shabby mountebanks, who boasted to the judges of
their proficiency in astrology, cartomancy, alchemy and phrenology,
and of the "scientific potions" they concocted from a predictably horrible list of ingredients such as bat's blood, toad's bones and Spanish fly,
were really capable of communing with any dark powers. They traf-
ficked their concoctions to credulous upper-class women who believed them to be aphrodisiacs, mystically empowered by being passed
"under the chalice" by Mariette, who was a bona fide priest. By and
large, the sorcerers claimed, these noblewomen had wished for charms

to make the King fall in love with them, so that they could succeed Louise de La Vallière in the coveted role of *maîtresse déclarée*. Among their hopeful customers had been the Marquise du Baugy, the Comtesse de Roure, the Comtesse de Gramont, the Vicomtesse de Polignac, the Duchesse de Vivonne and the Marquise de Montespan. Shocked to hear his daughter and her sister-in-law named in connection with such blasphemous activity, the Président pressed Mariette further. He explained that Lesage had recruited the clients, telling them that the powers of a priest could be put to use for their own ends. Without the benefit of a stole or a surplice, or even of a church, Mariette could make an incantation over their head and their prayers would be answered. Over whom had Mariette recited this inverted gospel? "All those persons whom Lesage brought to me: Mme. de Baugy, Mme. de Raffetot, Mme. de Montespan . . ."

Both Lesage and Mariette were lucky, considering that a conviction for sorcery carried the death penalty, and by burning rather than hanging. Lesage got away with nine years in the galleys, Mariette nine years' banishment. Prudently, the names of Mme. de Montespan and the Duchesse de Vivonne were forgotten after the first interrogation. Since Louise de La Vallière was still the official mistress, the two prisoners could not have hoped to gain anything by implicating Mme. de Montespan in their "powder" trade, but given her real position at the time, it would obviously not have done for the Président de Mesmes to have involved her in any form of scandal. Soothsayers were rather a vogue among the ladies of the court, and there was no real harm in fortune-telling or buying charms. But love potions to ensnare the King? The Vivonnes stood to benefit if Mme. de Montespan retained her hold on the King, so the Président thought it prudent to leave her name out of things.

The case was never made public. Lesage's sentence was commuted in 1674, the same year that Louise de La Vallière finally left the court. Perhaps Athénaïs's "powders" had been efficacious after all . . .

It is quite understandable that Athénaïs would turn to supernatural aid in her pursuit of the King's constancy. Lucifer was still a force to be reckoned with in the Grand Siècle. Just as the clear lines of the King's new house at Versailles were blurred by the more sinuous rhythms of the baroque style, so the incipient classicism of the times was grafted on to the superstitions of an older, darker world. It was not yet quite the age of enlightenment. Science had not yet emerged from the polymorphous explorations of the Renaissance "natural philosopher," the magus, the mystic. The Church gave great credence still to the person of Satan and to his power: in the Catechism, the name of Satan was invoked sixty-seven times — four more than the name of Christ Himself. The Devil and his legions of demons were as real and as powerful as the Holy Saints, good and evil illuminated side by side in the candlelight of the churches, worked in the damp stone in a familiar iconography of martyrs' hearts and cloven hoofs, suppliant eyes and devilish horns. The Devil's work was seen everywhere: in blighted crops, in the wailing of a sick child, in the coldness of a lover's glance. Each of life's misfortunes had its own particular saint and a different magical remedy. The rites of Catholicism, which relied on images and the mystical intervention of the priest, encouraged such reliance on the supernatural. If something was lost and St. Anthony was deaf, then the ritual of the sieve and the shears might recover the object. While St. Claire heard appeals for the blind, a cat's eye worn on the chest could also improve the sight. Bad luck at cards, a spotty complexion, an inconvenient husband or an empty purse — each problem was the province of a saint, and if there was no specific saint to deal with it, then a charm, a powder or a visit to the sorceress might solve it. La Fontaine wrote an amusing riddle on the subject:

> *Whether you lost an earring or a lover*
> *Had a husband who refused to die*
> *A jealous wife, a possessive mother*
> *Or any suchlike bother*
> *Straight to the soothsayer you'd fly.*[1]

One of the most popular and successful soothsayers was Catherine Monvoisin, known to her elegant lady customers as La Voisin. In the 1670s, her business was booming. Despite her useless husband, a cowed and incompetent merchant, La Voisin had acquired a pretty suburban villa and bragged of her considerable earnings. A supplier to duchesses, La Voisin was herself a duchess among witches, presiding over her ceremonies in her fantastic "emperor's robe" of purple velvet tooled in gold, which cost over 10,000 livres. She had many lovers from the more respectable levels of society, including a count and a marquis, and boasted that she had received invitations from the King of England and the Hapsburg emperor to demonstrate her skills. In her garden she had constructed a convenient little oven in which she baked what she coyly referred to as her *petits pâtés;* in fact, the ashes of over 2,000 aborted infants lent their richness to the soil in which her roses flourished. All the little inconveniences of a fashionable lady's life could be resolved with a visit to La Voisin. She could make a bosom more bountiful, or a mouth more diminutive, and she knew just what to do for a nice girl who had got herself into trouble. It was common to see a carriage arriving at her villa from Versailles or St. Germain, full of masked and giggling ladies in search of a palm-reading or a love charm. The Duchesse de Bouillon came for a consultation about her rather meager décolletage, the Comtesse de Soissons for a "powder" to restore a certain man's affection. And if La Voisin, with her laboratory of chemicals and her panoply of charms, failed to oblige, she would, for a fee, call upon a power stronger than her own.

La Voisin's skills were legendary within her own trade, and she was particularly well known for the swift dispatch of rivals or spouses in love affairs. "What a boon it is to our profession," she famously remarked, "when lovers resort to desperate measures." Desperate measures usually called for something more potent than a charm, and this is where La Voisin's activities as a "sorcerer" took a sinister turn. The boundaries between "white" and "black" magic were blurred, and practitioners like La Voisin were prepared to make use of both types to procure results for their clients. It was quite plausible to create a novena for the disappearance of, say, a troublesome husband, and if this did not work, to progress to performing an inverted or "black" Mass for his disposal. In this area men were often involved, frequently hypocritical priests willing to pervert their sacred power, as in the case of Lesage and the Abbé Mariette. A further and more worldly remedy was poison, which was often associated with and produced by the practices of black magic. A huge variety of different poisons were used by witches or soothsayers: arsenic, sulphur, diamond powder, opium, mandragora, vipers' venom, the juices emitted by a rotting toad.

Poison had always lurked in the background of politics, since as a murder weapon it was virtually undetectable by the physicians of the time. The only method of determining whether or not poison had been administered was to give a sample of the substance in question to a dog and see if it died. As we have seen, Henriette d'Angleterre, on her deathbed, was convinced she had been poisoned, and her daughter, who became Queen of Spain, was to die of poison in 1689. It was rumored that Catherine de' Medici, a queen who placed great faith in the power of the occult, had imported her own Italian poisoners in her train.

If poison was sometimes seen as a political expedient, it had always, like witchcraft, been considered the peculiar province of women. It was most commonly the weapon of the weak, of those who had no protection in law and no recourse in physical strength. Regardless of the sophisticated debates of the *précieuses,* outside the self-contained feminine communities of the convent, with the rare exception of extraordinary women like Athénaïs de Montespan who were not only wealthy but in control of their own finances, most women were vulnerable and powerless, dependent on the goodwill of their male relations. Married women owned no property, and if a marriage failed between a couple too poor to keep a civilized distance on their respective country estates, a wife had no option but to remain with her husband, however drunken, lazy or brutal he might be. A proverb from southern France sums it up: *"Les femmes ne sont pas gens"* — Women are not people. This lack of status was evident in every aspect of society, from the practice of wife-selling, which flourished into the nineteenth century, to the country tradition that women never sat down to eat with men. There are frequent references in proverbs and songs to wife-beating being a normal, even desirable activity, and whereas male infidelity was the norm, an adulterous wife could be publicly whipped or incarcerated in a convent. It is hardly surprising that, among the lower classes, "most wives seemed to have lived in fear of blows, but many a husband ate and drank in fear of poison."[2] Among wealthier women, poison was a means not only of escaping a tyrannical husband or father, but also of obtaining a fortune — indeed, poisons were often euphemistically dubbed "inheritance powders."

The sorceresses who produced poisons for their upper-class clients were usually much less successful than La Voisin. In 1679, a list of over 400 "fortune-tellers" was produced, all women operating in Paris accused of everything from relatively innocent white magic to criminal activity such as abortion and poisoning. Studies of witchcraft show that alleged witches were often impotent and desperate, poor and marginalized, and the Parisian poisoners follow this pattern in that they were nearly all middle-aged women, single or attached to men unable to keep them, hovering in minor trades and permanently on the brink of beggary. Many were drunkards or part-time prostitutes; most were itinerant if not actually homeless, circulating in the miserable flophouses and gin palaces of the Parisian slums. This is not, of course, to suggest that misery and poverty were exclusively female afflictions, but it is interesting that so many women, rich or poor, saw witchcraft and poisoning as an answer to their plight. The "typical" fortune-teller, then, was not an independent businesswoman like La Voisin, whose clients were wealthy, frustrated and ambitious women, but a small-time witch.

In 1679, La Voisin was the principal suspect in a police investigation into crimes of poisoning among the upper classes. The inquiry unearthed a scandal which, through the person of the King himself, threatened the security of the nation. The "Affair of the Poisons" was compared to an outbreak of plague within the most elevated section of French society, and its potential effects were perceived as even more catastrophic. It became an international event, the most alarming revelation of corruption within the aristocracy ever known in the courts of Europe. Something was rotten in the state of France, something which had slithered from the slums of Paris into the drawing rooms of Versailles; something which threatened to taint indelibly all the power and prestige the Sun King had labored to achieve. The Affair of the Poisons was the stuff of political nightmare, and Athénaïs de Montespan was implicated at its very heart.

It began quietly, with Mme. de Sévigné indulging in a macabre little joke about the most notorious scandal of 1676. "Well, it's all over and done with," she wrote. "Brinvilliers is in the air. Her poor little body was thrown after the execution into a very big fire, and the ashes to the winds, so that we shall breathe her, and through the communication of the subtle spirits, we shall develop some poisoning urge which will astonish us all."[3] The Marquise de Brinvilliers, an obviously deranged woman with a sad history of sexual abuse, had been executed for poisoning her father, along with numerous other victims, and for attempting to poison her husband. She had perfected her murderous skills by practicing them on the unfortunate inmates of Parisian hospitals during her charitable visits. Conspiring with her lover, one Sainte-Croix, she aimed to dispatch her husband in order to free herself to remarry, but her intended fiancé, reflecting on the risks of marriage to such a black widow, lost his nerve and began to administer a course of secret counterdoses. Much to the delight of the chattering classes of Paris, who reveled in black humor, the poor Marquis de Brinvilliers had lingered for months, never knowing whether he was dying or recovering, until he was finally saved by his wife's arrest. With the dissipation of the Marquise's ashes, the affair seemed finished, a shocking crime to be sure, but one of little real consequence. It appeared, however, that the Marquise de Sévigné's grisly joke contained a germ of truth, since before her death Brinvilliers had claimed that "there were many people engaged in this miserable traffic of poisons, and people of condition, too." In 1676, it was still possible to dismiss such an allegation, but the following year, the Parisian chief of police, Gabriel-Nicolas la Reynie, found himself investigating another case of poisoning which appeared to threaten the King himself.

Among Colbert's many excellent innovations during his long service to Louis XIV was the establishment of a police force in Paris. The city then bore no resemblance to the sanitized metropolis created by Haussmann in the nineteenth century, but remained largely medieval, a noxious cat's cradle of narrow streets where criminals ruled unmolested by the law. "Day and night they rob and kill here . . . We have reached the dregs of the centuries," wrote one despairing commentator before the Fronde wars.[4] Thanks to Colbert and his lieutenant-general of police, crime in Paris was greatly reduced by the end of the reign. La Reynie's job was in fact more akin to that of a modern American mayor than to that of a policeman. He was responsible for street lighting and refuse collection as well as law enforcement, and had jurisdiction over the trade guilds, public sanitation and new buildings. Colbert believed in a relationship between public order and the development of industry, so La Reynie was given carte blanche to intervene in trade, for example, by forcing tailors to use silk buttons to promote the Lyons silk market. He was also granted the powers of a magistrate to investigate and prosecute his own cases.

In 1677, with the successful prosecution of the Marquise de Brinvilliers behind him, La Reynie turned his attention to the case of a young woman known as Mlle. la Grange. A widow from Anjou, she had been set up in some style as the mistress of a wealthy Parisian lawyer, who tired of the relationship after eight years and talked of retiring to the country. This plan was thwarted by his sudden death, whereupon La Grange presented herself to his relatives in the role of grieving widow. The family were suspicious, especially as the household servants reported signs of poisoning, and they demanded an investigation. It was discovered that La Grange had fraudulently married her lover, a corrupt priest named Nail, who had impersonated the late lawyer in the marriage ceremony in a plot to gain his fortune.

The case took a serious turn when La Grange wrote to the war minister, Louvois, from the Châtelet prison, claiming to possess crucial information indicating that the King's life was in danger. Such claims were not uncommon, but since Louis had been suffering in recent years from violent headaches and fits of the "vapors," for which he took tea, Louvois was sufficiently alarmed to have La Grange brought to his house in Paris for interrogation. She clearly revealed something of consequence, as she was immediately removed to the Bastille prison, largely reserved for political prisoners. Louvois then authorized La Reynie to begin a thorough investigation into poisoning cases, at the King's request: "His Majesty has commanded me to tell you that he expects you to pursue this affair with application, and that you shall omit nothing in bringing it to light." Something in the case was giving the highest authorities in France cause for concern.

In September 1677, a Jesuit priest at the church of St. Antoine, near the Bastille, handed in a piece of paper he had received from an unknown woman at the confessional, which she said she had found in the walks at Palais-Royal, Monsieur's Paris residence. Via the King's confessor, Père la Chaise, it arrived at La Reynie's office. It appeared to be a letter from a woman to her lover and accomplice. In it she cautioned him about "this white powder that you wish to put on the napkin of we-know-who," then warned him that she would marry his rival if he did not succeed. Further on, she wrote: "I am extremely frightened that our letters are seen and that people will think me guilty . . . Because in all other crimes one has to be an accomplice to be punished, but with this one it is necessary only to have known." The sole crime for which knowledge amounted to complicity was lèse-majesté — treason. So was "we-know-who" perhaps the King, or maybe the Dauphin? Had the letter been planted by La Grange in order to substantiate her claim to secret knowledge of a plot against Louis, or was it genuine, and was La Grange acquainted with the writer? Despite twelve hours of interrogation and torture, La Grange denied all knowledge of the letter, as did her lover, Nail, and they

were both condemned to death. Only in the cart on the way to the
scaffold did they admit to understanding the mysterious references,
but they still refused to make a formal statement, and were hung
without revealing whatever knowledge they had.

Just after La Grange's arrest, La Reynie apprehended another group
of suspected poisoners, the "Vanens gang," a miserable troupe of
forgers, "alchemists" and other charlatans led by Louis Vanens, an
adventurer with aristocratic pretensions who styled himself "Chevalier." Vanens, a known criminal, was suspected of having been
involved in the death by poison of the Duc de Savoie some years earlier. La Reynie felt certain that this group was in some way connected
with the La Grange case, a belief reinforced by the testimony of a
maidservant in Vanens's house, who maintained that her master had
known La Grange. One member of the gang, Marie Bosse, who had
been arrested for trafficking in toads, a well-known ingredient of
poisons, also claimed to have been acquainted with the mysterious
letter-writer, but when pressed, she defended herself saucily by asking La Reynie why he didn't leave petty people like herself alone and
concentrate on what was happening "high up." She bragged that she
knew the names of several upper-class people who had bought
"charms" to use against the King. Curiously, she added that one particular woman had done so. The identity of this aristocratic customer
was provided by Vanens's valet, Jean Barthominat, who said that his
master knew Mme. de Montespan, and furthermore that Vanens
"ought to be torn apart by four horses" for the advice he had given
the Marquise.[5] But since he immediately retracted this extraordinary
claim, La Reynie dismissed it as bravado. Still, it must have been
highly disconcerting to hear the name of the King's favorite in such a
context. He continued his inquiries, hoping to establish a connection
between La Grange, the mysterious letter and the increasingly
repeated assertion that poisoning was occurring among the aristocracy.

Trawling through the layers of petty criminals, sorcerers and
poison-sellers who bubbled in the rank stews of St. Denis, La Reynie
turned up several cases of poisoning, as well as strange tales of baby-
snatching. Infants, it appeared, were disappearing. Horrible rumors of
child murder, satanic rites and sacrifice were suddenly everywhere.
Paris seemed to be swimming in a hysterical sea of poison, swarming
with stories of murders, kidnappings and black Masses. Mme. de

Sévigné's son Charles describes the atmosphere in a letter to his sister: "Here I am back again with our darling *maman,* but so far no one has accused me of trying to poison her, which, I can assure you, the way things are going presently, is no small tribute to my reputation for filial devotion!"[6] Yet until the end of 1678, La Reynie's investigation seemed to be making little headway.

Then Marie Bosse reappeared. The police had a visit from one of their *mouches,* undercover agents, who had dined at the house of a fortune-teller called La Vigoureux, where Marie had been among the guests. Obese and drunken, she had boasted between slugs of wine: "What a marvelous trade it is! What a clientele I have — duchesses, marquises, princes! Only three more poisonings and I can retire with my fortune made!" From the obvious fury of the hostess, the agent realized that this was more than mere braggadocio. A policeman's wife was sent incognito to Mme. Vigoureux for a palm-reading, and easily obtained a vial of poison for the proverbial "troublesome husband."

La Reynie moved quickly now, and on 4 January 1679, La Vigoureux, La Bosse and her three children were captured at the fortune-teller's house, where they were all asleep in the same bed, and imprisoned in the Bastille. They swore that their activities were no more than harmless quackery, and the semiliterate La Bosse insisted, implausibly, that she used the laboratory equipment found in the lodgings for her "chemistry studies." As well as acids and mercury, the police recovered a small vial of menstrual blood, which La Reynie, who had begun to study texts on witchcraft such as the *Malleus Maleficarum,* knew to be an ingredient used in black magic practices. The connection between poisoning and witchcraft was thus established in the case, and if La Bosse was to be believed, the Marquise de Brinvilliers had been proved correct. "People of condition" were apparently employing witches, and a trail of sorcery was being revealed that La Reynie feared might rise as high as the King at Versailles. Hoping to procure themselves a degree of leniency, La Bosse and La Vigoureux began to name names. It was they who produced the list of over 400 fortune-tellers, from which La Reynie made over a hundred further arrests.

On 12 March, the infamous La Voisin was arrested, in a neat irony, just as she was returning from Mass. The police searched her house and found tiny human bones in the little oven in the garden, as well as a whole laboratory of poisons and an elaborate treatise on physiognomy, along with all the hocus-pocus paraphernalia of fortune-telling. Three days later, Athénaïs de Montespan left the court, precipitately and inexplicably, for Paris. Bussy-Rabutin attributed her sudden departure to a quarrel about Mlle. de Fontanges. "They are saying that there has been some quarrel in the household, and that this comes from jealousy that she has of one of Madame's maids, called Fontanges, with whom the King, it is said, has already taken his pleasure." Athénaïs returned only after the arrest of one of La Voisin's lovers on 17 March. Together, La Voisin and this man had provided a full range of services, from abortions to curses and interviews with Satan. His name was Adam Coueret, alias Athénaïs's old friend Lesage.

As soon as they were both at Vincennes, La Voisin and Lesage began a desperate process of mutual accusation, each hoping to escape blame for the heinous crimes of the other. La Reynie now had over a hundred witches in prison, of whom the most important were Lesage, La Voisin, La Bosse, La Vigoureux, a woman named La Trianon, Lesage's former accomplice Mariette and another priest named Guibourg. All of them were jabbering the names of their clients and the horrible services they had demanded, and La Reynie's ears were ringing with some of the most famous names in France. Poison had become a fact of life in every strand of society. "Men's lives," he wrote despairingly, "are up for sale as a matter of everyday bargaining; murder is the only remedy when a family is in difficulties. Abominations are being practiced everywhere — in Paris, in the suburbs, in the provinces."

On the same day as Lesage's arrest, Louis informed La Reynie that he intended to establish a special court to deal with what appeared to be a veritable epidemic of poisoning. The Chambre Ardente, as it became known, was inaugurated by letters patent of 7 April 1679 and held its first sitting three days later. An extraordinary tribunal seemed necessary firstly because of the large number of cases to be tried, and secondly because it appeared that many of the suspects were drawn from the upper echelons of society; if there was going to be a scandal, Louis wanted to have as much control over it as possible. The court was to sit for three years, issuing 319 subpoenas, arresting 194 people and sentencing 104 of them. Thirty-six prisoners were condemned to death, four to the galleys, thirty-four banished or fined and thirty acquitted. Mme. de Sévigné commented: "There is no other topic of conversation. No such scandal as this has ever been known in a Christian court."

It is important to establish, however, that the Chambre Ardente was not intended to be a "secret" court. The precedent for the creation of special tribunals had existed in French law since the Middle Ages, and the use of such a tribunal in the Affair of the Poisons was not in itself an attempt by the authorities to hush up the cases by removing them from conventional jurisdiction. It is likely that the investigators were initially unaware of the potentially explosive nature of the business in hand. In bypassing Parlement, with which most of the aristocracy, of both the sword and the robe, were connected, it was in fact more likely that unbiased judgments could be passed on the upper classes. At a conference at Versailles on 27 December 1679, Louis personally instructed La Reynie to administer "absolute justice" to anyone found guilty, "regardless of rank or sex or position," a public declaration of impartiality which would be sorely tested and swiftly compromised.

In January, the scandal broke. Arrest warrants were issued for some of the most prominent members of Louis's court, among them the Maréchal de Luxembourg, the Princesse de Tingry, the Duchesse de Bouillon, the Comtesse de Soissons (Louis's former lover Olympe Mancini), the Marquis de Cessac, the Vicomtesse de Polignac and the Marquise d'Alluye. The Duchesse d'Angoulême was accused, as well as the Comte de Gassily, the Duc de Vendôme and the Marquis de Raffetot. Of these, the Comtesse de Soissons and her accomplice, the Marquise d'Alluye, were certainly guilty. Louis, out of tenderness for his old love, warned her secretly in time to allow her to escape with the Marquise d'Alluye into exile, but on the condition that if she ever returned to France she would have to stand trial. The Comtesse had already been suspected of causing the death of her husband in 1673, but La Voisin claimed that Mme. de Soissons had originally approached her to ask how to recover the King's love, which she had lost to his first *maîtresse en titre* Louise de La Vallière. La Voisin had read her fortune and found it was connected with that of a "great prince" who, to the fury of the Comtesse, would never return to her. The lady was provoked to declare that "if she could not get revenge on Mlle. de La Vallière, then . . . she would do away with both one and the other." Louis's leniency, given this reported intention to murder him, testifies to an occasionally dangerous sentimentality, for he was in no doubt of the Comtesse's guilt and well aware that he would have to answer for her escape to God and to his people. The Comtesse's reputation was so damaged that when she arrived in Flanders with the Marquise d'Alluye, the towns of Antwerp and Namur closed their gates against them and the people pelted them with squalling cats. Later, when Marie-Louise, the young Queen of Spain, was poisoned in Madrid, no one was at all surprised to learn that the Comtesse had recently paid a visit there.

The Marquis de Cessac also compromised himself by fleeing into exile, as did the Vicomtesse de Polignac, who made a dramatic escape from her country house just minutes before the royal guards arrived. The trials of those aristocrats who were innocent or arrogant enough to remain in France were, naturally, a huge sensation. The Duc de Luxembourg dutifully accepted his prison sentence, determined to obey the King in every way, and passed his time between interrogations in prayer, much to the disgust of Mme. de Sévigné, who felt he had compromised his ducal dignity by accepting trial in a bourgeois court rather than by his peers in Parlement. He was accused of using witchcraft to dispose of his wife and the guardian of a woman he wanted to marry, and, rather greedily, to make his sister-in-law, the Princesse de Tingry, fall in love with him into the bargain. Other accusations were ridiculous and melodramatic, involving orgies with dozens of naked women, satanic sabbats and the procuration of abortions for the Princesse. After fourteen months the Duc was acquitted, as was the Princesse, and after a week's exile in the country, he returned to Versailles, where everyone behaved as though he had never left. Louis rewarded his stoicism with various important commands, in which the Duc gained enormous credit for himself and significant victories for France.

Some of the trials provided high comedy. The unfortunate Duchesse de Foix was most embarrassed at the revelation of a note she had written to La Voisin complaining about a breast-enhancing potion — "The more I rub, the less they grow!" The third Mancini sister, the Duchesse de Bouillon, was accused of buying poison from La Voisin to dispatch her boring old husband so that she could marry her lover, the King's young cousin the Duc de Vendôme. All Paris was thrilled as she arrived insouciantly in the courtroom with her lover on one arm and her patient husband on the other. She was quite unabashed about her consultations with La Vigoureux and La Voisin, claiming that she had visited the latter "to see those Sibyls she had promised me, a company well worth the journeys." The judge asked her if she had also seen the Devil. "Yes," she replied, "and he was small, dark and ugly, just like you." She was acquitted, and left the court gaily, remarking, "Really, I would never have believed that wise men could ask so many silly questions."[7] Her sauciness delighted Mme. de Sévigné but irritated Louis, and the impertinent Duchesse had to spend several years in the country as punishment for contempt of court. As the trials continued, art inevitably imitated life as record audiences gathered to watch the marvelous special effects of Corneille's smash hit *The Fortune-Teller,* which featured plenty of sulphur and explosions.

La Voisin's trial proceeded, and there were suggestions of even more skeletons in the cupboard. Once again, Athénaïs de Montespan was linked with the circle of poisoners. La Voisin was accused by other prisoners of having delivered "love potions" to Athénaïs's sister-in-law, the Duchesse de Vivonne, at the palace of St. Germain, where they had been placed into the hands of one of Athénaïs's personal maids, Mlle. des Oeillets. It was of course no crime to procure harmless charms from a fortune-teller, but the thought that so serious a criminal as La Voisin had been able to come so close to the King was troubling. Wary that the mention of Athénaïs's name in the context of the trials would provoke a furor, Louis had rather compromisingly written to La Reynie in September 1679: "I herewith instruct you to proceed as speedily as possible with such interrogations, but to make transcripts of these responses on separate folios, and to keep these folios apart from the official records of the rest of the investigation." When the arrests began early in 1680, with the Duchesse de Vivonne under suspicion thanks to the confessions of the prisoners at Vincennes, Louis stayed her arrest, since she was effectively a member of his family. To deviate quite so obviously from his public declarations in his private actions was not typical of Louis, and suggests that he was already afraid of what the public inquiry might reveal.

Finally, Lesage made a concrete accusation against Athénaïs. He claimed to have assisted La Voisin in 1667 when Athénaïs had supposedly consulted her for a spell to get rid of Louise de La Vallière and ensure her own place as favorite. Lesage also alleged that La Voisin had attempted to present a poisoned document to the King, and that she and Mme. de Montespan had plotted to murder Mlle. de Fontanges, who had been at the height of her favor the previous year. Although La Voisin confessed to numerous serious crimes, including that of helping the distinguished writer Racine to murder his mistress, the actress Mme. du Parc (Racine was cleared of the charge), she consistently denied any connection with Mme. de Montespan, or any attempt on the King's life. Interrogated by Louvois himself, she insisted that she had had no commerce with Mme. de Montespan's maid, Mlle. des Oeillets. She did admit to saying a blasphemous novena at the request of a girl named Cato, who wished to enter Mme. de Montespan's service as a maid, but claimed that the spell had failed and that she had never seen the girl again, and had no idea whether she had in the end joined Mme. de Montespan's household. The "petition" she had tried to present to Louis had been an innocent request, such as every French subject had the right to put to him on certain special days. La Voisin, a more skilled practitioner than Lesage, would in any case certainly have known that percutaneous poisoning, whereby the chemical enters the body through the skin, was largely an ineffective fantasy, producing at best an irritating rash which could become infected. La Voisin spent her last few days in prison drinking and carousing, unrepentant, and even when put to the "question extraordinary" she refused to name Mme. de Montespan.

The procedure followed by the Chambre Ardente was that La Reynie would submit the names of suspects to the prosecutor-general, after which they would be arrested, interrogated and perhaps paraded before other prisoners to be identified. Then they would either be freed or progress to a second examination. If they were still under suspicion, they could be put to torture, on the result of which "extraordinary" questioning the final sentence would be delivered. At each stage of the investigation, the findings of the preliminary questioning and the questions ordinary and extraordinary were put to the judges, who would decide whether to acquit or to continue the trial. Various revolting forms of torture were used, such as forcing gallons of iced water into the gullet to cause the victim to burst, the rack and branding irons. La Voisin was condemned to interrogation with *les brodequins,* a process in which the legs were crushed between wooden planks and systematically broken with hammers. One source of the confusion surrounding the testimonies of the accused of the Chambre Ardente is that confessions extracted during such appalling agonies were often subsequently retracted by condemned prisoners unwilling to die with a lie on their consciences. La Voisin, it was claimed, held firm, but a note from La Reynie shows that in her case the authorities merely went through the motions of applying the dreadful *brodequins,* causing no real damage. Why? Only Louvois or Colbert could have ordered such a special dispensation. Was this evidence of favor in high places, suggesting that La Voisin's silence was a loyal one, and that she was hopeful of a last-minute reprieve? Or was the torture countermanded through fear of what she might reveal under duress? Whatever the case, La Voisin followed her colleagues La Bosse and La Vigoureux to the fire drunk and defiant, although some witnesses claimed that as smoke began to engulf the pyre in the Place des Grèves, she whispered urgently to her confessor that "a great number of persons, of all sorts of conditions addressed themselves to me to ask for death and the means to procure it . . . it's debauchery which is the first cause of all this disorder." If this is true, was it a reference perhaps to the King and his famous double adulteress?

La Voisin's death on 4 February 1680 seemed to liberate the tongues of the witches imprisoned at Vincennes. Suddenly, they began to pour forth a flood of accusations against Mme. de Montespan. The first to speak up was Marie Monvoisin, La Voisin's daughter, who claimed she had been too terrified of her mother to confess previously, and who had already tried to commit suicide in her cell. Her charges against Athénaïs fell into three categories, first, that she had used on the King "powders" obtained from La Voisin, second that she had conspired to murder Mlle. de Fontanges and the King, and third that she had participated in black Masses to gain the Devil's help in keeping the King's love.

With regard to the "powders," Marie said:

Every time something new happened to this lady and she feared the good graces of the king were diminishing, she advised my mother of it so she could bring a remedy. My mother therefore said Masses over these powders destined for the King. They were powders for love. There were black ones, gray ones, and white ones. My mother mixed them. Some were passed beneath a chalice by a preacher. Yes, it happened that I carried these powders to the lady myself. The first time, if I remember properly, was two and a half years ago [this would place the events in 1678, around the time of the birth of the Comte de Toulouse].

The lady came to my mother's house and, after having spoken together, my mother brought me to the lady and said to her, "Madame, will you be sure to recognize this girl?" The lady said, "Yes, if we arrange some signal." It was arranged that day, a Thursday, I think, that the lady would come the following Monday to the Petits-Pères, and that I would have a mask, that I should kneel and pretend to pray, when I saw the lady I would rise and, without stopping, put into her hand the hidden packet of powder which my mother had given me. Another time, it was between Ville d'Avray and Clagny . . . that I met this lady to put into her hands a powder that had been passed beneath the chalice.

Marie also maintained that on another occasion she had gone with her mother and a group of others to Clagny to deliver fifty louis' worth of powders, though she herself had not gone inside. At every one of their supposed meetings, "Mme. de Montespan" had been masked. Most of the powders had been delivered to the maid Mlle. des Oeillets, and Marie had only learned the name of this mysterious, cloaked brunette through a slip of the tongue by her mother.

The conspiracy against Mlle. de Fontanges was developed, according to Marie, at the end of 1679. Marie's former fiancé, a man named Romani, was to gain entry to La Fontanges's house by posing as a silk merchant. Romani's brother was the priest who confessed Mlle. des Oeillets, so access was to be arranged through her. Romani's testimony corroborated these details. The plan was to poison La Fontanges with silks impregnated with arsenic, and for good measure La Voisin was said to have provided a pair of poisoned gloves as well. Marie also claimed that Athénaïs de Montespan, in a rage at having been discarded for La Fontanges, had plotted against the King. "My mother told me that the lady wanted at that time to go to extremities, and tried to induce her to do things for which she had much repugnance. My mother gave me to understand that it was against the King, and after hearing what took place at Trianon's, I had no doubt about the matter."

La Trianon was another "artist in poisons" who had been arrested on the evidence of Marie Bosse. She had often worked with La Voisin, and the alleged attempt to assassinate Louis was supposedly formed at her house in the Rue Beauregard in Paris, where the witches decided that Trianon would prepare a poison-soaked petition, which La Voisin would put into the King's hands at St. Germain. Marie Monvoisin was under the impression that her mother and La Trianon would be paid 100,000 ecus for the task.

Marie's third series of accusations concerned the black Masses Athénaïs was alleged to have commissioned, and in which it was claimed she had also participated, in 1673. The ceremonies were performed using the naked body of a woman as the "altar," and "communion" was celebrated from a chalice containing wine mixed with the blood of a newborn infant. Three or four babies had purportedly been sacrificed on Athénaïs's behalf. Marie claimed that she had seen "the lady lying on a mattress, her head hanging, a napkin on her stomach and on the napkin, a cross, at the base of the stomach, and the chalice on the stomach." The first Mass had taken place, she said, at the chapel of Villeboursin, near the château of Montlhéry. The woman Marie believed to be Athénaïs de Montespan had recited the incantation for the ceremony: "Astaroth, Asmody, Princes of Friendship, I conjure you to accept the sacrifice of this infant I present to you for the things which I ask, which are that the friendship of the King and Monseigneur the Dauphin should continue towards me, that I should be honored by the princes and princesses of the court, that nothing I demand from the King should be denied to me, as much for my relations as for my household." After this Mass, Marie claimed, her mother had decided that two more would be necessary, but Mme. de Montespan had said she really did not have the time, and so they had been conducted on her behalf, with a witch substituting for her. The second had been held at St. Denis and the third at La Voisin's house, several weeks apart.

The priest who performed the ceremonies was the Abbé Guibourg, who had also been arrested. Marie Monvoisin added that Guibourg had told her he had performed a similar Mass in 1674, on a woman "whom he did not know and who everyone always told him was Mme. de Montespan." Guibourg had served as chaplain at Montlhéry since 1664. The château was owned by M. Leroy, a relation of Mlle. des Oeillets, governor of the pages of the Petit Ecurie, a significant court post. The château, with its high, dark walls and deep moats, was an appropriate setting for Guibourg, whose face was so hideous that it terrified people and who, if the accusations against him were only partly true, was an appallingly evil man. He broadly confirmed Marie's accusations, but said that the first Mass had taken place in 1667 or 1668, in the rooms of Mme. de Thianges at St. Germain. He quoted the incantation from memory: "I ask for the friendship of the King and that of Monseigneur the Dauphin, and that it should continue towards me, that the Queen should be sterile and that the King should leave her table and her bed for me; that I should obtain of him all that I ask for myself and for my relations; that the King should leave La Vallière and look at her no more, and that, the Queen being repudiated, I can marry the King." Guibourg also supported the contention that Mlle. des Oeillets had been the go-between for La Voisin and Mme. de Montespan.

This was all unimaginably horrible. La Reynie might overlook some imprudent fooling with love potions, but sorcery, child murder, treason? What would happen if it became known that the mother of the King's legitimized children had been dealing with witches and conducting satanic ceremonies within the walls of a royal palace? Was it conceivable that the legendary beauty who had governed the court with such spirited tyranny was capable of such repugnant crimes? Evidence from the other prisoners at Vincennes seemed to suggest that this was so.

Jeanne Chanfrain, one of Guibourg's mistresses, testified that she had given birth to seven children by him, of whom three or four had been sacrificed to the Devil. Madeleine Gardey, the wife of François Chappelain, chief almoner to the King, claimed to have participated in a black Mass at St. Sulpice, where a note saying that Mme. de Montespan "wished to be loved by a person of consideration" had been passed beneath the chalice. Two of her servants, Françoise Filastre and La Dumesnil, had also been arrested. Dumesnil said that she had distilled the entrails of a baby whose throat had been cut to prepare a potion on behalf of Mme. de Montespan. Françoise Filastre had a lover named Coton, yet another corrupt priest, who had also taken Marie Bosse and Madeleine Gardey as mistresses. Coton had performed abortions and sacrificed his children by Françoise Filastre. Filastre maintained that she had practiced poisoning, and that, with Madeleine Gardey and Guibourg, she, too, had sold powders to Mme. de Montespan. Furthermore, she confessed under torture that Madeleine Gardey had asked advice on Mme. de Montespan's behalf as to how to murder La Fontanges and remain in the King's good graces. Together, they had provided a poison for Mme. de Montespan to give to her rival, and planned to try to smuggle La Filastre into Mlle. de Fontanges's household. They had also intended to poison Colbert.

The other witnesses were Bertrand, who admitted to being part of the conspiracy with Romani to kill Mlle. de Fontanges; Delaporte, a witch who claimed to have witnessed a black Mass said by Guibourg for Mme. de Montespan, and La Duverger, yet another witch, who was the mistress of the Abbé Mariette. She lodged in the same house as Lesage, and testified that her room in the Rue de la Tannerie had been used for a black Mass said for the death of Louise de La Vallière in 1667. Mariette reiterated the evidence that had been suppressed at the Châtelet investigation in 1668, which La Reynie summarized:

> Mariette, wearing his surplice and stole, sprinkled holy water, and read a Gospel over the head of Mme. de Montespan, while Lesage burned incense, and Mme. de Montespan recited an exorcism, which Lesage and Mariette had given her in writing. The name of the King occurred in this exorcism, and that of Mme. de Montespan, as well as that of Mme. de La Vallière. The exorcism was intended to obtain the favor of the King and the death of Mme. de La Vallière: Mariette said it was merely to get her sent away.

Mariette also explained that they had taken away two pigeons' hearts, given by Mme. de Montespan, which were passed under the chalice at a Mass said by Mariette at St. Severin some days later, attended by Mme. de Montespan.

Such an incestuous labyrinth of corruption and murder might, in the following century, have sprung from the imagination of the Marquis de Sade, but there is no doubt that La Reynie, at least, took the witches at their word. From this complex web of evidence, it was possible to build up a picture of witchcraft that corresponded with the crises of Athénaïs's relationship with the King over twelve years, from 1667–8 when she had consulted Lesage and Mariette about retaining the King's love and disposing of Louise, to the apparent triumph of La Fontanges in 1679.

Had Athénaïs really resorted to black magic, infanticide even, in desperate pursuit of her ambition? An examination of the evidence suggests that Athénaïs was as innocent of the major crimes of which she was accused as she was guilty of the minor ones, and it is therefore surprising that a good many historians have chosen to accept the words of the witches as truth, and to paint Athénaïs as black as her accusers. It is not, however, difficult to exonerate her of the charges of murder and satanism if the testimonies of the prisoners are examined alongside the circumstances of Mlle. de Fontanges's death, the involvement in the case of Louvois and the ever-present Mlle. des Oeillets, and finally the reaction of Louis himself. The Affair of the Poisons, and the relative degree of Athénaïs's part in it, is crucial to any understanding of her life as *maîtresse en titre,* and the historical significance of her role at Louis's court would be compromised without confirmation of her innocence.

The use of torture must cast doubt on many of the confessions. Marie Monvoisin was not tortured, but she was suicidally depressed, and the years she had spent as her mother's assistant must surely have distorted her grasp on reality, a supposition borne out by her hysterical belief that her mother could attack her with spells from a separate prison cell. With her mother dead, there was no one to dispute her evidence. Françoise Filastre retracted her entire confession, elicited by the terrible *brodequins,* on the way to the scaffold, saying that she did not wish to die with such a vicious lie on her conscience. One theory as to the epidemic of confessions that emerged after La Voisin's death was that the prisoners attempted to prolong their lives by mentioning Mme. de Montespan, as the investigations this would necessitate would keep them from the pyre. Although it has been proved that the security at Vincennes was not sufficiently lax for this to have been a collective plan — and indeed the coherence of many of the testimonies suggests that a lot of the prisoners believed themselves to be speaking the truth — it is notable that not one witness was able to swear that he or she had actually seen Mme. de Montespan, in spite of their eagerness to bring up her name.

Both Marie Monvoisin and Guibourg said that they "believed" that the naked woman serving as the altar for the black Mass had been Mme. de Montespan. The only physical picture provided was that of Marie Monvoisin, who described the masked woman who visited her mother as a "tall brunette." Athénaïs was medium-sized and blond, and Marie agreed that the woman she had seen was in fact Mlle. des Oeillets. Guibourg was not able to prove that he had seen Mme. de Montespan, either — even at the Mass supposedly celebrated in

Mme. de Thianges's rooms, he had only been "told" that the woman who had participated was Athénaïs. His memory of the incantation repeated on this occasion, in 1667 or 1668, seems suspiciously clear and, most importantly, the date he gave contradicted that supplied by Marie Monvoisin, who placed the Mass in 1674. If Marie's date was correct, then the request that the King should abandon Louise de La Vallière would have been superfluous, since she had not only already been dismissed but had left the court. If Guibourg's date is accepted, then although the La Vallière argument would stand, the request for the friendship of the Dauphin would seem odd, as he was only six years old at the time. Moreover, the incantation seems to have been concocted by someone with no knowledge of court affairs or customs. The Queen had already proved that she was not sterile, and since this was the only acceptable reason for a monarch to repudiate his wife, the request that Marie-Thérèse be discarded for Mme. de Montespan is ridiculous. Besides, Athénaïs herself would have known that even if the Queen were dismissed, she herself could not marry Louis unless her own husband, from whom in 1667 she was not even formally separated, was to die. It is inconceivable that Athénaïs would have recited such stupidities, however nefarious her intentions.

Further doubts on the reliability of the Vincennes confessions are cast by the role of Louvois, whose presence in the Affair of the Poisons was prominent from the start. More properly, such matters should have been within Colbert's jurisdiction, and the progress of the investigation may in some ways have been influenced by the rivalry between the two ministers. Louvois's thirst for power was notorious — Saint-Simon goes so far as to suggest that he may have encouraged Louis to go to war simply to ensure his own primacy. The conclusion of the Dutch wars in 1678 meant that, for the present, domestic affairs, and therefore Colbert, took first place. Colbert had always been an ally of the Mortemart family, and was a particular friend of Athénaïs's. Mme. Colbert had cared for the youngest of the mistress's children, Mlle. de Blois and the Comte de Toulouse, and in 1680 Colbert's third daughter, Marie-Anne de Seignelay, had been married to Louis de Rochechouart, the eldest son of Athénaïs's brother the Duc de Vivonne. Apart from their brief coalition in the Lauzun affair, Louvois had always disliked Athénaïs, and, sensing the way the wind was blowing, had already openly declared himself a "Maintenoniste" (he was subsequently to be a witness at Louis's second, secret, marriage). Louvois therefore had a good deal to lose if, as had happened so many times before, Athénaïs once again succeeded in making Louis return to her. If, on the other hand, her reputation should be irreparably blackened, Louvois, via Mme. de Maintenon, would have a great deal of influence over the King.

When Louvois, who had been following La Reynie's investigations ever since the La Grange case, heard of the arrests of La Bosse, La Vigoureux and La Voisin, he wrote to Louis expressing his concern at the "extraordinary" revelations that were appearing. He interviewed Lesage in his cell, and offered him a pardon if he would talk. As the arrests began, it was notable that many of the accused were friends of Colbert — the Duchesse de Bouillon, the daughter of Louvois's deceased rival the Maréchal de Turenne; the Duchesse de Vivonne, mother-in-law to Colbert's daughter; the Duc de Luxembourg, whom Louvois hated because of Louis's faith in his generalship. When the news of Luxembourg's arrest began to circulate, Louvois rushed to him and offered to help him escape, saying that he would be mad not to flee into exile — a flight that would of course have been most convenient for the minister.

It is quite possible that Louvois manipulated the other prisoners as he manipulated Lesage, and encouraged them to name Mme. de Montespan. Louvois was certainly spreading rumors that someone close to Louis was involved in the poisonings. On 3 February 1680, before Marie Monvoisin began her revelations, he wrote to La Reynie: "With regard to that person to whom the use of poisons is not unknown, that person whom you consider dangerous to allow to remain at court, the King has judged it appropriate to receive you and hear you on that matter." Given that the arrest warrants for those aristocrats involved in the case had already been served, on 23 January, and that Mlle. des Oeillets had left Athénaïs's service in 1677, there could only be three possible identities for this person. The maid Cato, whose position La Voisin had tried to help her secure, but who, she claimed, knew nothing about any of the witches' other activities; the Duchesse de Vivonne, who had now been twice accused of dabbling in the occult; or, as Louvois's self-conscious discretion seems to insinuate, Athénaïs herself. It is implausible to go as far as to suggest that Louvois was in fact the author of the whole Affair of the Poisons, but two remarks he made do prove that he was aware that the prisoners were lying. To the governor of Besançon, in 1682, Louvois said that

Lesage "could never have said a word of truth,"[8] and to M. de Chavelin, Intendant of the Franche-Comté, he confessed that all the *sottises* (idiocies) uttered against Athénaïs de Montespan were without foundation. So was Louvois pushing Louis to believe the worst about his former favorite? Since September 1679, Louis had been anxious enough about possible scandal to have some of La Reynie's documents kept apart, as instructed in his letter of the 21st. Marie Monvoisin had accused Athénaïs on 26 July 1680, and on 2 August, Louis wrote again to La Reynie:

Having seen the declaration made on the twelfth and twenty-sixth of last month by Marie Marguerite Monvoisin, a prisoner in my château at Vincennes . . . I write this letter to tell you that it is my will that you make every effort within your power to get to the truth of the statements made in her declarations and in her answers to your questions. It is my intention that you take every precaution to make sure that all reports dealing with this particular inquiry be filed in special dossiers, kept separate from the records of the investigation.

At this point, the relationship between Louis and Athénaïs had reached an all-time low. They had not slept together since the birth of the Comte de Toulouse, and had not met in private for months. In the spring, they had had an embarrassing public quarrel sparked by a complaint by Louis about the strong perfume Athénaïs had taken to using. Was he becoming paranoid about the source of his mysterious headaches? Athénaïs snapped back that if she had those imperfections of which he accused her, at least she had no offensive smells about her. They quarreled again when Louis refused to take supper at midnight in her rooms, as had been his custom for years. Colbert intervened, and Louis was persuaded to change his mind, though only on condition that the whole court was present. Was he afraid of Athénaïs's temper, or of the dangers of her table? Despite the tensions, however, appearances were kept up, and Athénaïs and her six-year-old daughter Mlle. de Nantes had been included that summer in the customary progress to Flanders.

On 1 October 1680, the day that Françoise Filastre was burned alive in the Place des Grèves, Louis called a halt to the proceedings of the Chambre Ardente. No such action had ever been taken before, but it seems that both Louis and La Reynie were convinced of the impossibility of continuing the tribunal without further compromise to Athénaïs de Montespan. At this stage, the chief of police seems to have been firmly convinced of her guilt, and to have been torn between his duty and his loyalty to the King. "I affirm that my spirit is confounded," he noted, "in the discussion of all the reasons that I have tried to examine, as subject and as judge, and what an effort I make to keep nothing before my eyes but my duty." As far as La Reynie could see, there was no way around the conundrum. "I have done what I can since I examined the proofs and the accusations to assure myself and to remain convinced that these facts are true, and I could not get to the bottom of it. I have researched, on the contrary, all that could persuade me that they were false, and this has been equally impossible for me."

La Reynie continued his investigations privately, on Louis's behalf, and began to consider the involvement of Mlle. des Oeillets. When questioned, she denied all knowledge of the poisoners, and defied them to identify her, but when she was presented to them in November 1680, all the living prisoners who claimed to have known her identified her correctly. For La Reynie, this seemed to be the definitive proof that Mme. de Montespan was guilty of sacrilege, of the attempted murder of Mlle. de Fontanges, of the murders of children and of treason for giving aphrodisiacs to the King and for attempting to murder him. In La Reynie's opinion, she deserved the fire. Mlle. des Oeillets, though, was never punished, and died a comfortable and wealthy woman in 1687. If La Reynie had pursued the accusations about her more closely, he might have come nearer to what seems the only likely solution to Mme. de Montespan's involvement in the Affair of the Poisons.

Claude de Vin des Oeillets was born in 1638, and entered Athénaïs's service in about 1668, thanks to the support of the Duc de Mortemart, who was a protector of her mother, a well-known actress. She remained in service until 1677, when she retired to her fine *hôtel particulier* near Clagny. On her death, she left two other properties in Paris, a country house, a carriage, expensive Dutch china, plenty of diamond and pearl jewelry, rich Flemish tapestries and over 2,000 gold louis. She had not come by such wealth entirely through her services to Athénaïs. According to Primi Visconti, "This lady gave out that she had had commerce with the King several times. She also claimed to have had children by him. She was not beautiful, but the King often found himself alone with her when her mistress was busy or unwell. La des Oeillets tells me that the King had his troubles, and that he would sometimes spend hours before the fire, pensive and sighing."

Perhaps Louis was sighing about what Athénaïs would say when she learned that he had indeed had a child by Mlle. des Oeillets. There was no question of his recognizing the little girl, who was given the name of Louise de la Maisonblanche and baptized as the child of false parents. She was married to the Baron de la Queue, and Saint-Simon notes priggishly that the Baron had been made captain of the guards and was provided with money in exchange for having married a daughter Saint-Simon believed Louis to have had by a gardener. Louise was very jealous of her glamorous half-sisters, who became the Princesse de Conti, the Duchesse de Bourbon and the Duchesse d'Orléans, whereas she was consigned to a quiet, rather sad life in the country, though her marriage was successful and she had several children. Her mother had entertained high hopes of replacing Athénaïs as *maîtresse declarée*. Visconti recalled that "there was a Mlle. des Oeillets, the daughter of an actress, who fixed the attentions of the King for a time considerable enough for her to be able to hope to become mistress, but the taste of the King changed, which caused her such chagrin that she died of a languishing illness."

If Mlle. des Oeillets did die of love in 1687, she spent plenty of time trying to avenge herself first. It is unlikely that her hopes were ever justified, since Athénaïs would hardly have retained her services after the birth of Louise in 1676 if she felt she had reason to be concerned about Louis's loyalty. In relation to the accusations against Athénaïs, Mlle. des Oeillets was said to have been the courier of the love powders and an assistant in the plot against Mlle. de Fontanges. In 1675, she apparently approached La Voisin on her own behalf and asked for advice on how to murder the King by magic. The job was given to Lesage, but he lost heart when he heard that Louis had been experiencing attacks of the "vapors." This date is confirmed by the *Journal of the Health of the King,* which notes in October that Louis was suffering from violent headaches accompanied by breathing difficulties and shivering. A few days later, he was feverish, with burning skin and inflamed eyes, all of which was enough to scare Lesage off. His place was taken by another poisoner named Vautier. If this was true, it seems that Des Oeillets, presumably incensed by Louis's decision not to acknowledge their unborn child, had become furious enough to attempt to murder him herself.

According to Marie Monvoisin, Des Oeillets had been accompanied to her mother's house by a mysterious English "milord." Hence the origin of the story about the poisoned petition and the payment of 100,000 ecus. It is extremely doubtful that Athénaïs, even with her enormous wealth, could have raised such a sum, and even less likely that a ladies' maid could have produced it. Athénaïs's pension at the time was only 2,000 ecus, raised to 5,000 when she became superintendent of the Queen's household. Indeed, the entire budget for the state in 1679 was only 42 million ecus. This, however, was said to be the sum offered to La Voisin, Trianon and Vautier to help Des Oeillets and the Englishman flee to England if the plan succeeded. At the time, La Voisin was known to have been boasting of imminent enormous wealth and spending lavishly. Marie Monvoisin also claimed that when her mother was arrested, the Englishman offered to help her to escape. Was Des Oeillets therefore involved, knowingly or not, in some wider political plot to assassinate Louis?

Marie Monvoisin said that the Englishman was Des Oeillets's lover, and that he had promised to marry her. Was their relationship the secret behind the mysterious letter handed to La Reynie during the La Grange case, whose authoress spoke of the crime of treason and who threatened to marry her correspondent's rival if he did not succeed? It is conceivable that the Englishman, and the mythical 100,000 ecus, were part of some international conspiracy to murder Louis XIV, whose recent victory in Holland had made him the most powerful monarch in Europe. His son, the Dauphin, now a docile and indolent teenager, would be far less of a danger to the other European powers. At the time, in England especially, there was a good deal of anti-Catholic hysteria centered on the Catholic King James II, Louis's cousin, who had been deposed in the glorious revolution of 1688 and had taken refuge at the French courts, and his descendants were to plague the rulers of England with "Popish plots" for another sixty-five years. Louis's loyalty to his embattled Catholic cousin was perceived as a real threat to the Protestant cause in England. (Interestingly, the best claim to the English throne after the overthrow of James was La Princesse Palatine's, but since she had converted to Catholicism, of which she never really approved, in order to marry

Monsieur, the crown went instead to her cousin, Louis's future enemy William of Orange.) That the English "milord" might well have been using Des Oeillets's disappointed passion for the King to further the aims of a Protestant power can be no more than speculation, but the fact remains that his existence in the Affair of the Poisons has never been satisfactorily accounted for.

The conspiracy of the poisoned treaty, if it took place, did not succeed, and Des Oeillets then apparently turned to Guibourg, who mixed her a poison in the chalice consisting of her own menstrual blood, flour, bat's blood and the Englishman's sperm, claiming it would kill the King slowly. Des Oeillets's subsequent visits to La Voisin were supposedly made on the Marquise de Montespan's behalf, but Lesage confessed that "the plan was to give [the poisons] to Mme. de Montespan, and to poison the King by this means, through Mme. de Montespan, without her thinking that she was doing it." If Des Oeillets really did plot to murder Louis — and the evidence of the prisoners is much more cohesive on this point — then she played perfectly into Louvois's hands in his scheme to disgrace Athénaïs.

At the time of her questioning, Des Oeillets claimed to a friend that the King would never dare to prosecute her, and she wrote to Louvois claiming that it was Mme. de Montespan's other maids, who hated her, who were responsible for the slanders against her. Some historians view the identification of Des Oeillets by the Vincennes prisoners as a farce stage-managed by Louvois, for she was not presented to them anonymously as part of an identity parade, but merely shown, alone, to the witches. Could it not be that Des Oeillets had Louvois, rather than Louis, to thank for her immunity? That, having trapped her by having her identified, he then offered her protection to remain silent about the truth of Athénaïs's involvement with the poisoners? After all, Louvois was the only person who said definitively that he knew the accusations against the King's mistress to be false.

The last part of the accusations against Athénaïs concerned the attempt to poison Mlle. de Fontanges, and here again, Des Oeillets was involved. The King's mistress herself, and many of the court, were convinced that she was being poisoned. After her death, Madame made several references in her correspondence which show that she was certain Athénaïs de Montespan was responsible. "She died under the firm persuasion that the Montespan had poisoned her along with two of her women. It is said publicly that they were poisoned." *The Familiar Spirit of Trianon, or the Phantom of the Duchesse de Fontanges, recounting the Secrets of her Loves, the Particulars of her Poisoning, and her Death,* one of the scurrilous pamphlets circulating in Paris, featured a diatribe from La Fontanges against Mme. de Montespan: "It is you who poisoned me to satisfy your envious rage! . . . Tartary awaits you, tigress, that terrible place where all poisoners are found, frightful with the cries and the contortions made by these unfortunates! You will be placed in the same rank as Brinvilliers and the others who have attempted the lives of innocents!" What Athénaïs made of this terrible slander is unknown, and she made no public effort to defend herself. But Louis expressed a wish that no autopsy be performed, which shows that he, too, was suspicious.

It is unlikely, though, that Athénaïs, however infuriated she was by Louis's temporary obsession with La Fontanges, would have taken her seriously enough to consider stooping to murder. She had triumphed over the Princesse de Soubise and Mme. de Ludres with her wit, and La Fontanges was so notoriously stupid that it was obvious Louis would tire of her once the novelty wore off, which is exactly what happened. Moreover, as Athénaïs was famously the last person to learn of their relationship, in April or May 1679, it is impossible that she could have been involved in a murder plot which, according to Marie Voisin, was hatched in December the previous year. Des Oeillets, though, was apparently determined to do away with Fontanges, and the connection between Athénaïs and the plot of the poisoned silks can be explained by the fact that either Marie Monvoisin, knowing that Des Oeillets had previously acted as a go-between, simply assumed that this was still the case after 1677, or that Des Oeillets deliberately used her mistress's name as a cover for her own plans for poisoning La Fontanges in 1679.

The second poisoning attempt, recounted by La Filastre, also exonerates Athénaïs from any involvement. Aided by Madeleine Gardey, La Filastre had tried to enter service at the court to get closer to La Fontanges, but the attempt had failed. If Mme. de Montespan was really employing the two witches to poison her rival, it would have been nothing to her to gain them entry to the court. Des Oeillets, by contrast, no longer had any influence there. In August 1679, La Filastre left Paris for the Auvergne, to look for the ingredients for a new poison for La Fontanges, but she was short of money, and Madeleine Gardey had to sell some jewelry to pay for the journey, and then go around borrowing to pay for her friend to return. It seems strange that a woman as rich as Athénaïs would have left her coconspirators financially in the lurch. Finally, why would Athénaïs have continued her contact with the witches when La Voisin had been arrested several months earlier, and Madeleine Gardey was under police surveillance? Even if Athénaïs had wanted to poison La Fontanges, she was too intelligent to have persisted when the chances of discovery were so high. Mme. de Caylus was convinced that the rumors about Athénaïs were "without foundation," and she was undoubtedly right. All the blame for the conspiracy must surely lie with Mlle. des Oeillets, to whom posterity has not been nearly so unkind.

If it is relatively simple to acquit Athénaïs of the charge of attempted murder, while conceding that she did buy aphrodisiac powders from the witches and may have participated in some sinister though harmless rituals, the vision of her participating in the black Mass is extremely disturbing, and one which most historians, even those with a care for her reputation, have accepted as true. Three other witnesses, Mme. d'Argenton, Mme. Badouin and Dupin, an actress, claimed that Guibourg had celebrated such Masses for them. However, it is quite possible that the black Mass was a fabrication produced by the witnesses, encouraged by the prejudices of their interrogators.

Modern scholarship often takes the view that the practice of witchcraft was largely an invention of its prosecutors. The Church, after all, sanctioned belief in witchcraft — in the seventeenth century it was heresy not to believe in it, and witchcraft confessions demonstrate a consistency which suggests that formalized Devil-worship, as opposed to the "cunning" of superstitious folk practices, was learned behavior, the performance of a role prescribed by scholars and theologians. "The modern myth of Devil-worship, with its night-flying and sabbats, was a gross invention of friarly authors, an amalgam of papal fabrication with ancient pagan superstition."[9] Again and again, witch-trial confessions all over continental Europe attest to the preoccupations of the prosecutors, reflecting the educated assumptions of the authorities who controlled the law courts. The idea of the black Mass appears in theological literature in the mid-fifteenth century, and was refined by the seventeenth into such texts as Pierre Lancre's *The Tableau of Inconstancy of Wicked Angels and Demons* (1613), which provides what is practically a recipe for the alleged activities of the La Voisin circle: "To dance indecently, to banquet filthily, to couple diabolically, to sodomize execrably, to blaspheme scandalously, to pursue brutally every horrible, dirty and unnatural desire, to hold as precious toads, vipers, lizards and all sorts of poisons." The use of torture would of course exact precisely the sort of confession the inquisitors believed they needed, but "there is no good evidence that a single coven ever existed, or that witches ever participated in a sabbat of any kind."[10] Guibourg and his fellow prisoners may have been screaming out, as the mallets shattered their bones, no more than a formula already well known. "A kind of scholarly pornography was generated, while the use of torture secured the right confession."[11] It is by no means certain, then, that Athénaïs de Montespan ever laid out her perfumed flesh to serve as a bloody altar anywhere but in Louvois's imagination.[12]

It was not, however, such speculation that saved Athénaïs's public reputation and protected her from prison or worse, but the intervention of her friend Colbert. Perhaps Colbert suspected that Louvois's involvement in the case was less than disinterested. In any event, he was not prepared to let Athénaïs go undefended. He sent all the papers La Reynie had collected to an independent counsel, a lawyer named Claude Duplessis, who had recently published a treatise on criminology. Duplessis considered that, quite simply, La Voisin had no motivation for not mentioning Athénaïs (unless she had been bribed with the offer of a last-minute reprieve) and, most plausibly, that Athénaïs had no motivation for harming Louis. Colbert summarized Duplessis's analysis in an eloquent document for Louis. First, he appealed flatteringly to Louis's own judgment. "Could there be a witness more reliable or a better judge of the falsity of all this calumny than the King himself? His Majesty knows in what sort of a way Mme. de Montespan has lived with himself, he has witnessed all her behavior, all her proceedings at all times and on all occasions, and a mind as clear-sighted and penetrating as Your Majesty's has never noticed anything which could attach to Mme. de Montespan even the least of these suspicions." He goes on to discuss the impossibility of the attempted murder, discreetly observing that it was not in Athénaïs's interests to poison the man to whom she owed everything and upon whom the future of her children depended. As for "those little anxious moments of jealousy, which her affection could have produced in the mind of Mme. de Montespan," these had begun only in 1679. Colbert concludes with an appeal to Louis's affection: "Such things are inconceivable, and His Majesty, who knows Mme. de Montespan to the very depths of her soul, could never persuade himself that she could have been capable of such abominations."[13]

Given that Athénaïs was to remain at court for another eleven years, it appears that Louis was convinced. He had a stormy interview with Athénaïs who, with typical Mortemart élan, "first cried, then made reproaches and finally spoke haughtily."[14] It was at the zenith of the scandal, in 1680, that Athénaïs was appointed superintendent of the Queen's household, an honor which Louis would hardly have conferred on a dangerous woman who had plotted to poison him. After the suspension of the investigation, Athénaïs received a gift of 50,000 livres, which shows that if nothing else Louis was still prepared to pay her gambling debts, and in 1681, she appeared with Louis at a ball for Mlle. de Nantes, a surprising show of parental solidarity if Louis really believed she was a child murderer. The two youngest of their children were also legitimized that year, a gesture of respect, if not of love, and for some years at least Athénaïs maintained her position as the leading woman at court, very much a presence in Louis's daily life.

Perhaps the King had a more private reason, too, for believing she was innocent. During his involvement with La Fontanges, the royal virility had apparently needed a boost, and Louis's valet Vienne (who owed his appointment to Athénaïs — another of her ill-judged protégés) had been supplying him with aphrodisiacs. Louis also had a private medicine cabinet where he prepared his own concoctions, and if the *Journal du Santé du Roi* is to be believed, his frequent fits of the vapors may have had as much to do with his doctors' prescriptions or his own self-administered doses than any powders Athénaïs slipped him. If the King's head had ached recently, it might well have been simply because he was overindulging in Spanish fly.

So Athénaïs was protected, but the price of preserving her reputation was a grave miscarriage of justice. Just as it was impossible to condemn the guilty without compromising the *maîtresse en titre,* it was equally impossible to acquit the innocent. Having been closed by the King as the accusations against his mistress began to emerge, the

Chambre Ardente reopened in 1681 and continued its trials until 1682, when La Reynie, who considered it a dishonor to the King to have to interfere preferentially in the proceedings, had to concede defeat. It was proving impossible to try the 106 remaining prisoners without resorting to the evidence Louis was determined to suppress, and La Reynie therefore suggested that the only solution was to use lettres de cachet to lock them up for life. Of course, this meant that many potentially innocent people would live out their days chained to the walls of Besançon or Belle Ile, while others who were certainly guilty, including Guibourg, Lesage and Madeleine Gardey, were spared the fire. Some of the leftover prisoners from the Chambre Ardente were still alive thirty-seven years later, still being whipped if they spoke to their jailers, for fear that they might mention Madame de Montespan's name.

The exact contents of the documents delivered to Louis concerning Athénaïs de Montespan's involvement in the Affair of the Poisons can never be known, because he burned them with his own hands. It is uncertain, for example, how much he knew of the plotting of Mlle. des Oeillets. Was there other evidence which gave him reason to doubt Athénaïs? And if his reason convinced him of her innocence, did his superstition, his susceptible imagination, lead him back to terrible scenes of debauchery and slaughter? She was, after all, enough of a witch to have enchanted the King, and now that her spell seemed irretrievably broken, he was never quite able to trust her again. Innocent as Athénaïs surely was, there was yet sufficient ambiguity surrounding her dealings with the witches to destroy the remains of Louis's love, and to haunt her reputation forever.

Chapter Thirteen

"Hope may be a lying jade, but she does at
any rate lead us to the end of our lives along a
pleasant path."

Louis de France, the Grand Dauphin, known as Monseigneur, had
very different tastes in women from his father. Indeed, this dull,
indolent young man cheerfully married one of the ugliest princesses
in Europe, Marie-Victoire of Bavaria, and on her death in 1690 contracted a secret marriage with her even uglier lady-in-waiting, Mlle.
de Choin. It was fortunate both for him and for the Bourbon bloodline that his inclination was so in step with his duty, for when the time
came for him to be married in 1680, Marie-Victoire was the only real
choice. The Grand Dauphin's mother, Queen Marie-Thérèse was,
along with her sister the Archduchess of Austria, the last truly sane
member of the Spanish royal family which, by the end of the seventeenth century, had really become very peculiar indeed.

Since it was known that the King wished Marie-Victoire to be
admired, no one ever mentioned her plainness. Her teeth were rotten, she had a sallow complexion with brown stains set off by a huge
nose, and the rough red hands of a kitchen maid. The Dauphin,
though, was quite delighted with his Dauphine, and as she compensated for her looks with intelligence and education, the court universally approved of the match. Mme. de Maintenon was particularly
delighted, as the Dauphin's marriage was an opportunity for Louis to
heap more attention on her. After the Affair of the Poisons, it seemed
that there was no chance of Athénaïs recapturing his heart.

In 1679, even as the King's romance with Mlle. de Fontanges was in full bloom, it had appeared that *les deux sultanes,* as Athénaïs and La Maintenon were known, were neck-and-neck in the race for the royal favor. Perhaps La Maintenon would replace La Fontanges to gain the ascendancy, or perhaps Athénaïs would make a late comeback. This competitive ambiguity was preserved by the prestigious posts Louis bestowed on each of them. For some time, Athénaïs had been soliciting for the job of superintendent of the Queen's household. This was the highest-ranking position for a woman at court, and was one of the few things that Louis, out of good taste, had ever denied her. To calm her wrath over his infatuation with Mlle. de Fontanges, Louis bought the commission for her from his old flame the Comtesse de Soissons (who left Versailles as a result of the poisons scandal) for 200,000 ecus. But the fact that Athénaïs had been barred from receiving a duchesse's *tabouret,* and that the duchesses were still able to take precedence over her, continued to rankle. Louis solved this by inventing for her the title of chief adviser to the Queen, a position which was to carry a duchesse's privileges, including at last the blessed *tabouret.* Surely Athénaïs must have felt, as had Louise de La Vallière and as would Angélique de Fontanges, that being officially permitted to sit down in the presence of a man by whom she had had seven children was a poor exchange for the loss of his affections.

La Maintenon, by contrast, had every reason to feel encouraged. When the household for the new Dauphine was created in 1679, Louis took the unprecedented step of creating a second post of *dame d'atour* specifically for the former governess. This meant that La Maintenon would now be a member of the Dauphine's household, requiring her to be officially in Louis's company, which was not the case for the superintendent of the Queen's household, a more administrative post. Both marquises were included in the royal party that set off to greet Marie-Victoire, but when the court returned to Versailles, the sharp eyes of the *Gazette* noticed that it was Mme. de Maintenon, not Mme. de Montespan, who occupied the coveted seat next to the King in the royal carriage.

Mme. de Sévigné's letters are now full of the growing influence of the King's new favorite. On 5 June 1680, she notes: "The credit of Mme. de Maintenon still continues . . . She goes to visit him [Louis] every day, and their conversations are of a length which give rise to numberless conjectures." On 9 June: "Mme. de Maintenon's favor is constantly increasing, while that of Mme. de Montespan is visibly declining." A court joke had the two marquises meeting on the Queen's staircase at Versailles. Says La Maintenon to La Montespan, "What! Are you going down, Madame? I am going up."

At court, people recalled the Grand Divertissement of 1668, at which Louise de La Vallière, Athénaïs de Montespan and Françoise Scarron had all been present together. Had they but known, ran the joke, that here were the past, the present and the future seated at the same table. Mme. de Sévigné reported of "Mme. de Maintenant": "Nothing now but perpetual conversations between her and the King, who gives all the time he used to bestow on Mme. de Montespan to Mme. la Dauphine" (and, by implication, with La Maintenon, her *dame d'atour*). If Athénaïs had cherished the hope that Louis would return to her after he tired of Fontanges, she knew she could no longer sustain it after the stresses of the Chambre Ardente or in the face of such obvious neglect. She refused, however, to take the traditional route to the convent. Her only chance of remaining at the court which had been her life for twenty years was to displace La Maintenon by any means available. Mourning the loss of her looks with the melancholy peculiar to the beautiful, she "was ready to die with mortification at the influence obtained by wit and conversation"[1] and, embonpoint or no, was determined to trump La Maintenon's wit with her own. But what Athénaïs had not realized was that times had changed. She had always been more concerned with amusement than with truthfulness and, having once bested Louise de La Vallière's dull earnestness with her own fantastic humor, she found herself as bewildered as her old rival now that La Maintenon had been clever enough to make sincerity a fashion. Appearance had been everything to Athénaïs in her desire to impose her *gloire* on the world, but she had allowed appearance and artifice to become conflated. So, though she remained Louis's mistress in name, she was horrified to discover the frailty of her true position.

One small reassurance was that Athénaïs's erstwhile employee was unpopular with much of the court. La Maintenon's secretiveness and ostentatious piety, as well as the long hours she was spending closeted with Louis, gave rise to fear and distrust. And amid the obsession with etiquette and precedence which was becoming the main occupation of many of the aristocrats enclosed in this city of the rich, the governess's humble birth and rather dubious history counted against her.

It was on this front that Athénaïs launched her first attack. Madame Scarron's bohemian marriage of convenience, her early poverty and her pretensions to an aristocratic lineage had already disgusted the Dauphine and her cousin Madame. Both German ladies were intractable on the subject of breeding, and one of their pleasures was making life a misery for those courtiers with flimsy quarterings. Gratifyingly for Athénaïs, they both hated La Maintenon for her upstart influence over the King, and in this they were joined by the Duc de Saint-Simon who, while he came to resent Athénaïs for the precedence her bastard sons were given over the dukes of France, did respect her for the purity of her own lineage. For good measure, Athénaïs made sure that the governess's sexual history was also called to account. "Could she suppose that people would always remain in ignorance of the first volume of her life?" mused Mme. de Sévigné, and while it appears unlikely that La Maintenon had indeed led the life of a merry widow, there are certain ambiguities in her history which lent credence to Athénaïs's malicious insinuations. It was rumored, for instance, that she had had a lesbian relationship with the great courtesan Ninon de Lenclos. The basis for this gossip was a pornographic novel, *L'Ecole des Filles,* published in 1655, in which the experienced Suzanne initiates the timid Fanchon, said to represent the young Mme. Scarron, into the delights of sapphism (the English diarist Samuel Pepys bought a copy in secret and pronounced it "a mighty lewd book"[2]). Ninon's own recollections do not confirm this, but Voltaire notes that the two were intimate friends, and slept together for several months, this being "a fashion in friendship."

An unexpected ally in Athénaïs's campaign against the governess was Charles, Comte d'Aubigné, La Maintenon's brother. Although he was to benefit from his sister's position in acquiring the governorship of Aigues-Mortes, this poor and cowardly soldier was constantly carping that he had not been made a duke, or even a *maréchal.* Although the Comte was a boastful, pompous spendthrift, he shared his sister's intelligence, and the court delighted in his witty remarks, particularly when they concerned the history of the widow Scarron in her days at the Hôtel d'Albret. Saint-Simon recalls that he "used no restraint when he described her amorous adventures, and contrasted them with her present piety and majesty." He was to refer insolently to Louis as "my brother-in-law," which caused La Maintenon enormous embarrassment. Altogether, he was a thorn in her side, "forever chasing after whores in the Tuileries and spending a vast deal of money on them."

If Aubigné was a burden, his wife was even worse. The marriage had been arranged as a favor by Mme. de Montespan in 1678, when La Maintenon was still officially governess to Athénaïs's older children, but it may have been something of a backhanded gift, for Mme. d'Aubigné, the daughter of a Parisian doctor, was, in Saint-Simon's snobbish words, "if possible, even more plebeian than her birth . . . marvelously stupid, of commonplace appearance, and so totally devoid of any social sense that Mme. de Maintenon found it equally embarrassing to receive her in company or refuse her admittance." Mme. d'Aubigné retreated into the company of her vulgar Parisian friends, but constantly disgraced La Maintenon with her public complaints about her husband's extravagance and ill-treatment. La Maintenon, ever ready to manipulate religion for her own convenience, complained to the priests at St. Sulpice, who managed to talk d'Aubigné into entering a "gentlemen's retreat" where he could live quietly on his pocket money in lodgings. Poor Mme. d'Aubigné was persuaded into a convent, which, according to La Palatine, she thought "very hard lines after all that had happened, and that they might well have spared her that." Much to Athénaïs's glee, the Comte d'Aubigné, an unwilling captive, told everyone what a liar his sister was for boasting of his conversion. He escaped to his Tuileries whores as often as he could, but was always recaptured by the priests, and eventually put under the surveillance of a "companion," an extraordinarily dull priest named Madot, who quite literally bored him to extinction. La Maintenon's only use for Christian charity, it seemed, was control.

With Angélique de Fontanges now weeping and fussing because she was no longer loved, and Louis spending ever more time in the governess's room, it was apparent that he cared nothing for such calumnies, and Athénaïs changed tack. Perhaps the ruse of distraction, though it had admittedly misfired with La Fontanges, would now serve to rid her of both of her rivals at once. Mme. de Caylus reports that Athénaïs attempted to draw Louis's wandering eye to her own young niece, Mme. de Thianges's daughter the Duchesse de Nevers, "in order to preserve the royal favor in her own family." Mme. de Sévigné confirms that on one visit to Versailles with her mother, her aunt and Louis, the Duchesse was so bedecked with flowers that she rivaled Flora herself. De Sévigné, who perceived

Athénaïs's game very well, adds archly: "How dangerous such a jaunt would be to a man who had anything of the libertine in his composition!" The plan was not a success — perhaps Flora's charms were too demure, too springlike, to ignite the aging royal imagination — and Athénaïs next attempted to push one of her own household, a voluptuous creature named Mlle. d'Ore, upon Louis's affections. Mme. de Maintenon was by now alarmed, noting in her correspondence: "I have been suffering terribly from melancholy vapors . . . I believe you already know Mlle. d'Ore. On Saturday she partook of *medianoche* with the King. They say she has a sister even more beautiful than herself, but that is no concern of ours." Whether or not "*medianoche*" is used here as a polite euphemism, Mlle. d'Ore was no more of a hit with Louis than the Duchesse de Nevers. Maybe the ailments of La Fontanges and the carping of La Montespan were more than even the King's celebrated libido could withstand.

Yet in spite of the plotting and the rivalry between them, the two Marquises hated one another with the greatest cordiality. Athénaïs was fundamentally too good-tempered to allow a feud to interrupt a good conversation, and on one famous occasion when the two ladies were obliged to take a carriage journey together, Athénaïs suggested as they set off: "Let us not become the dupes of this affair, but converse as if we had no cause to quarrel. Of course, that will not necessitate our loving each other any the more, and on our return we can resume our former relations."[3] Perhaps, since there were now younger courtiers, such as the Dauphine, who had not known her in her days of triumph, and who saw her merely as the disgruntled mother of the King's bastards, Athénaïs needed La Maintenon as a link with her past, someone who would respect her for what she had been. Although she was consumed with jealousy and distress at her rival's role in Louis's life, her feelings were of the type which ignite passionately and dissipate quickly, and she was not inclined to remain in a state of constant anger. La Maintenon describes one occasion when they took a walk together in the gardens of Versailles "arm in arm and laughing heartily, but we are on none the better terms for all that." Athénaïs continued to mock La Maintenon's *dévot* circle. She went, along with other court ladies, to one meeting in La Maintenon's rooms where each contributed a monthly purse of alms for the poor. Seeing the long-faced nuns and priests waiting outside,

Athénaïs remarked: "You could not hope for a better attendance in your antechamber, Madame, were it the day of your funeral."[4]

The most exciting event at court that year, 1680, was the birth, in a sweltering August, of the Dauphine's first child, the Duc de Bourgogne, the heir to the throne in the third generation. As the Dauphine went into labor, messengers gathered outside the palace, ready to gallop the news all over France, and when the child was born the cries of delight could be heard at the other end of Versailles. The Abbé de Choisy recorded the universal joy at the event in his memoirs: "We became almost crazy . . . everyone took the liberty of embracing the monarch, who gave his hand and kissed everybody. The common people seemed out of their senses." The courtiers ripped up the parquet in the Galérie des Glaces and piled it with whatever else they could find — furniture, sedan chairs, old clothes — on to a huge bonfire to celebrate. Perhaps the only people who were not beside themselves were the poor Dauphine who, after a thirty-hour labor in a room crowded with ambassadors — who by custom were permitted to witness royal births — lay stifling in a freshly flayed sheepskin, and Athénaïs. "She evaporates our joy, she dies with jealousy," crowed La Maintenon, as though she herself were a member of the royal family, suggesting that Athénaïs was annoyed because this birth was not as shameful as those of her own children. Once again, Athénaïs was forced to acknowledge that she was no longer the cynosure of Louis's eyes.

The following year, 1681, did bring some consolation to Athénaïs in the final removal of La Fontanges and the legitimization of Mlle. de Blois and the Comte de Toulouse. As well as a mark of Louis's continuing regard, if not of his love, this was a strong indication, if any were needed, that he considered her absolved from any incrimination in the Affair of the Poisons. Yet that same year also delivered a crushing blow in the death of the six-year-old Mlle. de Tours on 15 September, despite (or perhaps, given his subsequent record, because of) the attentions of the new royal doctor, Fagon. The court was at Fontainebleau, from where Louis instructed the monks of the priory of St. Pierre de Souvigny to bury his "*très chère fille*" in the vault of the Ducs de Bourbon. The funeral took place on the 19th, and the child was carried to the tomb in her little coffin, draped in white satin with a silver cross, by the light of 600 candles. Athénaïs's grief at her daughter's death has already been described in her letter to her son the Duc du Maine. Cruelly, she was not able to attend the funeral, as she had to depart for Bourbon on a mission to negotiate on Du Maine's behalf with the Comte de Lauzun, the former friend she had betrayed, who had finally been released from Pignerol.

Lauzun had Athénaïs to thank for his freedom, though her motives in procuring it do her little credit. Du Maine was undoubtedly Louis's favorite child, and both his parents felt that he required titles and estates to befit the position he would hold at court as an adult. Since the boy was illegitimate, there was a limit to what Louis could do for him, and the only other member of the royal family with sufficient wealth at her disposal was Louis's cousin Mademoiselle, whose marriage to Lauzun the King refused to allow at the eleventh hour. The still unmarried granddaughter of Henri IV remained the richest woman in France, with the principalities of Dombes and La-Roche-sur-Yon, the duchies of Montpensier, Chatellerault and St. Fargeau, the earldom of Eu, the barony of Thiers and numerous other fiefdoms at her disposal. Marie-Thérèse was hoping that this vast inheritance would be left to her own son, the Dauphin, but since Mademoiselle loathed her after the Queen had sided against her in the Lauzun affair, this was unlikely. Athénaïs, however, had remained on good terms with Mademoiselle. Fortunately for Mme. de Montespan, Mademoiselle had never suspected her involvement in Lauzun's disgrace, and had continued to treat her as a confidante.

With Louis's implicit encouragement, Athénaïs had set to work on Mademoiselle in the hope of obtaining lands for Du Maine. She had hinted that perhaps it might still be possible for the thwarted marriage between Lauzun and Mademoiselle to come off. Louis's anger towards Lauzun had cooled, and Athénaïs, who was now in need of as many allies as she could find, guessed that Lauzun's enmity towards her for having him put in prison would probably dissolve in his gratitude to her at obtaining his freedom. What could Mademoiselle do, she had wondered, to please Louis enough to grant "her heart's desire"? Mademoiselle had soon perceived the aim of Athénaïs's insinuating flatteries, the invitations to carriage and boat rides and the friendly intimation that, "in time, circumstances change." One of Lauzun's friends, Pertuis, put the point more bluntly. "Make them hope that du Maine will be your heir."[5] To convince Mademoiselle that she still had enough power to secure Lauzun's release, Athénaïs had had Colbert intervene at Pignerol for an amelioration of the terms of Lauzun's imprisonment, and from 1679 onwards, he had been permitted to take walks and receive visits. Colbert, using a friend of Lauzun's named Barrail as a go-between, had conveyed the Marquise's terms clearly to Mademoiselle.

Athénaïs was asking for the two juiciest titles of Mademoiselle's estate, the principality of Dombes and the earldom of Eu, for her son. She wheedled and charmed and coaxed so energetically that she wore Mademoiselle down. The King's cousin begged for time to recover from her troubles. When she heard that Athénaïs wanted the titles bestowed immediately, rather than as a posthumous inheritance, she was outraged. She felt too well, she said, to see any present advantage in dying. Worried that the plan might collapse, Athénaïs hinted at ever more favorable terms — who knew whether the lovers might not be reunited at last? On 2 February 1681, Mademoiselle, too exhausted to resist any longer, and pinning all her hopes on the possibility of happiness with Lauzun, signed away Dombes to Du Maine and bestowed Eu upon him, in a false sale, for the sum of 1,600,000 livres.

Athénaïs probably knew all along that Louis, who was too nice to play any active part in such a despicable swindle, had never had any intention of permitting Lauzun to return to court, let alone to the welcoming arms of his cousin. All Mademoiselle received in exchange for her king's ransom was Lauzun's release and permission for him to live as an exile on his estates. Athénaïs, though, was quick to blame Louis's strictness for the failure of a plan conceived out of her own dishonesty. When she was finally forced to admit to Mademoiselle that there was still no question of a marriage, she tried to pretend that she had never made such an extravagant promise. "What, he will not come straight here, after all I have done!" gasped Mademoiselle.

"How difficult you are to please," drawled La Montespan.

The coup de grâce came on a walk in the park at St. Germain, when Athénaïs airily mentioned that "the King also asked me to tell you that he does not wish that you should think of marrying M. de Lauzun." Officially, then, Lauzun would not be recognized, but Athénaïs carelessly suggested that he and Mademoiselle could perhaps marry in private. Mademoiselle was furious, since it would be impossible for her to live openly with her husband if they were not equally publicly wed. Athénaïs was hardly in a position to pronounce on the propriety of anyone's marital situation, and she dismissed Mademoiselle's conscience with the argument that in fact she would be much happier, as Lauzun would love her even more if their relationship were clandestine. "Secrets add to the taste of things," she added wistfully.[6]

Mademoiselle was not a Bourbon for nothing, and she had kept one trick up her sleeve. She had granted Athénaïs's request only on the understanding that Lauzun would be able to return to her, and now, she announced, she would have to compensate him, for during his imprisonment she had "sold" the earldom of Eu to him. In September 1681, therefore, mourning her daughter, Athénaïs was dispatched to Bourbon to try to persuade Lauzun to surrender the title. She proposed to grant him lands worth 40,000 livres a year in exchange, but Lauzun demanded the restoration of his post as captain of the bodyguard, a gift from the treasury of 200,000 livres and for the pensions he had missed while in prison to be backpaid. Since Mademoiselle was complaining that she had already given enough, Athénaïs had to pay dearly to secure her son's future. Lauzun eventually received the barony of Thiers, the estate at St. Fargeau and a further revenue of 10,000 livres as joint compensation from Mademoiselle and Athénaïs, who was now obliged also to negotiate between the King and his cousin. Having been duped once, Mademoiselle was determined that this time she would get her way, and that Lauzun should be allowed to return to court. If he wasn't, the grant to Du Maine would not be permitted to be made public. Louis wrote a hypocritical letter to Colbert, feigning surprise at Athénaïs's intervention on Mademoiselle's behalf, and reiterating that while "I am upset when I do not know how to do what she wants," his cousin had been shown amply "my pleasure in granting to Lauzun what I have just granted him."[7] Athénaïs finally managed to bring Mademoiselle around, and Du Maine publicly received his estates, yet neither she nor Mademoiselle was ultimately rewarded for their efforts. With hindsight, Mademoiselle admitted that she had been checkmated by Athénaïs, who was far more skilled in court politics, but Athénaïs herself gained no real satisfaction from her shabby victory. Du Maine felt no gratitude to his mother, and turned against her viciously in favor of his old governess, while Louis, whatever the extent of his collaboration in Athénaïs's efforts on their son's behalf, was not prepared to acknowledge her help. Lauzun, whose eventual rehabilitation at court was due in a large part to Athénaïs, married not poor Mademoiselle, but the fourteen-year-old sister-in-law of the Duc de Saint-Simon. In private, he would squeeze himself into his old guards uniform and dream of what might have been.

The episode demonstrated all too plainly just how marginal Athénaïs's role at court was becoming. The King did visit her in her apartments, between Mass and dinnertime, and briefly after supper with the Dauphine, but he now restricted their private contact to conversations of only a few minutes' duration. The only truly intimate moments in the day of a man who lived his life before a permanent audience of 5,000 people were the two or three hours he spent between working or hunting and in the evening with Mme. de Maintenon.

With the permanent establishment of the court at Versailles, Louis solidified the rigid, ritualistic timetable for which he became so famous, known as *le mécanique du Roi*. Anyone in the country could look at a clock at any given hour and know exactly what the King of France was doing. He rose at eight o'clock sharp, awakened by his valet and those privileged mortals who had the right of the Grande Entrée. After prayers and brief ablutions came the Seconde Entrée, which consisted of the most assiduous courtiers competing fiercely to attract a word, or even a look, from the King. The day after his father's death, Saint-Simon was ecstatic when Louis favored him with the remark: "Ah, here is the Duc de Saint-Simon." It was one of just three occasions on which Louis spoke to him.

After a brief session with his ministers, the King proceeded to Mass. During his walk to the chapel, any courtier was permitted to speak to him, though since he kept up a brisk pace, their inquiries had to be brief, and were invariably met with a laconic "I'll see." After Mass, Louis was closeted with his ministers, and the courtiers had to hang around waiting to bow to him as he left his Cabinet for the Petit Couvert, his first meal, which he ate alone, or occasionally with Monsieur, though in full view of the court. Then it was time for an outing. The King, in a new suit and wig, would set forth in his carriage to inspect the park. Another change of clothes, and he retired to his rooms, or Mme. de Maintenon's, with his family and his dispatch box. At ten in the evening there was the ceremony of Grand Couvert, in which the King dined with his family, and which anyone in France had the right to observe. Then, until midnight, Louis withdrew to his rooms, again with La Maintenon, everyone sitting stiffly on their armchair, straight-backed chair, or stool, the princes on their feet. The King's official bedtime brought a reverse of the morning's ceremony, with one gentleman selected for the honor of holding the royal candle for the reading of the evening prayer.

The royal family now presented a most edifying spectacle of orderly domestic life. The King seemed to be converting sincerely to religion. He was spending those hours he did not bestow on Mme. de Maintenon with his wife, and the neglected Queen blossomed beneath this unexpected attention. "I am informed that the Queen is very well at court, and that the complaisance and interest she has shown during the journey [to Flanders in 1681] . . . have gained her a thousand marks of regard," reports Mme. de Sévigné. In a scheme of consummate hypocrisy, it was Mme. de Maintenon who had encouraged Louis to finally pay attention to his little Spanish wife. Marie-Thérèse was pathetically grateful to the woman who had once conspired to keep her husband's illegitimate children invisible. "She was touched to the very verge of tears, and exclaimed in a kind of transport, 'God has raised up Mme. de Maintenon to bring me back the heart of the King!'" La Maintenon worked on the poor Queen's timidity with no disinterested motive, happily accompanying that lady to pay a call on the King when she was too overawed by her magnificent spouse to do so alone. The Queen's gratitude was very public, and La Maintenon notes that she has been presented with the royal portrait as a mark of esteem, adding gleefully "Mme. de Montespan never had any such thing."

In the eyes of her supporters, Mme. de Maintenon was achieving marvels, restoring order and respectability at last to the libertine court. "All good men, the Pope, the bishops, applauded the victory of Mme. de Maintenon, and considered that she had rendered a signal service to the King and to the State," comments M. Lavallée.[8] Pope Innocent XI did indeed take an interest in the activities of Louis's self-appointed spiritual mentor, hoping that the King's conversion might pave the way to a reconciliation between the Vatican and the French court, between which relations were strained. La Maintenon received various gifts of relics and prayer books from His Holiness, the most appropriate of which was surely the preserved corpse of a martyr. La Maintenon was in paradise at this gratification of her immense spiritual pride, but she was careful to represent her joy to her confessor, Abbé Gobelin, as mere satisfaction at discharging her pious duty. "I am but too much extolled," she wrote to him, "for certain good intentions which I owe to God." The only outward signs of her changed position were her indulgence of a hitherto dormant taste for finery and an increased haughtiness in her manner, though she continued to behave sycophantically to the Queen.

The court was bewildered by their monarch's attraction to this quiet, mysterious, middle-aged lady. How had she come to have such an influence over him? Primi Visconti summarizes their theories:

> No one knew what to believe of it, because she was old: some saw her as the confidante of the King, others as a procuress, others as a skillful person to whom the King was dictating his memoirs of his reign. It is certain that with regard to the change in her clothes and manners, no one could explain what had taken place. Many were of the opinion that there are men who are drawn much more towards older women than to younger ones.

This last suggestion hints at the truth. For despite the pomposity of her pronouncements on sin, her harrying of Athénaïs over her adultery, and her rejoicing in the conversion of her monarch, which she had been trying to effect for the previous seven years, Françoise d'Aubigné had become the King's mistress. If he had not previously had a taste for mature charms, Louis seems to have developed one.

It seemed to be Marie-Thérèse's eternal fate to be deceived by those who professed friendship towards her. As Athénaïs had done long ago, La Maintenon impressed the Queen with her demonstrations of piety and used her encouragement of a reconciliation between the royal couple as a cloak for her own machinations. But why had she chosen to make what was clearly a tactical surrender? Interestingly, her correspondence with the Abbé Gobelin for that year has been lost, but the letters she exchanged with her siblings seem to impart a new sense of joy and confidence. It is uncertain exactly when their sexual relationship began, and therefore impossible to know whether the post of *dame d'atour*, for example, was a reward or a bribe. Since there was no new official mistress after the fall of Angélique de Fontanges (although Athénaïs still nominally held the title), it seems probable that Mme. de Maintenon took her place in about 1680. It is improbable that such an energetic forty-two-year-old as Louis would remain chaste for long, and likely that La Maintenon felt it was more prudent to succumb to his advances than to risk losing her hold over him to yet another mistress. The conclusive proof that she had become his lover is a remark she subsequently made to Mme. d'Aumale: "I was happy, and only concerned to amuse him, to remove him from women, which I could not have done had he not found me complaisant and always ready. He would have sought his pleasure elsewhere if he had not found it with me."[9] Perhaps this chilly widow of forty came to regret this "complaisance," since she found herself fulfilling her conjugal duties into her seventies.

How, though, did she reconcile her own adulterous behavior with years of condemnation of that very sin? The *correspondance générale* of Mme. de Maintenon gives some clue, although these papers should be read always as a contrived exercise in posthumous public relations rather than the ingenuous revelations of the lady's private thoughts. Since Mme. de Maintenon professed to believe that she had been chosen by God to bring the King, and thus the realm of France, back to the path of virtue, she saw the sacrifice of her own virtue as a necessary and therefore forgivable inconvenience. This long explanation by M. Lavallée, one of her most ardent supporters, suggests as much.

> People saw with dismay that this Prince had not yet abandoned the irregularities of his youth, that he was becoming more and more the slave of his pleasures, and that he was advancing towards a disgraceful old age, in which his own glory and that of his country would be tarnished. Now the King was not only the head of the state, but its very soul; he was the country incarnate, a sort of visible Providence and the lieutenant of God on earth . . . What would have become of this royalty of divine essence and its divine and glorious mission with a Prince neglectful of his first duties, whose passions rose superior to all the laws of God and man, surrounded by women imploring a glance from him and by courtiers who had built up infamous hopes on the future scandals of a licentious reign? . . . Out of this slough Mme. de Maintenon drew Louis XIV; she brought him back to his duties, to the assiduous care of his realm, to the good example which

he owed his subjects; she dissipated the clouds of pride which enveloped him, and made him descend from Olympus to inspire him with Christian sentiments of repentance, of moderation, of tenderness . . . and, above all, of humility.[10]

What price a little extraconjugal sex in return for such miracles? It might be argued, however, that since Mme. de Maintenon's tenure as mistress coincided with the most disastrous wars, ruinous expenses and isolationist hubris of the reign, Louis might have been better to remain a Jupiter in the pagan realms of Athénaïs than to descend into Catholic bigotry in the virtuous bed of his pious widow. La Maintenon's own perception of her role in Louis's life, however, corresponds with Lavallée's invocation of the divine role of the King. It would be no exaggeration to say that she believed herself to have saved France, as well as her monarch, from the lubricious embrace of Athénaïs de Montespan.

On 30 July 1683, Mme. de Maintenon's expectations changed dramatically. In May that year, the court had departed on the summer progress to inspect the troops stationed in Burgundy and Alsace. The Queen returned to Versailles in July with an abscess on her arm, from which she developed a fever. Doctor Fagon, the King's new physician, bled her, and then, against the advice of the other surgeons, administered a huge dose of emetic. Marie-Thérèse went into violent convulsions and it became clear that she was going to die. Courtiers idling in the Galérie des Glaces were astonished to see Louis sprinting towards the temporary chapel to fetch the viaticum, tears streaming down his face. The Spanish Queen died peacefully, with the Grand Dauphin at her bedside weeping and kissing her hands. Through his own tears, Louis declared remorsefully: "This is the only grief she has ever caused me."

The Queen was the only one of Louis's women he had never loved. Such a sad, quiet, dutiful little life she had lived, the least vivid satellite in the Sun King's orbit. In the last year of her life she had had the pleasure of her husband's increased gentleness, but her existence had always been a marginal one, rewarded by the court only with dim respect rather than with love or indignation. Before she died, she whispered pathetically that she had known only one happy day since she became Queen. Was it perhaps her wedding day? Marie-Thérèse was a hopeless Queen for such a King, and not having done any harm is a sorry royal epitaph, but at least she died under the happy delusion that her husband had returned to her at last.

After visiting the corpse and sprinkling it with water, Louis departed immediately for Monsieur's house at St. Cloud, since etiquette did not permit the monarch to remain in the same house as a corpse. He then repaired to Fontainebleau, where he was joined by Mme. de Maintenon as part of the Dauphine's suite. The governess was attired in such voluminous mourning, and wore such a lugubrious expression, that Louis had to laugh at her excess of sincerity, and indeed it seemed that he himself had completely recovered from the death of his wife. He was sporting a fetching purple half-mourning, and appeared disinclined to relinquish the delights of the new hunting season out of respect for Marie-Thérèse.

Between La Maintenon's affected gloom and Louis's callousness, the only person who appears to have behaved with a proper sense of decency was Athénaïs de Montespan. She was disgusted by the lack of distress exhibited by the King, Monsieur and Mademoiselle. The latter, chastened, remarked that during Marie-Thérèse's illness, Athénaïs had tended her faithfully, and that after her death she showed all her Mortemart breeding in the way she performed her duties. Unlike La Maintenon, smug in her billowing black, Athénaïs behaved like a great lady, possessed, as Mme. de Caylus put it, of "an elevated spirit," who knew the value of her public role regardless of any compromised private integrity. Marie-Thérèse would have understood.

After the Queen's heart had been embalmed and taken to Val de Grâce, her corpse was carried through the silent, black-draped rooms of Versailles and taken to St. Denis. On the way back, recalls Mademoiselle in her memoirs, everyone laughed a good deal in the carriages, while the accompanying musketeers amused themselves by hunting the plentiful game on the surrounding plain. No one was present to see the body interred. With Marie-Thérèse already forgotten, what was to become of Athénaïs, whose post as superintendent of the Queen's household no longer existed?

Perhaps if it had not been for the Affair of the Poisons, Athénaïs might now have been granted her dream of becoming the King's wife. It was clear that Louis, still a relatively young man, would marry again, but equally it was unlikely that he would choose to make a state alliance. No particularly alluring foreign princess was available, the

House of Bourbon seemed assured of two generations of heirs, and Louis's arrogance sought no strategic alliance in Europe (given the state of the treasury, it is just as well for his pride that he did not attempt to seek one). Bossuet was in despair lest the King's new freedom inaugurate another phase of licentious behavior, and Athénaïs, having abandoned hope of becoming Louis's wife herself, found that she agreed with her old enemy. "We must think of remarrying him as soon as possible," she said. "Without that, so well do I know him, he will make a bad marriage sooner than none."[11] It was time for Louis to abandon public sins and sinner-esses and set an example befitting His Most Christian Majesty. It seemed sensible, therefore, for him to marry someone he liked, so that he should not be tempted into adultery once more. It was hardly difficult to identify the obvious candidate.

Many courtiers had already allied themselves to La Maintenon in anticipation of the King making her at least his official mistress. As Mme. de Maintenon left the Queen's deathbed, the Duc de la Rochefoucauld had whispered to her, "Do not leave the King now, Madame. He needs you more than ever." One faction at court was clearly confident that the governess's power would now be formalized. The Abbé de Choisy explains why Louis would have made such a choice.

> He was unwilling to marry through consideration for his people, and wisely judged that the princes of a second marriage might, in the course of time, cause civil wars. On the other hand, he could not dispense with a wife. Mme. de Maintenon pleased him greatly. Her gentle, insinuating wit promised him an agreeable intercourse capable of regenerating him after the cares of royalty. Her person was still engaging and her age prevented her from having children. To which we may add that Louis was sincerely desirous of leading a regular life.[12]

The Affair of the Poisons had brought home to Louis quite how desperate some women at court were to become his lover, and he was appalled by the stories of poisons and potions aimed at the possession of his person. His increasing religious faith was offended by the lurid revelations of the trials, and the reflection they cast on a society of women whose moral decline seemed to have descended beneath gallantry and gourmandizing, and yet whose behavior could be seen as having being encouraged by his own sinful example. The state had been compromised by the investigations and, as Louis saw it, he had therefore been compromised as well, which was intolerable to his self-esteem. A wife to whom he could be faithful would prevent him from falling in with the murderous schemings of the court ladies.

La Maintenon herself, however, was by no means certain of her position. Was it conceivable that the greatest monarch in the world could ally himself with a woman of very dubious pedigree, the widow of a disreputable poet and a former servant in his household? As long as Marie-Thérèse had been alive, Mme. de Maintenon was able to continue her mission for the domination of the King's soul under the protection of his marriage. Without the Queen, she was dangerously exposed, a contingency she had apparently never accounted for. She wrote to her brother: "The longer I live, the more clearly I recognize the futility of making plans and projects for the future; God nearly always brings them to nought, and, as He is hardly ever taken into account when they are made, He does not bless them." One senses that she felt aggrieved that God should have put her in such an inconvenient position. Her behavior in the weeks following Marie-Thérèse's death indicates a great agitation of her normally tranquil spirits. She wandered about Fontainebleau at odd hours in floods of tears, complained of headaches and attacks of the vapors, and paid no attention when anyone spoke to her. The only power she had was to withhold herself sexually from Louis, perhaps in an attempt to force his hand, and a letter written to Mme. de Brinon a fortnight after the Queen's death discreetly suggests as much. "I implore you to pray for the King, as he has more need of grace than ever to sustain a state contrary to his inclinations and habits." No great sacrifice this, since for La Maintenon sex was always a weapon, never a pleasure.

What were Louis's feelings at the time? Throughout the twenty-three years of his dynastic alliance with Marie-Thérèse, he had struggled with the conflicting exigencies of duty and desire, unable to lead the ordered personal life he longed for within the confines of his loveless marriage. Aged forty-five and becoming more and more pious, he was aware of the conflict between his own virility and the necessity of living an orderly public life. He had been troubled previously by his relationship with a married woman, but as Voltaire later remarked, "When he was no longer in love, his conscience made itself felt more keenly."[13] Athénaïs was no longer the tempestuous, enchanting beauty of the 1670s and even if he had wished to marry her, matters would have been complicated by the fact that Montespan was still alive. A wife he desired would save him from the temptations of the court, and now, since another state marriage was neither necessary nor particularly feasible, and Athénaïs no longer considered, it seemed reasonable that he should please himself. Moreover, Louis was methodical in his habits, and selecting the Marquise de Maintenon would continue two of them that were long established: replacing the current mistress with one of her ladies, and trusting as his confidants ministers who owed their status to merit rather than aristocratic birth. And as Lamartine suggested, "An attachment to Mme. de Maintenon seemed almost the same thing as an attachment to virtue itself."

Louis's natural choice was therefore the Marquise. However, to marry a commoner would be a violent assault on the God-given hierarchy of the French monarchy, and thus upon his own status and power. It was precisely such a disruptive misalliance that he had forbidden in the case of Lauzun and his cousin Mademoiselle. Françoise Scarron could never be an acknowledged Queen of France, taking precedence over the princesses of the blood — it would be an outrageous affront to what was perceived as the natural order of society. During his relationship with Athénaïs, Louis had learned that the law and public opinion could, if necessary, be swayed to his will, but marriage to La Maintenon required a more private acceptance.

That Louis had hit upon a solution is clear from the change in tone of La Maintenon's letters. Rumors were already circulating about the King's intentions, and La Maintenon was happy to encourage them. "There is nothing to reply on the subject of Louis and Françoise; those rumors do circulate — but I'd like to know why she would be unwilling?" wrote Mme. de Sévigné. "I should never have believed that difficulties in this matter should have come from her side." This comment has been interpreted as an indication that La Maintenon had refused a proposal of marriage and was anxious to set the matter straight, but it is also likely that she would have started such a rumor precisely by denying it, in order that once again her public conduct should be seen as a model of modest discretion. Either way, the ex-governess can barely contain her joy. "Do not forget me before God," she wrote on 20 September 1684 to Abbé Gobelin, "for I have a great need of strength to make use of my happiness." The "vapors" from which she had been suffering departed, according to Mme. de Caylus, at the same time as the court from Fontainebleau.

The exact date of the marriage between Louis XIV of France and the quondam widow Scarron is uncertain. Mme. de Maintenon's own letters suggest that it took place in June of 1684, when she writes to her brother with her usual mixture of humility and arrogance, "Our positions in life are different, mine brilliant, yours calm. God has put me where I am, I must do as best I can. He knows that I have not sought my position; I shall never rise higher, that is something I know all too well." The Abbé de Choisy also places the marriage in 1684, noting that he presented Mme. de Maintenon with a copy of his book *Journal du Voyage en Siam* in 1687, "three years after her marriage."[14] Saint-Simon suggests that it occurred earlier, in the winter of 1683, and this is supported by the Abbé Langlois, who claims that the ceremony was conducted on the night of 9 October 1683. Such early dates are rather surprising given that Louis continued to wear his violet mourning for some months after the Queen's death. Whenever it was held, the marriage ceremony was conducted in the chapel at Versailles, which had been prepared by Bontemps, Louis's valet de chambre. The Mass was said by the ever-complaisant Père la Chaise, and the blessing by the Archbishop of Paris, Harlay. The witnesses were Louvois and the Marquis de Montchevreuil, whose wife was a good friend of La Maintenon. No documentary evidence of the marriage has ever been found.

Louis's solution, then, was a simple one. His morganatic marriage, during which he may well have offered his bride his left hand, rather than the right, was simply to remain a secret. He could thus achieve his ends with no danger of public compromise. Perhaps no other woman could have endured such a burden, as Mme. de Maintenon did, for thirty-two years, and this strength and discretion, more than anything else, may have been the reason she was allowed to become his wife. The court was never sure that the marriage had taken place. Writing in 1686, La Palatine declared: "As long as there is no declaration, I find it difficult to believe." The next year, she commented:

I have not been able to discover whether or not the King has married Mme. de Maintenon. Many people say that she is his wife, and that the Archbishop of Paris married them in the presence of the King's confessor and Mme. de Maintenon's brother;

others deny it and it is impossible to know which view is correct. But what is certain is that the King has never had, for any of his mistresses, the passion that he feels for her; it is really curious to see them together. If she happens to be in the same place he cannot remain a quarter of an hour without whispering something to her or speaking to her in secret, although he has spent the whole day with her.

Perhaps it was the necessity for secrecy which added such piquancy to the union, for whatever its consequences for the life of the court and for France, it must be conceded that the marriage was a happy one for Louis. Mme. de Maintenon remained impenetrable on the subject, though the slight hints she dropped over time show that she was anxious that people should infer the legality of the union. To Mme. de Perou, a nun at the convent school founded by La Maintenon at St. Cyr, she observed that there was a great difference between her position and that of other mistresses of the King, such as Mme. de Montespan, since his friendship towards her was "based on sacred ties."

Louis was even able to remain faithful to La Maintenon, even if it was effectively by default, since in the 1680s his health began to fail and he grew tired of the exhausting lovemaking he had once found so rapturous with Athénaïs. Perhaps he even believed that Athénaïs's insatiability had contributed to his ailments, since medical writing warned that the effects of over-frequent sex on men were "gout, constipation, bad breath and a red nose,"[15] all of which were now spoiling his earlier handsome looks. After 1686, "the year of the fistula," Louis was really more in need of a nurse than a lover.

The anal fistula for which Louis was operated on became that year a rather humiliating matter of international interest. The English writer Jonathan Swift alluded to it satirically at some length in his description of

a mighty king who, for the space of above thirty years, amused himself to take and lose towns, beat armies and be beaten, drive princes out of their dominions, fright children from their bread and butter; burn, lay waste, plunder, dragoon, massacre subject and stranger, friend and foe, male and female . . . the philosophers of each country were in grave dispute upon causes natural, moral and political to find out where they should assign an original solution of this phenomenon. At last, the vapour or spirit which animated our hero's brain . . . seized upon that region of the human body so renowned for furnishing the "zibeta occiden-talis" and gathering there into a tumour, left the rest of the world for that time in peace. The same spirits which, in their superior progress would conquer a kingdom, descending upon the anus conclude in a fistula.[16]

Swift's reduction of Louis's mighty warrior pose to the "vapours" of his anus gives an impression of just how much the French King was loathed by his neighbors across the Channel at the time, though one story, which must have amused Louis, has it that his infected funda-ment was the inspiration for the English national anthem "God Save the King." In 1686, Mme. de Maintenon decided to give a party to celebrate the King's recovery from *la grande opération* on the problem. It was to include music composed by Lully and sung by the girls from the school at St. Cyr. Apparently, an Englishman who just happened to be passing the convent as the girls were rehearsing liked the tune so much he wrote it down, and then just happened to play it to Louis's old enemy, King William, and Queen Mary, who admired it enough to adopt it as their anthem . . .

Louis's operation was performed by the royal surgeon, Felix, who was ennobled for his success. The King bore the intervention of the scalpel with fortitude, receiving an envoy immediately afterwards, racked with pain but betraying no sign of discomposure apart from the sweat on his brow. Nevertheless, the operation signaled a change in the extraordinarily robust health he had previously enjoyed, and with it came an increasing dependency on Mme. de Maintenon. According to the *Journal du Santé du Roi,* the King's doctors were obsessed with his digestion throughout the remainder of his reign. Fagon waxed positively lyrical on the color of his excrement. Louis's huge appetite, combined with the courses of "purges" upon which Fagon insisted, left him constantly plagued by the need to relieve himself. One day, for instance, he evacuated "eight times before his dinner, twice during his council and the last, an hour after the *coucher* . . . for which he woke several times."[17] Opiates and purgative broths, bleedings and emetics kept him almost constantly uncomfort-able. The royal teeth were a mess, too, all the upper ones having been extracted the previous year in an operation which broke Louis's jaw .

and ruined the symmetry of his face, causing his cheeks to bag and jowl. Athénaïs must have been as saddened by her once beautiful lover's physical decline as she was by her own increasing amplitude.

Frustrated by the physical limitations imposed on him by his poor health, the King turned to food for comfort, and gorged more than ever, thus exacerbating the problem which had reduced his virility in the first place. La Maintenon's body thus became the means by which the Church could control the King's aging flesh. Although Louis was only forty-eight at the time of the fistula operation, from then on the *Journal* makes him sound like an aged invalid, an impression La Maintenon encouraged. However, the legendary Bourbon libido had not entirely surrendered. As has been noted, much to her disgust, the King's wife was required to submit to conjugal relations right up to the end of Louis's life, sometimes, as she complained to her confessor, as often as twice a day. She was encouraged to acquiesce dutifully, accepting with "grace and virtue" what Athénaïs had once performed with passion. Louis had once teased Athénaïs in a letter, "You are no good whatever as a nurse, being extremely hasty and impatient in everything,"[18] and she now found herself excluded from the bed of his sickness as she was from that of his pleasure.

La Maintenon's nursing may well have been a source of psychological as well as physical comfort for Louis. Family relations in seventeenth-century France were typically quite formal among the upper classes, with the "natural" role of the mother often being taken by a child's wet nurse. Louis's own nurse, a woman named Pierrette du Four, retained the extraordinary honor of being the very first person to greet the King in his state bed each morning, a recognition of an emotional connection which superseded the stringent court hierarchy. This distinction, described by Philippe Beaussant as "*du sang et du rang*," blood and rank, continued into the circumscribed dichotomies of adult life. As a mother was a social, rather than a physical nurturer, so a wife was for duty, a mistress for love. Civilized behavior is by definition in some senses unnatural, so emotional needs were distinguished from social obligations as expressions of the self. For Louis, whose every action was calculated as part of his "performance" as King, it must have been a relief to find a woman in whom both roles could be legitimately united.

Was Athénaïs, who belonged to the former pattern of Louis's emotional thinking, aware of how irrevocably she was now barred from his favor? Did he explain the marriage to her? How else could Athénaïs have begun to understand how the King of France could prefer a poor nobody to a Mortemart? They certainly had some sort of scene, because Athénaïs slammed her door in the King's face, screaming, "And what should I call Madame de Maintenon? That goose girl, that arse-wipe!" and retired with one of her migraines for some days. Despite this, on the surface nothing changed immediately, and the King continued his routine visits to both ladies as before. In 1684, however, he announced that he wished to enlarge his own apartments by annexing those of Athénaïs. For her new quarters, she was given the renovated Appartement des Bains on the ground floor, where once she and Louis had played in their octagonal pool, Venus and Neptune infinitely reflected in the mirrors Louis had positioned for their mutual delectation. The new rooms were therefore a constant reminder to Athénaïs of what she had lost, all the more so when La Maintenon took advantage of the King's convalescence after the fistula operation to have the communicating staircase between the King's apartments and Athénaïs's bricked up. Looking glasses and fountains, their beautiful insubstantiality now mirroring her loneliness, were all that remained to Athénaïs. From living next to Louis, Athénaïs was now placed directly beneath him, and although she quitted her beautiful rooms gracefully, it was a sad sign of the times. Louis had her former apartments turned into a *cadre prestigieux* where he could display his precious objects, which clearly no longer included his "real Queen."

Chapter Fourteen

"Hypocrisy is an homage that
vice pays to virtue."

Prestige at Versailles was very much determined by a person's location within the internal geography of the palace, so Athénaïs's
descent to the Appartment des Bains was interpreted by the court as
the first step towards her disgrace and her estrangement. La Maintenon had already given a not too subtle hint of the reversal of status
between herself and her former mistress. On the court visit to Chambord in September 1684, the King's secret wife had traveled in the
first carriage with Louis and the Dauphine, followed by the *dames
d'honneur* in the second. Athénaïs, accompanied by her elder children
Mlle. de Nantes and the Duc du Maine, had to content herself with
third place. She bore this slight, as she bore the loss of her apartments,
with perfect self-discipline. She realized that tantrums and rages were
no longer effective, only undignified in the face of Louis's indifference, and she called upon her well-bred self-control to deny her rival
the satisfaction of seeing her misery. Indeed, the two marquises maintained an appearance of great cordiality, even going so far as to
embrace one another in public, and seemed to take such pleasure in
one another's conversation that anyone who had seen them without
being up to date on the intrigues of the court would have believed
they were the best friends in the world.

Now that there was clearly no longer any question of Louis
returning to her, Athénaïs was desperate to preserve the role she loved
and fulfilled so admirably at court. She was still officially the reigning

favorite, and as the mother of Louis's legitimized children she still commanded a good deal of influence. Moreover, La Maintenon still preferred to keep to the shadows, and in any case had no talent for organizing the brilliant entertainments that were such an important part of the public image of Versailles. Athénaïs, by contrast, had been the center of court society for fifteen years and was adept at creating the balls, masques and parties that not only dazzled foreign ambassadors but were necessary for keeping the captive aristocrats amused. It seems that Athénaïs now accepted her defeat for first place in Louis's heart, but tried to carve out a career for herself with the skills she had practiced for so long. She kept her composure after the embarrassment of losing her apartments, and offered her former lover a stunning New Year's gift of an album of illustrated miniatures representing the sieges of the 1672 campaign in Holland, with a text by Racine and Boileau. Bound in gold, it was worth over 4,000 pistoles, a clever, tasteful and provocative present that called to mind such happy memories for Louis that he returned her generosity with the gift of the estate at Clagny to Athénaïs's children after her death.

For some time, then, Athénaïs continued to lead her usual life at court, driving out occasionally with Louis in his calèche or discussing with him the program of entertainments for the winter season; organizing parties, masquerades and card games; dressing beautifully, amusing everybody. One of her great enjoyments was driving for promenades or suppers to Louis's new pleasure house at Marly, which had been begun by Hardouin-Mansart in 1679 and which was now nearing completion. The King had consulted Athénaïs about the designs for the new house, a compliment magnified by the fact that La Maintenon, who had no sense of aesthetics, saw Marly only as an irritating extravagance. "Marly will soon be a second Versailles," she grumbled in a letter to one of her cardinals. "There is no help for it but prayer and patience."

The atmosphere at Versailles had changed since the days of Athénaïs's ascendancy. Since the court's permanent establishment there in 1682, life had taken on a greater formality, a stiffness, that even Louis found oppressive. To some extent, the rigid etiquette maintained at Versailles was a practical necessity, since without firm rules of conduct the vast household of 5,000 people would have descended into chaos, given the crowded and very public conditions of daily life there. La Maintenon once apologized for the state of a letter by explaining that it was being written at St. Germain in a room containing twenty women, three children and seven dogs. Louis's insistence on absolute control of his courtiers' lives was also admirably served by a system that kept them squabbling over the minutiae of precedence. This structure could be compared to the hierarchy used to control the ranks of an army, and it was not without a certain elegance; Saint-Simon summed it up by saying that the King existed at the heart of the greatest, strongest and most refined society that civilization could create, and yet there was something cold and inhuman about this enclosed world where every action was performed with the precision of the ballet, something that stifled spontaneity and energy. Athénaïs, to the manner born, was comfortable with the infinitesimal knowledge of detail required of a courtier, and her *esprit* and initiative could create vivaciousness within it, but La Maintenon was too mindful of her own parvenu dignity, too concerned with the secret machinations of her own power, to stimulate any lightness in those around her. Under her influence, the intractable decorum of secular etiquette was compounded by a dolorous and stringent piety. La Palatine complained constantly to her German relations that "the pervasive hypocrisy has made this court so dull that one can hardly stand it any more."

Marly was to be a retreat from Versailles, a small, informal house where the courtiers could behave a little more like human beings. People would be able to sit down in the salons, and the men permitted to keep their hats on when the company took a tour of the grounds. It looked less like a royal palace than a charming village, arranged on a new design based around a two-story, square house for the King, named, unsurprisingly, The Sun, with two flanks of six small villas, called after the signs of the Zodiac, to house those lucky enough to be invited to accompany him there. Between the main house and the pavilions were parterres and arbors filled with Louis's favorite scented shrubs, and two long pools inhabited by his favorite carp, each individually named — Proserpine, Dauphine, Dawn, Flax, Pearl, Topaz, Golden Sun, Beautiful Mirror. The park was filled with statues, and fully grown trees transported to create instant forests. Eighteen million tulip bulbs were brought there in four years to fill the flower beds with color.

An invitation to Marly was a tremendous honor begged for by the courtiers with the simple question, "Sire, Marly?" as Louis made his way down the Galérie des Glaces. Louis could relax here in a way that was impossible at Versailles, where hundreds of people witnessed his every daily action, and inevitably, the competition to join the monarch in such an easy atmosphere was fierce. Marly represented such a paradise of favor that the Abbé de Polignac, strolling with Louis in the hallowed gardens during a shower, dismissed a friendly remark from the King about the inadequacy of his coat with the gloriously absurd statement that this was nothing, since "the rain at Marly is never wet."[1]

Athénaïs's spirit was visible at Marly, in the capricious, eccentric style of the house, in the deliciously scented park and in the gaiety they inspired. Offering her views on the plans with Louis and his architect was the last contribution she made to the buildings which characterized the reign, and it is sad that Clagny, the first Trianon and Marly no longer stand as a monument to her talents. According to contemporary descriptions, there was a unity, an elegance of scale and a whimsicality in these buildings which created a beauty never achieved by the heavier magnificence of Versailles. The house was not completed until 1686, but Louis still used Marly, as he had Versailles, for parties and excursions before it was finished. Athénaïs organized the official opening party, which included a ball and a jolly concert at which everyone joined in the singing, as well as little stalls selling trinkets in four of the apartments, each named after the seasons. Spring was served by her youngest daughter, and Summer by Mme. de Thianges, while Athénaïs symbolically reserved Autumn for herself, and with a pleasing irony, Winter for Mme. de Maintenon.

Athénaïs's children were now the greatest evidence of her authority, as well as her main source of emotional succor. Following the death of his sister Mlle. de Tours in 1681, the little Comte de Vexin had died, aged twelve, in 1683, the same year as Queen Marie-Thérèse, mourned by Mme. de Maintenon as well as by his mother. Athénaïs's four surviving children were now more precious than ever. There is no doubt that she suffered dreadfully over the loss of the other two, whatever the suggestions of some hostile historians that she was an indifferent or neglectful mother. It is true that she often displayed a *laissez-aller* attitude towards her offspring. On one occasion, while she was away at St. Germain, she was told that a fire had broken out at the Rue Vaugirard house. In response to this news she merely observed that it would bring the children luck, and carried on playing cards. Perhaps this seems extraordinarily unemotional, but there was, after all, very little she could do from St. Germain, and she was obviously sensible enough to realize that since the message was from Mme. Scarron, she and the children could hardly have burned to cinders.

Any judgment of Athénaïs as a mother must be made in the context of the mores of her time. Childhood, as the term is now understood, was a modern concept in the seventeenth century. It has been suggested that prior to the eighteenth century there was a marked parental indifference towards children dying young, rooted in a pessimism about their chances of survival and manifested in a stoicism in the face of their deaths. Because of the fragility of children's lives, as infants they "didn't count" as people, a concept illustrated in Molière's play *Le Malade Imaginaire,* in which the hero, L'Argan, is said to have only one child, his daughter Louison being too young to be considered an individual. Aristocratic babies were sometimes given titles, but not a Christian name, for similar reasons. The first daughter of Athénaïs's granddaughter the Duchesse de Chartres, for example, was known before her death in infancy only as Mlle. de Valois. This attitude was essentially medieval. What might look to us like indifference may have been the best response in a world in which infant mortality was an everyday tragedy, since in fact there is ample evidence to suggest that grief, rather than mere resignation, was a common response. "I have lost two or three children not without regret or sadness," writes Montaigne in the sixteenth century (though admittedly his lack of precision rather belies his concern).[2] The Church discouraged the mourning of a baptized child on the basis that the infant's innocence would guarantee a swift passage to heaven, but the poignant rituals enacted in the French countryside on the deaths of mothers and children attest to the desperate strength of the maternal bond. In Alsace, a woman who died in childbirth would be buried with a sturdy pair of shoes, to allow her to make the long trek back from purgatory to feed her baby. In Provence, if a mother and child died before "churching," the godmother would bring a pair of shoes to the house and announce: "Mother, the Mass is going to begin. You must get up and walk." If the floorboards creaked, it meant the mother was following to watch over her child's soul.

So there was, by the seventeenth century, a growing sense that children were psychologically separate from adults, unique individuals with characters of their own. This new attitude coexists with the medieval one in *Le Malade Imaginaire,* in which Louison, who "doesn't count," is nevertheless given a speaking role. When Bishop Bossuet was trying to persuade Athénaïs to give up the King and retire from court, she protested that she would not be able to take her children with her. "Your children," answered the Bishop, "are not necessary to you; Madame de La Vallière managed to leave hers."

"Yes," replied Athénaïs, "and in forsaking them she committed a crime."[3]

People were beginning to take pleasure in the prattling company of small children for its own sake; a pleasure expressed in the French word *mignotage.* Mme. de Sévigné writes with a note of surprise of the delight she finds in being with her little granddaughter. "I amuse myself for whole hours!" Both Louis and Athénaïs loved spending time with their children, something which had annoyed the Queen. On one occasion, when she heard some courtiers discussing the charming *mignotages* of the Duc du Maine and the Comte de Vexin, she blushed with jealousy, remarking, "Everybody goes into ecstasies about those children, while Monsieur le Dauphin is never even mentioned."

With the idea that children were individuals came a move away from the older communal tradition of child-rearing among the upper classes towards a separate upbringing. In consigning her children to Mme. de Maintenon, Athénaïs was in fact doing no more than following the fashion of the day, even if in her case — given the demands of the court on the *maîtresse en titre* and the initial discretion required to conceal the illegitimacy of the children — it was a particular necessity. The practice of wet-nursing has also been cited as evidence of maternal indifference. It is true that upper-class women believed it to be better for their figures not to breast-feed. However, more important considerations were the practical problems it presented for a woman expected to live the public life of a courtier and the fact that a wet nurse was felt to be in the best interests of a child. The milk of upper-class women was thought to be inferior, partly out of class snobbery — the delicate, well-born lady was seen as almost a different species from the more physically robust peasant woman — and partly because tight lacing and a rich diet were believed to impair the milk. The optimum start in life for a child, it was agreed, was provided by a healthy country woman with good milk. Aristocratic ladies were very fussy about the credentials of their nurses. Red-haired nurses, for example, were unpopular, because it was believed that redheads were a product of sex during menstruation and mothers feared that the suspect morals of the nurse's parents might be conveyed via her milk to the child. The painting of the birth of the Virgin by the Le Nain brothers in Notre Dame de Paris illustrates how inconceivable it was for privileged women to feed their own children at the time. Here St. Anne is relegated to the background, while the holy child is being suckled by her nurse. Breastfeeding was promoted among the aristocracy in the 1690s, but it never caught on, and the practice of wet-nursing continued well into the nineteenth century.

There was nothing, then, in Athénaïs's behavior towards her children that departed from the customs of her time or her class. If the upper-class mother played a lesser role during her child's infancy, her ultimate task was to maximize his or her prospects on reaching maturity. The socialization and the social success of daughters in particular was her primary responsibility. So Athénaïs became more involved in her children's lives as they grew up out of duty as well as self-interest, though in her case, since they were now the fulcrum of her remaining power over Louis, their success was intimately connected with her own survival.

Athénaïs took care to display her offspring to advantage. For Carnival in 1685, she gave a ball in her apartments for which Louis lent her his own musicians and dancers. The rooms were charmingly transformed into a replica of the fair at St. Germain, with the prettiest young girls of the court, masked, tending stalls selling flowers, exotic fruit and trinkets. Du Maine, Mlle. de Nantes, Mlle. de Blois and the little Comte de Toulouse all attended, publicly demonstrating Athénaïs's continuing link with the royal family. That summer, this distinction was confirmed with the engagement of her eldest daughter Louise-Françoise, Mlle. de Nantes, to the grandson of the Prince de Condé, Louis de Bourbon.

Louis's decision to marry his various illegitimate children into the royal family was one of the most controversial of his reign. Saint-Simon never got over it. His memoirs are infected by his constant invectives against the "bastards" and the way they usurped the proper prerogatives of the ancient nobility. He is in a constant frenzy of disgust at "their birth, which is blasphemy, and their rank, which is a

scandal." Not everyone felt quite as strongly as the ferocious little
duke, but even so there had been some surprise at court when Marie-
Anne, the first Mlle. de Blois, Louis's daughter by Louise de La Vallière, had been married, aged thirteen, to the Prince de Conti. In her
time, she was the loveliest woman at court, distinguished from her
sister-in-law by being known as "the beautiful Princesse de Conti."
Once, seeing the Dauphine asleep, the beautiful princess remarked
that she looked even uglier than when she was awake. She was greatly
discomfited when the Dauphine opened one eye and retorted that
she did not have the "advantage" of being a love child. Marie-Anne's
marriage made her one of the first-ranking women at Versailles but,
having inherited her mother's dullness along with her looks, she
failed to take advantage of her position; she neither charmed the
court with her society, nor, finding herself a widow at nineteen, did
she amuse it with a scandal. She did, however, show a good deal of
taste in the eyes of some in loathing Mme. de Maintenon, who grew
more haughty, scheming and imperious by the day. When her
brother-in-law was away at the front, Marie-Anne wrote to him saying that she was obliged to drive out with La Maintenon and "an old
freak" called the Princesse d'Harcourt every day. "Judge what fun this
must be for me."[4] Louis, informed by his mailbag spies of the insult,
was furious with his daughter, and La Maintenon bore her a grudge
ever after.

Like the Contis, the Condés were of the blood royal, descended
from an uncle of Louis's grandfather Henri IV. The head of the family, the Grand Condé, had been a distinguished soldier, but had never
quite rehabilitated himself after fighting on the opposite side to
Mazarin and the Queen Regent in the Fronde. The engagement of
his eldest grandson and heir, Monsieur le Duc, to Mlle. de Nantes,
the King's daughter by Athénaïs de Montespan, was therefore an
important symbol of a return to Louis's favor which outweighed the
embarrassment of the bride's illegitimacy. Indeed, "The Grand
Condé and his son left nothing undone to testify their joy, just as they
had left nothing undone to bring about the marriage."[5] Whether the
twelve-year-old bride, whose new title was to be Mme. la Duchesse
de Bourbon, was equally joyful is less clear. She was a beautiful girl,
with a truly exquisite face, and was to blossom into a curvaceous and
sexy woman, whereas her seventeen-year-old bridegroom was most
unattractive, a midget with a huge overdeveloped head (a result, it was

said, of his mother being gazed at lustfully by her pet dwarf when she was pregnant with him). Still, Louis gave a splendid party for their engagement, presenting his daughter with an enchanting dress of black taffeta overlaid with gold and pearls for the occasion. There was a promenade to Trianon in gondolas, where supper was served in pavilions of flowers while the court watched a firework display on the water. Louise-Françoise had a dowry of 1 million livres, with 100,000 a year as her personal income, while her husband received a pension of 90,000.

Despite some unkind remarks about the miniature couple — one witness described the ceremony as a "ridiculous marriage of marionettes"[6] — the wedding, on 24 July 1685, was even more spectacular. The Duc wore a coat of mauve satin, and the new Duchesse was resplendent in silver brocade with silver lace covered in emeralds and rubies. She appeared to be almost crushed by the weight of the jewels in her hair. After the ceremony, the couple were put to bed, the Dauphine handing the Duchesse her nightgown, and Louis doing the same for the Duc. Athénaïs had rather uncharitably hoped that the marriage would be consummated immediately, since she feared that the Condés might change their minds about her daughter, but since Mme. la Duchesse had not reached puberty, the bedding remained symbolic, and the next day the bride and groom returned to their respective schoolrooms. For Mme. la Duchesse, this meant returning to Mme. de Maintenon. Her mother and her governess had called a truce for the wedding day, overcome by the emotion of the occasion, and had surprised the court by greeting the couple together at the chapel door, but the next day normal hostilities were resumed. Voltaire declared the wedding Athénaïs's "last great triumph at the court of France."[7] Afterwards, the delicate porcelain Trianon was pulled down.

"Born of love and made for love,"[8] the new Duchesse de Bourbon had inherited all her mother's charm. She was "the wittiest, most malicious of women,"[9] one of those whom Saint-Simon recollects as continuing to use the particular Mortemart language and manner of speech after her mother had left the court. Even La Palatine, who hated Athénaïs's bastard children, had to admit that "she ridicules everything in such a droll manner that one can't help laughing . . . in all her life she has never had a bad-tempered moment." Unlike Athénaïs, Mme. la Duchesse left some record of this distinctive style, in a scandalous novel set in the time of the Roman emperor Augustus, with the characters drawn from the court at Versailles, which she wrote to amuse herself. Though as diminutive as her little husband, she towered over him intellectually, and it was not long before she began an affair with Marie-Anne de Bourbon's brother-in-law, the far more dashing Prince de Conti, while the Duc was away at the front. Later, she had a long-standing affair with the Marquis de Lassay, which endured until her death in 1743. She built an enormous house, the Palais Bourbon, on the banks of the Seine, with a smaller residence next door for her lover.

Although she proved a less than faithful wife, Louis always approved of his elder daughter. In 1686, she and her sister Mlle. de Blois both fell ill with smallpox at Fontainebleau. Athénaïs, in one of her last seasons at court, nursed them both round the clock. The Grand Condé, who was deeply attached to his granddaughter-in-law, also insisted on attending her bedside, where he was joined by Louis himself when her condition appeared grave. At the door of her bedroom, Condé, anxious that the King should not jeopardize his own health, tried to prevent him from entering, and "a great struggle ensued between parental love and the zeal of a courtier, very glorious for Mme. la Duchesse."[10] But Louis was so concerned that he insisted on being with his daughter, and did not return to Versailles until the Duchesse had recovered. Sadly for the elderly Condé, the strain was too much, and his exhausting devotion to the little girl cost him his own life.

Despite her frequent presence at Marly in 1686, Athénaïs endured further humiliations that year. In May, Louis departed to take a course of waters at Barèges in an attempt to cure the famous fistula. Athénaïs was not invited to join the party, and collapsed in a fainting fit when she heard that she had been excluded. Leaving for Paris in a temper, she came back a few days later to collect the Comte de Toulouse, who she planned to take with her on a visit to Rambouillet while the King was away. Just as the boy and his mother were stepping into the carriage, a spiteful message arrived ordering Toulouse to stay and accompany his father to Barèges. The cure was eventually postponed, and Athénaïs remained at Versailles with her children, but it had been a nasty reminder of the new order of things for the woman who had once commanded the King. In October at Fontainebleau, Athénaïs was lodged as an ordinary courtier, while La Maintenon enjoyed the fine suite of apartments next to the King's, where Athénaïs had made Louise de La Vallière comb out her hair so long before.

One of the most painful snubs La Maintenon inflicted on Athénaïs was publicizing the treachery of her old friend Racine. As the writer grew older, he had returned to the Jansenist beliefs of his youth, and became suspicious of his own genius, abandoning the drama because he thought it was sinful. Instead he contented himself with his role as royal historian and with the writing of occasional pieces such as inscriptions for medals. But when Mme. de Maintenon decided that the schoolgirls of St. Cyr should have a suitable religious play to perform as part of their education, she persuaded Racine to make an exception in this worthy case.

St. Cyr displayed all the best qualities of the Marquise de Maintenon's character — her cultivation, her love of learning and her talent for education. She had founded the school with Louis's help in 1686, in specially constructed premises not far from Versailles. It was intended to offer an education to poor girls from noble families — they had to prove sixteen quarterings of nobility on the father's side — whose maintenance and dowry would be provided by the monarchy. For girls from the *hobereau* class, the poorer nobility who could neither afford to come to court nor make their fortune in any profession, it was a wonderful opportunity. Unfortunately, since the school immediately became fashionable, the poverty ideal did not endure for long, but the education provided by St. Cyr for the lucky ones was sensible and enlightened, with none of the pious limitations of so many girls' convents. Athénaïs was one of the school's first visitors, accompanied by the ten-year-old Mlle. de Blois, and she admired the girls in their black dresses and aprons, with colored ribbons on the bodices to distinguish the different forms. St. Cyr endured unchanged until the French Revolution. La Maintenon was to spend the last years of her life here, and when she died she was buried in the chapel. Her pride did get the better of her a little, though: Horace Walpole, visiting the school in 1769, observed that the infirmary was adorned with "every text of scripture by which could be insinuated that the foundress was a Queen."[11]

La Maintenon was particularly concerned that the pupils should excel at French composition, and she thought that acting would improve their style. Racine obliged them with his penultimate play, *Esther*, in 1689, and the performances were a tremendous success, with Louis attending the first and last nights. But it was obvious that the piece was a thinly disguised allegory of the current state of affairs at Versailles, and in the discerning opinion of the novelist Mme. de Lafayette, it was a contemptible piece of flattery designed to bolster La Maintenon and humiliate Athénaïs. In the play, the holy, humble Esther triumphs over the imperious Vashti, and the identity of the king, Ahasuerus, needed no explanation. The wits joked that in locating St. Cyr so close to Versailles, old Esther was creating a harem for Ahasuerus, but the fact that anyone with taste declared the piece a nonsense can have been of little consolation to Athénaïs. Now that Racine had returned to religion, his loyalties were all with the enemy of his former patron, and in changing his allegiance he made Athénaïs an object of very public ridicule.

She still had her children. Athénaïs was close to both of her daughters, though in later years her maternal role evolved into that of mediator, since after the marriage of Mlle. de Blois, the two sisters became, for the most part, deadly rivals. If the court was surprised that two of Louis's illegitimate daughters had been married to princes of the blood, they were speechless at the King's choice of husband for his youngest. Françoise-Marie was to marry Philippe, Duc de Chartres, the son of Monsieur and La Palatine, and the eventual head of the house of Orléans, whose rank was grandson of France, from his descent from Louis XIII. At the time, no one suspected that her husband would ultimately become the Regent of France.

Mlle. de Blois had not, unlike her elder sister, been brought up by La Maintenon, for although she had been born at that lady's château in 1677, during the alliance Athénaïs had made with the governess to dispose of Mme. de Ludres, La Maintenon had refused to have anything to do with her, or with the Comte de Toulouse, who were, of course, the result of Athénaïs's reunion with Louis after his religious crisis in 1676. La Maintenon, cheated in her attempt to conquer the King's soul, "did not spare her exhortations and remonstrances"[12] at the birth of Athénaïs's youngest daughter, and she and her little brother were brought up in the old house at Rue Vaugirard in Paris, where La Maintenon had begun her career. Although rather too plump, Mlle. de Blois was pretty, with perfect skin and her father's melting eyes. She suffered from the defect of having one shoulder higher than the other, which Mme. de Caylus interpreted as evidence that she bore "the conflict between love and duty" in her person.

Philippe, Duc de Chartres, who became Regent of France on Louis's death in 1715, was far more talented than his indolent cousin the Dauphin or his cowardly cousin Du Maine, and suffered as a consequence. He was clever, cultivated and brave, interested in science as well as the arts. But Louis very unwisely allowed himself to be prejudiced against his nephew, and Philippe was kept kicking his heels at Versailles, forced to hear inflated accounts of the Duc du Maine's exploits on campaign and going mad with frustration. Not having inherited his father's penchant for boys, he vented his humiliation in a string of affairs with women (he became a father aged thirteen after impregnating the daughter of the concierge at the Palais Royal), drinking, gambling and dabbling in such dangerously unorthodox sciences as alchemy. Louis was perhaps rather intimidated by Philippe's promise, and forcing his daughter upon him as a backhanded honor was one way of demonstrating his power over the lesser House of Orléans.

A good deal of plotting was necessary to bring about the marriage. In 1688, Louis announced that he intended to raise a few lucky men to the Order of the Holy Spirit, one of the highest honors in France. Among the nominees were Monsieur's boyfriend the Chevalier de Lorraine and his brother the Comte de Marsan. Monsieur also submitted the names of two more of his favorites, the Marquis d'Effiat and the Marquis de Chatillon. This outrageous nomination of flagrant homosexuals to the holy order was Monsieur's pay-off for his support of the marriage. On Athénaïs's suggestion, he was also given the Palais Royal, which had previously been leased from the Crown. The real opposition to the match, however, was likely to come from Madame, La Palatine, who would never stomach such an insult to her proud German blood.

Madame had a curious relationship with the King. Like her predecessor, Henriette d'Angleterre, she was more than a little in love with him, as her obsessive reportage about his activities, preserved in her voluminous correspondence, shows. These letters, the writing of which consumed hours of Madame's day, give one of the best portraits of life at Versailles, although inevitably they are as full of gossip and prejudice as they are of hard facts. Madame and Athénaïs may not have had much in common, but they both appreciated that the most interesting part of a person's character is often the untruths attributed to it. The letters were opened by the King's spies, as Madame well knew, and she used them to make criticisms of Louis that his terrifying manner would have prevented her from making to his face. When she got wind of the marriage plot in 1688, she made her opinions clear in a letter to her aunt Sophie, the Electress of Hanover.

> I must confess to my dearest Tante that I have been most distressed lately . . . I have been made privy to the reason why the King treats the Chevalier de Lorraine and the Marquis d'Effiat so well; it is because they have promised him that they would persuade Monsieur to ask the King most humbly to marry the Montespan's children to mine, that is, the limping Duc du Maine to my daughter and Mademoiselle de Blois to my son. In this case Maintenon is all for the Montespan, since she has brought up these bastards and loves the limping boy like her own . . . Even if the Duc du Maine were not the child of a double adultery but a true prince, I would not like him for a son-in-law, nor his sister for a daughter-in-law, for he is dreadfully ugly and lame and has other bad qualities to boot, stingy as the devil and without kindness. His sister, it is true, is rather kind . . . But most of all, they are the children of double adultery, and the children of the most wicked and desperate woman on earth . . . whenever I see these bastards, my blood boils over.

Whatever her view of Athénaïs, La Palatine was quite accurate in her estimation of Du Maine. He was eventually married to a daughter of the Condé family, who was popularly thought to resemble a black beetle. The couple were so very short and so very proud that Du Maine's sister referred to them contemptuously as *"les poupées du sang,"* the dolls of the blood. Madame, relieved that her own daughter, Elisabeth-Charlotte, had been spared such a fate, explained in a letter: "I believe that the King's trollop must have been told what the populace of Paris is saying, and that must have frightened her. They are saying very loudly that it would be shameful for the King to give his bastard daughter to a legitimate prince of the house." Madame may have been pleased to flatter herself that she had public opinion on her side, but in truth Athénaïs was not in the least bit afraid of the Parisians, or of Madame, come to that, especially as Louis had already married one illegitimate daughter to a Conti.

Madame's son, however, did not escape. On 10 January 1692, she wrote again to her aunt, with "eyes so thick and swollen that I can barely look out of them," with an account of how the betrothal had come about. Apparently, Monsieur had come to her room and said, "Madame, I have a message from the King for you, which will not be too pleasing to you, and you are to give him your answer in person tonight. The King wishes me to tell you that since he and I and my son are agreed on the marriage of Mademoiselle de Blois to my son, you will not be foolish enough to demur."

Madame was far more at home on the hunting field than in the hushed antechambers where intrigue bred, but in this extremity she had bestirred herself to play the courtier. After Philippe had been talked around by his tutor, the Abbé Dubois, La Palatine had attempted to persuade him to stand up to his uncle and refuse the match. But given that Louis's manner famously reduced everyone, especially his relations, to a state of terrified agitation, it was hardly likely that he would refuse his "consent." So when Madame was summoned to Louis's Cabinet, it was to be presented with a fait accompli. She was so appalled that she barely managed a wobbling curtsey, and immediately withdrew. The engagement was announced that evening at Appartement, and the court rushed to congratulate the couple while reveling slyly in Madame's delicious discomfiture. La Maintenon could hardly disguise an air of triumph. Although she must have hated the elevation of Athénaïs's daughter, whom she had refused to raise, she had endured so many insults from Madame's pen that her delight at La Palatine's humiliation overcame her jealousy of Athénaïs. No one, however, dared to approach poor Madame, who strode weeping noisily along the Galérie des Glaces, sniffling into her handkerchief and looking, according to Saint-Simon, like Ceres after the abduction of her daughter Proserpina. At supper, neither Madame nor Philippe could eat, always a sign of extreme distress for the Bourbons, and Mlle. de Blois was so nervous in her gaudy outfit that her governess had to take her on her knee. Saint-Simon adds that the next day Madame answered her son's nervous greeting with a powerful slap in the face.

Gleeful descriptions of the affair soon sped in dispatch bags around all the courts of Europe. Madame, aware that she had made an embarrassing public spectacle, resolved to put the best face she could manage on the wedding. After all, as she wrote to her aunt, "I will have no trouble getting used to [my daughter-in-law], for we will not see each other often enough to annoy each other . . . Saying *bonjour* and *bonsoir* each morning and night won't take long."

The bride's sister, Mme. la Duchesse, was nearly as furious as Madame, and even less restrained. In marrying Philippe de Chartres, Mlle. de Blois would become a granddaughter of France through her husband's rank, and would therefore take precedence over her elder sister, a mere princess of the blood. Mlle. de Blois would have a longer train and be permitted to sit in an armchair in the presence of the King, while Mme. la Duchesse would have to writhe with envy on a straight-backed, armless chair. Even worse, Mme. la Duchesse de Bourbon would have to address the new Mme. la Duchesse de Chartres as "Madame." Neither of these great ladies was yet out of her teens. Mme. la Duchesse was so peeved that she could not bear to attend the ceremonies which, as Saint-Simon records with gloomy satisfaction, had more splendor than pleasure about them.

The betrothal took place on the evening of 17 February 1692 and the marriage the following day. At the engagement Mlle. de Blois wore a dress of gold, embroidered all over with tiny black flowers, trimmed with gold Spanish lace and decorations of diamonds and rubies, with more diamonds in her fair hair. Her fiancé was magnificent in gold brocade with pink and gold ribbons. The bride's dowry was an astonishing 2 million livres (more fuel for the rage of Mme. la Duchesse, who had received only 1 million), a pension of 150,000 livres a year and jewelry worth 600,000 livres.

For the wedding, Mlle. de Blois wore silver, while the Duc de Chartres appeared in black velvet — perhaps his mother's choice — and marvelous shoes encrusted with pearls and diamonds. At the "bedding" ceremony, the Duc was given his nightshirt by King James II of England, who had been exiled to the French court since 1688, and Madame, with gritted teeth, presented the new Duchess with hers. The next day, the fourteen-year-old girl received the congratulations of the court as she lay in bed. "Sodomy and double adultery had triumphed," wrote Saint-Simon disgustedly.

The new Duchesse de Chartres took a pragmatic view of her marriage. "I don't care if he loves me, so long as he marries me," she said of Philippe. The marriage was not really a happy one, although the couple eventually had seven children. Françoise-Marie felt isolated in her husband's family, and looked to her Mortemart cousins for support, which infuriated her hostile mother-in-law. From the beginning,

Philippe's infidelities were legion, and after the birth of his first legitimate son, Athénaïs's grandson, he installed his mistress, Marie-Louise
de Séry, in a house right under his wife's nose at the Palais Royal. He
insulted his wife further by having Marie-Louise act as hostess during
the state visit of the Elector of Bavaria. Philippe was not really a wicked
man; he was just young, frustrated and unhappy, largely thanks to the
unfair treatment meted out to him by his jealous uncle Louis.

The *"esprit Mortemart"* was discernible in Françoise-Marie, but it
was combined with a laziness and a lack of interest in court life
unknown to Athénaïs. Madame complained that her daughter-in-law
spent all her time reclining in her salon, too idle even to dine with her
family, as this would have meant sitting on a stool rather than lolling
on a sofa. The Mortemart tendency to plumpness manifested itself
early in Françoise-Marie, for she was really a glutton, and drank to
excess as well. Her pride was notorious, and she incensed Madame by
suggesting that it had really been rather kind of her to agree to
become Duchesse de Chartres, as her husband was only the King's
nephew, while she was his own daughter.

The marriage held, and a show of loyalty was maintained, at least
in public. Eventually, Madame and her daughter-in-law were reconciled, united in their hatred of the scandalous Marie-Louise. After
Philippe's mistress died, the couple grew closer, and Françoise-Marie
reigned supreme at the Palais Royal until her death in 1749.

But where, during all the scheming and plotting that surrounded
her daughter's marriage, was Athénaïs? She was not even invited to
attend. Athénaïs had to read about her daughter's marriage, and that
of Du Maine a month later, in the *Mercure Galant,* like any bourgeois
housewife hungry for a bit of upper-class gossip. Sadly, this was largely
the work of her disloyal son the Duc du Maine. Early in 1691, Louis
had announced that he intended to leave for the siege of Mons and to
take the Comte de Toulouse with him. Athénaïs was particularly upset,
since she had just learned that Mlle. de Blois was to be taken from her
charge and placed in the care of the wife of the Duc du Maine's tutor,
Mme. de Montchevreuil. To deprive her of her children was to
deprive her of her only reason for remaining at court, and Athénaïs
was deeply offended and hurt. In desperation, she asked Bossuet to
inform the King that since he obviously had no further use for her,
she required his permission to retire from court to the convent of Les
Filles de St. Joseph, in which she had been charitably interested for

some time. Perhaps she was dusting off Louise de La Vallière's old tactic to revive some flame of Louis's love. Whatever her reasons, she immediately regretted her impetuousness, for Louis received the news with perfect equanimity, and announced that this was most convenient, since he had intended to give her apartment to the Duc du Maine and to pass on the Duc's to Mlle. de Blois. Mortified, Athénaïs gathered up her baggage and her dignity and retreated to Clagny, from where she coolly announced that in fact she had not really intended to leave the court for good, and that she thought it rather hasty of him to have had her furniture removed.

It was the Duc du Maine who, far from begging his mother, the *"belle madame"* of his childish letters, to remain at his side, had gleefully sent on her things with all speed. He had also been seen throwing Athénaïs's delicate furniture out of the windows of her apartment. Du Maine had long since realized that he had more to gain from his beloved governess, the King's secret wife, than from his troublesome, embarrassing mother, and had plotted with her old enemy Bossuet to take advantage of her careless remark. What better way of ingratiating himself with La Maintenon than by sacrificing his mother? La Maintenon loved Du Maine as her own son, and they were both greedy for power and keen that the Duc should position himself as the leader of the factions that were forming among the younger generation of courtiers. Athénaïs's presence was too much of a reminder to Du Maine of his compromising birth, and in his ambition, La Maintenon found the ally she needed to achieve what she had been hoping for for twenty years.

Du Maine really was a revolting little individual. He felt no loyalty to his mother for her work in securing him the great fortune on which he founded his fantasies of power, or for the tenacity with which she had insisted on remaining at court to safeguard his future and that of his siblings. When he realized she could be no more use to him, he packed her off like a sacked chambermaid. Saint-Simon is not the most reliable judge of the characters of Athénaïs's children, but in the case of Du Maine his description seems accurate. He compares the Duc to the Devil

in malice, in perversity, in unkindness to all and good to none, in sinister plotting, in sublime vaingloriousness, in conceits without number and endless dissembling; yet with much seeming amiability, especially in the arts of pleasing and entertainment, for when he wished he could charm. Being the most arrant coward in heart and mind, he was also most dangerous, for provided he could manage it unseen, he was ready to go to dreadful lengths to escape what he feared, and would lend himself to the meanest and most despicable actions, by which the Devil lost nothing.

Du Maine's cowardice was a devastating blow to his father, who revered martial prowess, and who hoped that as his own years of campaigning drew to a close he could live his battles vicariously through his son. Louis created a special precedent to allow Du Maine to lead an army by promoting the Duc de Vendôme, the dashing, illegitimate grandson of Henri IV, to a general's command, in which, unlike Du Maine, he proved most able.

Du Maine took up his post at the head of the left flank of the Maréchal de Villeroy's army in 1695. On 14 July (not a happy date for the French monarchy), the Maréchal sent orders to Du Maine to attack the enemy, who were greatly disadvantaged, being outnumbered, out-armed, exhausted, and trapped in an open position on a plain, their only hope of escape the cover of a wood three leagues away. It would be a sure and simple victory for the French troops. Du Maine procrastinated. He had to go to confession, to reorganize his camp, to reconnoiter the position again. Six times the orders were sent, and all the while the enemy were sneaking closer to freedom. Du Maine's dithering lost the day for the French. No one at court dared to tell the King of this shocking display of cowardice, particularly as the dispatches were usually full of sycophantic exaggerations of Du Maine's heroic exploits. Louis finally learned the truth from his valet, Vienne, and "his distress was more than he could bear."[13] That night at Marly he lost control of himself in public, venting his fury on a waiter at table whom he had spotted filching a petit four. Louis leaped to his feet and rushed at the man, beating him with his cane, which was, luckily, made only of bamboo. The company, horrified, were quick to shout out their anger at this "rascal" to prevent the King from even more undignified rage. Later, the Marquis d'Elbeuf slyly asked Du Maine in public where he was planning to serve next, explaining that he meant to accompany him, since anyone who stayed close to the Duc would be sure of preserving his life.

Notwithstanding the efforts of Mme. de Maintenon, Louis had never been able to bring himself to order Athénaïs from court, but between them her own son and Bishop Bossuet managed it. "Mme. de Montespan left the court in a storm of tears and never forgave M. du Maine, who, by this monstrous service, won for himself the love and perpetual devotion of Mme. de Maintenon." Du Maine's deceitful treatment of his mother should perhaps have alerted Louis to the nasty side of his son's character, but with the King's secret wife as his champion, Du Maine knew he would remain safe from censure. He was even to deprive Athénaïs of her refuge at Clagny, despite the fact that it had been promised to her mother until her death. Du Maine demanded Athénaïs's lovely house as a wedding "gift," suggesting to La Maintenon that now his mother was banished, it would be embarrassing, and too tempting for the King, to have her so close to Versailles.

In her last days at Clagny, Athénaïs must have been surprised that she had gone on living. Suddenly, and by what seemed a banal accident, she had lost the life which she had so loved for twenty years. As long as she remained at Versailles, visited by the King, respected by the court, she could believe that in some measure she was significant. Now she was little more than the ghost of herself, "one of those unhappy souls who return to expedite their faults in the places they used to inhabit."[14] The morning of her final departure, 15 March 1691, she had wryly announced to Bossuet that he could, at last, pronounce her funeral oration. "Yes, Madame la Marquise. The King no longer loves you." The King no longer loves you, you are as good as dead.

As she wandered in the gallery at Clagny, Athénaïs may have smiled at the fresco she had chosen in the days when her whim was Louis's command. Dido, the beautiful Queen of Carthage, who is loved and then abandoned by Aeneas, mourned from her walls. In Virgil's poem, Aeneas begs Dido to save his fleet, then leaves her desolate when he sails away to found Rome, and Dido commits suicide. "Why should I palter?" she storms at Aeneas. "Why still hold back for more indignity? / Sigh, did he, while I wept? Or look at me? / Or yield a tear, or pity her who loved him?"[15] Athénaïs had held on for as long as she could, but was she, like Dido, granted at least the chance to confront her lover? Was there some final parting scene between the

King and his mistress? It appears not. That Athénaïs left Versailles in tears is all that is known.

Embodied at Versailles in the intrigues of the *dévot* party, the strictures of Bossuet and the triumphant hypocrisies of Mme. de Maintenon, the Catholic Church would perhaps seem an unlikely source of refuge for Athénaïs in her exile from court. However, that strong faith encouraged by her mother Diane in her childhood had remained a constant throughout her life, and in the years after 1691 she came more than ever to rely on it, though typically, it was in the form of action rather than the cloistered contemplations of Louise de La Vallière, that it manifested itself. Athénaïs had, as she famously remarked, never taken the liberty of committing all sins simply because she was guilty of one, and in fact had often left the King to pray privately. She had never missed a fast day or doubted the certainty of her beliefs. Now middle-aged, and deprived of much of her celebrated troubling beauty, she had nevertheless retained all her energy, and she threw herself into good works with all the zeal she had formerly spent on arranging entertainments for Louis. She was determined, it seems, to prove to the world that although she had left Versailles, her life was not over.

Athénaïs had become involved with the Filles de St. Joseph during the difficult period of the King's religious crisis in 1676, quite possibly, given Bossuet's attempts to persuade the King to break with her, in the hope of providing herself with a refuge in the event that the bishop's mission had succeeded. The order was made up of nuns who devoted themselves to the education of poor or orphaned girls, and so generous were Athénaïs's donations that by 1681, the order passed an act recognizing her as their "superior" and giving her the power to organize the rule of the order, to choose its nuns and boarders and to supervise "the well-being and utility as much spiritual as temporal of the said Maison de St. Joseph." Even if this is viewed as a shrewd acknowledgment of the "temporal" benefits Athénaïs's wealth might bring to the order, it was also a recognition of the strength of her faith, despite her status as France's most public, and in 1681, as yet unrepentant sinner.

There was a particular irony in the order's selection of Athénaïs as its patron, for one of its principal aims was the promotion of modest behavior in young women. The Filles de St. Joseph, who had been installed in Paris since 1639, were a common sight in the streets of the capital, the nuns in their black dresses with square white collars and wimples, the boarders in dull, gray serge. The uniforms were hardly consistent with Athénaïs's own extravagant tastes, and she must have been amused by the fact that in their promenades through Paris, the nuns taught the girls to walk "modestly," and not to flirt with or ogle passersby. More practically, the boarders were instructed in housework, knitting and dressmaking, so that when they left the convent at seventeen, they would have a means of supporting themselves in the "honest families" where the nuns placed them. Inspired by this useful program, which sensibly recognized that material support, as well as faith, could help women to a virtuous life, Athénaïs founded a similar society of her own in 1686. She made a large donation to set up a hospital in Fontainebleau, which became known as the Hôpital de la Ste. Famille, with the aim of providing sixty orphaned girls, aged about six or seven, with instruction in religion, writing, dressmaking and lacemaking.

In the same period, Athénaïs formed two other charitable orders, the Hôpital des Viellards in St. Germain in 1678, and a boarding house for young girls at the Ursuline convent there in 1681. She spent 17,000 livres on the hospital building, and six years later acquired land to extend the accommodation and to add a church. She was acknowledged as the "founder" of the Ursuline school by letters signed by the King and in 1685 provided the funds for new lodgings for the convent. Unlike La Maintenon, whose school at St. Cyr demanded sixteen quarterings of nobility from its students, Athénaïs was too socially secure for snobbery, and her charities were genuinely concerned with helping the poor, and women in particular. She encouraged practicality as well as piety, and she was able to ally her love of artistic patronage with her charitable aims.

Under Athénaïs's direction, the Filles de St. Joseph began to produce really beautiful needlework, from designs by celebrated artists such as Simon Delobel, tapestry-maker to the King. As well as embroidered religious vestments, described as "superb" and "perfectly beautiful" by contemporaries, the girls sewed covers for the furniture of the state apartments at Versailles, including — and again Athénaïs must have smiled — a *lit d'ange* for the King's bedroom. Other pieces included armchairs, tapestries and screens, stools and folding chairs, all worked in embossed brocade several centimeters thick. The blue velvet and gold embroideries given by Athénaïs to the Grand Dauphin were also a product of St. Joseph, and were included in a piece created by the famous furniture-maker Boulle. Ever one to claim a good idea as her own, La Maintenon presented Louis in 1689 with a bed decorated in embroidered screens from her rival's workshop: a beautiful gift, though the ambassador of Siam found the subject of the commission — all the kings and queens of France, with the princes and princesses of the blood in the costume of their times — in rather surprising taste. The fact that the school at St. Cyr later became famous for its embroideries may be largely due to La Maintenon's desire to compete with Athénaïs on yet another front.

The most impressive work of St. Joseph was perhaps the entablement created for the throne room at Versailles, which was supported by eighteen pilasters of cloth of gold on embroidered bases. In the winter, the spaces between them were hung with red velvet, in summer with hangings upon which flowers, garlands and cupids were chased in 20,000 livres worth of gold and silver. Truly fit for a king, or a queen of France. Did Athénaïs recall, in the days she spent at the convent after her ignominious flight from Versailles, that she had once dreamed of sharing that delicate, glimmering shade? What mortification to know that La Maintenon now lurked legitimately in its shadow!

It is hard to know whether the pious life towards which Athénaïs seemed to be moving in her charitable activities was motivated by anything more substantial than an observance of the conventional route for women in her position. Discarded mistresses, unmarried girls and widows all found their way to the convent, after all. Yet her energy, as much as her vanity, was unable to accept a quiet, cloistered retreat from the world, and so far as was possible, she made her penitence as public and as splendid as her disgrace. Mme. de Caylus conceded that she was possessed of a "grandeur of soul," and however limited the scope of her actions, she attempted to achieve something lasting and substantial in her pragmatic charity, something more enduring than a few decades' worth of Hail Marys. She spent her money as enthusiastically as when it had streamed across the gaming tables of Versailles; she built and organized and bossed her paupers with the same gusto she had once used to construct Clagny and order the courtiers about. Since she could no longer have the King, her vanity needed another outlet, and she was determined to be as successful as a benefactress as she had been as a mistress. Or perhaps her agony was too great to endure the silence of a convent cell.

Too proud to accept charity at La Maintenon's hand, Athénaïs requested nothing, either for herself or for her family, when she left the court. She did appear there a few more times, ghostlike: in August 1692, when the Duchesse de Bourbon gave birth to Louis-Henri, her first grandchild, Athénaïs presented her with one of her own sets of pearl and diamond jewelry, and she attended the child's first communion in 1698. In 1695 she was a guest at a supper in Paris given for her daughter and son-in-law the Duc and Duchesse de Chartres. The host was Langlée, who had once bestowed upon her that gold dress fit for a fairy empress.

Chapter Fifteen

"Old people are fond of giving good advice:
it consoles them for no longer being able
to set a bad example."

As director of the order of St. Joseph, Athénaïs was able to take an apartment in their Paris convent in the Rue St. Dominique, near to the church of St. Sulpice, where she had been married nearly thirty years before. From there, it was a short journey through St. Germain and the Quartier Latin to the Carmelite convent in the Rue St. Jacques, where Louise de La Vallière was waiting out the long years of her repentance. Drawn, perhaps, by a hope that they would find some solidarity in what was now a shared loss, Athénaïs paid her old rival a visit, and burst into tears at the sight of her.

"You weep," said Louise, smug to the last, "but I weep no longer."

"You weep no more?' asked Athénaïs sadly. "I will cry forever."

True, though, to the dignity which had supported her through so many reversions of Louis's affection, Athénaïs shed her tears in private. It seems that she and Louis had no personal contact after their separation, not even when she proudly returned her jewels to him. Perhaps she had hoped that this gesture of independence would impress him, or move him to pity. As it was, Louis merely returned to Athénaïs what was hers, keeping back only a pearl necklace which he presented to the mother of the future Louis XV, Marie-Adelaide de Savoie, wife of his grandson the Duc de Bourgogne. Court life, propelled by the unchanging rhythms of etiquette, simply moved inexorably on without her.

Athénaïs, meanwhile, held a little court of her own at St. Joseph, and if the surroundings were rather more humble than the state of Versailles or the luxury of Clagny, its mistress had retained all her famously imperious airs. "All France went there," records Saint-Simon. "She spoke to each one like a queen. Everywhere about her there was an air of widespread grandeur . . . She received, but never paid visits, not even to Monsieur, or to Madame, nor to Mademoiselle, nor to the Hôtel de Condé." The only exception Athénaïs made was for Louise. Her callers were, rather pathetically, expected to treat her with the same ceremony as they would have done at court, and even her children who, with the sad exception of Du Maine, she saw frequently, were expected to perch on flimsy little folding chairs while she reclined in state in the room's only armchair, set at the foot of her bed. Visiting her crowded little apartment was fashionable, since she was as charming and witty as she had ever been, and the ladies of the court would remind their daughters of the importance of calling on Mme. de Montespan whenever they went to Paris.

Along with the Comte de Toulouse, the Duchesse de Bourbon and the Duchesse de Chartres, Athénaïs could now count the Marquis d'Antin, her legitimate son by Montespan, among her social circle. Athénaïs had been unable to see Louis-Antoine, who had been taken to Bonnefont at the age of three by his father in 1668, for eleven years. They were reunited when, aged fourteen, D'Antin fell ill at his school, the Collège de Juilly near Versailles, and Athénaïs paid him a discreet, anxious visit. In his journal, D'Antin described his emotions at the time: a mixture of delight at her warmth and resentment at her long absence. He was perhaps unaware of how difficult it would have been for her to arrange a meeting without arousing the temper of her still irate husband. She did manage to visit the boy secretly two or three times during the following years, as he passed through the Jesuit college in Paris and then a military academy. Once he was an adult, it was easier for Athénaïs to help him, and in 1683 she had obtained for him a lieutenant's rank in the King's regiment and (with the unlikely assistance of Mme. de Maintenon), a place in the household of the Dauphin. Her caution about Montespan was quite justified. When D'Antin was injured in a hunting accident in 1686 and taken to Clagny to recuperate, Athénaïs nursed her son attentively, and he wrote rather sadly in his journal that he was all the more touched because he had never expected any show of affection from her. Montespan, rather less charmed by Athénaïs's sudden interest in their son, decided to use the excuse of the hunting accident to make an appearance at Versailles. Terrified that he would make a scene that would damage her precarious status at court, Athénaïs dispatched her son's confessor to intercept her husband with the excuse that a stormy scene between his parents might disturb D'Antin's recovery. The priest halted Montespan's carriage and, amid some shocking language from the Marquis, persuaded him to turn back. He retreated to Sèvres and whiled away his son's convalescence recounting scandals about his wife to anyone who would listen.

Athénaïs adored matchmaking, and now, overjoyed to be able to take a role in her son's life, she set about arranging his marriage, which took place later that year. Whether or not Montespan's untimely appearance had weakened her status still further, the wedding proved to be a mortifying demonstration of the low regard in which she was now held at court. Athénaïs had selected as her son's bride Julie-François de Crussol, eldest daughter of the Duc d'Uzès, and the granddaughter of Athénaïs's friend Julie de Montausier, who had contrived her early meetings with the King. (What must the bride have thought about marrying the son of a man who had quite literally scared her grandmother to death is not recorded.) Athénaïs was livid when Julie-François's family objected to the match. She was appalled that the Uzès overlooked not only her own position but D'Antin's precious share of Mortemart blood, seeing him as merely the son of an impecunious Gascon gentleman and a discarded royal mistress. This time her tantrums were of no avail, and the Uzès held firm, refusing to provide their daughter with a dowry until after their own deaths. M. de Montausier was more generous, donating 20,000 ecus and a lieutenant-generalship in Alsace, with an income of 8,000 ecus, for D'Antin. Athénaïs gave her son a pension of 2,000 ecus and furnished an apartment for the young couple. Her wedding gift to the bride was a marvelous necklace of diamonds and emeralds worth 40,000 ecus, and she also thoughtfully presented Julie with a huge bowl filled with everything an elegant woman would need at court: ribbons, gloves, scent and fans. The ceremony itself, though, was another disaster. It was held in August 1686 at the bride's family house in Paris, the Hôtel de Rambouillet, where the famous salons had been held, but despite Athénaïs's anticipation of a splendid party, no one came, not Monsieur, not any of the important courtiers, and certainly not Louis.

D'Antin had inherited his mother's ambition to succeed at court, and Athénaïs, spurred on by the humiliation of the wedding, was determined to assist him. In 1695, after her retirement from Versailles, she purchased the estate of Petit-Bourg for her son for 40,000 ecus, and engaged the architect Lassurance to dismantle the existing house and build a smart château with a mansard roof and two wings connected by a doric portico in its place. She was concerned, though, that another inherited passion, gambling, would dissipate the fortune she was spending on D'Antin, and furthermore stand him in poor stead at court, which was far less permissive now that La Maintenon had the ear of the King. She tripled her son's pension in exchange for a promise that he would surrender his ruinous habit, and commissioned Toulouse to tell the King of the young man's reformation. Louis greeted the announcement with sarcastic indifference, merely shrugging his shoulders to whoops of malicious laughter from the courtiers. Athénaïs had sunk a long way from the time when her displeasure could invoke terror. To the younger generation, in fact, her attempts to impose herself appeared pathetic and ridiculous.

With the exception of Toulouse, who was perhaps the dullest but the most decent of her children, Athénaïs was unlucky with her sons. Although D'Antin was happy to make use of her wealth to fund his extravagant tastes, his gorgeous equipage and his prodigious Mortemart appetite (he, too, grew fat from his gourmandizing), he made no real headway at court until he formed an alliance with La Maintenon after his mother's death. Mme. de Maintenon had originally hated and feared D'Antin as "the son of an enemy who might conceivably return to favor, whom she could not forgive for what she had been to her, for what she owed her, nor for the coin in which that debt had been paid," according to Saint-Simon. In other words, D'Antin was a reminder that the poor widow Scarron had repaid her benefactress with treachery and spite. Later, though, La Maintenon came to believe that as the half-brother of her beloved Du Maine, D'Antin would provide a useful ally if he were rewarded with advancement, and she set about rehabilitating him, much to his disloyal pleasure.

D'Antin's half-brother-in-law, the Duc de Chartres, once described him as "exactly as a real courtier should be, without humor and without honor." He was certainly a breathtaking sycophant. Only a matter of months after Athénaïs's death, D'Antin's new friend the Marquise de Maintenon contrived that Louis should spend a night at the house Athénaïs had bought for her son. At Petit-Bourg, Louis found "the furnishing of the rooms, the comforts of all kinds, the abundant and delicate fare served at a vast number of tables, the profusion of all manner of refreshments, the prompt and willing service at the turn of one's head, the care, the forethought, the luxury, the charming novelties, the excellent concert, the games, the ponies, and numerous decorated carriages for driving in the grounds . . . everything to indicate most tasteful and elegant extravagance."[1] The only royal objection was to a beautiful chestnut avenue, a fine feature of the grounds but one that unfortunately obstructed the view from the King's bedroom. When Louis awoke the next morning, the avenue had vanished, apparently soundlessly: there were no cart tracks, or anything at all in fact, to suggest that it had ever existed. D'Antin was made governor of Orléans for his toadying, exclaiming when he heard the news: "I am thawed at last!" and eventually achieved the summit of his ambition with a dukedom and a street named after him in Paris. Athénaïs, though, would probably have found the gesture unworthy of the dignity of a Mortemart.

Athénaïs retained her enthusiasm for building, and her most important purchase of the years following her removal from Versailles was also made in D'Antin's name, though she retained a life interest in it for herself. This was the château of Oiron in her ancestral province of Poitou, which she bought for 340,000 livres in 1696 from the Duc de la Feuillade, son of her brother Vivonne. Like all of Athénaïs's houses, it was beautiful, dating in part from the Renaissance, when it had been improved by Artus Gouffier, chamberlain to François I, who added a grand staircase to the north wing and an arcaded gallery. In the seventeenth century, the main house was remodeled in the fashionable classical style and supplemented by two pavilions, joined by a doric portico. Athénaïs was responsible for the reconstruction of the buildings, which had fallen into disrepair, including one of the two bell towers that surmounted each wing. Along with the house, Athénaïs bought the estates of Curcay and Moncontour, adding a third, Tersay, six years later. The expense consumed a considerable part of her fortune, but D'Antin agreed to pay her an annual rent of 3,000 livres in exchange for his eventual ownership of the property, as well as 100,000 livres to be distributed among charitable causes selected by his mother.

If the exterior of Oiron was impressive for its size and its beauty, the interior was a sadder, more personal reflection of the life Athénaïs lived there. In the gallery, the stucco ceiling, inlaid with flowers, fruits and pastoral scenes, echoed Oiron's idyllic position amid the placid beauties of the Poitou countryside. On the walls, frescoes told the story of Helen of Troy, a salutary reminder of the humbled pride of their faded owner. To these ornaments Athénaïs added many pictures of her own — of her children, of her sister Mme. de Thianges, and of the royal family, but mostly there were pictures of the King. Louis was everywhere in the house: framed in ormolu, silver or enamel, rearing in sculpted miniature on his horse or gazing translucently from an engraved goblet. The centerpiece was the King's bedroom, featuring a great oak bedstead with a gilded rail, a black velvet canopy and curtains embroidered in silver and gold. There were ten arm-chairs of gilded wood, upholstered in a tapestry showing the Sibyls, the oracles of ancient mythology, and a green chalcedony table with a pedestal of gold. Athénaïs had a bust made of Louis in silver, with gold hair, and at Beauvais, she commissioned tapestries showing him as a young man, charging on his horse in a plumed hat, victorious on the battlefields of Flanders where he had first loved her. In her bed-room alone, there were four portraits of Louis. Indeed the whole house was a shrine to the love that for twelve years had astonished and scandalized the world.

Despite the sumptuous décor, and the ceiling so bedecked with garlands and voluptuous goddesses that visitors feared it might fall on their heads, the King's room had a funereal air about it, which was not surprising, considering that it was never used. Louis never slept there, never admired his portrait with the feather in his cap. Two pic-tures of Athénaïs showed her not as *la reine sultane,* the real Queen of France, but as Mary Magdalene, weeping and repentant (though it must be said that, true to form, the Mignard version is more erotic than regretful). In the new bell tower, blue and white tiles in the Delft style showed a pattern of waves which recalled the Mortemart family motto, *Ante mare undae.* Was Athénaïs trying to remind herself of her

family's "superiority" even as she recalled the blue and white porce-
lains of her pleasure house at Trianon?

If the apogee of Louis's reign can be said to have been 1678, then the
following decades might broadly represent a slow process of reversal
and decline, marked by compromises to French military strength
abroad and economic collapse within the nation, largely as a result of
the cost of the King's ambition. The royal family also suffered: from
four generations of Bourbon heirs at court in 1704, by 1715 the line
had dwindled to Louis himself and his sickly five-year-old great-
grandson. Versailles was becoming so paralyzed by the rigidity of its
etiquette that even Louis was glad to escape more and more often
to Marly, and the chilly influence of La Maintenon spread through
the drafty corridors of the great house, petrifying the court into
monotonous and grudging devotions animated only by a mechanical
round of "pleasures" as predictable as the litany of the Mass.

Politically, this new era had begun in 1686 with the Revocation of
the Edict of Nantes. Ratified in 1598, the edict had given French
Protestants the right and liberty to worship, preach, marry and work,
and though the prejudices of both Catholics and Protestants prevented
it at times from functioning properly, there was nevertheless a new
degree of religious toleration in France that was considerably more
enlightened than, for example, attitudes in Holland or England in the
same period. Cardinal Mazarin had adopted a broadly pro-Protestant
policy, guaranteeing the acceptance, if not tolerance, of the Protestants, and until the conclusion of the Dutch wars, Louis had taken a
similar line. However, spurred on by La Maintenon and the *dévots,*
their influence now unchecked by the stabilizing voice of Colbert,
who had died in 1683, Louis was encouraged to revoke the agreement. Since the collapse of the Spanish bloc, France had represented
the main stronghold of Catholic power in Europe, and Louis was
concerned at the increasingly hostile Protestant ambitions of William
of Orange, soon to reign in England as William III in place of Louis's
deposed Catholic cousin James II. Louis declared that he would give
his life to see his subjects united in the bosom of the Church, and the
flattering entreaties of the *dévots* persuaded him that the conversion of
Protestants was the greatest work so great a king could accomplish.

The period after the revocation was one of the most shameful in
the history of France, but while atrocities were being committed against

the Protestants in the provinces, Louis's ears were being filled with triumphant tales of conversions by the thousand, and Masses were said in thanks at Versailles for the souls of those who were in fact desperately attempting to escape with their lives. Altogether, 200,000 Protestants fled into exile, 1 per cent of the entire French population, as the revocation helped to draw France into yet another war.

On the death of Elector Charles von Simmern, ruler of the Palatinate, in 1685, Louis made an aggressive move on the small Rhineland state. In the same way as he had demanded Spanish territories in the Netherlands on behalf of Queen Marie-Thérèse nearly twenty years earlier, he now claimed about half of the Palatinate for his sister-in-law, the Princess Palatine. To oppose him, William of Orange formed the League of Augsberg, an alliance consisting of Spain, the Hapsburg Empire, Sweden, and a number of smaller German states, joined by England in 1689 after William came to the throne there. Louis welcomed to France his exiled cousin James and his Queen, Mary of Modena, put St. Germain at their disposal and set about burning the Palatinate to ashes. La Palatine was heartbroken at the destruction of her homeland, and could never reconcile her affection for Louis with the ruin of her country, preferring to blame Louvois for the scorched-earth policy pursued by the French. Louvois died in 1693, largely unmourned — thanks to La Maintenon, who had turned against her former crony when he begged Louis not to make his marriage public, offering the King his own sword with which to kill him rather than make him witness such a disgrace — and from then on Louis decided to command his armies himself. The war dragged on, successfully for the French with the captures of Mons and Namur, but disastrously for the Catholic cause in England after James was defeated by William III at the Battle of the Boyne in 1690. A peace of sorts was concluded at Ryswick in 1697, but the whole of Europe held its breath, knowing that there would be more conflict to come when the King of Spain died.

In 1693, at the age of fifty-five, Louis decided to retire from accompanying his armies on campaign. Marie-Thérèse's cousin with the blue feather would ride no more to war. Unfortunately, the Duc de Luxembourg, whom Louvois had jealously tried to compromise in the Affair of the Poisons, died two years later, having never lost a battle in his long and distinguished career as a general, to be replaced by Villeroy, who was frankly incompetent. (More of a *bon viveur* than a soldier, Villeroy, it was said at court, was irresistible to women, but never to the enemy.) Without their King or their greatest general, the French armies were no longer invincible.

Charles II of Spain died in 1700, bequeathing the crown of Spain as well as Spanish dominions in Italy, the Netherlands and the New World to Louis's eighteen-year-old grandson the Duc d'Anjou. (The Spanish King had no children from his marriage to Monsieur's daughter Marie-Louise since, as she reported dutifully before her suspected death by poison, he was impotent.) It was an incredible compliment to Bourbon power, and after lengthy consideration, Louis decided that D'Anjou should accept. In a dramatic announcement, he had his council chamber opened to the whole court, and presented D'Anjou as the new King of Spain. The Spanish ambassador fell to his knees to kiss the new monarch's hand, murmuring, "The Pyrenees have ceased to exist."[2] The next day, their Most Catholic and Most Christian Majesties arrived for Mass side by side, as equals, and Louis offered his grandson his own cushion to kneel on. D'Anjou, who had been disregarded by most of the court, shyly demurred, and the two kings knelt side by side on the bare floor. It was a beautiful scene, a fitting close to the last century of undisputed Bourbon power in France. Protestant Europe was already rallying itself for a challenge to the Catholic hegemony established on the continent by the Spanish succession. By 1702, London, the Hague and Vienna were filled once again with declarations of war on France, and Denmark and the German princes quickly followed. The principal objective of the new alliance was to bring about the abdication of the new King of Spain in favor of the Austrian Emperor Charles, and the recognition by Louis of the rights of the house of Hanover (France still supported the Stuart claim to the English throne).

The next eleven years were disastrous for Louis as his glorious armies suffered defeat after defeat. The losses of Malplaquet and Oudenaarde destroyed French confidence, the country was bankrupt, the soldiers unpaid. A series of terrible winters brought famine year after year, and half the livestock in France was lost. Louis melted down his gold plate to pay the troops, and issued desperate proclamations to the provinces, urging his subjects to yet further endurance. Many people blamed Mme. de Maintenon's bad influence for the King's apparent loss of judgment, and a parody of the Lord's Prayer was recited on the streets, which ended, "Deliver us from La Maintenon."

By the time the Peace of Utrecht was signed in 1713, France was on its knees. Although Louis had not succeeded in enforcing the Catholic claim to the throne of England, his grandson remained King of Spain, so the war of succession had to some degree ended honorably. Louis, however, was a dying man. He had not doubted himself since Athénaïs de Montespan had first taken him in her arms nearly fifty years before, but now he was deeply troubled that his obsessive pursuit of *la gloire* had reduced his people to beggary. Louis the Great continued his unerring daily routine, but the Sun King's radiance was irrevocably dimmed.

At Versailles, Louis was finding it difficult to keep his large and increasingly unruly family under control. By the turn of the century, the royal household comprised not only Louis, Monsieur and La Palatine with their daughter Elisabeth-Charlotte, but the Grand Dauphin and his three sons, the Duc de Bourgogne and his wife, the Duchesse Marie-Adelaide de Savoie, the Duc d'Anjou and the Duc de Berry. Also living at court were Monsieur's son, Philippe de Chartres, his wife, Louis and Athénaïs's daughter the former Mlle. de Blois, and their daughter Marie-Louise-Elizabeth, who would become Duchesse de Berry, and Louis and Athénaïs's elder daughter, now Mme. la Duchesse de Bourbon, and the Duc, not to mention the Princesse de Conti, the King's daughter by Louise de La Vallière. The Duc and Duchesse du Maine and the Comte de Toulouse made up the younger generation. All these young people — and they were very young, Athénaïs's daughters having been married in their early teens — found the changeless round of the court extremely dull. Since Louis had continued with his policy of absolute control, even the Dauphin, in theory the next King, was barely allowed to speak a word at council meetings, and the other young men had nothing apart from soldiering to occupy them. In 1698, the Dauphin sketched pen portraits of his sons and daughter-in-law.

Bourgogne, a masterpiece. Delicate health. Very gay but not very chatty. Loves to study science, languages, philosophy, mathematics and history ancient and modern . . . rather proud and intimidating.

Anjou, sweet nature and also a clever boy. People prefer him to Bourgogne.

Berry, very chatty, lively and full of promise.

Duchesse de Bourgogne. Sharp and spiteful . . . She and Bourgogne completely indifferent to one another. Servile to Mme. de Maintenon.

The young ladies had even less to amuse them than their husbands. They gossiped and gambled and stole one another's lovers. The Princesse de Conti and Mme. la Duchesse were jealous of the Duchesse de Bourgogne, who would one day be Queen of France. They considered her spoiled and precocious, and their own beauty was insulted by the King's favoritism, which required that the ugly little Duchesse, with her monkey face and snaggle of teeth, be regarded as a beauty. Mme. la Duchesse was also annoyed by her younger sister's enormous pride. "She is granddaughter of France even on the privy," people said of her. But with the exception of the Duchesse de Bourgogne, who had been educated by La Maintenon when she came to Versailles aged twelve, and called her "Aunt," everyone was united in one activity: complaining about "the old woman."

La Palatine's letters give a picture of the dreariness of Versailles after Athénaïs had retired. "There is an old German proverb," she wrote, "that comes to mind now. 'Where the devil cannot go, he sends an old woman.' This is something that all of us in the royal family have come to experience." In another: "Court life is becoming so dull that one can hardly stand it any longer. For the King imagines that he is pious when he sees to it that everyone is properly bored and bothered." Even elegance seemed to have become a thing of the past. "I am certain," declared La Palatine to her aunt, the Electress of Hanover, "that if Your Grace could see the great care and trouble that the women are now taking to make themselves repulsive, Your Grace would have a good laugh . . . the coiffures are getting higher every day. I think they will finally have to make the doors taller, for otherwise these ladies will no longer be able to go in and out of the rooms."

The natural coiffure à la Fontanges was out of fashion now. Instead of imitating the spontaneity of the hunting field, the women were plastered in paint and hair grease, and creaked through the Galérie des Glaces like wooden dolls. It was a pity that La Maintenon should have ended her life with a crusade against everything that was beautiful and joyful, for her intelligence could have been channeled into creating an elegant and amusing court, of which Versailles was sorely in need. Instead, having spent the years of her youthful poverty in the salons of some of the most intelligent and educated conversationalists in France, in her powerful old age, La Maintenon chose the most ignorant and vulgar for company, and the shrieking nonsense that replaced cultivated conversation at the court became known as *babil de St. Cyr* in a dubious tribute to the school's founder. Saint-Simon notes that Athénaïs's salon had been the center of *esprit* at court, and there was no one to take her place.

Among the bored younger members of Louis's family, the libertine spirit of the Regency seemed already to have taken hold. When they could, they escaped from Versailles to Clagny (now occupied by the Du Maines) or St. Cloud, or, increasingly, to Paris. La Maintenon was disgusted by their behavior, particularly that of the female courtiers: "The women of these days are insupportable to me," she declared, "with their immodest dress, their tobacco, their wine, their greediness, their coarseness, their laziness." She banned opera at Versailles and allowed only "respectable" plays to be performed in an effort to improve morality, but this policy served only to make the young people more frustrated and badly behaved. They responded by giving private entertainments of their own: Lully's *Alceste,* for example, was performed at the Princesse de Conti's little house in Versailles, the Grand Dauphin staged opera at his house at Meudon, and Molière's early comedies, which had once delighted the King, were now performed in secret at the Palais Royal. Mme. de Maintenon had never approved much of the theater, but deep embarrassment was added to her antipathy when, much to the amusement of Athénaïs's daughters, some of Scarron's comedies were played at Versailles.

Athénaïs's daughters, the Duchesse de Chartres and Mme. la Duchesse, were the leaders of this scandalous younger set. "No one is safe from their ridicule," criticized La Palatine, "and all this under the pretext of amusing the King." They did not give a fig for La Maintenon, and outraged her by taking what Saint-Simon politely calls "long repasts' together. At Marly, the teenage duchesses were caught smoking pipes they had begged from the Swiss guards, given away by the smell, but when La Maintenon summoned them for a scolding, Mme. la Duchesse laughed in her old governess's face. Despite their deadly quarrels over which of their daughters should marry the Duc de Berry (Mme. de Chartres eventually won), they joined forces to tease their beautiful but slow-witted half-sister, Louise de La Vallière's daughter the Princesse de Conti. One evening, Mme. la Duchesse, rather drunk, was playing at olive-spitting with her father, to the Princesse's evident disgust. Louis remarked that her sobriety hardly fitted their cheerful drunkenness, to which the Princesse retorted that she "would rather be a sobersides than a chronic boozer." Mme. de Chartres replied in her slow, quavering voice, her mother's voice, that she would rather be a wineskin than a tart. When the Princesse could find no witty riposte to this, Mme. la Duchesse vanquished her completely by writing some bawdy verses to the effect that Mme. de Conti had not inherited her mother's modesty, and that the guards were always having to be sacked for being caught in bed with her. And so it went on.

Athénaïs, meanwhile, continued to immerse herself in her charitable work. She too had been affected by the Spanish wars, having had her royal pension of 100,000 livres reduced by two thirds, but she was worried only about the effect this would have on the paupers she assisted. When she had first left Versailles for St. Joseph, Athénaïs had had several conversations with a lady celebrated for her devotion, Mme. Miramion, to whom she had explained that she sincerely wished to repent, and expressed hope for that lady's good influence. Through her tears, Athénaïs had told Mme. Miramion, "Ah, Madame, he treats me like the least of women, nevertheless since the Comte de Toulouse, I have not so much as touched the tip of his finger."[3] Mme. Miramion, whose charitable interests were particularly concerned with "fallen women," accepted that France's most famous sinner was in earnest, but suggested that although Athénaïs wept much, her tears were "those of weakness and despair, not yet of penitence." Perhaps inspired by Mme. de Miramion, who had founded a convent in Paris, Athénaïs decided that good works would be the first stage in conquering her still rebellious heart.

Having come to believe that there was no better way to please God and be forgiven for her sins than to support the poor, Athénaïs had decided to transfer the refuge she had set up under the sisters of St. Lazare nearer to her new home. So she established a new hospital at Oiron, which still exists today, complete with a portrait of its founder by Mignard. The buildings were "furnished with beds, linen, crockery and everything necessary for the maintenance and lodging of poor people," and in 1704, a foundation deed was passed which decreed that the hospital was to care for one hundred poor people of both sexes, six each from Curcay and Moncontour, sixteen from neighboring parishes, six from Fontrevault, where Athénaïs's sister Marie-Madeleine was abbess, two nominated by the Bishop of Poitiers, and the remainder from Oiron itself. The directors were the Bishop of Poitiers, the owner and her successors of Oiron, the dean and priest of Oiron, and the *seneschals,* the royal lieutenants, of Oiron, Curcay and Moncontour. Twenty-four old men were also supported, with the express purpose of praying privately for Mme. de Montespan. Athénaïs had already instituted a private Mass for her family at Fontrevault, known as the "Mass of guardian angels." It was celebrated daily, on Monday for all the children, on Tuesday for the Duc du Maine (who in 1684, when the Masses began, had not yet become estranged from his mother), on Wednesday for Mlle. de Nantes, on Thursday for Mlle. de Blois, on Friday for Athénaïs herself, on Saturday for the family again and on Sunday for the Comte de Toulouse. Athénaïs gave 5,000 livres for the purchase of land whose revenues would support the chaplains who said the Masses. Even before she left the court for good, it seems, then, that she was increasingly concerned about the state of her soul. Unkind tongues suggested, with reference to the rumors of the poisons scandal, that having made a friend of the Devil for so long, Athénaïs was now anxious to avoid his company for eternity.

Athénaïs donated more than 110,000 livres to her pet project at Oiron, as well as some of her own plate and furniture carved with her coat of arms, and took a personal interest in every aspect of the hospital's organization, from the decoration of the rooms to the timetable of the boarders' days. She was pleased when in 1705 Louis confirmed the foundation with letters patent, and the hospital was officially opened with a Mass soon afterwards. As tribute to the owner of Oiron, the community was to pay an annual "rent" of a half-louis, and the first ripe grape from its vines. On the feast of St. François (Françoise was, of course, Athénaïs's Christian name), the superior of the order of nuns which ran the hospital presented the host at the parish Mass, and presented the priest with an offering of a gold louis. The hospital was an imaginatively compassionate project, but Athénaïs seems still to have felt the need to impose herself upon it just as she had with the convent of St. Joseph. Her charity was far from discreet, as though she wished to advertise that she was now spending her ill-gotten gains for the good.

While the Oiron plan was being realized, Athénaïs took to spending a good part of the year with her sister at Fontrevault, and Marie-

Madeleine remarked with pleasure that her sister's presence attracted many other visitors who helped her to evade what would otherwise have been a heavy solitude. It seemed that Athénaïs had still lost none of her capacity for drawing people to her. She did not reside in the convent itself, but in a small house in the grounds known, in a cruel reminder of former times, as the Petit Bourbon, though she participated in the routines of prayer and work of the nuns, taking particular pleasure in spending time with the younger novices and an interest in new vocations. She described Fontrevault to her friend the Duchesse de Noailles, whose daughter planned to enter the convent. "I have shown your letter to my sister, who thanks you for having decided to send her your daughter . . . As to the vocation, I can answer for that. This is a convent where no novice refuses to take the vows, and with reason, for it is most holy and most beautiful, and one where the nuns are a thousand times more happy than in all the rest of the world."[4] Is there a note of wistfulness here? Might Athénaïs, in the peaceful country surroundings of the abbey, have reflected that she might have been happier if she had followed her sister to the veil, rather than choosing the turbulent life of the court?

She certainly loved the company of her learned, charming sister; indeed, Marie-Madeleine's society was perhaps Athénaïs's greatest consolation for the loss of her beloved Louis. She never displayed her notorious temper to Marie-Madeleine, instead treating her deferentially, with a solicitous regard for her health and the exhausting effects of her duties as abbess. Together, the sisters could indulge in the whimsical conversation of their shared *esprit Mortemart* for, as Saint-Simon commented, Marie-Madeleine was "more witty than any of them, with that same turn which no one but themselves, or those who were continually in their society, have ever caught." The sisters grew closer than ever after their brother Vivonne died in 1688, followed by that masterpiece of nature Mme. de Thianges in 1693.

It was to Fontrevault that the Marquis d'Antin rode in the winter of 1701 to announce the death of his father to Athénaïs. Montespan had died in his son's arms, and D'Antin had missed the interment to race to his mother's side. Athénaïs responded very correctly, donning mourning and having a funeral Mass said, but she must have been astonished at what she discovered when the Marquis's will was opened. For it was not until then that it became apparent that Montespan had been tormented for thirty-five years by his frustrated love for his wife. The document, witnessed by M. de Faulquier, the royal notary of the district, on 23 October 1701, requests that Athénaïs pray for her husband, and reminds her of "all the tender friendship that she well knows he has always had for her" and of his confidence in her piety on such a grave occasion. Despite his threats, his insults and his abuses, Montespan had preserved an untarnished image of the beautiful young woman he had once vengefully buried in effigy. He actually made Athénaïs coexecutrix of his will, emphasizing his "trust in her charity" and begging her to accept the charge for reasons of the "friendship and sincere tenderness" he felt for her.[5] That this was more than a sentimental dying whim is confirmed by Montespan's clear statement that these requests had been made in his other, preceding testaments. Athénaïs's reaction to her husband's posthumous declaration is unrecorded.

Montespan's fortunes had improved since the sorry inventory of his possessions at the time of his separation from his wife in 1674. In 1687, his uncle the Duc de Bellegarde had died, and although the Montespan claim to the title was dubious, since he was descended through the female line, Montespan eagerly assumed it, and removed from his château at Bonnefont to the Bellegarde residence at St. Elix, near Toulouse. Despite the fact that the title was never officially recognized outside the province, Montespan adopted the role of regional patriarch with gusto, dispensing justice on his estates and receiving his annual tribute of two capons from the councillors every All Saints' Day. He improved his new property by adding an orangery, a formal garden and some fine statuary, in imitation of the fashion at Versailles. If this was a poor attempt to re-create the milieu in which his wife had so recently moved, Montespan was soon gratified by a taste of the real thing: by the 1690s he had finally become persona grata at court, much to the amusement of La Palatine, who described his card games with his "daughters" with much amusement. Montespan and D'Antin would be seated opposite one another, with Madame la Duchesse de Chartres on one side and Madame la Duchesse on the other, as Montespan dealt the cards most respectfully, amid much hand-kissing of his wife's adulterous offspring.

Montespan's freedom did not, however, extend to the possibility of his marrying again. When he courted Mlle. Riquet, the daughter of a celebrated Toulouse engineer, announcing in characteristically theatrical style that he intended to write to the Pope to have his marriage annulled, the plan was given short shrift by Louvois, for even now the taint of Louis's double adultery was a sensitive subject. And clearly it remained so for Montespan who, if he was able to play the fluttering gallant at Versailles, reverted to his usual manners in the provinces. In a game of *lasquenet* in Toulouse, Montespan lost his king of hearts. "Ah Monsieur!" piped up a witty lady. "That is not the king of hearts which has done you most harm." The company sniggered, but Monsieur le Marquis was not amused. "If my wife is worth a louis, Madame," he punned, "then you are valued at thirty sous." Some days later, Toulouse held one of those masked balls where clumsy provincials aped the wicked behavior of the glittering denizens of Versailles. Taking advantage of their mutual anonymity, Montespan rewarded the witty lady with a good kick.[6]

Montespan's tumultuous existence settled towards the end of his life into apparent contentment; he divided his time between his château, Toulouse and the court, enjoying the increasing success of his son D'Antin and amusing his country guests with bear hunts and amateur theatricals.

Even so, it is not difficult, given the romance of his lingering love, to pity Montespan. It was hardly his choice to play Amphitryon to Louis's Jupiter. While it is tempting to cast him as a victim of his wife's ambition, it must be recalled that Montespan had been an appalling husband: extravagant, neglectful, abusive and violent, behavior for which adultery, even on such a spectacular scale, seems, if not an equable, then at least an appropriate return.

The contents of Montespan's will are all the more surprising considering that, some time earlier, Athénaïs's confessor, Père de la Tour, had exacted an act of penance in which Athénaïs had had to humbly beg her husband's forgiveness. Athénaïs had chosen La Tour, whose sermons were well known in Paris, as her spiritual adviser as he was both devout and sufficiently worldly to be good company, but in the matter of her moral duty he was exigent and strict. It is a measure of Athénaïs's sincere desire to repent and return to God that she accepted a humiliation that would have been intolerable to her pride a few years before: she had written to Montespan not only apologizing for the wrongs she had committed, but even offering to resume their conjugal life if he wished it, or alternatively to retire to any place he chose for her. Perhaps this submission was not entirely disingenuous, for even after such a long separation, Athénaïs knew her husband,

and must have counted on his pride making such a reconciliation impossible. If so, she was proved right. Montespan replied tersely that he wished neither to see her nor to direct her in anything, nor indeed to speak to her for as long as she lived. What Athénaïs could not have known until after his death was how much such a renunciation must have hurt him.

Of Athénaïs's circle at court, the first to die was Monsieur, in June 1701. The royal brothers had dined together at Marly, but had quarreled about the extramarital activities of Athénaïs's son-in-law the Duc de Chartres. Louis had become insufferably pompous on the subject of adultery now that he was piously married to La Maintenon. The Duc was having simultaneous affairs with one of his mother's ladies and a Parisian actress. The latter presented the Duc with a son at exactly the same time as the Duchesse de Chartres produced a daughter, Charlotte-Aglae, Athénaïs's granddaughter. The Duc made no secret of visiting both new mothers in Paris together, much to the annoyance of his wife, who complained to Louis about the insult. Louis attempted to remonstrate with Monsieur, who pointed out that the King was hardly in a position to throw stones. What about the times he himself had driven Louise de La Vallière and Mme. de Montespan through Flanders in the same coach as the Queen? Louis was outraged that his brother should dare to allude to his past, and they both grew so angry that a servant had to remind them that the company in the next room were hanging on to their every word. Monsieur returned to his château at St. Cloud in a rage, and rather overrefreshed himself in an attempt to calm his nerves. When he suddenly collapsed, a thin trickle of blood oozing from his nostrils, a messenger was sent to Marly. La Maintenon, fearful and bitter towards a man who had always despised her, persuaded Louis that there was no immediate danger, so the King did not leave for St. Cloud until three in the morning, by which time his brother had fallen into a coma from which he never awakened. The deathbed scene was not edified by the spectacle of La Palatine, waddling about in terror in a nightgown, shrieking "No convent for me!"

Louis wept publicly, and was for once unable to eat, but after an early night he seemed quite composed, and could be heard humming opera tunes the following morning. That evening, the Duc de Montfort expressed his disgust at Louis's grandson the Duc de Bourgogne, who had set up a card table in the salon while his great-uncle was practically still warm. The young man blushingly exclaimed that he was acting on orders, since "the King wishes that no one be bored at Marly." Soon the room was full of tables and the gaming went on as usual.

Athénaïs was deeply saddened by the death of Monsieur, her friend and ally for over forty years. Of course, her daughter the Duchesse de Chartres would now become Duchesse d'Orléans, since her husband inherited his father's title, and therefore one of the most important women in France, but Athénaïs could feel no pleasure in this triumph, as much now as a result of her inclination to dissociate herself from the world as of her absence from the court. Uncharacteristically, she took long walks in the fields, remembering Monsieur and the life they had shared. With the death of her husband that same year and, tragically, that of Marie-Madeleine in 1704, Athénaïs was becoming obsessed with the prospect of her own end. The loss of her sister left Athénaïs prostrate with grief, and her spirits never really recovered. When Louis heard the news, at supper, he expressed his "extreme regret" at the passing of a woman he had esteemed as a friend, but he made no offer of condolence to Athénaïs, even though she was nearby in Paris when the word arrived.

Athénaïs returned to Oiron and unpacked her clavichord and her writing desk, her four dozen plates embossed with her arms, her white taffeta bed curtains. With the exception of the "King's bedroom," she furnished the rest of the house with tasteful simplicity, choosing elegant pieces such as her marquetry dressing table, but avoiding the excessive luxury of Clagny. She unfolded her dresses, in gold and silver lace, in purple damask, in satin and velvet; her thirty corsets, coats brocaded in gold, embroidered skirts and taffeta gowns in blue, violet and lemon yellow or cerise-striped, blue and silver, green with silver working, white or blue covered with meadows of seamstresses' flowers. Beneath her gorgeous Queen's gowns, she wore a hair shirt to chafe her white skin, cruel belts and bracelets of steel with iron spikes to torment that "too beautiful, too weak flesh."

That year, Athénaïs expressed her new spiritual awareness in a long letter to a friend.

For much of the time, we are to ourselves a great world, and we often converse in our souls with a numerous populace of passions, desires, plans, inclinations and tumults which agitate us with their worries, trouble us with their disobedience, and prevent us from hearing God, who speaks to our hearts, and who alone ought to be our world and our everything . . . there is no more time to lose, because if this grievous night surprises us, all is lost for us, without reprise . . . look for God while he can be found, for fear of searching for him uselessly at the end of a life which will not be very long, and shrink from dying in sin and disorder.[7]

Now aged sixty-three, and seeing the tomb closing on her beloved friends and relations, Athénaïs was struggling to prepare her soul for death. Such preparation (which is a central theme of Saint-Simon's memoirs, to give one example) was a convention, but one viewed as vital, since a sudden, ill-considered death was considered both tragic and shameful. Its importance can be gauged from contemporary inventories of the possessions of those who had died. In 1700, 80 percent of such inventories contained some sort of essay or pamphlet on what was known, quite seriously, as "the art of dying," and many more people than those represented by such figures would have heard such works read aloud.

After the death of Marie-Madeleine, Athénaïs began to reflect on the principles of Jansenism, the puritanical, severe order that had once caused her husband's family such embarrassment. Since Jansenism taught that "works," that is, charitable activities, were insufficient in themselves to secure a salvation only obtainable through grace, Athénaïs, who had recently devoted so much of her energy and fortune to precisely such activities, had to accept that her struggle for reformation would be much more private and difficult. That the majority of the works in her library at Oiron were religious, if not Jansenist texts, attests to her search for the elusive spiritual essence of grace. They included writings by St. Augustine and David's Psalms, Grenade's Catechism in four volumes, a *Guide for Sinners* and the works of Jansen, along with at least eight other theological collections. Such texts were crucial to the essential preparation for death, which necessitated a gradual drawing away from the distractions of the world and a humbling of the flesh in readiness for communion with God. Athénaïs, never one to do things by halves, took her new studies very seriously, now directing her intelligence and energy to this austere discipline as well as to the supervision of her charities.

She was helped by an old friend, Daniel Huet, Bishop of Avranches, whom she had encountered at court during his time there as an undertutor to the Grand Dauphin. Huet was an appealing character, not sour and joyless like Bossuet, but almost as learned — a talented mathematician and philologist as well as a skilled theologian — and it is a testament to Athénaïs's intellectual ability that he was prepared to correspond seriously with her. It was with Huet that she debated the value of letters over conversation. Athénaïs, that great talker, suggested that there was necessarily something rather static and lifeless about letter-writing, while the Bishop countered that conversation was too anarchic and spontaneous, that the cleverest remarks could fall unrecorded on the stupidest ears, or worse, that the speaker might express himself thoughtlessly merely in order to amuse. This objection encapsulates both the charm and the deficiency of Athénaïs's conversational gift, for its ephemerality was the very source of its wit. Another discussion recalled the *précieuse* questions that had entertained Athénaïs and her friend Mme. Scarron many years before at the Hôtel d'Albret, such as "Which is better, illusion or truth?" Predictably enough, Huet expostulated at length on the desirability of the truth, but perhaps Athénaïs, who had lived for so long within the theatrical myth of the Sun King, saw some whimsical advantage in the attractions of illusion.

The correspondence did not always take such an elevated turn. Sometimes the friends exchanged poems, as they did when Huet wrote in verse to tell her that he could not visit her until the following spring.

> *N'attendez pas donc mon retour*
> *Qu'au retour de chaleurs nouvelles.*
> *Je n'irai vous faire ma cour*
> *Qu'au premier vol des hirondelles.*[8]

By way of reply, Athénaïs tries to tempt him to come sooner:

> *Là, vous receviez de mes mains*
> *Fruits, pois verts, artichauts, salades*
> *Tandis que tous les médecins*
> *Les defendoient a leur maladies.*[9]

Elsewhere in her letters to Huet, and in those to her friend the Duchesse de Noailles, Athénaïs is anxious to emphasize that she has conquered her love of the world, embodied for her in the life of the court. "Of the intrigues of the court, I no longer wish to hear talk of them," she asserts, or, "I assure you, I have no ambition in this world, and I dare say that I am empty of desires, and that this spares me from all sorts of pains."[10]

In spite of such protestations, there is a lingering sense of need in her letters to remain informed of the events at Versailles, partly because she missed Louis and her children so terribly, and partly to reassure her that she had chosen a better path in retiring from the world. "When one acts in good faith, one would rather be far away than near, and I have found in the short time I have spent in Paris so much need for care and circumspection, especially in regard to appearances, that it seemed to me the pain greatly exceeded the pleasure."[11] Is Athénaïs speaking here of *apparence,* the duty to preserve a good social face, or of the mortifying efforts required to make her dead beauty presentable? The need to step away from worldly concerns also meant the relinquishing of vanity, at once a relief and a torment for a woman whose beauty had once been a legend in Europe.

La Palatine, who had always been cheerful about her own absolute lack of attractions, nevertheless exulted in Athénaïs's vanished looks. "I see that those whom I used to see when they were so beautiful are now as ugly as I am: Mme. de La Vallière no one in the world would know any more, and Mme. de Montespan's skin looks like paper when children do tricks with it, seeing who can fold it into the smallest piece, for her whole face in closely covered with tiny little wrinkles, quite amazing. Her lovely hair is all white, and her face is red, so her beauty is quite gone."

According to Saint-Simon, however, Athénaïs remained "divinely beautiful" until the day she died, so perhaps it was still possible to see the vestiges of the imperious young goddess in the placid elderly woman. And however faded her beauty, Athénaïs certainly retained her air of majesty, a truly royal mystique which proclaimed her, always, queen of her surroundings. This new placidity, the sense of peaceful resignation that Athénaïs tried to cultivate in her correspondence, was sometimes little more than a mask for the torments she created for herself in pursuit of a state of grace. While appearing ready to welcome death with an easy countenance, she was terrified of dying and seemed to be attempting quite literally to outrun her own mortality. Suffering at the same time from a disgust with the world and a horror of being alone, Athénaïs careered all over France in an effort to escape her fears. One year she moved from Clagny to Paris, from Paris to Fontrevault to Saumur to Jargueneau; after a brief pause at Oiron, it was off to Bellegarde, now the residence of D'Antin, then back to Clagny before a season at Bourbon. The very difficulties and rigors of traveling were perhaps a blessed distraction from her preoccupations. Athénaïs was still famous enough for her activities to attract attention. "I am not surprised that she has run off to the country," remarked La Maintenon of the precipitate journey she undertook after the death of Monsieur. La Bruyère, in his *Characters,* satirized Athénaïs under the name of Irene, who travels to Epidaure (Bourbon) to consult an oracle about her ailments. First she says that she is exhausted, which the oracle attributes to the ardors of the journey; then that she has no appetite, for which the cure is to dine lightly; then that she has insomnia, that the wine is undrinkable, that she has grown too heavy, that she has indigestion, that her sight is failing, to all of which the oracle responds with practical advice. Then Irene complains that she is feeble and unhealthy.

"That is because you are aging," replies the oracle.

"But by what means can I cure this languor?" asks Irene.

"The quickest cure, Madame, is by dying."

Afraid that she would indeed die before she had expiated her sins, Athénaïs redoubled her efforts to ensure her salvation. As a form of penitence, she worked for several hours a day with her ladies at rough tasks such as shirt-making for the paupers, punishing her white hands with the stiff needles. She prayed incessantly, and while keeping up the elegance of her social position on the surface, she imposed secret privations on herself. Not content with the hair shirt and steel belts and bracelets, she now slept between the coarsest linen sheets under her luxurious bedcovers, exchanged her lawn petticoats for unbleached shifts beneath her fine clothes, and took to wearing a spiked girdle. She also renounced her sensual love of eating, sticking with difficulty to a simple and sparing diet, punctuated by frequent days of fasting.

Yet even such extreme gestures were not enough to convince her that she would not go straight to hell. Saint-Simon heard that as her fear of solitude increased, so she employed women to sit up with her at night, lying "with her bed curtains drawn back, her room ablaze with candles, her watchers around her, whom, whenever she woke up, she wished to find talking, playing cards, or eating, to assure herself they were not drowsy." Thus the long nights dragged their way towards dawn punctuated by the gentle slap of a card as the ladies propped up their sagging heads. No fortunes were thrown on Athénaïs's table now, no provinces won or lost, and the only louis in the Marquise's chamber were the four who observed the dreary gathering from the walls. Did Athénaïs remember little Marie-Thérèse, with her shy allusions to "my cousin with the blue feather," now that she, too, was reduced to loving a portrait? Or perhaps, since the King was not permitted to remain in the presence of a corpse, the portraits were talismans against the horror that crept in among the shadows as the candles burned low, insinuating itself through the thick curtains of the bed. Was Athénaïs frightened because she had indeed dabbled with the friendship of the Devil in Lesage's room in Paris in 1668, and had no wish to renew their acquaintance? Or maybe the fear of death was so strong because Athénaïs knew in her heart that despite her prayers and her mortifications, her repentance remained insincere. She could regret the vanity and extravagance of her court life, her duplicities, the fact of her double adultery, but could she truly renounce her great love for Louis, claim that she did not care for him, that she wished she had resisted his affections? She may have been unable to reconcile her knowledge that their love had been a sin with her feelings for her lover; may have seen herself as an Eloise, caught between the denial of one form of grace or the other. If so, according to the spiritual rules she had imposed upon herself, she had every reason to fear that she would be damned.

Chapter Sixteen

"Neither the sun nor death
can be looked at steadily."

O ne night in 1705, Louis was seized with a fit of the vapors as he
looked through a sheaf of faded, highly scented papers. The
heady perfumes that had once been his delight now sickened him so
much that no one would dare to approach him wearing scent, so why
did he risk an attack of nausea to burn the papers himself? In the solitude of his wife's sitting room, he was amusing himself by reading his
old love letters, for La Maintenon had not been able completely to
eradicate his nostalgia for his old mistresses. Four years later, again
alone with his wife, Louis burned with his own hands secret records
of the verbal processes of the Chambre Ardente, which he had kept
in their black leather coffer to protect Athénaïs during the Affair of
the Poisons. How did he remember Athénaïs, this old, sick man, his
country bankrupt and beleaguered, his ministers, Colbert and Louvois, both dead; this warrior prince who no longer rode to war but
remained closeted in his vast, cold house, a prisoner of his decaying
body? Did he recall, sentimentally, the beautiful young woman in
Flanders in the days of his first great victories, when he rode beside
her carriage sweeping off his hat to sing to her in the sunshine? Or
did he recoil in horror at the insinuations in La Reynie's pages that
the woman he had made his true consort had also consorted with
Satan? Did he remember the furious pleasures of her bed, her sweet
mouth and her scented hair? "I want," Athénaïs had said. "I want, I
want." And Louis had given her a Queen's fortune and a palace, made

princes of her sons, defied the Church, scandalized the nation, created miracles in her honor in the passion of his great love, whose mementos were now charred in his hands. Yet when he had heard the news of her death, he had not given her so much as a tear.

Athénaïs-Françoise de Rochechouart de Mortemart, Marquise de Montespan, died at about three o'clock in the morning at Bourbon on 27 May 1707. She had arrived at the spa early in the month, in the company of Lucie-Félicité d'Estrées, Maréchale de Couvres, the twenty-four-year-old daughter of her friend the Duchesse de Noailles. Perhaps Athénaïs had had a presentiment that this journey would be her last, as before she departed she had arranged her affairs, doubling her alms-giving and dispatching all the pensions she had bestowed two years in advance. She was well enough when she arrived at Bourbon to attend the blessing of a bell at nearby Couzon with Lucie-Félicité and her brother, but on the night of the 22nd she was taken ill with a fainting fit. Her ladies called for vinegar and cold water, but she remained unconscious, and Lucie-Félicité was summoned. In the absence of a doctor, Lucie and Athénaïs's attendants attempted to cure what they suspected was apoplexy by the amateur administration of emetic. The dose was so powerful that the *Mercure Français,* still fascinated by Athénaïs, reported without much consideration for her dignity that she had vomited sixty-three times. When doctors eventually arrived they declared the case to be hopeless, and Lucie sent a messenger to fetch D'Antin. Athénaïs rallied, and was able to ask for a priest to hear her confession and furnish the sacraments. D'Antin arrived, having interrupted a hunting trip with the Grand Dauphin, on the 26th. Athénaïs told him wryly that he found her in a very different state from when they had last been together at Bellegarde.

As the end approached, Athénaïs seemed less frightened. Lonely for so long, perhaps she believed she was to be reunited with her sisters, her brother and the many friends she had outlived. She called together her household servants and asked their pardon for her bad temper and for the scandalous life she had lived "with so deep and penitent humility that nothing could be more edifying."[1] She thanked God for permitting her to die far away from "the children of her sin,"[2] and begged the priest who confessed her to do so simply, as though he were dealing with an ignorant person. She did not speak of her family or her affairs, beyond some instructions for her charities, trying to keep her mind fixed on the mercy for which she hoped so fervently. D'Antin recorded her last moments. "Arrived at Bourbon the evening before her death, I made the sad witness to the most firm and Christian death that one could see, and the merits of good works and of a sincere penitence have never been raised so high as in her favor."[3] In her death, Athénaïs seemed finally at ease, concerned only with the expectation of salvation — "a hope," remarked Saint-Simon tartly, "with which [they] were pleased to flatter her." Athénaïs had always been excellent at getting what she wanted, and after years of discipline and struggle, it seems she realized even the most unworldly of her ambitions.

As for her material hopes, many people had continued to believe, right up until her death, that Athénaïs might once more triumph over La Maintenon. The Noailles family had certainly shared this delusion, for although they were already related to La Maintenon by marriage, they were prepared to risk her wrath by marrying their youngest daughter to Athénaïs's grandson by D'Antin in the hope of the return of the favorite to power. This explains the presence of the Maréchale de Couvres at Bourbon. The family flattered Athénaïs with these "expectations" to the last, but she was merely amused, treating the Maréchale like a doll and sending her out of the room for chattering. She would have been gratified, though, to know that her influence was still considered important enough for the marriage to come off after her death.

And what of Athénaïs's ambitions for those "children of her sin"? As Louis's formerly indomitable strength waned, and with it his authority, the cabals of the court began to realign themselves in preparation for the reign to come, and as is clear from La Palatine's letters, those children were in the thick of the plotting.

> The entire court is in a ferment. Some are trying to gain the favor of the all-powerful dame, others that of Monseigneur, others again that of the Duc de Bourgogne. He and his father do not love each other, the son despises him, has ambitions of his own, and wishes to rule. The Dauphin is completely dominated by his bastard half-sister, Mme. la Duchesse. All of them are against my son, for they fear that the King may look upon him kindly and arrange an alliance between his daughter and the

Duc de Berry. Mme. la Duchesse would prefer her own daughter to marry the latter, and she therefore monopolizes him. The Duchesse de Bourgogne wishes to rule both the Dauphin and the King; she is jealous of Mme. la Duchesse and has made a pact with the Duchesse d'Orléans in order to thwart her . . . Meanwhile, the old woman sets one against the other and rules all the stronger for it.

The Duchesse de Bourgogne, Marie-Adelaide de Savoie, was the last love of Louis XIV's life. The child of Monsieur and Henriette d'Angleterre's second daughter, who had married the Prince of Savoy, she had been given to Bourgogne aged twelve. Monsieur sulked because his granddaughter would now take precedence over Madame la Palatine, who had been the first woman at court since the Dauphine's death, but Louis was besotted with her. He took a walk with her every day, on private visits to Marly, he gave her a little zoo and her own theater, and for a while she was the star of the court, bringing new energy to its tired routine. She was not universally popular, but when anyone criticized her she merely pirouetted about, singing, "What do I care? I shall be their Queen!" However, the little Duchesse did not live long enough to achieve such a triumph, her death being one of a series that nearly destroyed the royal family.

The events of the years following Athénaïs's demise were to see the legitimate line of the Bourbons poised for extinction, with the result that, for a while, only one little boy stood between Athénaïs's eldest son and the crown of France. At the beginning of 1711, the succession looked strong. Everyone assumed that Louis XIV would in due course be succeeded by his son, the Grand Dauphin, and he in turn by the Duc de Bourgogne. The heirs in the third generation, the children of Marie-Adelaide de Savoie, were aged four and one respectively, and even if they did not live, the Duc de Bourgogne could be succeeded by his brother the Duc de Berry, who was married to Athénaïs's granddaughter Marie-Louise, the eldest daughter of the Duc and Duchesse d'Orléans. (The Grand Dauphin's second son, the Duc d'Anjou, had renounced his rights to the French succession when he ascended the Spanish throne.) Louis could therefore be satisfied that his dynasty was assured, despite the fact that only one of his legitimate children had survived into adulthood.

In 1711, however, it became clear that all the power-broking between the different court factions in anticipation of the succession would have to begin again. First, the fifty-three-year-old Grand Dauphin died at his country house at Meudon, the victim of a heart attack after a bout of smallpox. Then in 1712, Marie-Adelaide, the Duchesse de Bourgogne, was lost, ostensibly from an attack of measles, but probably as a result of the enormous doses of emetic which were administered to cure it. Her husband died of the same complaint within days. Now the two children of the Bourgognes were all that remained of the succession, and they too had fallen ill. The newest little Dauphin was seen off by the doctors just as his mother had been, and two-year-old Louis, now styled the Duc d'Anjou, survived only because his sensible governess had pretended that he was quite well and had hidden him in her own room, away from the fatal medicines, until he recovered. Three Dauphins of France were dead in less than a year, and it was whispered that they had been poisoned by the Duc d'Orléans, the husband of Athénaïs's daughter, in a plot to have his own daughter, the Duchesse de Berry, ascend the throne with her husband. These rumors were undoubtedly unfounded, just as those surrounding the death of Monsieur's first wife Henriette had been years before, but Berry would now be Regent and, since it was by no means certain that the infant Duc d'Anjou would live, probably the future King. Yet Berry, too, was to die, in a hunting accident in 1714, and his wife was delivered of their last child, stillborn, a few weeks later. Did it seem to Louis a punishment for his double adultery with Athénaïs that his illegitimate children flourished, while his heirs, even into the third generation, were cut down? If the little Duc d'Anjou died, the throne could be contested between Philippe d'Orléans and his cousin, now reigning as Philip V of Spain, and France might have to face another Fronde.

The death of the Duchesse de Bourgogne caused Louis, in Saint-Simon's words, "the only real depression of his life." That terrible, tragic year "eclipsed all joy, pleasures, amusements, and all kinds of grace; gloom covered the whole court." Indeed, the King never recovered, and La Maintenon reaped the fruits of her condemnation of all entertainments as she battled to amuse a man who was no longer amusable. All gaiety had departed, first with Athénaïs, and then with Marie-Adelaide. Now an old woman, La Maintenon seemed to realize how little the fierce ambition of the previous forty years had brought her. "We lead here a strange life," she wrote. "We wish to display gallantry, wit and invention, but all this is wanting; and we have given it up. We play, yawn, gather some trifling folly from those around us, hate each other, envy each other, flatter each other, abuse each other." The only source of exciting speculation was the succession, which seemed likely to pass to Philippe d'Orléans.

La Maintenon had other ideas. She was instrumental in persuading Louis to take the unheard-of step of altering his will, so that if D'Anjou died, Louis's sons Du Maine and Toulouse could succeed. La Maintenon hated the Duc d'Orléans, not only for his dissolute lifestyle, but because of his progressive, some said atheistic, beliefs. The Duc was talented and energetic, a fine soldier, and, as he was eventually to prove, an able politician, but Louis was prejudiced against him because of the threat he posed to the cringing, creeping Du Maine, and had, as we have seen, foolishly allowed this prejudice to influence his judgment. Kept in the background and denied a proper role at court, it was hardly surprising, as Monsieur had once observed, that D'Orléans had sought distraction in drinking, gambling and women. The Edict of Marly, signed in 1714, was designed to limit D'Orléans's power when he became Regent by creating a Regency Council of fourteen aristocrats, among them Du Maine and the Comte de Toulouse. D'Orléans would merely preside over what was effectively a cabinet, where decisions would be taken by majority vote, while the personal care and education of the little Duc d'Anjou were to be the sole responsibility of Du Maine. And if the child died, Du Maine, not D'Orléans, would have the right to succeed. This controversial will was hidden in a wall of one of the towers of the Palais de Justice in Paris, behind an iron grille within an iron door, and the keys deposited with three separate members of the Parlement.

Although Louis's will did not produce another civil war, a succession crisis was avoided only by the strength shown by D'Orléans when he eventually became Regent in 1715. Under the arrangements of the Edict of Marly, Du Maine and Toulouse imposed themselves as a new rank between the princes of the blood and the ducs, who were outraged by their effective demotion, for as peers of the realm they expected to take precedence over illegitimate royal children (for Saint-Simon, the recovery of the ducs' rightful status became a cause célèbre). Held in low esteem by the higher echelons of the aristocracy, Du Maine, encouraged by his wife to defend his rights, sought support among the lower ranks of the nobility, creating a division which made him even more unpopular. He was perceived as a bastard upstart, La Maintenon's creature, and it was not long before D'Orléans, with the support of the ducs and the Parlement, sought to overturn Louis XIV's will. Louis had recognized such a possibility, perhaps because in his heart he was aware of the shortcomings of his favorite but cowardly son, predicting to Du Maine: "However great I may make you during my lifetime, after I am gone I can do nothing for you." Du Maine compared himself morosely to a flea caught between two fingernails, the princes of the blood and the ducs.

Despite the fact that the Du Maines had positioned themselves as champions of the people, and the true representatives of Louis XIV's legacy, by 1717, D'Orléans was secure in the belief that he could have the Marly codicil overturned a posteriori, and passed an act stripping the legitimized princes of their right to the succession. In future, they would rank lower than the ducs, as their status would be determined by the date of the creation of their titles. Toulouse was spared this humiliation, being allowed by courtesy to retain his privileges during his lifetime in recognition of the solid service he had given to France, but Du Maine was not to escape it.

The Regent's revocation of the Edict of Marly also made Athénaïs's sons the inadvertent instruments of the legal precedent that would eventually be employed to abolish the monarchy itself: "If the French nation should ever experience this misfortune [the extinction of the legitimate royal line], it belongs to the nation itself to repair it by the sagacity of its choice."[4] Effectively, the overturning of Louis XIV's will asserted the right of the state to dispose of the throne, and thus by extension to control its power, a claim which was developed and clarified during the eighteenth century and reached its revolutionary fulfillment in 1789.

For Saint-Simon, Du Maine's demotion was a cause for jubilation. "I was dying of joy," he recalled. The Duchesse du Maine still fancied herself as a great politician, although it was said of her that even if she held a scepter in her hand, she would manage to transform it into a baby's rattle. Her ambition simply made her ridiculous. The Du Maine house at Sceaux was a symbol of her "shame and embarrassment, the ruin of her husband by the huge sums of money expended there, the spectacle of the court and the city, who thronged there and mocked."[5] The Duchesse tried to engineer a coup d'état by plotting with the King of Spain, but d'Orléans discovered the plan, known as the Cellamare conspiracy, and the Duchesse succeeded only in getting herself and her husband arrested.

They were imprisoned for two years, the Duchesse at Dijon and the Duc at the fortress of Doullens, where he passed his time translating Lucretius. Perhaps he was relieved when La Maintenon died, aged eighty-four, in April 1719, her epitaph pronounced triumphantly by La Palatine: "The old whore has kicked the bucket." There had been no love lost, either, between La Palatine and Athénaïs de Montespan, but they did at least agree on their choice of adjectives to describe their mutual enemy, "arse wipe" and "manure heap" being two favorite selections. Although the Du Maines had three children, the Prince des Dombes, the Comte d'Eu and Mlle. du Maine, none of them left any heirs. It was perhaps appropriate that the legacy of Athénaïs's ambition should not, after all, be carried through Du Maine, who had always been far more La Maintenon's child.

Nor did Mlle. de Nantes, Athénaïs's elder daughter, carry her mother's bloodline to posterity, despite having nine children by her husband. After the deaths of her husband, the Duc de Bourgogne, and her lover, the Prince de Conti, she took to eating, drinking and intrigue more than ever, and began her very public affair with the Marquis de Lassay. "She sought to drown her sorrows," commented Saint-Simon, "and she succeeded." She continued to quarrel with her sister the Duchesse de Chartres, now queening it as the Regent's wife, and it is likely that her famously sharp and spiteful tongue was responsible for the rumor that D'Orléans was having an incestuous affair with his daughter the Duchesse de Berry.

Athénaïs's other son, the Comte de Toulouse, made a slightly eccentric, if happy marriage. His bride, Marie-Sophie de Noailles, was the widow of D'Antin's son the Marquis de Gondrin, and hence Athénaïs's granddaughter-in-law, so Toulouse effectively married his own niece. They were a devoted couple who, most unusually for the time, shared the same bed for fourteen years and were hardly ever separated. Their son, the Duc de Penthièvre, became one of the richest men in France, having inherited the estates of the Comte d'Eu, his cousin through his uncle Du Maine — the fortune that his grandmother had wangled out of Mademoiselle in return for Lauzun's release so many years before. Penthièvre married his cousin, Marie-Thérèse d'Este-Modena, the granddaughter of the Duchesse de Chartres (and Athénaïs's great-granddaughter). Although Toulouse's offspring did not enter any of the royal houses of Europe via the male line, Penthièvre's son was the Prince de Lamballe whose wife died so horribly for Queen Marie-Antoinette in the French Revolution.

It was through her youngest daughter, Mlle. de Blois, Duchesse d'Orléans, that Athénaïs's great-great-great-grandson became King of France, the nation's only constitutional monarch. The eldest son of the Duc and Duchesse d'Orléans, known as Louis the Pious, married a German princess with whom he had a son, Louis-Philippe, Louis the Fat, who in turn married Louise-Henriette de Bourbon-Conti, and produced yet another Louis-Philippe d'Orléans, who became famous as Philippe Egalité. This great-great-grandson of Athénaïs married her great-granddaughter, Marie-Adelaide de Bourbon-Penthièvre, the daughter of Toulouse's son Penthièvre, and their child, born in 1773, became King Louis-Philippe, directly descended from Athénaïs de Montespan and Louis XIV on both sides.

Louis-Philippe married one of Marie-Antoinette's nieces, once again a cousin, Marie-Amélie de Bourbon-Naples. Before their wedding in 1809, Marie-Amélie noted in her diary that the Duc had shown her a spiked iron bracelet worn by Athénaïs de Montespan in the days of her repentance. He had carried it over the Swiss border when he escaped from the revolution, using it, along with some letters from Henri IV, as essential proof of his ancestry and his claim to the French throne. By way of Louis-Philippe's ten children with Marie-Amélie, Athénaïs's blood made its way into the veins of many of the royal houses of Europe. The royal families of Spain and Portugal, the Dukes of Wurtemberg, the monarchs of Belgium, Italy, Bulgaria and Luxembourg can or could be traced back to Athénaïs and Louis XIV. She may have been the real Queen of France only in name, but it is Athénaïs, not poor, forgotten Marie-Thérèse, who is the ancestress of some of the most important dynasties in Europe.

By the time Athénaïs died in 1707, to the remaining members of the world she lived in — with the exception, perhaps, of the paranoid La Maintenon — it must have seemed that she had already been dead for many years. No service was held for her at Clagny, at St. Germain, at

Versailles or even at Oiron. The death notice written by the curé of Bourbon was curt and inaccurate: "Today the 28th May 1707, by I the undersigned, was brought to this church the body of Marie [sic] Françoise de Rochechouart de Montespan, superintendent of the Queen's household, deceased in this town on Friday the 27th after receiving all the sacraments, where it will rest until otherwise disposed of." It was left to the *Mercure Français,* whose gossipmongering had been as faithful to her in exile as it had been in the days of her glory, to issue her obituary.

> She received almost every month a considerable sum, and one could say of it that never had money been better employed. It was almost all destined for hospitals and the poor . . . One could also say of this lady . . . that she only sought to do good during the time when she could be useful to her friends, to persons of distinction, to men of letters, and in general to all those who possessed some merit. She was a benefactress, she never sought to harm anyone.

The piece also mentioned Athénaïs's particular interest in the fine arts, and her role as patron to those artists who excelled during her time at court. It was a generous thank-you to a subject who had provided the *Mercure* with some of its most sensational stories.

The Marquis d'Antin left Bourbon before his mother's corpse was cold, claiming in his memoirs to have been so overcome by grief that he was forced to retire for some days to Bellegarde. The truth, according to Saint-Simon and the diarist Dangeau, was considerably more squalid. During the night after Athénaïs's death, D'Antin left his horse at the door of her lodgings, marched into her room, wrenched a key from the neck of the corpse and opened a locked drawer in a cabinet, from which he seized a box and made off to Paris without a word. D'Antin was apparently afraid that his half-brothers and -sisters would profit from his mother's will at his expense, whereas if she died intestate, he would be the sole legal beneficiary. Saint-Simon asserts that Athénaïs definitely made a will, but none was ever found, which suggests that this was the document kept in the mysterious box, and that D'Antin, as venal as his brother Du Maine, was prepared to rob his mother's body in order to secure her fortune.

Since D'Antin had left no orders, Athénaïs's funeral was left in the charge of the most menial of her servants. The Comte de Toulouse, who had set off for Bourbon from Marly, had been given the report of his mother's death at nearby Montargis and, apparently in great distress, had turned back to Rambouillet, perhaps from a misplaced concern for D'Antin's feelings. Lucie-Félicité de Couvres had taken refuge in a nearby Benedictine abbey, exhausted and overcome with guilt that her attempts at a cure had probably contributed to Athénaïs's death. Athénaïs had left some instruction as to how she wished her body to be disposed of — her heart was to be embalmed and placed at the convent of La Flèche, her entrails likewise at the priory of Ste. Menoux, and her body at St. Germain — but there was no one to take responsibility for seeing that her last requests were fulfilled. Her funeral thus became a macabre comedy, with the priests of two local houses, the Ste. Chapelle and the parish of Bourbon, quite literally fighting over her corpse at the very door of the parish church. The coffin was set upon the ground and the church doors closed until the dispute as to who should have the honor of conducting the funeral Mass was resolved. It was finally decided that Athénaïs's body would be deposited in the common Chapel of Rest ("just like the least bourgeoise," huffed Saint-Simon, ever conscious of the privilege due to his class), until D'Antin could be found to make a decision. A perfunctory Mass was held in the almost deserted church. More horribly, Athénaïs's once beautiful body, the body that had been stroked and kissed by the King himself, had been left to the clumsy devices of an amateur surgeon, Mme. Legendre, the wife of the intendant at Montauban, and as it lay neglected in the church, her entrails were given to a porter in a badly sealed casket to be carried to Ste. Menoux. The weather was bad, and the man, disgusted by the odor from the urn, was not inclined to bother with the journey. Peering inside, he was so revolted that he kicked Athénaïs's remains into a ditch, much to the delight of a group of rooting pigs, who made a fine feast of them. When this story reached Versailles, one Mme. Tencin remarked languidly, "Her entrails? Really? Did she ever have any?" It was, if nothing else, the kind of joke that Athénaïs would have appreciated.

It was not until July that D'Antin bestirred himself to attend to his mother's interment. It is probable that the newly rehabilitated courtier was afraid of offending La Maintenon by asking for his mother's body to be placed at St. Germain, so, even in death, Athénaïs was not permitted to return to court. Instead, the coffin was taken to the church at Cordeliers, where the Rochechouart de Mortemarts had buried their family since 1595, and where Athénaïs's mother and brother were interred. On 4 August, in a torchlight procession, her body was finally laid to rest beneath the black marble monument of her family mausoleum. After this humiliating end, Saint-Simon finally did justice to the mother of his mortal enemies, the royal bastards: "The poor of the province, on whom she had rained alms, mourned for her bitterly, as did vast numbers of other people who had benefited by her generosity."

At Versailles, the reaction to the death of the former favorite proved entirely typical of the callous, superficial life of the court. Du Maine could hardly conceal his joy at his mother's decease. While the Duchesse de Chartres, Mme. la Duchesse and the Comte de Toulouse grieved deeply, they were unkindly forbidden by their father from wearing mourning. But Athénaïs's daughters did not conceal their grief, and for some time they dispensed with their beloved finery and stayed in their rooms, avoiding social life and dancing, even gambling, as a mark of respect. Their mourning, La Maintenon complained, began to seem excessive after a month, since, she added wryly, "We don't like long afflictions at court."

The King had heard the news in a letter from D'Antin at Marly as he was about to go hunting. The company heard him read several lines aloud: "In dying, the Marquise de Montespan manifested the most Christian sentiments . . ." and then he told everyone to mount and they set off as usual. But when the party returned, Louis went to his rooms without even removing his riding boots and said that he wished to be alone. His footsteps could be heard pacing restlessly until night fell. In public, however, not a tear escaped him. His favorite, the Duchesse de Bourgogne, dared to ask him why he did not even sigh for a love that had endured so passionately for so many years. "When she retired," he replied, "I thought never to see her again, so from then on she was dead to me."

And La Maintenon? Did she rejoice that the woman she had driven from her love and her home was finally gone? Some days after hearing the news, she described her reaction to a correspondent. "The death of Mme. de Montespan has not left me unable to write to you, but it is true that I was strongly moved, because she was a person who could never leave me indifferent at any time of my life." Even after Athénaïs had left the court, she and La Maintenon had remained fascinated by one another, unable, whatever their own protestations, to release themselves from the close and intense rivalry of twenty years. In 1691, La Maintenon had written to Athénaïs's sister the Abbesse de Fontrevault: "I am overjoyed, Madame, to have received some tokens of remembrance from Madame de Montespan. I feared she was annoyed with me. God knows if I have done anything to merit that, and how my heart is hers!" On the face of it, such declarations may seem merely typical of the former governess's customary breathtaking hypocrisy, yet they also attest to that fascination which neither woman could quite bear to break. In 1698, Athénaïs, in turn, wrote to the Duchesse de Noailles:

> I wrote today to extol your merits to Madame de Maintenon and to felicitate her on the pleasure which she must find in your society . . . You will remember what I said to you about it at St. Joseph, and I repeated it today to Madame de Maintenon in the effusion of my heart which her letter has provoked, for she has told me all that I desired of her, which consisted merely in showing me very plainly that intercourse with me is not agreeable to her. Such may well be the case, and so well do I understand it that I ask nothing else to set my mind and heart at rest about a person who has made too deep an impression upon both not to retain her place there. Nor can I sufficiently impress on you, Madame, the good you have done me by relieving me from so heavy a burden, which to endure or shake off entirely was always very painful. . . . It is done, and I ask nothing more, either from you or Madame de Maintenon . . . I have only to conclude your letter, as I have concluded hers, by saying that silence between her and me becomes agreeable to myself when I know that it is so to her.[6]

Three years later, though, La Maintenon was still writing to Fontrevault, "You do not often mention Madame de Montespan's name. She is too often present in my thoughts . . . believe both of you that the sentiments I entertain for you give me a claim to your regard."

For years, Athénaïs's love for Louis had been ossified, as empty and static as the unused bedchamber at Oiron. There had been no real intimacy or private moments between them since the birth of the

Comte de Toulouse in 1678, and even during her last decade at
court, Athénaïs had barely seen the King alone, surrounded as he was
by the crowds of Versailles and the impregnable barriers of etiquette.
He had receded into images, a young man on a painted white horse, a
cipher in an embroidered pageant on her wall. The sick, sad old man
in his chilly mausoleum of a palace had nothing in common with the
lover Athénaïs remembered, who had danced with her in the *Amants
Magnifiques* or galloped over to Clagny to make love to her while the
ambassadors waited at Versailles. La Maintenon, perversely, proved
more of a link with Louis than Louis himself, and the intensity of
their feelings for one another was perhaps greater, in the end, than for
the man who had ordered both their lives.

La Maintenon was always anxious to prove her disinterestedness in
Athénaïs's removal, as she is here in attempting to explain her motivations to the pupils at St. Cyr: "If loving Madame de Montespan as I
had loved her, I had launched an intrigue for wicked reasons . . . if
instead of urging her to break with the King I had shown her the best
way of keeping him, then indeed I would have given her the ammu-
nition with which to destroy me." But her protestations of virtue sat
uneasily with what was clearly a conflict between affection and ruthless ambition. She seemed unable to dissociate her "love" for Athénaïs
not only from what she saw as her worthy intent, but also from a fearful knowledge that their relationship would inevitably become a fight
to the death. It was, perhaps, not love that the two women shared, but
something akin to it, something forged by all their years of jealousy
and rivalry, by a shared affection for "their" children, by their thorough knowledge of all that was best and worst in one another; something, ultimately, that meant they could never be entirely free of their
own reflection in the other's eyes. By 1707, hardly any of their old
circle were living, either friends or enemies. Racine was gone, and
Molière; the King's artist Le Brun, Marie-Thérèse and Monsieur,
Louvois and Colbert, the Prince de Condé and the Duc de Luxembourg, Ninon de Lenclos, the scandalous friend of La Maintenon's
youth, and Bossuet, the pious ally of her old age, Athénaïs's brother
and sisters. The two marquises were bound in a curious isolation of
memory, their relationship a bond with their shared past.

In truth, La Maintenon's reaction to Athénaïs's death was not
nearly as measured as she gave her correspondent to believe. She
remembered her friend from the Hôtel d'Albret, her patron, her

companion on the weary journeys north to Flanders; she remembered that Athénaïs had given her her children and her husband; she remembered their quarrels and their reconciliations, Athénaïs's dazzling, willful beauty and her ferocious temper, their coalitions and their battles. She remembered Athénaïs in the days of her triumph at Versailles. "Seated in the ravishing pink marble rotunda of the Baths of Siam at Versailles, she held her court attended with all the arts: she commanded waterfalls, the Grand Canal, the tapestry of lawns, the groups of cupids, satyrs and nymphs. Leaning on the alabaster balustrade of the terrace, above the porphyry staircase, she hollowed out the Fontaine des Suisses, which refracted a shimmering reflection of the wood at Satory. Like a goddess, she rode in her gondola along the Grand Canal to the Ile des Cygnes . . ."[7]

In the end, perhaps no one mourned Athénaïs more profoundly than the Marquise de Maintenon. She ran away from Louis and from Du Maine, from her priests and her ladies and her ministers, from the world she had stolen from her oldest friend. Hidden in the privy, an old woman alone in the dark, she wept.

Epilogue

All his life, the King had measured out his days with music. When he rose, when he walked, when he ate, his twenty violinists accompanied him; the strains of his composers Lully and Quinault rendered a permanent ballet of his existence. Only at the end did the old man call for silence.

The King was dying. His bed was placed in the center of the room, his room was in the center of his house. For nearly fifty years, he awakened there, facing east; every morning the two monarchs of the sun saluted one another. If Louis were to have forced his senses, projected his hearing around the great labyrinth that surrounded him, complex as the whorls of a shell, he could have felt his people waiting. The stifling August rooms shuddered and sighed with the breath of their suppressed impatience. He had been the heart of his house, but now its gorgeous prisoners were bleeding away, reconfiguring themselves around a fresh nucleus. As the King rallied and relapsed, they surged back and forth from his chamber, the shuffle of kid on marble, the ebb and flow of a great tide of ambition. The little boy was carried in to say good-bye; the courtiers swarmed, somewhere in the distance, around his uncle. Did the King remember another child, perched on cushions in his coach and six, rattling through Paris on a bright May morning, the cacophony of bells and cries, the gaiety of the tired streets made bright for their tiny monarch? Were things still as they should be, as he had always ensured they had been?

Perhaps the King dreamed an old dream. As he twisted and murmured, the watchers drew near, no longer troubling to conceal their anticipation beneath a grieving countenance. A dark room, an altar of a mattress propped on chairs, a woman splayed naked in faltering candlelight. The hideous priest lays a cloth on the delicious convexity of her belly, arranges a chalice. Her face is masked, a glint of brazen hair beneath her mantle, as somewhere an infant begins to wail, its cries the crescendo of his frantic desire to see, to know, her face, where is her face? The crying is hideously abbreviated, the priest raises the dark, sticky chalice, and the old man writhes down the alleys of his memory, contorting the sheets in a sinuous mockery of sweeter battles, laboring after this enigma of nightmare.

Something, though, something yet that was still unpredictable. The King struggled to breathe, all his legendary energy diminished to this one quotidian action. Tiring, Louis looked up, and there she was, as radiant, as proud, as beautiful as when she first danced with him at the Louvre. Athénaïs as Venus, waiting for him. Someone overlooked the bed, the painted canopy where his old love hovered above him, eternally seductive, beckoning. Her face, then, was the last thing. Did he smile, the King, as his triumphant beauty closed his eyes?

Historical Sources

Many of the primary sources that must be drawn upon in any reconstruction of the life of Athénaïs de Montespan are considered in their own right to be some of the most important works of French literature of the seventeenth century. As such, they are not merely factual reportage, but subject to the same complexities of interpretation as might be applied to novels or plays. Academia speaks, for example, of Sévignéen poetics in describing a particular type of subjective language, while Saint-Simon's unusual manipulations of seventeenth-century French suggest that he was engaged as much on a work of art as on a gazette of his age. The reader must therefore be alert not only to factual discrepancies in the work of the writers of letters or memoirs, but also to the peculiar subjectivity of the authors, their personal motivations and characters, and the location of both letters and memoirs within a very specialized genre of communication which can be as expressive of the changing nature of the French language as it is of the events of the French court.

Letters and memoirs are obviously defined stylistically by the cultural climate in which they are produced, and their function can alter accordingly. In Mme. de Sévigné's letters, for example, it is possible to discern a change in register between the relatively intimate communication of her correspondence with her daughter, Mme. de Grignan, and the more "public" letters, to Bussy-Rabutin, for instance, which were written to be read aloud or shared, and therefore have a more dramatic tone, stagey descriptions and flamboyant language. Since even "personal" writing was performative and carefully designed to display the intellectual qualities and *esprit* of the writer, such sources cannot be taken at face value. The influence of the cultivated language of the salons meant that linguistic skill was linked to a moral capacity; *honnêteté* was demonstrated in the elegant use of words. The vogue for the pen portrait meant that even private descriptions of personalities were flavored by a need to conform to a certain style.

The bulk of memoirs in seventeenth-century France were written by men, with the notable exceptions of Mademoiselle, Mme. de Longueville, Mme. de Motteville and Mme. de la Guette, and they were frequently written partly or wholly after the events they record, which meant they could be polished to form a coherent narrative to present to the world. So vivid are the Duc de Saint-Simon's descriptions of the court of Louis XIV that it is easy to forget that he did not arrive there until 1691, and was therefore not an eyewitness to many of the events he detailed. Athénaïs de Montespan was little more than a memory at Versailles for almost all of the time Saint-Simon spent there. His personal agenda, and its political implications, are clear in his memoirs: he was committed to the ideal of a ruling aristocracy based on birth which had ceased to have any political potential after the suppression of the Fronde. So he loathed the snobbish aspirations of the *noblesse de robe,* believing emphatically in the social hierarchy ordained, in his view, by God, and his respect for the King was greatly tempered whenever he felt that Louis was betraying his kingly role by encouraging parvenus, or when Louis's autocratic ambition came into conflict with what Saint-Simon saw as the essential privileges of his class. The Duc was critical of anyone who offended his sense of the rightness of the social order, but he was also pious, hence his particular loathing for Athénaïs de Montespan's children, whose elevation was not only a glorification of a sin against the holy sacrament of marriage but an insult to the aristocracy from which he came.

Saint-Simon's memoirs can be read as a political manifesto, in that they invoke an ideal of government based on a monarch and a strong aristocracy that he hoped to see realized in the reforms of the next reign. Vincent Cronin suggests that "one can be fair to Louis only by treating with extreme caution the writings of a man so hostile to the King,"[1] and if "hostility" seems too strong a word for what was clearly a troubled fascination, Saint-Simon's criticisms of Louis must nonetheless be read in the light of his attempts to bolster the new order of the Regency under his friend Philippe d'Orléans. This might not seem terribly relevant to the Duc's assessment of Athénaïs's character, but in dwelling upon her vanity and pride, Saint-Simon is criticizing a social revolution (the legitimization of her children and their inclusion in the succession) that offended his most profound beliefs. It is testament to Athénaïs's famous charm, then, that Saint-Simon is able to overcome his loathing of the royal bastards to describe it at all.

Mademoiselle's memoirs, though created rather more spontaneously than Saint-Simon's, in three periods around 1660, 1677 and 1689–90, had just as much of a personal agenda. In her account, the Lauzun affair, as well as her involvement in the Fronde, are vindicated for posterity. The famous incident when she had the cannon of the Bastille turned upon the royal troops, to protect the Frondeurs, led by the Prince de Condé, is lengthily considered, and Mademoiselle is unable to suppress her satisfaction at her own heroism, even as she tries to attribute her actions to the weak prevarication of her father, Gaston d'Orléans. Even though it took some time for the truth to emerge, when it did she was never able to forgive Athénaïs de Montespan for her involvement in the conspiracy to prevent her own marriage to Lauzun, or to take into consideration the fact that Athénaïs was just as much a victim of Louis's deceitfulness in the business as she was. Mademoiselle's justification of her own actions was sufficiently critical of the regime for Philippe d'Orléans to ban her memoirs when they appeared in 1718 and, like Saint-Simon, she must be read with an awareness of a subtext.

Both Saint-Simon and Mme. de Sévigné have been used as sources and models for subsequent French writers, perhaps most famously by Proust in *A la Recherche du Temps Perdu*. He compares the style of Mme. de Sévigné's letters to the painting of the artist Elstir, suggesting that she is absorbed by the personal, subjective qualities of a situation and disregards its "reality" as perceived by others. Her subjectivity, Proust proposes, had nothing of the communal to it. It is concerned with creating an affective world, constructed from what acts upon the senses of the individual. Again, such a rarefied reading of Mme. de Sévigné might not seem relevant to her eager reportage of Athénaïs de Montespan's triumphs and decline, but this interpretation emphasizes the specialized individualism that makes Mme. de Sévigné's letters such an important literary work and such a problematic historical source. In a sense, her subjectivity presents an opposite problem from Saint-Simon's in that many of her letters were in a sense love letters, stemming from the urgent need to communicate with her daughter, whom she loved in a way that seems positively sinister to modern psychology, and not designed as a chronicle to be admired by posterity. Whether the Sévignéen tone is seen to be compromised by its intimacy or by its performative qualities, the relationship between the author of the letters and their recipients prevents them from ever being relied upon as an entirely objective historical source.

The nicknames employed by Mme. de Sévigné to such amusing effect signpost another problem with the primary sources of information about Louis XIV's court, for these also had a serious function as code names, required for the sake of discretion by a writer whose political sympathies had once been allied with the Fronde, and who knew about the spy network that operated at Versailles. Louis was famous as a king who "wanted to know everything," and letter-writing, as his daughter the Princesse de Conti discovered when she insulted Mme. de Maintenon, could be a dangerous business. The Princesse Palatine was fully aware that her letters were read by the King's spies, and her comments often got her into trouble. Yet she engaged in an indirect dialogue with Louis via the spies, using her letters to express feelings and criticisms that she would never have dared utter to his face. "I must confess," she huffed after a scolding from Louis, "that I am thoroughly angry with the King for treating me like a chambermaid, which would be more befitting for his Maintenon, for she was born to it, but I was not."

Madame used her letters to complain about the duplicities of the court, highlighting the atmosphere of verbal obscurity that was so alien to her straight-talking character. "Perhaps," she wrote about the rumors that her son was to marry Athénaïs de Montespan's daughter, "I shall be exiled over this . . . for I shall not fail to let [Monsieur] know my exact opinion, which, as usual, he will report to the King . . . And if the King himself, to intimidate me, should speak to me about this matter, I shall tell him in plain words that I do not like it at all." Of course, poor Madame never did any such thing, but her knowledge that Louis had access to her "private" thoughts created an opportunity for communication which was, paradoxically, more honest.

Philippe Beaussant's stunning analysis of the symbolic ritual that pervaded even the most quotidian activities at Louis XIV's court shows just how difficult it is to penetrate the hermeneutical labyrinth the King established around him, and the reservations about the objectivity of primary sources expressed here could be elaborated upon at length. The genre of the memoir, the public use of letters, as exemplified by Mme. de Maintenon's desire to manipulate her story for posterity, and the checks on personal expression imposed by censorship all contribute to the caution with which those sources must be approached, and yet, of course, they remain the only access we have to the world Athénaïs de Montespan inhabited.

"Secrets add to the taste of things," Athénaïs once remarked to Mademoiselle, and she was probably far better equipped than the modern historian to deal with a world where no one quite meant what they said.

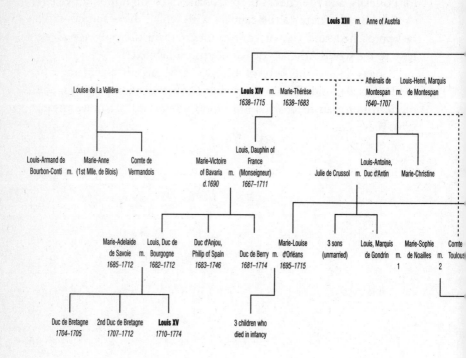

Louis XIII m. Anne of Austria

Louise de La Vallière ----------------- **Louis XIV** m. Marie-Thérèse   Athénaïs de   Louis-Henri, Marquis
                                        1638–1715   *1638–1683*   Montespan m. de Montespan
                                                                        1640–1707

Louis-Armand de   Marie-Anne   Comte de   Marie-Victoire   Louis, Dauphin of   Louis-Antoine,
Bourbon-Conti m. (1st Mlle. de Blois) Vermandois   of Bavaria   m.   France   Julie de Crussol m. Duc d'Antin   Marie-Christine
                                                      d.1690   (Monseigneur)
                                                                     1667–1711

                Marie-Adelaide   Louis, Duc de   Duc d'Anjou,   Marie-Louise   3 sons   Louis, Marquis   Marie-Sophie   Comte
                de Savoie   m. Bourgogne   Philip of Spain   Duc de Berry m. d'Orléans   (unmarried)   de Gondrin   m.   de Noailles   m.   Toulous
                1685–1712   *1682–1712*   *1683–1746*   *1681–1714*   *1695–1715*   1   2

Duc de Bretagne   2nd Duc de Bretagne   **Louis XV**   3 children who
1704–1705   *1707–1712*   *1710–1774*   died in infancy

The Royal Family Tree

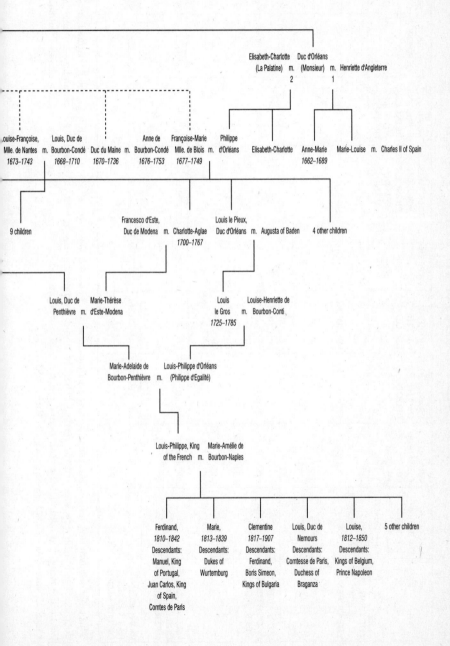

Système des Sièges (Seating System)

	DAUPHIN, DAUPHINE, SONS AND DAUGHTERS OF FRANCE	GRAND-CHILDREN OF FRANCE	PRINCESSES OF THE BLOOD	PRINCES OF THE BLOOD	CARDINALS	DUCHESSES, FOREIGN PRINCESSES, SPANISH GRANDEES	DUKES, FOREIGN PRINCES, SPANISH GRANDEES	LADIES OF QUALITY	GENTLEMEN OF QUALITY
THE KING									
THE QUEEN	STOOL	STOOL	STOOL	STANDING	STANDING BEFORE THE KING / STOOL BEFORE THE QUEEN	STOOL	STANDING	STANDING	STANDING
SONS AND DAUGHTERS OF FRANCE	ARMCHAIR	STOOL	STOOL	STANDING BEFORE SONS / STOOL BEFORE DAUGHTERS	STOOL	STOOL	STANDING	STANDING	STANDING
GRAND-CHILDREN OF FRANCE		ARMCHAIR	CHAIR	CHAIR	CHAIR	CHAIR	STOOL	STOOL	STANDING
PRINCES AND PRINCESSES OF THE BLOOD			ARMCHAIR	ARMCHAIR	ARMCHAIR	ARMCHAIR	ARMCHAIR	SEATED	SEATED

This table is drawn from Henri Brocher's *Le Rang et l'Etiquette sous l'Ancien Régime* (Paris, 1934), p. 28. How do the horizontal categories conduct themselves in the presence of the vertical? The table indicates the solutions, at least at Versailles. For example, a cardinal had to stand before the King, but could have a chair before a grandchild of France and an armchair before a prince of the blood. (Emmanuel le Roy Ladurie, *Saint-Simon ou le Système de la Cour*, Paris, 1997.)

Acknowledgments

I should like to thank Professor Anthony Nuttall of New College, Oxford, for his excellent advice, without which this book would never have been attempted. Many thanks, too, to Michael Alcock, at Michael Alcock Management, for endless encouragement and faith in the book. Alan Samson at Time Warner Books has been equally kind, and I am very grateful, as I am to my editor, Caroline North, whose patience and diligence have been so overwhelming that any remaining errors in the book are entirely mine. Linda Silverman was wonderful at tracking down pictures from all over Europe. Kinch Hoekstra, of Balliol College, was also kind enough to provide some obscure material: thanks for easing the tension. Without the scrupulous and dedicated attention of Asya Muchnick, this book might have proved as exasperatingly elusive as its subject. I am extremely grateful for her scholarly discernment. Thanks to Jack Murnighan, for Florence. Most of all, I would like to thank Dominique de Bastarrechea, for more inspiration, goodness and delight than I or this book can ever deserve.

Notes

GENERAL SOURCES

As certain sources have been quoted extensively, to avoid unnecessary repetition, these are not listed separately in the notes. Unless otherwise noted, Madame de Sévigné's correspondence is quoted from *Correspondance,* edited by Roger Duchêne (Paris, 1978) and *Lettres,* edited by Louis Jean Nicolas Monmerqué (Paris, 1866). The memoirs of the Duc de Saint-Simon are Lucy Norton's translation (London, 1967). Quotations from Bussy-Rabutin are from *Correspondance avec Sa Famille et Ses Amis,* edited by Ludovic Lalanne (Paris, 1858).

For Mme. de Maintenon (Mme. Scarron), the definitive source is the *Correspondance Générale,* edited by Théophile Lavallée (Paris, 1865). Quotations from Mademoiselle, Duchesse de Montpensier, are from the *Mémoires* edited by Christian Bouyer (Paris, 1985), while Mme. de Caylus is quoted from her *Souvenirs,* edited by Bernard Noël (Paris, 1965). Unless otherwise sourced, the quotations from Louis XIV are taken from his memoirs as edited by Jean Longnon (Paris, 1978). Primi Visconti is quoted from *Mémoires sur la Cour de France,* edited by Jean Lemoine (Paris, 1909). The correspondence of Madame, the second Duchesse d'Orléans (the Princess Palatine) comes from *Correspondance,* edited by Olivier Amiel (Paris, 1985).

Full details of these and other texts cited in the Notes may be found in the Bibliography.

EPIGRAPHS

The epigraphs that open each chapter are taken from the *Maxims* of the Duc de la Rochefoucauld.

POEMS

I do not pretend to be a literary translator, but except where translations are otherwise credited, I have tried to render the meaning of the poems I have quoted and, where I was capable, their rhyme and meter.

A NOTE ON CURRENCY

The basic unit of money at Louis XIV's court was the livre. There were 3 livres to 1 ecu, and 10 livres to one pistole, which was equal in value to a louis d'or. Three livres were roughly equivalent to $15 in today's money. So, for example, Marly, which cost 4.5 million livres to build, would have cost about $22.5 million in today's money. However, the purchasing power of the livre of course fluctuated widely during Louis's reign.

ON PRONUNCIATION

Athénaïs is pronounced A-ten´-ay-EES.

CHAPTER ONE

1. Primi Visconti. See General Sources above.
2. Be limping, fifteen, witless
   Ill-born, brainless, titless
   Have your children
   In a back room
   You'll have the best of lovers on my faith
   And La Vallière is the proof.
3. Cronin, *Louis XIV,* p. 70.
4. Mongrédien, *Madeleine de Scudéry,* p. 164.
5. Diderot and D'Alembert, "Article adultère," in *Encyclopédie, ou, Dictionnaire raisonnée des sciences, des arts et des métiers,* p. 128.
6. Melchior-Bonnet and De Tocqueville, *Histoire de l'Adultère.*
7. Quoted by Dulong in *Le Mariage du Roi Soleil.*
8. Louis XIV, *Oeuvres.*
9. Comtesse de Lafayette, *The Princesse de Clèves,* p. 46.

CHAPTER TWO

1. Mme. de Caylus. See General Sources.
2. Voltaire, *Le Siècle de Louis XIV.*
3. Duc de Saint-Simon. See General Sources.

4. Mitford, *The Sun King,* p. 45.

5. Cronin, *Louis XIV,* p. 33.

6. Mongrédien, *Madeleine de Scudéry,* p. 164.

7. Martine Sonnet, "A Daughter to Educate," trans. Arthur Gold-hammer in *A History of Women in the West,* ed. Davis and Farge, p. 122.

8. Mme. de Sévigné. See General Sources.

9. Mme. de Sévigné, *Selected Letters,* p. 203.

10. Madame. See General Sources.

11. *Mercure Galant,* 1660.

12. Quoted in *Memoirs of Madame de Montespan* (London, 1754).

13. Cousin, "Clef inédite du Grand Cyrus."

14. Leonard Tancock, "Introduction," in Duc de la Rochefoucauld, *Maxims,* p. 12.

15. George Eliot, "Women in France: Madame de Sablé," in *Selected Essays, Poems and Other Writings* (London: Penguin, 1990), p. 9.

16. Tancock, "Introduction," in *Maxims.*

17. Jean-Paul Desaive, "The Ambiguities of Literature," trans. Arthur Goldhammer in *A History of Women in the West,* ed. Davis and Farge, p. 264.

18. Lougée, *Le Paradis des Femmes,* p. 25.

19. Mme. de Sévigné, *Selected Letters,* p. 86.

20. Lougée, *Le Paradis des Femmes,* p. 192.

21. Mortemart, old fellow,
    Loves La Tambonneau
    She's a little yellow
    But he's an ugly beau.

22. Petitfils, *Madame de Montespan,* p. 10.

23. Anonymous, *Alosie, ou les Amours de M.T.P.*

24. Magne, *Ninon de Lanclos.*

CHAPTER THREE

1. Petitfils, *Madame de Montespan.*

2. And on my faith you will have the best of lovers.

CHAPTER FOUR

1. Mademoiselle. See General Sources.

2. Marquis de La Fare, *Mémoires et réflexions sur les principaux évène-ments du règne de Louis XIV.*

3. Tooth and nail.
4. Madame, quoted by Mademoiselle. See General Sources.
5. Petitfils, *Madame de Montespan,* p. 42.
6. Primi Visconti.
7. Truc, *Madame de Montespan,* p. 163.
8. Ibid., p. 171.
9. Poucher, *Les Trois Grands Divertissements de Versailles.*

CHAPTER FIVE

1. Blunt, *Art et Architecture en France.* For a discussion of Versailles and the theory of the baroque, see pp. 130–142, 302–311.
2. Sharing with Jupiter
   Has naught of dishonor
   And doubtless it can only be glorious
   With the King of the Gods to be rivalrous.
3. Louis XIV, *Oeuvres.*
4. Mme. de Caylus.
5. When Mortemart perceived
   Montespan had conceived
   He sang with his theorba,
   "Alleluia."
      A theorba is an obsolete form of lute.
6. Mademoiselle.

CHAPTER SIX

1. Quoted in Michel de Decker, *Louis XIV,* p. 119.
2. Voltaire, *Le Siècle de Louis XIV.*
3. *Memoirs of Madame de Montespan* (London, 1754).
4. Voltaire, *Le Siècle de Louis XIV.*
5. Petitfils, *Madame de Montespan.*
6. Mitford, *The Sun King,* p. 55.
7. Petitfils, *Madame de Montespan.*
8. Mademoiselle.
9. Madame.
10. Mme. de Sévigné, *Selected Letters,* p. 61.
11. Ibid., p. 63.
12. Marquis de Saint-Maurice, *Lettres sur la Cour de Louis XIV.*
13. Ibid.
14. Mme. de Sévigné, *Selected Letters,* p. 116.

CHAPTER SEVEN

1. Charlie Steen, chapter 4 in *The Reign of Louis XIV,* ed. Sonnino.
2. Ibid.
3. Saint-Simon.
4. Mme. de Maintenon. See General Sources.
5. Mme. de Lafayette, quoted by Mme. de Sévigné. See General Sources.
6. With regard to the names of Athénaïs de Montespan's children by Louis XIV, to avoid confusion, I refer to them by the titles which they were eventually given, e.g., the Duc du Maine. However, their titles were not officially bestowed until the children had been formally legitimated, though they were used prior to the conclusion of the legitimization process.
7. Quoted in Petitfils, *Madame de Montespan.*
8. Mme. de Maintenon.
9. The quotation is widely attributed to Ninon de Lenclos.
10. Saint-Simon.
11. Mme. de Maintenon.
12. Bossuet, *Oeuvres et Correspondance.*
13. Mme. de Sévigné.
14. Ibid.

CHAPTER EIGHT

1. Louis XIV, *Oeuvres.*
2. Ibid.
3. Mme. de Caylus.
4. Petitfils, *Madame de Montespan.*
5. Quoted in Beaussant, *Louis XIV, Artiste.*
6. Louis XIV, *Oeuvres.*
7. Attributed in numerous works to Abbé Testu.
8. Louis XIV, *Oeuvres.*
9. Ibid.
10. Quoted in Dunlop, *Louis XIV,* p. 217.
11. Louis XIV, *Oeuvres.*
12. Colbert, in a 1671 letter to the Duc de Chaulnes, then Ambassador of Rome.
13. Time, which destroys all, respecting your power,
    Allows me to clear the years of this work,
    Every poet who yet wishes to be immortal,

Must acquire your approbation.
There is no beauty in my writings,
Of which you do not know the least traces,
Oh! Who knows like you the beauties and the graces,
Words and looks, all is charm in you.

14. Hoffmann, *Society of Pleasures,* p. 58.
15. Letter to the Comte d'Olonne, 1656, quoted in *Recueil de Textes Littéraires Français, XVIIᵉ Siècle,* eds. Chassang and Senninger, p. 49.
16. Williams, *Madame de Montespan and Louis XIV.*

CHAPTER NINE

1. This anecdote is mentioned in many sources, and the case is discussed in detail in Guitton, "Cas de Conscience pour un Confesseur du Roi: Madame de Montespan," in *Nouvelle Revue Theologique* (Louvain, 1955).
2. Mme. de Maintenon.
3. Couton, *La Chair et L'Ame.*
4. Ibid.
5. Ibid.

CHAPTER TEN

1. Mme. de Sévigné, *Selected Letters,* p. 165.
2. Ibid., p. 194.
3. Ibid., p. 215.
4. Roche, *La Culture des Apparences,* p. 59.
5. Berthelée, *Inventaire des Documents des Archives Municipales de Montpellier.*
6. Mitford, *The Sun King,* p. 64.
7. Lewis, *The Splendid Century,* p. 41.
8. E. Bergler, *The Psychology of Gambling* (New York, 1958), quoted in Dunkley, *Gambling: A Social and Moral Problem in France 1685–1792,* pp. 5–6.
9. Quoted in Petitfils, *Madame de Montespan.*
10. Mme. de Sévigné.
11. Ibid.
12. The one limps and walks with a cane
The other is strong and rotund
The one is thin to the furthest point
The other bursts with embonpoint.

13. This study is quoted in Roche, *La Culture des Apparences.*
14. Mitford, *The Sun King,* p. 58.
15. Capefigue, "La Marquise de Montespan."

CHAPTER ELEVEN

1. The *chambre des filles* was distinct from the formal posts of *dames d'honneur* and *dames d'atour* given to noblewomen who attended on the Queen and other female members of the royal household. It referred particularly to the young unmarried women who attended on Madame, the wife of Monsieur, but also included young women who attended court, hoping to make their way in society and, aided by their families, to find a suitable husband.
2. Mme. de Sévigné, *Selected Letters,* p. 209.
3. La Vallière was common,
   La Montespan a peeress
   La Ludres was a canoness,
   All three were all for one.
   It is the greatest of potentates
   Who assembles all estates.
   The joke here is that Louis's choice of mistresses represents all three estates — Church, aristocracy and commoners — the divisions of French society from which its parliaments were drawn.
4. The Duchesse de Valentinois, Diane de Poitiers, was the famously imperious and avaricious mistress of Henri II.
5. Quoted in Richardt, *Le Soleil du Grand Siècle.*
6. Truc, *Madame de Montespan.*
7. Ibid.
8. The Duc du Maine's letters are discussed in Hastier, *Vieilles Histoires, Etranges Enigmes,* pp. 39–49. The existence of the little book is not mentioned by either Saint-Simon or Mme. de Sévigné, and there is a degree of controversy as to its authorship. Most people assume that it was dictated by La Maintenon, but Louis Racine claimed that his father, the great writer Jean Racine, was responsible.
9. Pevitt, *The Man Who Would Be King,* p. 249.
10. Lewis, *The Splendid Century,* p. 244.
11. Abbé de Choisy, *Mémoires.*
12. This pun on the Marquise's name renders it as "Madame Now" or, as we might put it, the woman of the moment.

13. Bussy-Rabutin. See General Sources.

14. From a contemporary pamphlet entitled *Le Passe Temps Royal, ou, Les Amours de Mlle de Fontanges* (The Royal Pastime, or the Loves of Mlle. de Fontanges).

     The first French newspaper, Renaudot's *Gazette* was founded in 1638 and was soon followed by the *Mercure Français* and the *Mercure Galant*. Since the press was censored, these newspapers tended to be rather innocuous in their references to the court, focusing on politely gossipy stories about high society. To cater to more lurid tastes, a burgeoning pamphlet industry provided information about politics, wars, the Church and criminal or sexual scandals, often with woodcut illustrations. Since the pamphlets were produced irregularly and often anonymously, they were harder to trace and were therefore far more satirical and disrespectful in tone than the mainstream press. As a gesture of caution, well-known figures were disguised with pseudonyms, just as Madame de Sévigné disguised the characters in her letters, but these aliases were so flimsy that the real identity of the subjects was usually obvious. It is suggested that one of the reasons Louis was so exigent in his demands to the Dutch after their defeat in the wars was his outrage at the portraits of him produced in the pamphlet press.

15. Charming object, gift worthy of the skies
    Your beauty comes from the hand of the Gods
    And is it not an image of Parnassus
    You shall see in the story I trace
    Since my verses present so much grace
    That to be offered to the tamer of humans
    Accompanied by a word from your mouth
    And presented by your divine hands.

16. *Chaise de commodité* literally means "chair of convenience," i.e., a lavatory.

17. Once at the court I was viewed as an equal,
    Mistress of my King, I defied a rival,
    Never did favor take such swift leave
    Never was fortune so swift destroyed,
    Oh, that distance is short
    From the home of the court to the horror of the grave.

18. Quoted in Davet, *Mademoiselle de Fontanges.*

CHAPTER TWELVE

All quotations in this chapter relating to La Reynie's investigation of the Affair of the Poisons are taken from Ravaisson, *Archives de Bastille,* t. IV à t. VII.

1. This English translation of La Fontaine's riddle is taken from Mossiker, *The Affair of the Poisons.*
2. Davis and Farge, *A History of Women in the West.*
3. Mme. de Sévigné, *Selected Letters,* p. 196.
4. Quoted in Niderst, *Les Français Vus par Eux-Mêmes.*
5. Cited in Lebigre, *L'Affaire des Poisons.*
6. Mme. de Sévigné.
7. The Duchesse de Bouillon's cheeky remarks were quoted with delight by many contemporary commentators, including Mme. de Sévigné, though it is suggested that the duchess polished them for posterity after her interrogation.
8. Petitfils, *L'Affaire des Poisons.*
9. Briggs, *Communities of Belief.*
10. Ibid.
11. Ibid.
12. Keith Thomas observes in *Religion and the Decline of Magic* that "acceptable evidence for the literal reality of ritual devil-worship, whether in England or on the Continent, is extremely scanty." One of the principal discussions of Madame de Montespan's involvement in black magic occurs in Francis Mossiker's *The Affair of the Poisons.* Mossiker's interpretation of witchcraft practices in seventeenth-century France is based on Margaret Murray's elaboration of the story of the pre-Christian witch cult suggested by Jacob Grimm in *Deutsche Mythologie* (1835), and yet the conclusions Murray drew from this were almost totally groundless. It is extraordinary that so many writers seem to have accepted such evidence as proof that the Black Mass occurred, let alone that Madame de Montespan was involved in it, when most historians of the subject concur that the evidence is dubious.
13. Quoted in Louis XIV, *Oeuvres.*
14. Mme. de Caylus.

CHAPTER THIRTEEN

1. Mme. de Sévigné.
2. From "The Diary of Samuel Pepys," 13 January 1662. Quoted in Stephen Coote, *Samuel Pepys: A Life* (London: Hodder and Stoughton, 2000), p. 85.
3. Mme. de Maintenon.
4. Mme. de Maintenon, quoted in Petitfils, *Madame de Montespan.*
5. Pitts, *La Grande Mademoiselle at the Court of France.*
6. Mademoiselle.
7. Louis XIV, *Oeuvres.*
8. Lavallée, *Memoires sur Madame de Maintenon.*
9. Mme. de Maintenon.
10. Lavallée, *Memoires sur Madame de Maintenon.*
11. Mademoiselle.
12. Abbé de Choisy, *Mémoires.*
13. Voltaire, *Le Siècle de Louis XIV.*
14. Abbé de Choisy, *Mémoires.*
15. Taillandier, *Le Grand Roi et Sa Coeur.*
16. Jonathan Swift, "A Tale of a Tub," in *Jonathan Swift: A Critical Edition of the Major Works,* ed. Angus Ross and David Woolley (Oxford: Oxford University Press, 1984).
17. Caroly, *Le Corps du Roi Soleil.*
18. Louis XIV, *Oeuvres.*

CHAPTER FOURTEEN

1. Quoted in Cronin, *Louis XIV,* p. 304.
2. Michel de Montaigne, *The Essays: A Selection,* trans. and ed. M. A. Screech (London: Penguin, 1987).
3. Saint-Simon.
4. Ibid.
5. Ibid.
6. Ibid.
7. Voltaire, *Le Siècle de Louis XIV.*
8. Mme. de Caylus.
9. Ibid.
10. Mitford, *The Sun King.*
11. Horace Walpole, *The Letters of Horace Walpole,* ed. Paget Jackson Toynbee and Helen Toynbee (Oxford: Clarendon Press, 1903).
12. Saint-Simon.

13. Ibid.
14. Mme. de Caylus.
15. Virgil, *The Aeneid,* trans. Robert Fitzgerald (London: Harvill, 1984).

CHAPTER FIFTEEN

1. Pevitt, *The Man Who Would Be King.*
2. Cronin, *Louis XIV,* p. 311.
3. Williams, *Madame de Montespan and Louis XIV,* pp. 351–2.
4. Petitfils, *Madame de Montespan.*
5. The will of the Marquis de Montespan is preserved in the Archives du Capitole.
6. Petitfils, *Madame de Montespan,* p. 278.
7. Petitfils, *Madame de Montespan.*
8. Do not, then, expect my return
   Until the return of spring.
   I will not come to pay my court to you
   Until the first flight of the swallows.
9. There, you will receive from my hands
   Fruits, green peas, artichokes, salads
   While all the doctors
   Forbid them to their patients.
10. Couton, *La Chair et L'Ame.*
11. Ibid.

CHAPTER SIXTEEN

1. Saint-Simon.
2. Ibid.
3. Duc d'Antin, *Mémoires.*
4. This edict, and the Parlement's traditional right of "remonstrance," is discussed in Pevitt, *The Man Who Would Be King.*
5. Saint-Simon.
6. Petitfils, *Madame de Montespan.*
7. Capefigue, "La Marquise de Montespan."

HISTORICAL SOURCES

1. Cronin, *Louis XIV,* p. 374.

Bibliography

Anonymous. *Alosie, ou les Amours de Mme de M. T.P.* Cologne, 1681.

————. *Madame de Sévigné and her Contemporaries.* London, 1861.

————. *Memoirs of Mme de Montespan.* London: Cooper, 1754.

Antin, Louis Antoine de Gondrin de Pardaillon, Duc d'. *Mémoires.* Paris: Société de Bibliophiles Français, 1822.

Aries, Philippe. *L'Enfant et La Vie Familiale sous l'Ancien Régime.* Paris: Editions du Seuil, 1973.

Beaussant, Philippe. *Louis XIV, Artiste.* Paris: Editions Payot et Rivages, 1999.

————. *Le Roi Soleil Se Lève Aussi.* Paris: Editions Gallimard, 2000.

Berthelée, J., ed. *Inventaire des Documents des Archives Municipales de Montpelier,* Vol. 4 (1665–1788).

Bertière, Simone. *Les Femmes du Roi Soleil.* Paris: Editions du Fallois, 1998.

Blunt, Anthony. *Art et Architecture en France, 1500–1700.* Translated by Monique Chatenet. Paris: Editions Macula, 1983.

Bonnassieux, Pierre. *Le Château de Clagny et Madame de Montespan.* Paris: Picard, 1881.

Bossuet, Jacques Bénigne. *Oeuvres et Correspondance. Edition critique de l'abbé J. Lebarq, revue et augmentée par* Charles Urbain et Eugène Levesque. Paris: Desclée, de Brouwer et cie, 1925.

Briggs, Robin. *Communities of Belief: Cultural and Social Tensions in Early Modern France.* Oxford: Clarendon Press, 1989.

————. *Witches and Neighbors: The Social and Cultural Context of European Witchery.* London: Fontana Press, 1997.

Bussy, Roger de Rabutin, comte de. *Histoire Amoureuse des Gaules.* Paris: Editions Gallimard, 1993.

———. *Correspondance avec Sa Famille et Ses Amis.* Edited by Ludovic Lalanne. Paris: Charpentier, 1858.

———. *Mémoires.* Paris: Charpentier, 1857.

Capefigue, J. B. "La Marquise de Montespan: Athénaïs de Roche-chouart-Mortemart," in *Les Splendeurs de Versailles.* Paris, 1868.

Caroly, Michelle. *Le Corps du Roi-Soleil.* Paris: Les Editions de Paris, 1999.

Caylus, Marie Marguérite Le Valois de Villette de Murçay, Comtesse de. *Souvenirs.* Edited by Bernard Noël. Paris: Mercure de France, 1965.

Chassang, Arsène, and **Charles Senninger.** *Recueil de Textes Littéraires Français, XVIIᵉ Siècle.* Paris: Hachette, 1966.

Chaussinand-Nogaret, Guy. *La Vie Quotidienne des Femmes du Roi: d'Agnès Sorel à Marie-Antoinette.* Paris: Hachette, 1990.

Choisy, François-Timoléon, Abbé de. *Mémoires.* Edited by Georges Mongrédien. Paris: Mercure de France, 1966.

Clarke, Mary, and **Clement Crisp.** *Ballet: An Illustrated History.* London: Hamish Hamilton, 1992.

Clément, Pierre. *Madame de Montespan et Louis XIV.* Paris, 1868.

Cousin, Victor. "Clef inédite du Grand Cyrus, roman de Mlle de Scudéry." *Journal des Savants,* 1857.

———. *Madame de Sablé,* 2 vols. Paris: Didier Librairie-Editeur, 1854.

Couton, Georges. *La Chair et L'Ame: Louis XIV Entre Ses Maîtresses et Bossuet.* Grenoble: Presses Universitaires de Grenoble, 1995.

Cronin, Vincent. *Louis XIV.* London: Harvill, 1964.

Davet, Michel [pseud.]. *Mademoiselle de Fontanges.* Paris: Albin Michel, 1941.

Davis, Natalie Zemon, and **Arlette Farge,** eds. *A History of Women in the West, Vol. 3: Renaissance and Enlightenment Paradoxes.* Series edited by Georges Duby and Michelle Perrot. Cambridge, Mass.: Belknap Press, 1993.

David, Elizabeth. *Harvest of the Cold Months.* London: Penguin, 1994.

Decker, Michel de. *Madame de Montespan: La Grande Sultane.* Paris: Librairie Académique Perrin, 1985.

———. *Louis XIV: Le Bon Plaisir du Roi.* Paris: Belfond, 2000.

Devismes, Roland. *La Cour à Versailles.* Paris: La Pensée Universelle, 1974.

Diderot, Denis, and **Jean Le Rond d'Alembert.** *Encyclopédie, ou, Dictionnaire raisonnée des sciences, des arts et des métiers.* London: Samuel Leacroft, 1772.

Du Crest, Sabine. *Des Fêtes à Versailles: Les Divertissements de Louis XIV.* Paris: Aux Amateurs de Livres, 1990.

Dulong, Claude. *La Vie Quotidienne des Femmes au Grand Siècle.* Paris: Hachette, 1984.

——. *Le Mariage du Roi Soleil.* Paris: Albin Michel, 1986.

Dunkley, John. *Gambling: A Social and Moral Problem in France, 1685–1792.* Oxford: University of Oxford, 1985.

Dunlop, Ian. *Louis XIV.* London: Chatto and Windus, 1999.

Feray, Jean. *Architecture Intérieure et Décoration en France des Origines à 1875.* Paris: Berger-Levrault, 1985.

Funck-Brentano, Frantz. *Le Drame des Poisons.* Paris: Hachette, 1900.

Gibson, Wendy. *Women in Seventeenth-Century France.* London: Macmillan, 1989.

Goubert, Pierre. *L'Ancien Régime.* Paris: Librairie Armand Colin, 1969.

Hastier, Louis. *Vieilles Histoires, Etranges Enigmes.* Paris: Librairie Arthème Fayard, 1957.

Hoffmann, Kathryn A. *Society of Pleasures: Interdisciplinary Readings in Pleasure and Power During the Reign of Louis XIV.* London: Macmillan, 1997.

Hufton, Olwen. *The Prospect Before Her: A History of Women in Western Europe, 1500–1800.* London: HarperCollins, 1995.

Keeble, N. H., ed. *The Cultural Identity of Seventeenth-Century Woman: A Reader.* London: Routledge, 1994.

La Fare, Charles Auguste, Marquis de. *Mémoires et réflexions sur les principaux évènements du règne de Louis XIV,* 3 vols. Edited by Michaud and Poujoulat. Paris, 1838.

Lafayette, Marie-Madeleine Pioche de La Vergne, Comtesse de. *The Princesse de Clèves.* Translated by Robin Buss. London: Penguin, 1992.

Lavallée, Théophile, ed. *Mémoires sur Madame de Maintenon.* Paris, 1863.

La Vallière, Louise Françoise de La Baume Le Blanc, Duchesse de. *Reflexions sur la miséricorde de Dieu.* Paris: Christophe David, 1740.

La Rochefoucauld, François Duc de la. *Maxims.* Translated and introduction by Leonard Tancock. London: Penguin, 1959.

Lebigre, Arlette. *L'Affaire des Poisons.* Brussels: Editions Complexe, 1989.

Le Nabour, Eric. *La Porteuse d'Ombre: Madame de Maintenon et le Roi-Soleil.* Paris: Tallandier, 1999.

Le Roy Ladurie, Emmanuel. *L'Ancien Régime: de Louis XIII à Louis XV, 1610–1770.* Paris: Hachette, 1991.

Le Roy Ladurie, Emmanuel, and **Jean-François Fitou** (collab.). *Saint-Simon, ou, Le Système de la Cour.* Paris: Librairie Arthème Fayard, 1997.

Levi, Anthony. *Cardinal Richelieu and the Making of France.* London: Carroll & Graf, 2000.

Lewis, W. H. *The Splendid Century: Some Aspects of French Life in the Reign of Louis XIV.* London: Eyre and Spottiswoode, 1953.

Lougée, Carolyn C. *Le Paradis des Femmes: Women, Salons, and Social Stratification in Seventeenth-Century France.* Princeton: Princeton University Press, 1976.

Louis XIV. *Mémoires.* Edited by Jean Longnon. Paris: Tallandier, 1978.

———. *Oeuvres,* 6 vols. Edited by Philippe-Henri, Comte de Grimoard, and Philippe-Antoine Grouvelle. Paris, Strasbourg: Treuttel et Würtz, 1806.

Magne, Emile. *Ninon de Lanclos.* Paris, 1948.

Maintenon, Françoise d'Aubigné, Madame Scarron, Marquise de. *Correspondance Générale,* 4 vols. Edited by Théophile Lavallée. Paris: Charpentier, 1865.

———. *Lettres.* Edited by Marcel Langlois. Paris: Letouzey et Ané, 1939.

Melchior-Bonnet, Sabine, and **Aude de Tocqueville.** *Histoire de l'Adultère.* Paris: Editions de la Martinière, 2000.

Mitford, Nancy. *The Sun King: Louis XIV at Versailles.* London: Penguin, 1994.

Mongrédien, Georges. *Madeleine de Scudéry et son Salon.* Paris: Tallandier, 1946.

———. *Madame de Montespan et l'Affaire des Poisons.* Paris: Hachette, 1953.

Montespan, Françoise Athénaïs de Mortemart, Marquise de. *Memoirs of Madame La Marquise de Montespan, Written by Herself,* a translation of the apocryphal *Mémoires* of 1829, attributed to Philippe Musoni. New York: Merrill and Baker, n.d.

Montpensier, Anne Marie Louise d'Orléans, Duchesse de (called Mademoiselle). *Mémoires.* Edited by Christian Bouyer. Paris: Albin Michel, 1985.

Mossiker, Frances. *The Affair of the Poisons.* London: Gollancz, 1970.

Newton, William R. *L'Espace du Roi: La Cour de France au Château de Versailles, 1682–1789.* Paris: Librairie Arthème Fayard, 2000.

Niderst, Alain, ed. *Les Français Vus Par Eux-Mêmes: Le Siècle de Louis XIV.* Paris: Robert Laffont, 1997.

Norton, Lucy. *The Sun King and His Loves.* London: The Folio Society, 1982.

Ojala, Jeanne A., and **William T. Ojala.** *Madame de Sévigné: A Seventeenth-Century Life.* New York: Berg, 1990.

Orléans, Elisabeth-Charlotte, Duchesse de (called La Palatine or Madame). *Correspondance.* Edited by Olivier Amiel. Paris: Mercure de France, 1981.

———. *A Woman's Life in the Court of the Sun King: Letters of Liselotte Van der Pfalz, Elisabeth-Charlotte, Duchesse d'Orléans 1652–1722.* Translated and edited by Elborg Forster. Baltimore: Johns Hopkins University Press, 1984.

Orsenna, Erik. *Portrait d'un Homme Heureux: André le Nôtre, 1613–1700.* Paris: Librairie Arthème Fayard, 2000.

Petitfils, Jean-Christian. *L'Affaire des Poisons.* Paris: Albin Michel, 1977.

———. *Madame de Montespan.* Paris: Librairie Arthème Fayard, 1988.

Pevitt, Christine. *The Man Who Would Be King: The Life of Philippe d'Orléans, Regent of France.* London: Weidenfeld and Nicholson, 1997.

Pitts, Vincent Jay. *La Grande Mademoiselle at the Court of France, 1627–1693.* Baltimore, Johns Hopkins University Press, 2000.

Poucher, A. *Les Trois Grands Divertissements de Versailles.* Paris, 1989.

Rat, Maurice. *La Royale Montespan.* Paris: Plon, 1959.

Ravaisson, François. *Archives de la Bastille, Paris,* t. IV à VII.

Richardt, Aimé. *Le Soleil du Grand Siècle.* Paris: Tallandier, 2000.

Roche, Daniel. *La Culture des Apparences: Une Histoire de Vêtement XVIIe–XVIIIe Siècle.* Paris: Librairie Arthème Fayard, 1989.

Saint-Maurice, Thomas-François Chabod, Marquis de. *Lettres sur la Cour de Louis XIV,* 2 vols. Edited by Jean Lemoine. Paris: Calmann-Levy, 1910.

Saint-Simon, Louis de Rouvroy, Duc de. *Louis XIV et Sa Cour.* Edited by Daniel Dessert. Brussels: Editions Complexe, 1994.

———. *Memoirs.* Translated by Lucy Norton. London: Prion, 1967.

Saule, Béatrix. *Versailles Triomphant: Une Journée de Louis XIV.* Paris: Flammarion, 1967.

Sévigné, Marie de Rabutin Chantal, Marquise de. *Correspondance.* Edited by Roger Duchêne. Paris: Gallimard, 1978.

———. *Lettres.* Edited by Louis Jean Nicolas Monmerqué. Paris: Hachette, 1866.

———. *Selected Letters.* Translated by Leonard Tancock. London: Penguin, 1982.

Solnon, Jean-François. *La Cour de France.* Paris: Librairie Arthème Fayard, 1987.

Sonnino, Paul, ed. *The Reign of Louis XIV: Essays in Celebration of Andrew Lossky.* Atlantic Highlands, N.J.: Humanities Press International, 1990.

Taillandier, Saint-René. *Le Grand Roi et Sa Cour.* Paris: Hachette, 1930.

Tannahill, Reay. *Sex in History.* London: Hamish Hamilton, 1990.

Thomas, Keith. *Religion and the Decline of Magic.* London: Penguin, 1991.

Toussaint-Samat, Maguelonne. *Histoire Naturelle et Morale de la Nourriture.* Paris: Bordas, 1987.

Treasure, Geoffrey. *Mazarin: The Crisis of Absolutism in France.* London: Routledge, 1995.

Truc, Gonzague. *Madame de Montespan.* Paris: Librairie Armand Colin, 1936.

Turner, James Grantham, ed. *Sexuality and Gender in Early Modern Europe.* Cambridge: Cambridge University Press, 1993.

Visconti, Primi Giovanni Battista, Comte de. *Mémoires sur la Cour de France.* Edited by Jean Lemoine. Paris: Calmann-Lévy, 1909.

Voltaire, François Marie Arouet. *Le Siècle de Louis XIV.* Edinburgh: M. de Francheville, 1751.

Walton, Guy. *Louis XIV's Versailles.* London: Viking, 1986.

Williams, E. N. *The Ancien Régime in Europe.* London: Pimlico, 1999.

Williams, H. Noel. *Madame de Montespan and Louis XIV.* London: Harpers, 1910.

Zeldin, Theodore. *The French.* London: Harvill, 1983.

Index

Athénaïs

The Life of Louis XIV's Mistress,
the Real Queen of France

by Lisa Hilton

A Reading Group Guide

A Conversation
with the Author of *Athénaïs*

Lisa Hilton talks with Megan O'Grady for Vogue

Most mistresses of French kings had themselves painted with religious paraphernalia, eager to improve their ambiguous position in society. Not Athénaïs de Montespan. The portrait of her in the Uffizi Gallery shows her reclining on a divan with her slippers kicked off, one breast exposed, boldly luxuriating in her sexual power. Now, for the first time in nearly a century, the most notorious mistress of Louis XIV is the subject of an English-language biography, Lisa Hilton's *Athénaïs: The Life of Louis XIV's Mistress, the Real Queen of France,* which provides the most revealing view yet of the woman who ruled Versailles with her dazzling wit and magnificent looks.

"I'd love to have her as a friend, but I don't know if I would trust her," laughs Hilton when asked about the beautiful young (and married) court attendant known as the Marquise de Montespan, who shrewdly entered into an illicit relationship with the Sun King to become one of the most powerful noblewomen in seventeenth-century Europe. Calling herself after the Greek goddess of virginity who carried the Gorgon's head on her shield, Athénaïs would prove to be an ideal match for the monarch in terms of ambition and appetite. Once she had succeeded in luring a still wet-behind-the-ears Louis away from his wife, Marie-Thérèse, and his official mistress, Louise de la Vallière (both of whom had considered the marquise their confidante), she devoted the next twenty years to pleasing him, ruthlessly defending her position against would-be successors.

It was while conducting research into royal furnishings from the same period at Christie's in Paris that Hilton, now twenty-eight, first began to wonder about the woman behind the audacious reputation. "I wanted to know the intimate stories, not just the lavish fetes and grandiose events," says the Oxford graduate and former model, who studied English and fine art, not history, prior to undertaking the weighty academic detective work required to trace Athénaïs's extraordinary influence as *maîtresse en titre.* "I wanted to write about Athénaïs as a mother who balanced her aspirations with child care, who battled her weight and told dirty jokes, who spoke her mind at a time when it wasn't becoming for her sex to do so."

Hilton's intensely personal approach lends a novelistic sweep to Athénaïs's tale, which unfolds, not coincidentally, against the rise of Versailles as a center of European politics and culture. Athénaïs, as Hilton depicts her, advised the king on virtually every matter of importance to the court and accompanied him on military campaigns, even while pregnant with two of their seven children (through whom she is an ancestor of most of the royal houses of Europe). An important patron of the arts in her own right, Athénaïs was among the first to promote Molière and Racine, whose plays so deftly satirized the hypocrisies of court life she often felt herself at the mercy of. She commissioned countless operas and ballets, dancing with Louis in several pastorals in which they cast themselves, somewhat predictably, as lovers. As hostess and decorator, she had ample occasion and the resources to show off her refined taste in the acquisition of tapestries and the planning of elaborate divertissements heralding France's newfound martial power. Whether Louis loved Athénaïs for herself or because she fit the image (as she was wont to accuse him), it is impossible to know, but she lived up to the glorious symbolism of her role so well that she became known throughout the kingdom as "the real queen."

Not the least of Athénaïs's contributions was her influence on matters of style: She served as a mannequin for aspiring couturiers' most extravagant designs, popularized the high-heeled shoe as an erotic accessory, and introduced the deshabille, a scandalously informal mode of dress that could be hastily removed to meet the passions of the famously insatiable king. Once the tongues had ceased to wag, a new trend was set. "Athénaïs established a relationship between fashion and celebrity that didn't exist up to that point," says Hilton. "The very idea of France as chic, as fashion's point of origin — this can be traced to her." If Athénaïs's boldly celebratory displays of her body are what set her apart most visibly from other royal mistresses, she was equally unashamed to show off her brains — in her day a far riskier breach of convention. In the later years of her life (after accusations of witchcraft forced her from grace), she established numerous girls' schools, which Hilton sees as the beginning of a rich feminine intellectual tradition in France.

It's little surprise that the young scholar who hopes that history will learn to respect Athénaïs de Montespan has forged her own less-than-traditional career path. Currently dividing her time between London, where she reviews French literature for the *Times Literary Supplement,* and the south of France, having impulsively spent her entire book advance on the ruins of a seventeenth-century pigeonnier (which she has since renovated), Hilton is hard at work writing about another comely scandal-maker, the duke-chasing eighteenth-century English actress Lavinia Fenton. "Historical women are fascinating because they are so marginalized — there's still so much to be said about their roles," she says of her affinity with the past, though it's clear her motives are unequivocally present-tense. "My hope is that readers will identify with the ones who broke the mold and see that in many ways they're modern characters. These are the women we want to know."

The complete text of Megan O'Grady's article on Lisa Hilton and Athénaïs *originally appeared in the December 2002 issue of* Vogue. *Reprinted with permission.*

Questions and Topics for Discussion

1. The author of *Athénaïs* explains that seventeenth-century standards of a mother's involvement with her children were very different from today's standards. Athénaïs turned over much of her children's care to their governess. Do you think there is merit to claims that she was a bad mother? Or was she constrained by the norms of the time? Can you identify ways in which Athénaïs expressed her love for her children?

2. Discuss the role of wit or esprit in the life of the court. Given the limited scope of girls' formal education at the time, how might a noblewoman equip herself for the expectations of court life? How did the famous Mortemart esprit help Athénaïs achieve her position?

3. As the author describes, Louis's court was governed by an almost dizzyingly complex set of social rules. Did Louis impose such a strict system on his nobles out of sheer vanity, or did he have other reasons? Why do you think the nobles of the time agreed to abide by such a regimented lifestyle?

4. Discuss the notion of marital fidelity as it applied to the nobility in Athénaïs's time. Among the upper classes, what was the expected relationship between husbands and wives? Was there a difference in society's view of women who took lovers as opposed to men who took mistresses?

5. Despite their supposed friendship, Athénaïs betrayed Lauzun's confidence not once but twice (pages 87, 93). Why? In what way does their relationship exemplify the politics of the court? When Athénaïs later aided in Lauzun's release from prison (pages 230–233), did she act out of remorse for her previous betrayals or from another motive entirely?

6. Athénaïs's dealings with her main rivals for Louis's affection, especially Queen Marie-Thérèse, Louise de la Vallière, and Mme. de Maintenon, were not uniformly hostile. Do you believe the occasional friendly encounters between these women were only hypocritical and calculated, or was there also a genuine compassion between them?

7. Athénaïs had a great deal of influence over the art, architecture, fashion, and what might be called taste of the time. What role did the arts play in the life of the court? If the works of Molière, Racine, and La Fontaine produced during this time are any indication, what was the relationship between the artist and his patron?

8. While Louise de la Vallière had been generally accepted as Louis's official mistress, Athénaïs's ascendance to this position drew the ire of Louis's religious advisers, especially Bishop Bossuet, and even temporarily forced the couple's separation. Why was Athénaïs's situation considered so shocking? What does this episode illustrate about the relative influence of the Church and the monarchy? Do you think the bishop's stand was a sincere or a politically motivated one?

9. For much of the second half of her life, Athénaïs was locked in a rivalry with Mme. de Maintenon, first for influence over Louis, and then for the loyalty of her children. Did Mme. de Maintenon gain the upper hand through circumstance or by outmaneuvering Athénaïs? What might account for the surprising betrayal of Athénaïs's children, especially the Duc du Maine?

10. The scandal created by the Affair of the Poisons shook the court and threw many nobles out of favor with the king. Do you believe there was a real plot to assassinate Louis? If not, are there other explanations for the accusations that came to light? If so, given the evidence presented on both sides, do you think Athénaïs was guilty of the charges against her?

11. Given Athénaïs's intense jealousy of other women who might have attracted Louis's attention over the years, does it surprise you that she seems to have known about his dalliances with servants and women of lesser rank but done nothing about them? Why did these liaisons not worry Athénaïs? What might her reactions indicate about the attitudes of the time regarding class and title?